Flight to Eden

Douglas Hirt

RIVEROAK®
Good News in Fiction

COOK COMMUNICATIONS MINISTRIES
Colorado Springs, Colorado • Paris, Ontario
KINGSWAY COMMUNICATIONS LTD
Eastbourne, England

River Oak® is an imprint of
Cook Communications Ministries, Colorado Springs, CO 80918
Cook Communications, Paris, Ontario
Kingsway Communications, Eastbourne, England

FLIGHT TO EDEN
© 2005 by Douglas Hirt

Cover Design by: Lisa A. Barnes
Cover Illustration by: Ron Adair

First Printing, 2005
Printed in the United States of America
1 2 3 4 5 6 7 8 9 10 Printing/Year 09 08 07 06 05

ISBN: 0781438721

Thanks to my editor, Craig Bubeck, whose enthusiasm for wild conjecturings made this novel possible.

A special thanks to all those people who lent their love, prayers, support, and advice. First and foremost, to my friend and wife, Kathy, forced to read the manuscript piecemeal as it came weekly off the printer—a most frustrating way to read a book, she will tell you. Then to my daughter Rebecca, who scrutinized every word with a keen editorial eye. Mary Davis, Kristen Heitzmann, and Virgil Collins read the manuscript and gave me valuable suggestions for making it better. Thank you! And finally, my friend and colleague, Tiffany Colter, for her outstanding advice in an area where I had absolutely no expertise!

Pillars of the Sun

Atlan

Hodin's Passage

and of Havilah

D LANDS

s of Eden

Eve's Weep

Havil

Aron-ee

Marin-ee

Border Sea

Orin-ee

Derbin-ee

Dragon
Pass

Wen's Slip

Cheve-lee

Sarv-ee

Land of Nod

Dornsi

Vald-ee

Wayfarer Inn

Nod City

WILD LANDS

ngrun
strict

HEDDEKEL

DS

Morg'Jalek

Morg'Lavin

LITTLE HEDDEKEL

Illackin
Mountains

Illackin

Lee-lands

Morg'Seth

CRADLELAND

©2004 Susan Kotnik

1

The Webmaster

*T*he growing heat of the day drew a heady fragrance from the moist ground and mossy rocks, one Rhone might have normally relished. But just then, the mustiness of the forest was only a distant tug at the back of his brain. Something else had caught his attention: a vaguely bitter smell. The smell of money! In the dappled sunlight through a high forest canopy, he paused and sniffed again.

Javian!

The corners of his mouth hitched up, then his broad forehead furrowed. The spoor was old; a lingering scent. The spider was now long gone. Rhone moved toward the faintly tangy remnant in the air, ears alert, his brown eyes in constant motion. Many beasts had turned; it was hard to know which were still harmless and which were not. The Teeg'kits had changed—they were now called mansnatchers—and the hook-tooths, according to some reports. Change was in the air. A man had to tread cautiously these days—much more so than only forty or fifty years ago.

Filtered sunlight mottled the shadows around him, and broken glimpses of a soft blue sky flashed in the scattered leafy breaks two to three hundred spans above his head. Rhone had shed his shirt in the heat of the day. The long, sinuous muscles of his arms

stood out like cords of rope, and his bronze skin glistened with perspiration as he moved silently through the forest. He carried a
sturdy shiverthorn pack over his left shoulder and a proj-lance in
this right hand—though he still somewhat distrusted the new
weapon. The long sword at his left side was a more familiar and
reliable friend. In the top of his right boot resided a thin, sharp
webbing knife. His dark mane of brown hair hung free about his
shoulders, held only by a forest-green headband of cotton to keep
it from his eyes.

At the edge of a small clearing, he stopped. His frown deepened
at the sight of long silken strands dangling from the treetops, drifting
in the slight breeze. He'd found the web. Abandoned, as he knew it
would be. It wasn't the first.

The tattered silken funnel that filled the clearing was still
anchored to the trees on several sides. Only a partial chimney, beginning fifty spans above him, still remained of the clever trap. From its
wide mouth below, it narrowed upward, toward a swath of sky. Even
though abandoned and in ruin, a score of tough anchor strands still
held it in place.

As he studied the ragged chimney of silk, his head tilted back,
disappointment became a nearly tactile thing. The web had a long
tear down one side where some animal had chewed or clawed its way
free. The once-glistening sheets of javian silk were now dulled with a
layer of dust and the carcasses of moths and dragonflies unable to
escape the sticky strands. A necklace of puff-pollen, beaded into pre-
cise balls of silk, lay like fine, silvery pearls around the outside slope
of the funnel. The spider had left its food cache behind.

And that was the most puzzling of all. So many spiders had left
their treasured gatherings of food behind. What had driven them
off? Javian spiders never forsook their hoards unless driven from
them. Some had even been known to attack humans defending a
stash of puff-pollen. Were the spiders turning too? Was that causing

this mass exodus? Were they being affected by the same forces that were affecting the beasts of the field?

Rhone shrugged off the problem, putting it aside to ponder later. Collecting had been a poor business this trip out. The single spool he carried in his pack was only three quarters full where by this time he should have filled two. Setting the pack aside, he drew out his webbing knife and began the task of separating the walking strands out of the web. The walking strands were the strongest and easiest to handle, having never been coated in the spider's sticky droplets.

It was the second hour of the first quartering, and dusk had begun to cool the forest by the time Rhone finished the job. He carefully wrapped the silk about a stick and put it into the pack with the spool. He'd been away from Nod City almost two months, and with so little to show for all that time he was tempted to stay longer and push farther into the Wild Lands, but Ker'ack would be expecting him soon.

He found a spring flowing from the cracks of a stone ledge and stopped in the cool of the evening to make camp. The forest darkened around him. The flames of his fire pushed the shadows back a comfortable distance as he prepared a dinner. With the sizzle of mushrooms, onions, peppers, carrots, and savots in his skillet, sautéing in sweet tarra sap, Rhone set about the business of cleaning the web. He split a soap reed, inserted the javian silk between its frothy pulp, and fastened an end of it onto his spool. Working in the firelight with the silk anchored beneath a smooth stick in the flow of water from the spring, he slowly reeled it onto his spool, drawing it first through the soap reed, then drying it with a cloth as it came up out of the water.

It took longer to clean old silk, but Rhone was a patient man. With one ear tuned to the night sounds, he let his thoughts drift. This rash of abandoned webs bothered him. He was nearly to the Illackin Mountains, and still the spiders were scarce. But then all of nature seemed to be changing; once-tame animals turned from men, even attacked them. Could it be because men had begun eating animal years. He read them as if discovering them for the first time, though in truth he could have recited the poem from heart. As he read, images of youth and home filled his head. The poem always conjured memories. Perhaps that was why he read it often. The stanzas ran on page after page, but when he came to a certain verse, he skipped over it and went on. In spite of that, when he'd finished, his eyelids sagging with sleep and his heart heavy with memories, that one shunned passage came to him. He couldn't drive the memorized words from his head.

> One has departed, another holds the throne,
> Home and hearth are lost.
> A war is over, a land in despair,
> A grievous wage for kinsman to bear.
> A people count the cost.
> Bitter wails now fill once courtly halls,
> With cries to redeem a shadow land.
> Deliver us from beneath the tyrant's heavy hand!
> Makir and shield bearers rally to the call.
> The son had departed, a brother holds the throne.

Rhone shut the moonglass and forced himself to think of something else as he curled up in his blanket to wait for sleep.

A deep rumble shook the ground beneath his head. Then another. He glanced around his dark campsite.

The rumble grew louder and drew closer. Some beast of the forest was moving swiftly toward him. A branch snapped and frightened monkeys fled through the treetops. A cold warning finger dragged a nail up his spine and he sniffed the air. The breeze was coming out of the wrong direction. Had his fire attracted a turnling? He reached for his proj-lance.

Don't linger in your blanket, Rhone.

It occurred to him suddenly he'd be in a bad way found still curled up in his blanket. Throwing it off, he stood warily.

All at once, the night went silent. Nearby, the muffled rumble of deep breathing caught his ear.

Rhone strained to penetrate the blackness. The hairs at the back of his neck seemed connected to needles. The few red embers remaining of his fire and the pale glow of starlight through the scattered gaps in the canopy gave off enough light for his keen eyes to pick out a shape here and there.

The creature sniffed. Rhone wheeled toward the sound. Leaves crackled beneath a massive weight. A shadow, only faintly lighter than the rest of the forest, suddenly loomed overhead.

He heaved the proj-lance and recoiled beneath the weight of the creature striking it. The weapon lurched from his grasp. The blow propelled him backward into the tree he'd been leaning against. His sword was there and at hand. Instinct replaced conscious thought and old training, long unused but still programmed into his muscles, took over. He swung out. The blade struck something hard and skittered along its edge. A roar shattered the air. Rhone glimpsed teeth like daggers, and a momentary flash of a greenish eye shine. A stengordon! The giant stood ten spans tall, and its hot, humid breath reeked of a garbage pit!

Rhone ducked. A snap and the clash of teeth cracked near his ear. Turning and crouching under the beast, he thrust the sword upward, his muscles straining when the point struck home. Lifting with his legs and driving with his arms, he punched his sword through the leathery hide and found hard muscle beneath.

Its howl shook the trees and sent sleeping creatures scattering skyward. The beast twisted, wrenching the sword from Rhone's grasp. A tail the thickness of a small tree trunk whipped around and drove him into the ground. The wounded beast howled again, and in the faint light Rhone saw it come at him. He scrambled back and his hand touched something hard on the ground. His proj-lance! The weapon leaped around and fired. A blinding flash, a whoosh, and the muffled boom of a proj detonating deep within the animal's body came all at once.

The beast swayed.

Rhone rolled to one side and sprang to his feet as small trees snapped beneath the toppling monster's weight. The ground rumbled.

Rhone scrambled away and put a tree between himself and the creature, but the downed giant didn't move. Rhone leaned against the rough bark and slid down, sitting there, shaking and gulping massive drafts of air. His heart pounded in his chest and the proj-lance in his hands was slick with his perspiration.

Rhone waited for the creature's ragged breathing to cease and for its massive limbs to stop quivering before creeping back to the beast. A turnling? Sten-gordons had until now been shy and reclusive.

With no small struggle Rhone extracted his sword from the tough flesh. Had others of his kind turned too? There was no way to know for sure.

❈

The next morning he examined the sten-gordon. The dark skin had faded in death, its once-bright scarlet and lemon stripes now rust and amber. A deep gash showed where his sword had taken a chunk out of one claw. Rhone frowned, sobered by how close he had come to death.

If he'd harbored any uncertainty the night before, this had made up his mind. He must return to Nod City. Others needed to be warned to keep a wary eye on the sten-gordon. With a final glance at the slain giant, Rhone slung his pack onto his shoulder and turned his steps toward home.

❈

The great dragon, glinting gold and red in the sunlight, swept down through the city, gliding with wide spread wings above broad avenues, riding the gentle updrafts of the warming morning air. With a sudden flap, and a gust of wind that ruffled the colorful awnings of the vendors below, it climbed lazily toward the towering walls at the city's center. Another powerful lunge lifted it above the battlements. Black, curved talons reached out and clutched a stone merlon and its bulk settled lightly upon the pink granite that encircled the paved plaza of Government House far below.

Rhone glanced at the dragon winging its way into the city and dismissed it almost at once. His curiosity, like those of scores of citizens hurrying with him, had been excited by the commotion coming from Meeting Floor. He joined the crowd moving toward the six arches of pink granite twenty-two spans high and almost ten wide, opening onto the Meeting Floor. The place was already packed with men and women craning their necks and lifting themselves on their toes for a glimpse of the raised platform at its center.

The dragon gave a shake, as if flinging dust from its ruby scales, ruffled its leathery wings, and folded them along its sleek sides until their tips reached back to enshroud a quarter length of its tail. Then it lowered its long neck, canted its head, and blinked golden eyes at the throngs below. Sitting there as if part of the stonework, it almost appeared to be listening, as if it could understand the angry voices of the milling crowd below.

Perhaps it could.

Rhone shifted the shiverthorn pack to his other shoulder and pushed into the crowd. He could see over the heads of most of the people, catching a glimpse of the polished onyx dais which lay in the heart of the plaza. An emissary wearing the official purple robes of the House of Cain stood upon the dais, reading a proclamation to the crowd. Sound mirrors around the perimeter of the Meeting Floor amplified his voice, yet angry shouts broke into his reading more than a couple times. With the interruptions coming more frequently now, the man looked to be reaching the end of his patience.

Rhone pressed on across the crowded floor in spite of protesters whose complaints invariably died in their throats with one look at him. He stood almost four spans tall. A life lived mainly in the Wild Lands had left him well muscled with shoulders that stretched a full span and skin a warm hue of walnuts. At his side rode a blade forged of the finest steel. He carried his proj-lance in his left hand, held close to his body to keep it from snagging amongst the crowd that grudgingly gave way for him.

"… and this tariff, which the Lodath has most reluctantly requested, shall last only until the first temple is completed. At which time—"

"I've heard that before," a voice protested. "His harbor pledge was only supposed to last until the temple docks were finished. That was nine years ago!"

A few of the Lodath's supporters cheered the emissary on in spite of this new ploy to milk glecks from their purses. Voices of discontent swelled again.

The Lodath's emissary scowled.

Rhone glanced toward the Government House. A curtain in a third floor window had briefly lifted then dropped back in place.

"Silence! Silence! Allow me to finish!" The emissary cast about the crowd.

The protests diminished to a mumbling undercurrent that never fully ceased.

"King Irad has given his approval for the tariff. The levy will be 3 percent of all items sold in the land of Nod. It will be collected on the last day of the month by agents of the Lodath's Guards and deposited in the treasury of the House of Cain."

Rhone worked his way nearly to the front of the crowd, three or four ranks back from where the onlookers pressed hard against the polished bronze tubes encircling the platform. He didn't need to get any closer for a clear view of the emissary's strained face, or the stern set of his shaven jaw, as he held the proclamation before him.

"The monies collected will be used to offset the heavy cost of erecting the Oracle's temple."

"After King Irad skims off his share," someone shouted.

"Administrative costs only," the emissary clarified, clearly at the end of his patience.

"Why do we have to foot the bill?" another demanded. "Isn't the Oracle supposed to be coming to enlighten the world?"

The emissary glared at this new interruption coming from a man standing not far from Rhone.

"He comes for the benefit of the world, but we are the most fortunate people he has chosen to dwell with. You have all heard his teachings. The Lodath has revealed his words to you. How can you compare the small cost of funding his temple, his dwelling place among men, to the great honor of having the Oracle in your very midst?"

Rhone's view shifted to a man and woman standing just in front of him. They weren't from Nod City, or even any of the settlements nearby. Their clothes were foreign. *Lee-landers.* The faintest twitch tugged down the corners of his lips.

The man was tall, stiff-backed, and intent. He wore the practical trousers of a farmer: leather and wool, bearing pockets great and small, and split at the ankles to fit over his sturdy boots. A colorful woolen tunic covered his broad shoulders, falling to midthigh and gathered to a narrow waist by a wide belt.

The woman was nearly as tall—three spans or a bit more. She appeared younger than he, with a healthy glow to her attractive face. Her black hair, thickly braided, hung down to her waist where a loose plait of blue cord encircled her cotton-and-shiverthorn dress. Like the man's tunic, the dress had been woven of green and brown and yellow threads. Its hem began within a hand's breadth of the paving stones at her sturdy shoes, and ended in a tight collar at her neck. Very discrete and proper—very much in keeping with the traditions of Lee-landers. Its full cut revealed little of her shape beneath it, except that the woman was obviously with child.

He noted the occasional glance of disapproval the onlookers in the crowd directed toward these Lee-landers, particularly from the Covenant wearers. Rhone was seeing more and more people wearing the Oracle's crystalline Covenant pendants.

The Lodath's emissary droned on about the necessity of the pledge and the wonderful benefits of having the Oracle among them. Rhone cared little about either. The nature of his work meant the tax would hardly affect him. And as far as the Oracle was concerned, he was just another charlatan who'd found a people with itching ears eager to chase after the latest fad. The Lodath claimed the Oracle was from the stars. Some even believed the Oracle was the voice of the Creator, though that notion never came from the Lodath. The stuff of stories. Tales told to young ears at bedtime. Yet, the man and his wife seemed riveted by what the emissary was saying, their faces stern and eyes narrowed as if mentally challenging each and every word.

Definitely Lee-landers.

Rhone wondered briefly what they were doing here in Nod City, so far from their homeland. Nod City did not often attract Lee-landers—especially these days. Probably came to gawk at the spectacle taking shape just outside the city's gates. Isn't that what drew most folks here these days? His eyes hitched toward Government House, but from here the ambitious construction project, which now apparently needed another influx of funds, lay hidden beyond the smoothly curving gold-and-pink stone walls.

Rhone's frown deepened. The Lee-landers he'd met in his travels were opinionated and clannish—difficult to barter with. He dismissed the couple and turned back to the man on the dais.

"The Lodath extends his most heartfelt thanks in advance for your continued cooperation, and for those of you who have already pledged their service to the Oracle, he pronounces a special blessing for bountiful harvests and many—"

"How can the mouthpiece of the serpent pronounce a blessing!" a voice boomed.

A gasp ran through the crowd. The emissary's face went pale. It seemed to Rhone as if every eye there had suddenly fixed upon the Lee-lander who'd just spoken out.

The emissary stammered, "Th—that's blasphemy!" His eyes narrowed dangerously. "Such words can serve no useful purpose but to bring misery down upon you."

The onlookers gave way as the Lee-lander approached the bronze tube barrier.

The woman clutched at his sleeve. "Lamech!"

Lamech hesitated, clearly struggling, but something stronger than his wife's wishes seemed to urge him on. His face stern, his eyes smoldered as if a fire had suddenly been kindled behind them. "You speak of my misery but fail to understand your own wretchedness, or the destruction your folly will bring upon you and your children! Turn aside from this road while you still have time! Put your feet back on the way of righteousness before the Creator's wrath can be contained no longer!"

The emissary's laugh sounded strained. "Now you speak of fables. We've grown beyond those stories of gods and thunderbolts, meant only to keep people in subjection."

The rumbled agreement from the crowd showed the emissary he'd struck a favorable chord. "You can keep your ancient gods and musty legends. Maybe where you come from men still toil under the yoke of fear, but not here. Not in Nod City! Just look around at the marvels. Everywhere you look is a testament to the supremacy of man. We've conquered nature, and now with the Oracle's guidance, we will begin to conquer our final limitations—those we put upon ourselves. So don't think you can burden us again with your myths and fear-mongering! We'll have none of it here!"

The crowd surged toward the Lee-lander, but some of them seemed to hesitate.

Go to them, Rhone.

The woman grasped her husband's arm and cast about for a way out. Then her eye caught Rhone's. It was for only an instant that they looked at each other before the woman's gaze jumped away, but in that fleeting second he could have sworn a shimmering light had filled the space between them. He shook his head and looked again, but the air had stilled. Without knowing why, he started toward the couple.

"You Lee-landers go back to where you came from!" an angry voice shouted.

"And take your dusty fables with you!" another snarled.

The Lee-lander was not intimidated, but his wife huddled near to him, her dark eyes in constant motion. He put an arm over her shoulder and drew her close. His voice was deep and resonant, and it boomed with a clear sound that overpowered the angry jeers. "Your hearts run to folly! If you permit this deception in your midst, you will surely bring about your own end. And that end will come swift and sure, and all remembrance of you will be cleansed from the world!"

"I've heard those threats before," the first man yelled. "Three hundred years ago your people were lamenting the end of all civilization. But look at us now, Lee-lander. See what we've built in spite of doomsayers like you? Where is our end? I ask you! Show me how bad off we are! You can see only clouds where the rest of us see the sun!

You tell us we allow deception in our midst. Are the lofty words of the Oracle the deception you speak of? If so, then I'd rather be uplifted by what you say are his lies than smothered by the so-called truth your deity would force upon us."

What the emissary had not been able to do with his words, the Lee-lander had done with his contrary opinion. Nothing like opposition to unite people. Rhone threaded his way through the crowd.

The emissary had let the crowd speak for him, but now he stepped forward. "Away with those two! Run them out of the city!"

The crowd rallied. Someone drew a knife and lunged for the Lee-lander.

Rhone's fist shot out and caught his wrist. Standing a full head taller than the man, he placed himself like a wall between the assailant and the Lee-lander. The man began to quiver beneath the powerful grasp, slowly folding under the irresistible force. His fingers sprang opened, and the knife clattered to the stones. Rhone shoved him back into the crowd. For a moment, the Meeting Floor went silent, all eyes suddenly on him.

What was he doing? It was nearly as much a shock to Rhone to be standing there as it was to the sea of wide eyes that encircled him. "Since when are the people of Nod City afraid of ideas? Is that the way the masters teach their students—picking and choosing what they should believe? Or do they open up all ideas and examine them for truth?"

What was he saying? Truth? He no more believed in the Lee-landers' brand of truth than he believed in the Oracle's. His truth was what he could see and feel and smell; everything else was mere abstraction, something he had neither the desire nor the time to bother with.

"You stay out of this," someone shouted, but when Rhone looked, no one owned up to it. Across the wide plaza, the Lodath's Guards had begun to file out of Government House, starting down the steps. Rhone slanted an eye at the Lee-lander, keeping the other on the crowd. "Now would be a good time for you and your wife to leave."

The man seemed to hesitate.

Rhone nodded toward the soldiers wearing the emerald green tunics and purple plumed helmets of the Lodath's personal guards, filing out of the building. Each carried a proj-lance.

"Lamech." The woman tugged urgently at his arm.

Lamech's eyes seemed to ache for her even as his spine went rigid. But the struggle lasted only a moment. His gaze came back to Rhone. It was the intense, piercing look of a man of perception attempting to discern something. *And had he?* Lamech gave a brief nod.

The woman's dark eyes studied him as well, but not in the intense, surgical manner of her husband. They were wide, intelligent eyes filled with appreciation perhaps—or curiosity? "Thank you." She tightened her grip on her husband's arm and the air gave a faint shimmer again.

Curious, now the crowd parted for them.

The emissary tried to recapture the masses' attention, while amongst the crowd, green-cloaked warders spread, searching for the source of the disturbance.

Leaning upon the long tube of his proj-lance, Rhone considered the faces glaring at him. But no one seemed eager to make the first move. Just as well. He had no desire to cause any more of a scene here than he already had. Turning toward the nearest exit, he threaded his way through the throng to the street.

2

Discord in the Marketplace

With a hushed whisper, the tall double doors swung open and Da-gore, captain of the Lodath's Guard, strode into the third-floor gallery. The nearly empty space seemed to open up and expand beyond the walls of stone and dark wood. He hardly noticed the delicately detailed tapestries and bronze plaques with stones of emerald and topaz and sardonyx, each one softly pulsating to its own unhurried tempo. The cavernous ceiling, a mosaic of octagonal crystal lenses, filled the gallery with outside sunlight. Set into the east wall, carved into a floral pattern by the cleverest artisans in Nod City, towered a pair of doors through which Da-gore had entered. The doors reached nearly to the ceiling, flanked on either side with tapestries depicting the rolling hills beyond, the vast forests, and the great, lumbering beasts—huge shaggy elephants, lep-horths, and a herd of three-points.

Near the west wall stood a swirled spire of milky white mineral, thrusting upward from the granite floor, once again the height of a man and twice as wide. Somewhere deep inside the pearly crystal a faint red glow pulsated slowly, steadily, to a measured beat.

A dozen windows spilled more daylight into the gallery, and it was by one of these that Sol-Ra-Luce stood as Da-gore's footsteps echoed upon the polished stone. He removed his helmet and shoved it under his left arm as he approached. The Lodath of the Oracle had a pinched look about his eyebrows, and a frown tugged at his lips.

"We'll soon get to the bottom of that disturbance, Your Eminence. I suspect it has to do with your proclamation." He came to a stop, glanced briefly past the gossamer curtains out the window, then back at the Lodath. "I've dispatched the morning guard."

From the Meeting Floor below a tumult of unhappy voices rose toward the opened window. His guards, clearly visible by the bright green of their cloaks, were already filtering out through the people. Upon the dais, motioning with his hands, Emissary Daniek struggled to recover the crowd's attention.

"So I see, Captain Da-gore. But I think it has nothing to do with the tariff." Sol-Ra-Luce grabbed the lapels of his dark blue coat and turned back to the window. The morning sunlight struck the high collar of woven gold, encircling his coarse, straight, black hair in a halo of light. The coat's hem, which hung to a point just above his knees, was trimmed in the Mystery Symbols of the Oracle. The hem, like the collar, was woven with threads of solid gold and shone in the morning sunlight while the dark blue material of the coat and pants seemed to suck in all light. To Da-gore, the appearance was something of a man floating several spans above the floor, and he was quite certain the impression was intentional.

The Lodath extended a long finger, its blue nail filed into a blade-like point. "Those two just leaving. Lee-landers by their dress. The disturbance involved them."

Da-gore hitched up questioning eyebrows then followed the Lodath's glance. Sol-Ra-Luce took a brass tube from the windowsill, peered a moment through it, then handed it to him. "They're just crossing Barter Road now. See how angry the man is? The woman with him is trying to be conciliatory. They speak," he looked at Da-gore, a faint twitch lifting the corner of his thin lips, "of me, I think."

The Captain of the Guard put the glass to his eye and found the man and woman on the crowded street.

"You see how he frowns and points back this way?"

Da-gore adjusted the focus. "Yes, I see." He was vaguely aware of the tall crystal, the perceptible increase in the beating light and the faint hum of molecular vibration.

Sol-Ra-Luce closed his eyes. A thin smile worked its way slowly across his face. "Yes, they definitely speak of me. She is not pleased, and he is only biting his tongue."

"Do you want those two followed?"

He glanced at Da-gore. "Perhaps. But there is another." He turned back to the window and again the sharp nail pointed. "That one making his way through the crowd. He stands out, no? He has the look of a Hodinite."

Da-gore put the glass back to his eye. "His build maybe, and perhaps his bearing, but he wears the garb of a gatherer. I've yet to hear of anyone from the Family of Hodin who was not a Makir Warrior at heart, and a Makir would never stoop to collecting tree milk and web for a living." He looked back at the Lodath. "Of what interest is this stranger to us, Your Eminence?"

The Lodath watched the large man leaving the Meeting Floor. "Not certain." He stroked his black goat-beard, contemplating. "This … gatherer … took the side of the Lee-landers." The Lodath closed his eyes. "I get no feeling for him."

Da-gore located him again in the glass. "He makes for Weaver's Lane. I'll wager he's a webmaster. No Hodinite that one, in spite of his height and those broad shoulders."

"Humm. I wonder." In the center of the gallery, the swirl of opaque rock had begun to shimmer. The Lodath turned, and for a moment the crystal's throbbing seemed to repeat the Lodath's quickening breathing. Then the shimmering stilled and only the quiet red pulsing deep within it remained. Sol-Ra-Luce drew in a sudden breath. Da-gore took a step, prepared to lend a hand.

Sol-Ra-Luce staggered, stabbing out a foot to catch himself. He placed a palm over his own heart and nodded. A second breath seemed to settle him. He returned to the window and took a firm grip upon the sill. "Have the Lee-landers watched, Captain Da-gore."

"Yes, Your Eminence." He turned to leave. The Lodath's curious melding was always somewhat disconcerting.

"And that stranger. I want to know more about him as well."

"I will see it is done." Da-gore started for the door.

"Captain Da-gore."

He turned back. "Your Eminence?"

"See to the Lee-landers personally."

Personally? Da-gore stiffened. Tailing was a job for his men, not himself. He nodded curtly. "As you wish."

Sol-Ra-Luce returned his gaze to the window. Emissary Daniek had left the dais and the crowd below was breaking up. Da-gore caught a flicker of movement. A great ruby dragon lifted off its perch upon the pink granite merlon and winged away from the city, disappearing beyond the citadel's walls.

✿

"They don't understand, Lamech." Mishah spoke softly, taking her husband's arm into her own and giving it an affectionate squeeze. "And maybe they never will." A profound sadness made her hope that wasn't true.

They were making their way along a busy avenue, wide enough for traffic to travel in both directions. Pebbly-skinned three-points with blunted horns and noses pierced for a guide chain lumbered ahead of heavy carts, five spans wide, wheels standing shoulder high at the axle beams. Loaded with fruits and vegetables, or quarried stones for the temple project, they rolled slowly up from the river below, rumbling the ground with each step.

"It's too hard to know the truth and not speak it." He gave her a gentle smile. "Still, I have you to think about ... and our son."

A *son*. Lamech was so certain they'd have a son. Would he be disappointed if the Creator gave them a daughter? She squeezed his arm with affection. It was difficult for Lamech to be here, in the heart of all he considered evil, and not speak out against it. "No harm was done. We have the Creator to thank for sending someone to help us."

"Perhaps." He frowned.

"What's the matter?"

"I don't know."

They kept to the sidewalks, out of the way of the traffic as they strolled toward colorful tents dotting an open-air market ahead like flocks of parrots and butterflies. Beyond the market and down a gentle green slope lay the Little Idikla River, blue and wide, glinting in the sunlight beneath the soft blue sky. Across the Little Idikla, the landscape was mottled green and brown in a patchwork of farms stretching all the way to the dark line of forests at the horizon.

From here, Mishah had a full view of the wharves below, mounded with crates of cargo bound for various destinations up river and down. Boats small and large and of every shape waited at the sides of long piers jutting far out into the slow-drifting water. The faint odor of unburned 'gia reminded her of home.

The Little Idikla was a lazy river, so unlike its turbulent cousin, the Idikla. It began its journey here at Nod City and meandered through most of the inhabited lands to the south. It was hardly recognizable as a branch of the Idikla, which not far above this confluence became a mighty torrent, and in only a little less than a week's travel north of Nod City became unnavigable at a place called Far Port.

Mishah searched briefly for the little boat that had carried them up from Morg'Seth. Though they had spent nearly four days on it, she could not pick it out from among the many vessels moored there.

Lamech's eyes were wary, and in constant motion. The people passing by seemed wary of him as well. He was a man of deep convictions, and wasn't that one of the many reasons she loved him so? Just the same, he was suspicious by nature, and his hotly held beliefs made him a hard man to live with at times.

A little north of the commercial wharves stretched a string of docks and ramps built for the fleet of temple barges. Some of these rested deep in the water, their broad decks gleaming with stone quarried from the Hawk Ridge Mountains. Others, now unburdened of their heavy loads, rode high in the water, readied for the return voyage upriver. Huge scaffoldings hugged the riverbank and arched over the barges like skeletal storks. Trams pulled by three-points moved endlessly between river and temple site. Mishah's view shifted and she caught a glimpse of the temple's rising walls through a gap between two tall buildings.

Lamech's words pulled her view back to his face. "I don't see your grandmother or your brother, or Kleg'l."

She scanned the faces of the shoppers milling about the tables of corn, gamin, orfin fruits, and coffa. Piles of melons filled the back of carts. Bunches of ripe yellow bananas rose in mounds side by side with baskets of hard, crisp apples from the mountain slopes of Morg'Jalek. Barrels of savots, tomatoes, beans, and a score of different fruits and vegetables from the lowlands made the market as bright as her flower garden back home. The marketplace seemed to go on forever and the hodgepodge of smells would have made her ill only a few months earlier.

"They are about somewhere." She tried to put the encounter on the Meeting Floor out of mind. In Nod City, a careless remark could put a man in shackles and before an officer of the House of Cain in a heartbeat. She sighed. Such was the price of carrying convictions, a trait that ran strong in her husband's family.

She was anxious to be on their way for many reasons, not the least being to avoid another conflict like the one they had just escaped. And because they had such a long journey ahead of them. She wanted to complete her month long pilgrimage to the Mother and return home before she became too large and uncomfortable. She looked down at her expanding stomach. She had been reluctant to make this pilgrimage at all, but Lamech had convinced her to do so. And her grandmother had wanted it for her as well.

At least Amolikah was with her. Mishah took great comfort in having her grandmother along—a comfort that even Lamech could not provide. She and Amolikah had always been close. Amolikah had made this journey twice before; once when Mishah's mother had been born, and again before Mishah had been delivered into the world. Now Amolikah was making the journey a third time. It should have been Mishah's mother accompanying her. A pang stabbed Mishah's heart.

"This will be the last time!" Amolikah had declared before leaving their home in the Lee-lands of Morg'Seth. Not that she would have ever refused to accompany another granddaughter on the pilgrimage. But Amolikah knew that the Mother had grown very old, and must soon return to Adam's bosom.

"There they are." Lamech's hand tightened over Mishah's fingers where they wrapped his arm, and he guided her through the crowds of shoppers toward her brother and grandmother.

The market lay at the end of Barter Road, on a swath of ground that ran nearly down to the river. A thousand people, maybe more, were packed into an area larger than Mishah's village in Morg'Seth. The noise and activity were enough to boggle a country girl. Bartering in Nod City, it seemed, had developed into a high art. How did visitors from the outlying provinces stand a chance? Hearing the skillful deal-making going on around her, she was convinced even the mildest of these city women was more adept at the game than she could ever hope to be. More than ever, she was anxious to be on her way, and then on her way *home*!

Amolikah's face brightened when she saw them. The older woman carried a single small bag over her left arm, while Kenock, a few paces behind her, struggled with two enormous sacks. Mishah had no doubt the sacks carried little of anything her brother might have traded for. She smiled at him and he grinned back.

"Grandmother has yet to meet a banana or orfin she didn't like. And I'm sure we have enough keelits to see us through to the Mother and back home! She must have squeezed and thumped every melon between here and the river!"

"Oh, Kenock, you exaggerate." Amolikah took Mishah by the shoulders and affectionately pressed her aged cheek to Mishah's smooth face.

Lamech laughed. The reunion had apparently shifted his thoughts. He relieved Kenock of one of the packages. "What all have you got in here?" He staggered dramatically under the weight.

"Lamech! Now don't you start complaining too." Amolikah shot him a withering scowl, but a smile peeked out at the edges. Her pale green eyes shifted back to Mishah, turning suddenly puzzled. "Didn't you find the items on our list?"

"We didn't have time to even look."

Lamech rolled his eyes.

"Time?" Amolikah's questioning glance moved between her granddaughter and Lamech.

Mishah stifled a smile and took her husband's arm again. "Lamech thought the Lodath's emissary needed a lesson in theology."

"No!" Amolikah's surprise turned to shock, and then to concern. Her voice lowered. "You didn't, Lamech? Not here in Nod City!"

"These people have lost their heads over this … this *Oracle* business. And they will lose their faith too!"

"Yes, yes, I know." Amolikah's indulgent tone caused Lamech's muscles to tighten beneath Mishah's grasp. "But here—now? You know what I told you about these people."

Kenock cleared his throat and hitched his eyes toward some women at a nearby fruit stand who were standing unnaturally stiff, heads inclined their direction. "Perhaps we ought to continue this later—when we're alone?"

Amolikah surprised Mishah with one of her rare moments of restraint. She glanced about as if suddenly aware of the press of people around them. "Very well. This isn't the time or place."

Mishah looked around. "Where's Kleg'l?"

Kenock transferred Amolikah's package to his other arm. "He's trying to book us passage upriver."

The tone in his voice made her uneasy. "Trying? Is there a problem?"

Kenock shrugged. "Not many boats make the trip north from here. The river gets pretty rough, I'm told. It might be easier to find passage along the River Road with a trader's caravan."

Lamech frowned. "We may be stuck here a few days."

Mishah's stomach clenched. She could not expect Lamech to be anyone other than who he was. And that meant if faced with the Oracle's lies again, he'd speak out. Today was proof of that. But she kept her worries to herself. "Then we shall just have to make the best of it, won't we?"

Kenock laughed. "Mi, one might think we've just been marooned on some remote outpost along the Border Sea. This is the hub of the settled world! Enjoy it!"

"I don't want to enjoy it. I want to get this over with."

Concern deepened about Amolikah's eyes, adding years to a face still clinging to the fading beauty of its youth. "Mishah, it is a great honor to be given an audience by the Mother. A woman gets only one chance. The Mother is very old. Her rest is not far off. You are very fortunate. Of all the women in the world, only our family is permitted this privilege. The Mother will most certainly give a blessing to you and the child … and perhaps even a prophecy."

"I know, Grandmother." Mishah gave the old woman's hand a reassuring pat. "I intend to complete the pilgrimage. I'm worried, that's all. I don't like this place, and …," Mishah's words drifted off into thoughtful silence.

"And what?" Amolikah pressed. "What's troubling you, Mishah?"

"I had that dream again last night."

Sudden understanding softened Amolikah's face. She folded an arm around Mishah's shoulder and gave a squeeze. "Do you want to talk about it?"

"I just want to forget it." Mishah frowned. "No, that's not true. I want to *understand* it."

"Dreams can't hurt you, Mi," Kenock said.

In her heart, she knew that to be true. Yet of late, the night visions had become so frequent she was certain there *had* to be something to them.

Lamech cupped a reassuring hand about the nape of her neck. "If it will make you feel better, I will temper my tongue while we remain in the serpent's stronghold."

Mishah smiled at him. *Could fire ever burn cold?* "Thank you, Lamech."

He shifted the heavy bag in his arms. "Perhaps we should find Kleg'l and learn what our fate really is? He may have already found us passage clear to Far Port."

"I, for one, hope not. I'd like to poke around Nod City a few days." Kenock flung an arm in the direction of the great buildings. "After all, how often does a man get a chance to come this far east? To experience even a little of what Nod City has to offer."

Lamech scowled, but kept his voice low. "Nod City is a den of deception and irreverence. It's the home of thieves, and the capital city of this cult to the Oracle."

The women at the nearby fruit stand were openly staring now, contempt plain upon their tight faces. Lamech stared back. The women turned away and began talking among themselves. He lowered his voice further so they couldn't hear. "What part of Nod City does a Lee-lander have anything to do with? None! Kenock, your fascination has apparently muddled your good sense. You all are best away from here."

"Us?" Kenock narrowed at his brother-in-law. "And what about you?"

"I bear the truth, like my grandfather before me. These people need to hear what I have to tell them."

"And what happened to your grandfather?" It was a rhetorical question. They all knew how Lamech's grandfather had simply disappeared. The details of the story varied, but the ending always remained the same. Some said he was murdered for the warning he proclaimed of the judgment to come, a prophecy that pressed hard on the ears of the wicked. More fanciful legends had him stepping onto the Creator's open palm and being borne away. And still others took the practical stand that he simply became a meal for a hungry turnling. Whatever his fate, Lamech's grandfather had vanished, never to be heard from again.

"I cannot allow fear to stop me from doing the will of the Creator."

How about your wife's fears? Mishah wondered.

Kenock said, "And how can you know it's his will? Does he talk to you, Lamech?"

"You know the answer to that, Kenock." Lamech's impatience showed. He never could hide it well.

Mishah stepped between them. "I think we ought to find Kleg'l."

The two men backed off.

A glint of amusement briefly brightened Amolikah's face. She gave an approving nod meant for Mishah's eyes only. "This way." She took charge of the situation in her usual, no-nonsense manner. She marched the small party of travelers past the vegetable and fruit stands, onto a wide, well-groomed pathway that wound in gentle sweeps through low hedges of red, purple, and yellow flowers, down to the river.

As they left, Mishah couldn't help noticing the worrisome way the women at the fruit stand watched them.

※

Perplexed, Rhone turned his steps away from the crowd. What had come over him back there on the Meeting Floor? No sooner had he entered the city than he let himself get embroiled in the affairs of others. Those Lee-landers were no concern of his. He tried to put the incident out of mind.

It was midday with the sun high in a pale bluish-pink sky. Although Nod City had almost fifty thousand residents, the wildlife didn't seem to mind. Everywhere Rhone looked colorful birds flitted among the citizens, landing on walls and pecking for scraps of food among passing feet. The air was clean and sweetly scented by the flowers that encircled most every building. To his right, a hundred spans or so, was a square of land left wild where trees towered over the buildings. Gold, black, red, and yellow monkeys swung among the branches or hung by their furry tails to snatch food from the out-stretched hands of laughing children.

As he watched, a small red-and-gold pocket dragon soared across the sky, its shiny scales catching the sunlight as it descended. Only about two spans in length, not including the long, whipping tail, the dragon landed heavily among the upper branches and snatched up a ripe keelit in its clawed fingers. In a moment, sharp teeth had gnawed their way through the tough umber skin to the sweet green pulp beneath, and the dragon's long tongue began darting in and out of the hole it had made.

Rhone started down the walkway, his heavy boots clunking upon the neatly fitted paving stones. Merchandise carts drawn by oxen clattered past him in a regular procession down to the market. He paused to let a freight dray, pulled by a lumbering three-point, pass by. The dray held polished quarry blocks, and was making for the temple construction site, just beyond the city walls. The three-point's thick skin, the texture of a pebble-strewn beach, creased and folded with each rumbling step. A heady musk filled the air. The animal was overdue for a long soak in the river.

Crossing to a side street, he put the traffic behind him. At Weaver's Lane he turned left and stopped before a building with the words "Ker'ack's Cabling and Tackle" carved into a wooden sign. The iron grate hung open.

Inside, the sweet smell of javian cables and ropes and the oily tang of wooden block and tackle assailed his nostrils. Riggings draped like vines along the walls. The clatter and slap of weaving machines came from a back room. It took a moment for his eyes to adjust to the darkened interior. When they did, a jungle of blocks and tackle, great and small, emerged from the high, shadowed rafters. Some were fashioned of wood and others of iron. Wood was preferable for its durability, iron for its strength. There were oak and maple and cypress and gopher blocks. Some stood taller than himself while others were small enough to rest comfortably upon his open hand.

Rhone much preferred the tall forests of the Wild Lands to the city. There at least he was free to travel without jostling among a crowd for a place to put his feet down. But Nod City is where he must come to trade the precious javian silk—the threads of commerce, as Ker'ack called it—and Nod City is where he must come to replenish his equipment if he wished to keep at his trade. And a lucrative trade it was, especially during these days of ambitious temple building. Javian thread was in high demand, and fewer and fewer men seemed able to successfully collect it. The knowledge was on the wane.

The knowledge was not something one man could teach to another. You were either born with it or you were not.

"Rhone!" Ker'ack came smiling from around a mound of spools. He gripped the taller man's hand in his callused fist and gave it a hearty shake. "Good to see you back in town again. Have a profitable trip, heh?" Ker'ack's eyebrow arched upwards. He was a stocky man with broad shoulders, a thick neck, big arms, and an ample waist. He stood three and a half spans and weighed nearly as much as a small milk cow. Ker'ack claimed to have been born only five hundred years after the Banishment, back when there were still the First Children alive to declare the Banishment a real event. Today, most men had tossed the story upon the rubbish pile of myths.

He had begun life as a shepherd in the North Lands, then followed his family down to Nod City where he plied a dozen trades before becoming a supplier of spider silk. For years Ker'ack had managed a modest living by selling web to weavers, balloon makers, and the construction firms that were constantly expanding Nod City. Nestled between the Little Idikla and the Idikla, Nod City had expanded beyond the banks of the Idikla over a hundred years ago. It now sprawled north along its fertile shores for nearly six leagues.

Because of the temple project, Ker'ack had a flourishing business. Rhone was only one of Ker'ack's main suppliers of the fine, immensely strong fibers that went into the cables and ropes that he manufactured and sold to the Temple Company. They'd known each other since the days when Nod City was nothing more than a jumping-off spot at the junction of the Idikla and the Little Idikla; a place people paused to rest after the long journey south, and before continuing down into the Lands of Hope.

The Lands of Hope?

Rhone grimaced. There had been no more hope down south than there had been up north. The ground was just as unyielding, each crop rotation just as toilsome as all the others that had gone before. Nothing much ever changed.

Plows may become better, the iron in their blades tougher, but men still toiled sunup to sundown, and the weeds still invaded the hoed furrows, and the land went barren if not painstakingly maintained. He thought of the Lee-landers again.

"Come on back to the office, Rhone. I've a kettle of tea on the stove." He grinned then eyed Rhone's pack. "You can show me what you got in the sack, heh?" Ker'ack took him by the arm, weaving them between piles of ropes and spools of cables, past the spinning shop where a score of craftsmen were working over their clattering machines. Ker'ack's youngest son, Bar'ack, poised over a braiding frame, tossed Rhone a wave.

The older man turned Rhone into a room and shut the door, taking the edge off the slap-clack of busy machines. He motioned him to a chair across from the cluttered desk.

"I've been scrambling like mad, praise the Creator for the business, trying to keep up with the orders ... and the demand is only going to increase as that confounded monstrosity rises to the sky." Ker'ack lifted a kettle off the hot iron plate. "Ferrisroot tea?"

Rhone nodded and Ker'ack filled two cups.

"That 'confounded monstrosity' is making you a wealthy man, Ker'ack. Thanks." Rhone set the mug of tea on a low table at his right elbow.

"Maybe." The web merchant's mouth tightened.

"So, why the long face?"

"Korgran was in last week."

"How is he?"

"Well enough," there was a long pause, "I think."

"What is that suppose to mean?"

Ker'ack tasted the sweet brew. "It means I hope you have more in that bag of yours than good wishes and excuses."

Rhone nodded, all at once understanding Ker'ack's concern. Collecting had not been profitable this time out. He had thought perhaps it was only his bad luck, but if he correctly read between Ker'ack's concerned look, his bad luck was shared with others.

"Korgran claims the spiders have moved on. Moved on! Who's ever heard of such a thing?" Ker'ack huffed. "I figured he'd just spent the last three months off somewhere taking it easy. But then a web merchant in the Irad district over in Old Town got the same story from a fellow who collects for him." Ker'ack pursed his thick lips, his eyes compressing. "You don't have to say the words, Rhone. The look on your face tells me all I need to know."

"That fellow in the Irad district must have seen what I have, Ker'ack."

"I was afraid you'd say that." The web merchant dropped heavily into his chair and stared at the mug of tea. "Ort'leck should be back any day now, and Lem-il next month. If they've had no better success …," he shook his head. "I won't meet my contracts."

Rhone wished he could be the bearer of better news. He and Ker'ack had been friends a lot of years and he would have done anything to help the older man. He had planned to spend a couple of months in Nod City before returning to the Wild Lands, but how could he now?

"If you think it will help, I can head back out next week."

Ker'ack shook his head. "You've got a life of your own to live, Rhone. I'd never ask such a thing."

A life of his own? Rhone laughed inwardly. His life consisted chiefly of his work. Few friends, no family, no woman … he cut that line of thinking. "I know you wouldn't, Ker'ack. That's why I'm offering it."

Ker'ack bent forward, resting his meaty forearms upon the cluttered desk. "Tell me, Rhone. What's going on out there? We've come on lean times before, but never like this. Never the same bad news from every webmaster coming in from the Wilds."

Rhone tasted his tea, then cupped the mug in his hands, feeling the warmth of it upon his palms as he considered. "Something seems to have driven them off. I was clear to the Illackin Mountains and still finding abandoned webs."

"Could the spiders tell you what it was?"

"I didn't ask."

Ker'ack scowled.

"I doubt they would know themselves. They aren't thoughtful creatures, Ker'ack. They react, that's all."

"I know. Still, they must be aware of something—some change."

Rhone shrugged. "Would they be able to put it into thoughts—thoughts I could understand? Perhaps among themselves ..." He shook his head. It was a difficult concept to explain to someone who did not have the gift. "But I doubt it." He fetched his sack onto his knees, unbuckled the flap, and extracted a bundle wrapped in a heavy cotton cloth. "This is all of it."

Ker'ack unfolded the cloth with the eager fingers of a child with his first gift on Creation Evening, lifting the spool of web from the wrapping in both hands as if it were gold. He held it toward the bright, unshuttered window. The thread glistened in the sunlight like dew drops. He unfastened the end and drew out about half a span of the silken fiber. A childish smile spreading his cheeks in spite of his concerns. "Beautiful, is it not?" Sunlight played along the silvery filament not much wider than the thickness of his fingernail. Ker'ack gave it a sharp tug. His smile broadened. "Hard to believe, but size for size, this is eight times stronger than any iron threads that the Tubal-Cain company can produce. And it never rusts! Properly prepared, it will last two hundred years. Like to see iron do that!"

"T-C claims to have a new iron that will."

"Bah! Nothing man can make will compare to what comes from the hand of the Creator!" Ker'ack judged the weight of the spool. "What do you have here? About nine thousand spans?"

"Closer to eight."

A momentary frown marred the smile. "Good stuff?"

Rhone feigned a wounded expression. "Ker'ack. Would I bring you anything but the best? Pure walking strands, that's what you are holding there. Not a span of that other stuff. And it's been properly cleaned too."

The smile returned full force. "You're a good man, Rhone!" Ker'ack laughed and carefully wrapped the spool back in its protective cloth. "You've eaten?"

"No."

"You must come for dinner. Sarsee will prepare something special for you, my friend. You are always one of her favorite guests. And ...," his eyes shifted momentarily toward the closed door. "There is a little matter that Bar'ack and I want to discuss with you."

"A little matter?" A warning prodded at the back of his brain.

Ker'ack laughed. "We will talk of it later, heh? Tonight?"

Rhone was loath to miss a home-cooked meal, even if it did include a little subterfuge on Ker'ack's part. He said he'd be there.

3

A Little Matter

Rhone's small rented cottage stood on the outskirts of Nod City, located on the grounds of Master Mav-duruc, the owner of a livery stable. Rhone's heavy boots clunked the stone walkway to the house. Mav-duruc had kept the flowerbeds along the paved walkway to his door cultivated and free of weeds in his absence. It was a solid, square stone building with a roof of green tiles whose eaves overhung the door and cast a line of shade along the whole front of the place. Wandering vines crept up the walls, over the door, and around the corners, spilling pink-and-white flowers down the front of the cottage. Inside, the place was exactly as he'd left it, if somewhat more dusty and desperately needing an airing out. The tidy three-room dwelling consisted of a parlor/kitchen combination adequate for one person, a cramped bedroom, and another small private room.

He flung his pack onto a chair, shedding his shirt as he headed for the washbasin, vaguely annoyed at his suspicious nature. He'd been two months alone in the Wilds and was torn between the choice of a good meal and an evening of pleasant company, or his own comfortable bed and the promise of a sound night's sleep—one where he didn't have to keep an ear or an eye open. Not that he wouldn't be only a whisker's breadth from wide-awake here. Habits developed over the years were hard to break. But what was this "little matter" Ker'ack wanted to discuss with him? Something that concerned his son Bar'ack as well?

He dried himself and sprawled across the bed, inhaling the fragrance of Mav-duruc's flowerbed, which ran between his cottage and the big house to the east. He closed his eyes, and when he opened them again, shadows had taken up habitation in his bedroom and the sun hung low in the sky.

He pulled on a fresh shirt and pants, shrugged on his vest, considered his sword and proj-lance a moment, but left them leaning in the corner and slid a thin webbing knife deep into the top of his boot instead and went outside.

In the fading light, Mav-duruc was fussing over a bed of evening-peace lay-downs, scratching at the ground with a hand cultivator, plucking up weeds and depositing them in a pile. "Rhone!" he cried upon seeing him step out his door. "When did you get back?"

He strolled over to where the older man was working. Mav-duruc was a trim man with gray hair and a long white beard encircling his black chin. His eyes were leaf-green, flecked with gold. The eyes smiled, along with the rest of his face. The old man was full of years, but exactly how many, he had never said. Rhone bowed slightly at the waist. "Evening-peace. May your servant find favor in your eyes."

Mav-duruc smiled. "Your presence gladdens my heart."

"I got back into town late this morning," Rhone went on, the formalities out of the way. "I would have stopped by earlier, but my bed got hold of me first." He laughed. "Your flowers look well."

"I haven't spent the time with them that I'd like to. The curse of the weeds. If I leave my darlings unattended more than a few days the weeds take over." Mav-duruc sighed hugely and smiled. "But I do love tending them." He looked up at Rhone. "Have a successful trip?"

"I've had better."

"Sorry to hear that."

"But I made enough to pay my rent."

Mav-duruc chuckled. "I don't worry much about that, Rhone. I know you're good for it, eventually."

"Anything come for me while I was away?"

Mav-duruc thought a moment, then shook his head. "No, nothing. Were you expecting something?"

He hadn't really. Not anymore. He'd come to grips with what had happened years ago and had mostly put it out of mind. But still something deep inside clung to the hope that someday a letter might arrive. Word of his mother would mean a lot … even word of his brother would be something. He didn't let his disappointment show. "No, nothing." The breeze shifted, carrying a rank animal odor from the barns beyond the house. A three-point's shrill chortle rent the stillness, followed by the bugling of an elephant. "Sounds like someone is hungry."

"They never fail to let me know when I'm late with their supper." Mav-duruc grunted as he stood. He massaged his knees, collected the pile of weeds into his arms, bade Rhone evening-peace, and started toward the barns.

It was dark by the time Rhone headed toward Ker'ack's cozy place a quarter league from his warehouse and not far from Old Town. His footsteps echoed on the quarried blocks as he strolled along streets that led back into town. Nod City was lighting up for the night; moonglass in every hue of the spectrum had been skillfully crafted into geometric designs, or intertwining floral works, or sometimes murals of country life. Many of the designs had the names of businesses cleverly integrated into them. The city glowed softly as the night came on, still a bustling place with people and beasts moving about her broad streets and lanes.

Nightlife in Nod City took on a lusty note after the shops closed up and the festival halls flung wide their doors. Street prophets declaring the Oracle's message competed with women's laughter and men's coarse conversation from a dozen doorways. Lyre and drums and cali-bells blared out vulgar songs while drunken voices bellowed in accompaniment, oblivious to key or harmony. Rhone was ever a wary man, but particularly so when he ventured into Nod City after dark.

"You all alone tonight?" A sultry voice inquired near the doorway of a festival hall he was passing by. A heavy woman with florid cheeks and yellow diamonds painted across her brow winked at him. Her hair hung coarse and black about her shoulders, twisted into a dozen thick braids, each ending in a golden clip, each clip attached to a fine gold chain. The chains all came together at the front of her low dress in a wedge of gleaming greenish moonglass that spread a soft emerald glow across her bare shoulders, illuminating the point of her chin.

She was alluring in a curious, temptress way that he found intriguing. She reached for his hand, her grip firm and warm, urging him closer. Eager eyes of indeterminate color in the poor light were wide and inviting, painted in glitter that sparkled in the light from the open festival hall doorway.

"Come inside and buy me a drink. The ale is cold, and it will kindle a fire in that big, broad chest. A fire I know how to put out," she breathed warmly as her free hand climbed to his shoulder, finding its way softly around his neck. It was a reach, but she was determined, and his breath quickened as she drew herself closer … and then her perfume suddenly made his head swim. She was an *afaleigh*!

His senses reeled from the fragrance, his thoughts suddenly muddled. An afaleigh here, and freely plying her ware inside the city limits! Were even *those* restrictions being cast aside? Did the city fathers know this was going on? He suspected they didn't. A nagging at the back of his brain warned him he shouldn't stay. If a man is not careful, if he permits an afaleigh to entice him, she will worm her way into his soul. A weak man might be lost forever to her wiles.

The perfume filled his nose, seeped into his brain, smothering common sense. Only *they* knew how to distill the peculiar odor from a recipe kept secret by their sect; and only an afaleigh, after years of training, could wear it and not be affected. His head swam as faint yellowish lights began to dance before his eyes.

"No." He took her hand to dislodge it from his neck, but hesitated. Did he really want to leave her? How quickly one could lose himself! "No, I have other plans." Struggling against his will, he detached himself from her and stepped away.

"Such a pity," she sighed softly. Then with a quick, dismissive smile turned to another man passing by.

Rhone staggered away and didn't dare look back. She was another man's problem now—problem or delight, it all depended. Yet, as he willed himself away from there, it was with an overwhelming reluctance, and a drunken totter to his step.

Slowly the poison ebbed from his system, but not before he'd gone another two blocks without recalling a single window, doorway, or face between then and the moment he'd left her. When his head finally cleared, he found himself on a dark street, his back hard against the rounded corner of a building, a black alley to his right and a slash of open sky overhead between the two buildings. The moon's perfect porcelain surface, softly glowing, shone clear and large in that slash of sky, obscuring all but the brightest stars around it. Its light probed the mouth of the alley, leaving only the back of it in deep darkness that strained even his eyes.

He suddenly shivered and his shoulders tensed. He glanced back the way he'd come, listening. The next corner down, two men stood talking. Another sat in a darkened doorway, knees up and his head hung between them. A woman and man, arm in arm, crossed the street and were briefly caught in a sliver of light from a curtained window, then entered one of the buildings with the sound of a heavy door closing behind them.

Rhone remained motionless a moment longer trying to sort out what it was he had sensed. Was part of it the lingering effects of the afaleigh's spell?

He detected nothing unusual, yet his shoulders refused to relax. He got a fix on his bearings and resumed his trek to Ker'ack's home.

The streets quieted down as he left the busy festival halls behind. The web dealer's home was a wooden oval, resting upon a stout stone foundation, encircled in bright windows. It had a flat roof of baked tiles overlaying each other like tight-fitting scales. It was nestled among four other curved dwellings that together formed a cluster; one of two dozen or so links in a peaceful neighborhood of clusters, strung out along the sweeping street like a strand of beads cast carelessly aside. This part of Nod City was still mostly free of commerce.

He found Ker'ack's gate open, the low boundary wall lined with moonglass spreading a soft orange glow upon the curving pathway to the house. Rhone stole a final glance down the street before the chrodertherium bushes at the door blocked his view. A bit of moonlight touched something back there. He stopped. Something ducked quickly out of sight.

So, that explained the itch between his shoulder blades. Who would be following him, and why? In spite of this new puzzle, a tight smile creased his face. The itch, at least, was gone.

At his knock, Ker'ack appeared in a warm glow of lamplight from the doorway. "Ah! Rhone. My heart gladdens!"

He gave the curt bow. "Evening-peace. Your servant ..."

"Of course, of course. You are always welcome over this threshold!" He laughed. "No need for formalities here! Your manners as always are impeccable. You learned well at your mother's hand."

Training was one thing he had no lack of, though the memory of it often brought a wince at the clenching claw in his chest. Ker'ack stepped aside for him. Rhone smiled at Sarsee who stood right behind her husband.

"Honor our home, Rhone." She was a tall, thin woman with high, sharp cheeks, clear blue eyes, light brown hair, and smooth olive skin a shade or two lighter than his own. Ker'ack was a fair-skinned stocky man and between the two of them they'd procreated seventeen children who covered the gamut from the palest moon-glow white to the deepest obsidian black. All seventeen lived in Nod City with families of their own now, all but Bar'ack, the youngest, who at forty-two had yet to find himself a suitable wife and had steadfastly resisted every arrangement his mother and father sought for him.

The house had a cozy, lived-in feel; cluttered but clean. Sort of like Ker'ack's warehouse. Comfortably yet not lavishly furnished, with a sofa suspended from the ceiling along one wall, three wooden chairs, a table holding a lamp and some books, and an upholstered honorseat. Sarsee's exquisite needlework adorned the backs of the sofa and chairs and hung from the walls beside portraits of all seventeen of their children. The floor's stone-and-glass mosaic was an intertwining grapevine motif, covered with a large woolen Dorminite rug that Sarsee had brought with her from her homeland when she'd married Ker'ack.

The aroma of cooking filled the air and started Rhone's mouth watering in anticipation. After two months in the Wild Lands, he was weary of his own cooking, which consisted largely of a bland mix of fruits and vegetables, sometimes steamed or grilled, but most often eaten raw and on the move. The nature of his life was not a settled existence as was Ker'ack's. Like Bar'ack, he'd not taken a wife. It wasn't that he did not want to be more settled, or to raise a family of his own, but circumstances had not smiled upon him in that way.

He shifted his thoughts onto a different track before that clawed fist had a chance to clench again.

Ker'ack motioned him to the honorseat, though Rhone would have preferred a less conspicuous position. An honorseat, by custom, had to be elevated a bit above any other furniture in a room. Rhone, already larger than most men, was always vaguely uncomfortable in a home that followed the old tradition. A big, yellow-striped cat jumped up on the sofa where Ker'ack had settled, swinging it gently. Sarsee sat beside her husband on the sofa and asked Rhone how he had been. Bar'ack came in from another room carrying a heavy, leather-bound book. He grinned at Rhone and immediately began pummeling him with questions about the Wild Lands. Ker'ack indulged the young man's curiosity, allowing him to occupy his guest's attention, a small, tolerant smile upon his face. After hearing a brief description of his trip, Sarsee sniffed the air.

"Oh-oh. Dinner needs attending." She sprang from the sofa and hurried back to the kitchen.

Ker'ack followed her through the doorway and returned carrying a tray holding a stone pitcher of warm whiteberry tea and four mugs. He poured the tea and handed Rhone and Bar'ack a mug, taking a third for himself. He lifted his mug to Rhone. "To collecting. May you find the mother spider and may her children spin you a thousand webs!"

Bar'ack rapped the table in agreement.

Rhone took a long draft of the tea. It had just a hint of ginger and ferrisroot. He slammed down the mug, smacked his lips, and made a show of dragging his sleeve across his mouth.

Ker'ack smiled. "You honor me." He took a seat, glanced briefly at his son, then to Rhone, his face becoming earnest. "Do you think they will be back, or have they moved on for good?" His hand settled lightly upon the cat's head, fingers kneading the base of the ears. A raspy purr filled the room.

"It's difficult to say." He sweetened his tea from a bowl of honey on the tray. "I don't know what has driven them off. Something has changed, but what that is … ?" He shrugged. "I just don't know. Perhaps some change in the temperature."

"Temperature? Nothing has changed there since the beginning. The first quartering cools the air and brings out the stars, clear as dew drops. The second deepens the night's chill, just as the Creator meant. The third gives us the morning dew, and burns off the fog, and the fourth holds the heat of the day. What has changed?"

Rhone didn't have an answer. Whatever the cause, it was too subtle for him to detect. "It could be anything."

"Anything, indeed," Ker'ack huffed. He had the look of a man with serious worries. "What will I do if they don't come back? I've contracts to fill."

Rhone took a pragmatic view of the problem. "You'll end up hiring more webmasters, sending them further into the Wild Lands, and paying them more money. That's what you'll do." But finding more webmasters might be a tougher job than he made it out to be.

"And charging the Temple Company double for my products?" Ker'ack frowned. "That will make a lot of people happy." He gave a short, sarcastic laugh. "Especially when the Lodath decrees another tariff on the people to pay for it."

"He already has."

Ker'ack glanced up from his mug. "He has? I hadn't heard. When?"

"Announced it from the Meeting Floor this morning. I was just coming into town as his emissary was trying to convince a lot of angry folks it was necessary."

"Humm." Ker'ack's eyebrows knitted together, folds deepening in his forehead. "Curious timing. It's almost as if they know something we don't."

Rhone laughed. "Isn't that the reason this Oracle is coming? To teach us mortal men things we don't know?"

Ker'ack waved a dismissive hand. "I don't believe it for an instant, but let the people think what they will. And they will!" He grinned. "In the meantime, I'll keep the Temple Company in cables and blocks, raise my prices as need be, and collect a great fat pile of golden glecks. I'm a businessman, Rhone, not a philosopher."

Bar'ack was listening intently. There seemed to be something on the young man's mind, but he wasn't sure how to broach the subject. Was it Ker'ack's "little matter?"

"Dinner's ready," Sarsee announced. They followed her down a hallway to a dining area at the back of the house. Plates were set out on a long wooden table with platters and trays and steaming bowls lined up in the center. Amongst them was a basket of rolls and bread, a platter of rice, and a great heap of fruit in a terra cotta bowl.

Ker'ack took his place at the head while Sarsee and Bar'ack sat on either side, leaving the end chair for Rhone. After everyone was seated, Sarsee asked her husband to bless the food. Rhone bowed his head with the family. He was easy where the customs of others were concerned, even when they weren't his own. Part of that training, he mused wryly.

"Oh powerful Creator, whose mighty words spoke all that there is into existence, whose strong hands hold it all together and spin the stars in their courses. I ask you to smile upon us tonight, and especially upon our fine guest, Master Rhone. Bless this food, for our health, and for the fullness of years. Thank you for your provision. Praise upon you."

"Praise upon you," Ker'ack's family and Rhone repeated. It was a rote prayer, one easily modified to fit the occasion, one he'd heard a thousand times before, and was likely to hear a thousand times henceforth.

Sarsee slid the platter of elephant-tusk rice to Rhone. Rhone particularily relished this giant variety, grown in the fertile lands to the south of Nod City. With tongs, he picked out two thick grains and passed the platter to Bar'ack. Next came a bowl of hot vegetables. Slicing the rice lengthwise, he filled them to overflowing; red tomatoes and bud-buttons, white savots, bright orange carrots and laylows, and green peppers blended to perfection in a thick slightly sweetened sauce. Mugs of tea, and thick cream for the bread rounded out the dinner.

The fruit was for dessert. Rhone stabbed a strawberry off the platter, sliced it into wedges, and smothered it in the sweet cream. His stomach was pleasantly full by dinner's end, and he regretted having to leave the strawberry half eaten on his plate. His compliments to Sarsee brought a pretty smile in reply.

After dinner everyone retreated to the welcoming room. Ker'ack placed a bowl of mintroot candy on the table then handed Rhone a mug of mild, after-dinner tea.

"I ran into an afaleigh on my way here."

Ker'ack frowned and poured himself a mug of tea.

"Since when have they been allowed in Nod City? At least, since when have they been allowed to ply their trade openly in public?"

"It's this Oracle business. The Lodath made a proclamation a month or so ago. Ker'ack grinned irreverently and set the teapot back onto the tray. "Lifestyle differences were to not only be allowed, but honored. Honored! Seems depravity is now official policy here in Nod City." He rolled his eyes. "Next thing you know, some enterprising fool will open a festival hall and put out a sign saying 'Men Only'!" He laughed. "Then we'll have to open one for women only too, so we don't discriminate."

Rhone gave a wry grin. "I might move permanently to the Wild Lands. At least the beasts of the fields keep to the proper order of things."

Ker'ack chuckled and took the chair across from the honorseat. "Speaking of the Wild Lands," he leaned forward, his round face assuming an earnest expression. Bar'ack sat on the edge of the sofa next to the cat, a hand wrapped about that heavy leather book, his eyes wide. The young man seemed to be holding his breath.

Rhone had been expecting this moment.

"If what you say is true, Rhone," Ker'ack began, "about having to send more men farther afield to collect the web, then perhaps I should begin now looking for more webmasters."

"Good webmasters are hard to come by."

"Especially if this shortage continues," Ker'ack added. "Their services would be in high demand." He paused as if expecting a reply.

Rhone sipped his tea, allowing his friend to broach his "little matter" in his own way.

Ker'ack gave a quick smile. "You know, a man gets to a certain point in life where he has to make his own decisions, to go his own way."

"True."

"Take me, for example. I jumped from one occupation to another before finding my niche. My father was a herder of sheep and biliacs. He wanted me to work beside him on the hillsides and in the shearing pens, and I tried it for fifty or sixty years, but I knew from the start tending livestock was not for me." He laughed. "I'm sure you've also had many occupations in your three hundred or so years."

Rhone remained silent, giving only a slight nod.

Ker'ack cleared his throat and continued. "What I'm saying is we all grow and change, and go on to different things."

In the moment of ensuing silence, Bar'ack had begun to fidget. Ker'ack glanced to his son, then back. "Bar'ack has come to me expressing his desire to be released from the family bond."

"Oh?" Rhone knew what was coming. "And what plans have you made, Bar'ack?"

The young man was surprised to be addressed directly, but he grabbed the opportunity to speak. "I want to be a webmaster. Like you, Master Rhone."

Ker'ack seemed relieved to have the matter out in the open. He raised the mug of tea to his lips, no doubt as an excuse to let his son speak for himself.

Rhone said, "Why would you choose such a life?"

Bar'ack stood and set the book upon the table. He was taller than his father, with a slender waist, wide though somewhat bony shoulders, a thin neck and sharp features. He took after his mother, and his skin was nearly as dark as hers.

"I wish to learn to speak the language of the javians, Master Rhone. And I wish to see the world out beyond Nod City. Since the day I was born, I've not traveled more than fifty leagues beyond its borders. I've never even seen the Wild Lands." His enthusiasm mounted as he picked up the old book, his knuckles whitening about its binding. "I've read all of Master Frobin's stories: *Legends of the World, The Day Before Tomorrow, The Makir and the Shepherd.* I've heard about the hovering stones of Per'inon, the Pillars of the Sun, and the singing sky above the mountains of Olphus. I've seen Makir Warriors putting on demonstrations in the marketplace, but that sort of fighting is only to please the crowds."

Rhone's back stiffened, his lips compressed slightly.

"Frobin says a Makir's strength is unequaled. A single warrior a match for a dozen fighting men. I want to see their land."

Ker'ack chuckled. "Frobin's stories fill a young man's head with adventures and put fire in his soul."

"The Makir have all but faded from the Land of Hodin, but you would not have wanted to meet one," Rhone said, his voice flat, his eyes hardening ever so slightly. "To enter Atlan is foolishness now that Zorin rules it." He grinned. "Unless you're willing to compete in the Pit of Ramor."

Bar'ack's expression widened. "You've been to Atlan? You've met Makir Warriors?"

Rhone felt the muscles across his chest constrict. "The Makir of legend are no more than that ... legend."

"Bar'ack," his father said quietly to quell his son's eagerness for answers.

Bar'ack tempered his enthusiasm. "There is so much in our world to see, and I want to see it all, Master Rhone. You've been to the Border Seas, haven't you?"

Rhone nodded.

"I've read of the Towers of Nerph on its shores, and of the great monsters that roam the deep. I wish to see all these things. As a webmaster, I'd have the opportunity to travel to all the far-off places. I've read Frobin's *Words from the Cradle*, too."

Ker'ack smiled an apology for his son's eagerness.

Rhone nodded. "I've read the legends."

"They must be more than legends, Master Rhone. Some believe it is a true place, still existing today, yet hidden." He leaned back and gave a slightly embarrassed smile. "Of course, the Oracle has explained how that was all mere myth."

"You'll find not many believe in the Cradleland anymore," Rhone said.

"Yet someday I'd like to see for myself, but unless I know the ways of the Wild Lands, how can I?"

"Do you have the gift?"

The eagerness in his face dimmed. "I ... I don't know. Is it something I can learn?"

Rhone shook his head. "I've not heard of any who has been able to master the skill. If the ability is within a man or woman, it can be encouraged and made stronger. But if not, it is not something to be learned."

"But everyone had the ability at one time," Bar'ack protested. "That's what Frobin says."

"If so, then like many things of old, it is dying."

"Frobin says we've lost much because of what happened in the Cradle."

Ker'ack gave a short laugh. "Frobin writes books to spark the imagination of young men who wish to leave their father's sides and strike off on their own. His scholarship may not be all he presents it to be. Isn't that right, Rhone?"

"Your father has seen much. His days are long and full, and he speaks wisdom."

Bar'ack's glow dimmed further. "Yes. He is wise and I honor his words."

Rhone heard the unspoken "but." He glanced to Ker'ack, caught assent in the older man's expression. He didn't relish the idea of taking on an apprentice, but Ker'ack was a good friend. And the reality was, most aspiring webmasters, even those who possessed the gift, found the life too rigorous for their liking. After a few months of living alone in the Wild Lands, collecting web, cleaning it, and rolling it on the spools, most were ready to hang up their webbing knife and settle back in the comforts of civilization.

"If you don't have the gift, you'll find the work frustrating at best, and dangerous at worse."

"How will I know if it is within me if I never try?"

Oftentimes, the best way to discourage someone with Bar'ack's enthusiasm was to let him experience a taste of what was in store for him. He glanced at Ker'ack. "Your feelings?"

"It's your choice, Rhone. My son is old enough to make his own decisions. If he wishes to be set free of the family bond, I'll release him. Although, I will miss having him working at my side."

Bar'ack crowded the edge of his chair, holding his breath.

For his friend, he'd do it. This way Bar'ack would know one way or the other. "You'll need to be outfitted. I can make a list. Plan on leaving in three days."

The smile exploded across Bar'ack's face. "I'll be ready! Oracle be praised."

Ker'ack shot the lad a scowl.

"Err, I meant Creator be praised."

When Rhone left shortly after, he'd acquired a ward and Ker'ack had lost a master webweaver. He was certain neither had profited in the exchange.

At Ker'ack's gate, he paused and peered up into the heavens. To the north the night sky was flashing sinuous bands of red and gold and green; fluid magnetic colors that streamed and swirled across the heavens in an eerily beautiful dance. But it was the orange balloon to the west that held his eye.

Suspended before a backdrop of stars, it loomed motionless above the temple site, larger than some villages; anchored in place by great cables of web—some of which he'd likely collected and sold. Four thick umbilical cords connected it to furnaces on the ground, pumping massive volumes of hot air to keep it afloat.

From here Rhone glimpsed the massive sloping temple walls rising on the Plain of Irad, beyond the city's limits. The final temple complex was supposed to be over a league square, but as of yet, only a fraction of that much land had been cleared and leveled for the construction of the first building.

Tonight, the site was ablaze with reflected light from the furnace fires. Arrays of great mirrors and rings of focusing lenses, spaced strategically about, captured the firelight and turned the night into day, illuminating the underside of the great balloon that for the last few years had been tethered above the rising stone monument. Most of the heavy lifting was done at night when the air was cooler. Many of the massive stone building blocks were more than a match for the buoyancy the balloon could provide in the heat of the day, even when clamped into their magnetic lifting harnesses.

Watching the bustle of activity in the distance—the lumbering behemoths in their traces hoisting the stones aloft, the men upon the lifting crane suspended hundreds of spans in the air, leaning over its sides to direct their placement—Rhone could only shake his head and manage a faint frown. Something about all this disturbed him. Yet, whenever he took a moment to consider why it should, he was never able to put a finger on exactly what that *something* might be.

With a sharp, sudden breath, he turned away and searched the dark street leading back into the heart of Nod City. If they were still there, they were well hidden. His jaw took a firm set as he withdrew the webbing knife from the top of his boot. Thrusting it under his belt at the hollow of his back, he bent his steps toward his cottage on the other side of town.

4

Suspicion

Mishah stood upon the open balcony overlooking the wide ribbon of water below, silvery in the moonlight, catching some red and green flares from the northern display. Strewed generously about with moonglass of different hues, Nod City had a gay, forever-twilight feel to it. She looked to the heavens where the dancing lights leaped and swirled; an entertaining performance, although not one that would steal your breath away—not like some she remembered from her childhood.

"The Creator is giving us a show tonight," Lamech noted, stepping out onto the balcony behind her. He slipped his arms around her large belly and hugged, careful not to squeeze too hard. They'd taken a room at the River Edge Inn; a dated three-story boarding house of pink granite with arching doorways and round stained glass windows in the old style. Their room on the third floor offered a spectacular panorama at night.

"Hmm?" She felt safe in his arms. Lamech; husband, star gazer, prophet, and now father of her child. He smelled of rich black earth and newly sawn cedar. The strong fingers that gripped her shoulder were callused from hard, honest work. "Oh, the dancing lights." She sighed. "I've seen better." She looked back at the river and the boats lining its wharves. "Two more days." She took in a deep breath and let it out slowly, leaning her head against his chest. How she wished she hadn't let her grandmother and Lamech talk her into the pilgrimage. She wanted to be home, in Morg'Seth, where she could experience her pregnancy in familiar surroundings.

"They'll pass quickly," Lamech soothed. "On the bright side, our passage is all the way to Far Port. It will be a short journey from there to the Mother. Kleg'l was fortunate to find us such a boat. The Creator smiles upon us." He took the tickets from his vest pocket and turned them toward the light of a moonglass. "The *Osar Messenger*. Kleg'l said it's one of only a few river vessels that runs clear to the falls."

He was trying to sound encouraging for her sake. Did her moods show so plainly?

"It carries freight and letters bound for the outposts and lands beyond. Not many passengers make their way to Far Port. It's the beginning of Wild Lands, your grandmother says."

"I wonder which one it is." Mishah's view wandered along the collection of boats and barges below. Up the river a ways stretched the temple wharves where work fires burned brightly, their light concentrated by great lenses and mirrors. Smoke snaked above the river, trailing away from the city tonight. A crane was currently lifting a massive stone block from one of the barges and swinging it toward a waiting dray with eight iron-rimmed wheels, each as tall as a man's shoulders. A contented three-point waited in harness, grazing a bale of oatgrass.

"No way to tell from up here."

She stared at the river, the boats, the temple wharves, not really seeing any of it. Her thoughts were troubled, and she didn't understand why.

Lamech grew silent. When she looked back at him, his mouth had shifted off to one side the way it did sometimes when his analytical brain suddenly came upon a problem. He stared at the dancing lights.

"What is it?" she asked softly.

His view shifted from the night-sky display to the softly glowing moonglass upon a table near the balcony railing. "You know, Mishah, you're right."

"I am?"

"I mean, about the dancing lights. I've seen better too, a lot better. But not for a very long time." He peered at the moonglass and his frown deepened, as if puzzled by something he'd not noted before, something that had all at once become apparent. Then with a sudden rush of breath, he seemed to dismiss the puzzle and lifted his face back to the night sky.

"Look, Mishah. The Archer is watching over us."

She leaned into his arms encircling her, his hand upon her stomach, upon their child. In spite of all her misgivings, when Lamech held her like this she felt safe. She peered up at the star picture. "Yes, the Gracious One."

"Two natures. Noble in character yet divine in power. The Redeemer who will come conquering. See how his arrow points toward the heart of the scorpion?"

She'd heard him tell it often enough to quote what would come next. "At the center of the shining stars he stands radiant and pierces the scorpion with his arrow."

His arms tightened about her and he laughed. "You know the star stories as well as I, my love."

"But I love to hear you tell them." She turned and kissed him.

"I love you."

❦

The chill night air brought a welcome relief from the humid heat of day. Rhone usually enjoyed nighttime strolls, but tonight his ears were alert, filtering out the sounds of his own footsteps as he walked back into the heart of the city. The music of the festival halls had begun to drift through the dark streets. Distant voices mingled with the steady grind of his soles upon the hewn stone, and something else too …

He turned a corner. Ahead, the lights of the first of the festival halls brightened the street. People chatted and argued and schemed on the sidewalks, while out in the wide avenue stood beasts harnessed to stout drays and freight wagons, horses and lizards in the traces of lithe carriages.

They were still behind him, keeping their distance. He'd picked them up almost at once after leaving Ker'ack's home. Two men, judging by the sounds of their feet. Whoever they were, they were doing a good job tailing him. Anyone else might never have known they were back there, but Rhone had lived too many years in the Wild Lands for a pair of stealthy trackers, even two as subtle as these, to escape him.

He turned a corner and ducked into the narrow passage between the two buildings. Gaining a hand- and toehold in the joints of the stone wall, he swiftly climbed into the shadows and went absolutely still, as if part of the building.

Their hurried footsteps slapped upon the sidewalk a few moments later.

"Where the Tempter could he have gone?" a voice whispered.

"Captain's not going to like this," came a higher pitched and nervous reply.

Below, two forms silhouetted themselves against the faint lights of the festival hall down the way. Rhone's eyes had grown keen living in the Wilds where deep forests were in perpetual gloom. The uniforms of the Lodath's Guards were unmistakable. They each wore a sword, and the taller of the two carried a proj-lance. Whatever their purpose, they meant business.

What interest could the Lodath have in me?

The man with the Proj-lance also carried a shuttered moonglass. He twisted the lens cap open and showed a pale white light down the alleyway.

"Not down here," the high-pitched voice said, losing the whisper.

"Festival hall down the way." The taller one looked up and down the street. "Or that way, along Forge Road."

"We better split." High-pitched was a burly fellow, no more than three spans tall. His hair was cropped short. The cape of the Lodath's Guards spread across his shoulders like a green tent.

"We can't afford to lose him." The husky whisper held an edge of growing panic.

"We won't, we won't." Although the blocky man tried to sound confident, his tone had lifted even higher and his words wavered nervously. "I'll take the festival hall. You check out Forge Road."

Rhone dropped silently to the pavement a moment later and slipped free of the shadows, keeping the man with the husky voice in sight. The guard was a big fellow, though not as tall as Rhone. Few men were.

The guard half sprinted, dodging here and there up the street, hastily flashing his light down alleyways. His careless rush grew more and more desperate as the moments passed. Rhone could have strode boldly down the middle of the street for all the attention the guard was paying to what was happening behind him.

The guard had his head poked down one of those narrow side streets when Rhone stopped behind him. "I saw him go that way."

The man spun around, startled. "Where the Tempter did you come from?"

Rhone hooked a thumb over his shoulder at the street, now a good distance behind them. His size alone would intimidate most men. "You and your partner have been on my heels all evening. Why?"

"I don't know what you're talking about."

Rhone narrowed his eyes. "What does the Lodath want with me?"

The guard saw it was pointless to lie any further. "We are following orders."

"What orders?"

Finding Rhone behind him had momentarily knocked him off his stride. Now he squared his shoulders and took a firmer grip on the proj-lance. "An impertinent tongue will get you chained to the temple crew."

"Save your threats for someone who might be impressed. Why are you following me?"

The man slowly shifted the proj-lance to his other hand. "Orders." He grinned. "Suppose we go ask the captain why." The proj-lance leaped up.

Rhone caught the weapon in a blinding move, wrenched it free and turned it on him. "Suppose we don't."

The guard took two quick steps backward, eyes fixed, his breath frozen in his chest.

Rhone lowered the proj-lance, broke open the breech, removed a barbed projectile and tossed it into the shadows across the street. He hauled back and flung the proj-lance down the alley. It clattered against a stone wall somewhere out of sight. He advanced a step. "Next time I'll wrap it around your neck."

The man backed again. "The captain will have you in shackles for this." He grabbed his sword from the scabbard and it sung through the air. Rhone ducked. The blade swung back, lower this time. He leaped and it passed under him. As Rhone came down his foot shot directly at the sword. The blade soared into the air and the guard grabbed his wrist.

Rhone snatched the weapon by the hilt on its way down, and pressed the point against the guard's chest. "Why is the Lodath having me followed?"

"I … I don't know. Me and Deree'inor, we were just following orders. The Captain said to follow you, and … and that's what we were doing." His bulging eyes had fixed upon the blade as his tongue nervously moistened his lips.

He was too frightened to risk a lie.

The guard's eyes gave a slight lurch to the left, then came back to the sword. "It might have something to do with what happened this morning at the Meeting Floor."

"You mean with those Lee-landers?"

He nodded, some of his taut fear dissipating. He glanced past Rhone again, then quickly up into his face. "You know, I … I can claim we lost you. You can go on your way and no one will be the wiser."

"What will your Lodath say? I hear he doesn't tolerate failure. It could be you chained to the temple crew."

"Well," he spread his hands. "I'll take that chance."

Rhone spun to his right and the sword rang as it slammed into hardened steel. Stunned, the second guard stared at the sword vibrating in his hand. In a blinding move, Rhone twirled his blade and plucked the weapon from the man's fist, flinging it away.

The first guard leaped to Rhone's back, levering a thick arm around his neck. Rhone reached over his shoulder, caught a fistful of tunic and flung the man into a wall as if he'd been a mere child. The guard hit with an *oomph* and crumpled to the ground. The second guard scrambled back.

Rhone thrust the sword out like a warning finger. "Tell your captain of the Guard that if he has business with me, he can knock on my door. If I find you or any of his men following me again, I won't be so forgiving." He flung the sword down the alleyway and turned toward home.

Scowling at the condition of his men, disgust like acid bile rose in Da-gore's throat.

"Then he said to tell you, if you had business with him, you should knock on his door." As Deree'inor spoke, his view remained averted from the Lodath's penetrating stare.

"*I* should knock on *his* door!" Da-gore's eyes glistened like lumps of obsidian, his face flint, the downward slash of his lips turning purple with building rage.

Sol-Ra-Luce remained silently observing, no doubt to learn the character of these men, and yes, Da-gore surmised, to more critically assess the character of his captain of the Guard.

"And you let him get the advantage over you." Da-gore couldn't afford to show sympathy in front of his superior. His burning glare took in both of them. "Two warriors in the Lodath's Guards!"

Though hunched over and clearly still in pain, Mer'dor's voice was huskier, more sure than Deree'inor's. "He didn't fight like any man I've ever faced, Captain." Mer'dor's view shifted briefly to the tall presence who had remained silent. "Your Eminence."

Looking back to the captain, Mer'dor said, "He moves like a cat and he strikes quicker than a serpent. It was almost as if he knew what we were thinking. The man must have eyes all around his head."

Da-gore's eyes narrowing to slits. "Excuses for incompetence!"

"But, it's true," Deree'inor said. "He had Mer'dor backed up against the wall with a sword against his chest. I saw it all and came up behind him quiet as nettle-down on a breeze. He couldn't have heard me, yet before I could strike, he'd come about and disarmed me in the blink of an eye. I've never seen anything like it."

Da-gore's fists bunched. Sol-Ra-Luce put a hand to the captain's arm. "Did you learn this man's name?" The Lodath's voice was calming, and his smile not unfriendly.

"Tha—that would be Rhone, Your Eminence." Mer'dor said.

"Rhone. Interesting. Single syllable names are not common in Nod City. What else were you able to learn about this Rhone?"

"He's a gatherer, Your Eminence. He deals in web. He works with Master Ker'ack who owns a web and tackle warehouse off Weaver's Lane."

"A webmaster." Sol-Ra-Luce glanced at the captain. "So, perhaps you were correct, Da-gore." Then he put an edge to his voice. "But I have never heard of webmasters trained to fight as warriors, have you?"

"No, Your Eminence." Inwardly, Da-gore bristled at the Lodath's condescending tone.

Sol-Ra-Luce smiled. "I don't think we need to question these men any further. It is clear this webmaster is more than he appears to be. He should be," Sol-Ra-Luce paused to find the word, "kept under a watchful eye? Perhaps he might be useful. Unless you have any further instructions for your warders, Captain, they may go."

"I have, Your Eminence." Da-gore glared at the two cringing men. "You have brought disgrace to the Lodath's Guards, to His Eminence, and upon yourselves." He stripped the emerald capes from their shoulders and flung them at their feet. "Three months on the temple crew should give you a better appreciation for your responsibilities to the Lodath."

Once the two men had gone, Sol-Ra-Luce took Da-gore to a circle of chairs before the tall, milky obelisk. The Lodath sat, brushed smooth the hem of his blue vesture, then motioned Da-gore to one of the chairs. "Tell me what you have learned of the Lee-landers."

"They are staying at the old River Edge Inn; a young man and woman, another man, older, and a servant. The fifth is a woman full of years."

"Five altogether. Lee-landers are a stubborn, intractable folk. Perhaps these are of no real concern, yet a charismatic Lee-lander could stir a crowd's passions if permitted to speak of the old ways."

Sol-Ra-Luce's eyes narrowed. "I don't need the sort of trouble an outspoken Lee-lander might bring."

Da-gore read between the Lodath's words what he really feared. He didn't want to have to explain *his* failure to the Oracle should a disturbance weaken the Oracle's tightening grip.

"Did you learn who they were?"

Da-gore shook his head. "Only the name of the servant. Kleg'l, who booked passage for the entire party on a boat, the *Osar Messenger*, heading north, to Far Port."

"Far Port?" Sol-Ra-Luce's brow contracted. "What in Far Port might interest people from the Lee-lands of Morg'Seth?"

"Nothing much beyond it but the Wild Lands and a few far-flung villages. I will inquire further."

The Lodath's eyes seemed to momentarily go out of focus, then sharpen suddenly. "Yes, do so. This is most curious." His voice changed. "*Most worrisome.*"

Da-gore's attention riveted, but when the Lodath spoke again, his voice had returned to normal.

"When do these Lee-landers leave for Far Port?"

"I spoke to the boat's skipper myself. He shoves off in two days. He's waiting on an order of ax heads and scythe blades from the Tubal-Cain company. I'll keep them under a close watch, if you so desire it, Your Eminence."

Sol-Ra-Luce pursed his lips and thought a moment. "Perhaps it's nothing at all. Just the same, you should keep them under your eye. If that Lee-lander starts preaching or speaking out against the Oracle again, I want to know."

"He already has. After leaving the Meeting Floor they went down to the market on Barter Road where he made remarks against the Oracle."

"Is that so?" Sol-Ra-Luce's view drifted up to the softly illumi-nated ceiling, then with a sudden jolt came back to Da-gore. The pulsing deep within the milky crystal had begun to beat slowly. Red ... steady ... mesmerizing. It held the Lodath's eye for a long moment. The air between shimmered. The moment passed. He drew in a sudden breath and gave his head a shake to clear it. "Find a reason to arrest the man and bring him to me."

"As you order, Your Eminence."

Ekalon drifted across the vacant Meeting Floor and out onto Barter Road, moving purposefully toward the heart of town. Along the way he gave a nod in passing to other agents of his acquaintance. Barelon was working the Shieldback and Dragon Festival Hall, busily whispering into willing ears. Barelon gave Ekalon a tight grin and a quick salute.

Up the street, Loth and Imont prowled the sidewalks, spreading disillusion and discontentment. Ekalon continued on his way. It was the same story throughout all of Nod City, wherever a willing ear could be found. In spite of the shackled-ones protecting their own, the Oracle's agents where busily encouraging others to sample the new freedoms the Oracle advocated through his mouthpiece, the Lodath.

As he left the city behind, the Oracle's agents became fewer, but some still prowled the dark streets, peering into windows, trailing close behind the humans. Now and again he'd spy a traveler with a shackled-one and steer a wide course around him. His orders tonight were not to challenge the shackled-ones, but to mark Rhone and learn all he could about this man who'd had the misfortune to arouse the Oracle's interest.

At Dairy Road, Ekalon paused before a dark cluster of buildings before him. Mav-duruc's stable yard. He sniffed the air, identifying the smell of a dozen different creatures, most coming from the direction of the barns. The odor of human was strongest from the big house across from the small, dark cottage off to his right. His view lingered a moment upon the big house, but the one he sought would be found at the cottage.

A narrow lane led to the small building. Ekalon peered into a window. A bed stood against one wall where shadows upon a sheet vaguely defined the bulky form that lay upon it. He prowled around the building, sniffing, frowning. The air rippled and he was inside the small parlor. The place held the foul smell of human, mixed with the more palatable earthy odors of forestlands and wild beasts. Ekalon shifted his staff to his other hand, suddenly wary. Something else was here. His wide, unblinking eyes roved the dark cottage. The skin at the back of his neck crawled. His mouth curled at the corners like a she-lion catching the spoor of prey—or an enemy.

Cautiously, he moved into the bedroom, his nose tasting the air. He leaned over the bed. The human's even breathing purred on. A sword and proj-lance stood in the corner; clothes lay piled upon the seat of a wooden chair. A sliver of blue light peeked out from a slit of a shuttered moonglass on a small table at the head of the bed. He'd found him easily enough, and now all that remained was to mark him for the Oracle. His staff tilted toward the base of Rhone's neck.

"Up to mischief again, Ekalon?"

He spun around and stared at the shadowed corner. The air rippled, a pearly light filled the room and a stocky figure stepped through. He wore a dark jerkin over a robin's egg blue shirt. His britches and boots were black. He held a gold-and-ivory staff in his long fingers. The edges of his light gray cloak glowed a moment in the fading opalescent light as the rippling air dissipated. The shackled-one rapped the end of his staff down upon the floor and gripped it in his left hand at arm's length as he stood there.

Ekalon recovered quickly from his surprise. "Sari'el! I thought I smelled something odious about this place." He took a firmer grip upon his staff. "Why are *you* here?"

"Need I explain it to you?" Sari'el inclined his head at the sleeping man.

"Him? This human has a shackled-one to watch over him?"

"He does now."

"He's not yours! He's been handed over to me, to be marked for my master's service!"

Sari'el's ruddy face remained calm, a hint of a smile spreading his lips. Ekalon hated the way Sari'el's dark eyes considered him with that certain curiosity, that vague air of superiority. He hated all the shackled-ones, hated their easy smiles, as if it took no effort at all. He hated their laughter ringing high and clear, and their voices, at times as powerful as the sten-gordon's roar, and the next moment as soft as a kitten's purr. He hated every one of them because at one time he too had been able to laugh and smile, to roar and to purr. Now he knew no joy, no laughter. His undivided purpose was to serve his master, and if he did well, he was not punished. If that could be called joy, such was the extent of Ekalon's happiness.

Sari'el's view held him. "That is not to be."

"The Lord of the World has deemed it so!"

The shackled-one's expression flattened at the mention of the Oracle. So, he clearly understood the power he was trifling with. Ekalon managed a smile. "See, you have no authority here. In this place you are bound by the Lord of This World just as I am. Now be away with you." He turned to the sleeping form and thrust out his battle-staff. The tip of it came to a halt a hand's breadth from Rhone's neck as if it had struck an invisible wall. Ekalon wheeled back, eyes narrowing at the shining staff leveled at him. "I said away with you! My lord has given him over to me to be marked!" He spoke precisely, each word spat out in a tight, mechanical monotone, each given equal emphasis. He still had the upper hand here.

Sari'el considered him a moment then answered cautiously, as if careful not to direct an attack against the name of Ekalon's master.

"Even the Lord of This World has bounds upon him. Here he is permitted a free hand—most often. But this man, Rhone, will not be marked."

Burning rage flared across Ekalon's face—rage was one of those emotions he could easily conjure. His battle-staff struck out. Sari'el's golden staff swept up and intercepted it, filling the room with a blinding spray of blue and silver sparks and the roar of a quarry charge going off. Ekalon swung again, this time for Sari'el's head, the black rod in his fists glowing red now, spitting tongues of fire. It found only empty space.

Sari'el came up from below, golden light streaming off the tip of his staff. It buried deep in Ekalon's stomach sending a violent electric storm though his body, folding him in half. He gasped, for a moment engulfed in a glaring flash of blue light, then stunned Sari'el with a burst of white-hot energy from the end of his battle-staff. Sari'el caught the burst along the edge of his staff, deflecting most of the force of it, and the two clashed.

Sari'el flung Ekalon at the wall. The air shimmered, the wall faded, and Ekalon flew on through it, sailing into the flowerbed beyond the cottage. With a groan, he pulled himself up on his staff.

The cottage wall shimmered again, bathing the yard in a bright pearly opalescence. Sari'el stepped through the rift and the dancing light faded back to solid stone behind him.

Ekalon wasn't about to let a shackled-one best him, not here in the Oracle's city! He sprang from the flowers, shot up a hundred spans into the night sky and hurled himself back down, thrusting his staff out before him, leaving a spitting, volcanic tail behind him. Sari'el leaped to meet him in the sky. They collided in a blinding shower. Sari'el reeled into a stand of trees. Ekalon shook off the impact as Sari'el burst from the trees and streaked back.

A rumble shook the air and they tumbled end over end, speeding back to the ground. Ekalon got his staff against Sari'el's chest.

Sari'el twisted out from under it as a flash of energy shot past him, scorching his tunic. They slammed into the ground and Sari'el gained the upper hand on Ekalon and pinned him beneath the end of his staff. Ekalon growled and clawed as a golden net spun around him holding him tight against the ground.

"Now, my fallen friend ..."

There it was again! That hateful smile! Strain as he might, Ekalon couldn't break free.

"... here is the message you take back to your master. The human Rhone is beyond your touch. He is to be set apart."

"Set apart?" The words stunned the struggle from Ekalon. "He has not yet chosen! He is still ours!"

"He may be tested as a man is tested, but in our realm, you may not mark him or in any way touch him. He is beyond you, or your master."

"Who says?" Ekalon strained against the golden net. "You know as well as I you are powerless against my Master."

"The Elect One says."

Ekalon stopped struggling, stunned. What fight was left in him drained away leaving him weak and defeated.

Sari'el stepped back, restraining him beneath the tip of his staff. But it was unnecessary. Ekalon didn't think he could move even if freed.

"I see that you understand now." Sari'el lifted the staff. An ember of golden light sparked to life at one corner of the net and in a flash raced across it eating up the links and leaving a golden mist that lingered a moment then vanished. Sari'el placed himself between Ekalon and the cottage. "Now go."

Ekalon stood, snatched up his staff and glared at the cottage. Ranks of shackled-ones stood shoulder to shoulder around it. A bold display, but his time would come. Hatred welled up, strangling the words in his throat. "You've made your point, Sari'el—this time. We will meet again."

5

Farmer, Prophet, Stargazer

Once again Mishah was strolling among the stones of fire. Malik the Swift and Pulcra passed beneath her feet, balls of angry vapors bubbling from the cauldrons of death upon lifeless crusts. She paused and stared, but like a gentle wind at her back, the guide's hand urged her on toward the third orb. He placed Mishah upon the vast circle of the Earth and pointed at the fourth stone, spinning in its circle; Oric, where great red seas cooled distant shores, but no tree thrashed in the violent winds that stalked across the stone's face.

His finger shifted and steadied upon a point of light beyond the fourth. It was the fifth stone from the sun, Rahab. *The place of the Rebellion.*

"Rahab is broken, though it has not been so from the beginning. The fingers of the Creator made everything perfect. But then came the Rebellion, and the Blight invaded the farthest reaches of creation, corrupting perfection at its very heart, spreading deadly pestilence to all the Creator had made. It was to Rahab that the Evil One's hordes fled, and the weight of their transgression was as a stone mason's chisel, splitting it asunder. But the Creator stretched out his hand and drew the pieces back together. Judgment is still to come. For a little while, the transgression will be permitted. When all is complete, the Creator will release Rahab."

Mishah marveled at this, although she did not understand it. She never completely understood what it meant, but at times, in some dim recess of her brain, she could almost fold her fingers around the mystery and claw away its tough husk. If she could only just peel back that first layer of meaning, the rest would unravel like stripping the skins off an onion.

But whenever she tried, the onion would dissolve into a vapor and the worlds would spin away in their orbits ... and Mishah would suddenly find herself back on firm earth strolling amongst tall forests. They were always unfamiliar places; far from her home in the Lee-lands of Morg'Seth ... yet how she knew this, she could not say.

A deep shadow passed over the forest, darkening the trees as sometimes happens when the wings of a great dragon block the sunlight. Mishah shivered. Her heart began to race. She knew what must come next.

She sensed more than saw the malignancy settling behind her, creaking the treetops, rattling branches like a sack of dry bones. Then came the footsteps, heavy and powerful, crunching quietly but swiftly upon a carpet of dead leaves. All at once she was running, the hot breath of pursuit a roaring fire at her neck—not dragon breath, but something else ... something more ominous and foreboding.

Faster it came!

Fear twisted its fingers in her gut and reached a gnarled hand up to strangle the breath from her throat. She fought to escape the evil, flailing aside the clutching tree limbs, stumbling over twisted roots writhing across her path. Her own body betrayed her as legs turned leaden.

Something stirred deep within her belly. A child ... a son ... ? How could she know? Then she understood! It wasn't her the evil wanted, but him, her unborn son!

Her running slowed as though her legs had become mired in

thick mud, and still the unseen terror came on, its crashing advance louder ... nearer!

Time lost its meaning. Future and past spiraled into a sickening montage. The evil's pursuit stretched from the Creation's beginning and would continue until the end. In some vague way Mishah understood this, but her brain whirled. Nothing made sense. The baby that had been in her womb was now in her arms, and that she didn't think this strange was the oddest thing of all. Nor did she deem it remarkable when the baby was suddenly a man, tall and strong, and running at her side; swifter than she. Mishah urged him to flee—to flee from the evil!

Something rumbled beneath her feet. Blackthorn roots broke up through the stony pathway, serpent-like and spinning out prickly tentacles. Needles of fire wrapped her legs and she sprawled headlong, tumbling to the ground. What little light filtered through the trees faded completely as the formless shadow hovered over her, its hot breath fouling the air. It need now only to reach down and suck the life from her soul. And it would, she was certain of it ...

With a jolt, the Evil recoiled.

Blinding light filled the forest, a brilliance both fearful and comforting. In an instant, the darkness dissolved. The Creator's hand stretched between her and the Evil, and his enveloping love evaporated her fear.

Evil cowered from the goodness. It always did. Stunned, it fled into the forest. Yet Mishah knew the Evil had not been deterred. Its true quarry had never been her. Now she understood. The one it loathed was her son, and it would pursue him unto death!

In a rush, the earth fell away and Mishah again found herself walking among the orbs of heaven. The Creator placed her once more upon the circle of the world and showed her a vision of a man fleeing before the Evil.

"Will you save my son?"

"I will, and your son will preserve mankind."

"How can that be?" Mishah watched the lone, weak man. How could any human stand against this Evil that had infected all of Creation?

"Watch the mighty work I will show to you this hour!" His voice thundered the words out across the heavens … the sound fearful, yet at the same time removing all fear. "The hour of judgment has come. Now see the wonders of my fingers."

The Creator released his grasp upon Rahab, the world his power had held together since the Rebellion. Rahab shattered with a blinding flash and a roar that deafened even the fiery furnaces of Oric. Great chunks of ice and rock hurdled through space. The red oceans of Oric vaporized before the mighty winds of devastation, its waters crystallizing in the frigid emptiness of space. Mishah shuddered as the calamity raced toward her.

But the Creator's words comforted her again. "Watch, my child and fear not. See these wonders." The voice roared as a mighty river, yet at the same time gentle as a whispering rill. His words had barely been spoken when a hail of Rahab's rocks struck the moon's placid surface churning it to ruin. Fiery rain sped past her; a hundred thousand missiles plunging into the earth's atmosphere. Mishah watched, more fascinated than terrified. One fiery fragment streaked toward the Evil, striking the path just behind her fleeing son. Instantly the ground ripped asunder and a fount of water shot heavenward.

The Evil was thrown back by the torrent hurtling up through the cold reaches of the firmament and falling back through the windows of heaven as great chunks of ice. Mighty waters rose. Mishah's fascination turned to horror! Her son was being swept away on the waves.

"No!" Mishah bolted up from her pillow, that single, startled cry echoing in her ears. She sucked in a ragged breath, her sweat-drenched skin chilling in the darkened room.

Where was she?

❦

"Mishah?"

"Lamech?"

He was beside her. He took her into his arms until the shivering passed. Lamech; her strong arm to lean on. Everything was all right. Her breathing evened out as her eyes became accustomed to the dark. It was just a dream—*that* dream again. Across the room the faint glow of a shuttered moonglass showed the two other beds; Her brother, Kenock, in one, Amolikah in another. And curled up on a sleeping mat by the balcony door, snoring softly, lay their good-man, Kleg'l.

"You are all right now?" Lamech said softly. "Your hands are cold."

She trembled and lay back upon the pillow. Lamech propped himself on his left arm, looking worried. "It was that dream again?"

She nodded.

He grimaced, then gave her hand a reassuring squeeze. "Everything will be fine, Mishah."

"Will it, Lamech? What if these dreams are more than the workings of a worried mind?" Was the Creator trying to tell her something? *Your son will preserve mankind.* What could that mean? But she kept these concerns bound up inside her heart.

He hesitated and seemed to be searching for the right words. Failing to find them, he said simply, "Mention this to the Mother. She is wise with age, and often shown visions of things to come. Perhaps she can unravel this dream for you."

Mishah stared at the ceiling and dragged her lower lip between her teeth. "What if I'm not supposed to be taking this pilgrimage, Lamech? Maybe the dream is telling me to turn back." Her hand rested lightly upon her stomach. "I wouldn't want to risk our child."

"Nothing will happen to *our son*. The Creator has us safely in the palm of his hand."

She smiled at the comforting thought, but fear lingered. "I wish I had your faith, Lamech."

"You do, Mishah. You just haven't tested it."

He made it sound like the testing of one's faith was something to be desired. The very thought of being sifted by the Creator terrified her. She wanted none of that. She wanted only to return to the comfort and safety of their home in the Lee-lands of Morg'Seth; to be near her sisters and brothers and father in this time of change ... this new experience. She'd never had an adventurer's spirit. A pilgrimage to the Mother was a common enough event among the women of her family, not an *adventure* in the usual sense of the word. But it was more of a disturbance to her comfortable, if somewhat unexciting, existence than she cared for. Unexciting was good. She had to smile at that. If that were true, then how did she ever fall in love with Lamech?

"What?" he asked.

She looked at his earnest face and concerned eyes, at the dark beard neatly trimmed to follow the line of his square jaw. "You." Her strength ... her love. So long as Lamech was at her side she could believe this journey would turn out all right.

"Me?" He grinned.

"Yes, you." Her head rose suddenly off the pillow and she gave him a quick kiss.

He engulfed her in his arms and kissed her back. His hand began to wander.

"Not here," she whispered, glancing at the family members sleeping nearby. He restrained himself. She snuggled into his embrace, filled with contentment. "Evening peace."

"Evening peace," he breathed huskily.

❦

The blanket of early morning mist clung close to the ground; a gray shroud draped over the land, obscuring the river below and the land beyond. Mishah tried not to think of the dream, but remnants of it still frightened her. It was like that every time. She inhaled the moist, clean air, and forcibly put the dream out of her mind, watching the fringe of treetops in the far distance beyond the city and the farmlands that still lay hidden. Lamech would often remark that this heavy morning moisture was a gift from the Creator. It watered the whole land, a good land, bountiful and beautiful.

The moisture condensed in cool, crystalline beads upon the balcony's floor and handrailing. Mishah dragged a finger along the balustrade, running the beads together and watching them pool in the irregularities of the hewed stone. The air held a crisp, refreshing chill. She pulled the robe tighter and wiggled her toes in the dry, fleece slippers. She loved the morning quartering, before the heavy heat of day set in. Upriver, a column of smoke from the temple wharves punched a hole in the fog, climbing straight up into the sky then feathering out in the gentle breeze. The breeze had shifted sometime during the night, and now she caught the odor of burning cedar and pine, the faint tang of unburned 'gia. Somewhere in the distance a cycler chugged.

If she were home, she and her sisters would already have the stove hot and bread baking. Lamech, her father, and her brothers would be working in the vera-logia fields. Amolikah would be waking the nieces and nephews to break their fast and then to chores. Later, when the day warmed and work ceased, Amolikah would gather the children into the big common room for their lessons. Life in the Leelands of Morg'Seth was orderly and uncomplicated. It marched steadily along at a comfortable pace.

A flock of flame-red flamingos floated above the plume of smoke, their spindly legs stretched straight out behind them, long wings spread wide, effortlessly bearing them aloft.

She sighed as they winged lazily toward the far forest and

recalled how Lamech had come in from working the fields one day with that intense fire in his eyes. She knew at once he'd been deep in prayer and received another revelation.

"Mishah," he'd said taking both her hands in his. "The Creator spoke to me. We must make this trip."

Spoke to him? That was how he always began when he'd gotten a notion in his head and wasn't prepared to shake loose of it. She'd protested that her patients needed her. As the only healer in their village, her place was there, not on a pilgrimage. It wasn't required—this pilgrimage to the Mother—but it was expected.

Oftentimes she wondered, *why this continued devotion to the Mother?* Sometimes in the privacy of her thoughts, she questioned the old stories. They sounded too fantastic to the modern mind. Yet how could she deny the earnestness in the older ones' faces when they spoke of the Mother? They remembered. They believed. *They were there!* She was only fifty-three years old. Just a dozen years out of her apprenticeship; a healer, a wife, and soon to be a mother. A heaviness settled upon her shoulders. *Oh, to have Lamech's faith.*

Just then, Lamech and Kenock stepped out onto the balcony in the middle of a debate, shattering the morning's solitude, and her introspection. And that was just as well. The two men were eating orfins.

Lamech had peeled an extra one and handed it to her. "How are the thoughts of my wife this morning?"

She took the sweet fruit from him and peered a moment at its pale fleshy pulp. "Troubled."

His sympathetic smile told her he understood. "Dreams are a burden." He bit into the fruit.

She didn't want to talk about it. "What are you two arguing about … again?"

Kenock spoke before Lamech could swallow down the bite he'd

taken. "I want to explore Nod City. But *your* husband thinks he owns me."

"I'm only thinking of your well-being, Kenock."

"Let *me* worry about *my* well-being." He gave Lamech a hard-faced glare then looked pleadingly at his sister. "I just want to see what this city is like, Mi. I'm not looking for trouble—unlike some people who will remain nameless."

Lamech rolled his eyes.

Kenock looked to Mishah, then to Kleg'l who had stepped out to join them. "Well? It's true, isn't it?"

"Your brother-in-law holds strong convictions, Kenock. He has a close walk with the Creator. You should listen to him." Kleg'l was a slender man, nearly as tall as Lamech. His arms were long, his shoulders narrow, and his face a collection of sharp angles. It was a clean-shaven face, usually unflappable; neither quick to smile nor to frown. At the moment, however, it wore a sly grin.

Kenock huffed. "How much did you pay him to say that?"

They laughed. It warmed Mishah's heart to see that in spite of their differences, there was a strong affection between Kenock, Lamech, and Kleg'l.

Kleg'l had come out of Morg'Jalek, a poor young man, indentured to Amolikah's husband. Trained in household management, Kleg'l's faithfulness and honesty propelled him to the position of good-man, and he had been given charge over the families' household finances. He served them 250 years, the required time, and when the day came to grant him his freedom and a plot of land, Mishah remembered how Kleg'l, looking embarrassed, chose instead to have his left ear pierced and accept the family's ring, making him a member in all but blood and inheritance. His duties were light and his privileges practically the same as a natural born child. He'd retained charge of the families' purse and carried out the duties of good-man with unquestioning integrity.

Amolikah poked her head out the door. She wore a brightly colored sleeveless basque over a beige traveling dress. She'd braided her salt-and-pepper hair and wrapped the coils atop her head, spearing them in place with a pair of long ivory pins. "You can protest all you want, Lamech, but I for one don't intend to stay closed up in this room all day. I'm going back to the market, and I'll need Kenock to carry my packages." She gave the young man a wink.

Mishah couldn't stand the thought of being closed up all day either, especially during the fourth quartering when the blanket of heat descended over the land. "I'll go with you, Grandmother."

Lamech sighed. "I see I'm outnumbered. Someone will need to keep an eye on all of you."

※

When she paused to look, to *really* look, at Nod City, she was amazed at all the little advancements that set this place apart from her village in Morg'Seth. She marveled at the fountains gracing parks and patios, spaced at regular intervals throughout the city. The fountains back home captured water off high slopes then channeled it by way of long wooden pipes and forced it through nozzles. They were pretty little things, but they never sprayed very high or varied from a fixed pattern.

Here, the fountains danced in a swirling, leaping choreography of water to please the eye. And in other places where groomed lanes meandered through a gardener's love affair with flowers and vines, spurts of tinted water would suddenly leap to life and race along a pathway like a playful frog, always one jump ahead of her. She suspected somewhere beneath the streets were chambers holding mechanisms to energize the water; pumps powered by sunlight, or perhaps cyclers. She listened for a muffled thump, thump, thump somewhere beneath her feet.

Vera-logia, the fuel that powered the cyclers, was becoming more and more common through the lands. Lamech had been wise years ago in convincing the farms about the Morg'Seth region to make it their primary crop and major export. Today, the farms were growing wealthy marketing 'gia.

She and Lamech, in spite of his threat to "keep an eye" on them, drifted off by themselves in search of the beauty of Nod City. "Even the warty jump-plop carries the crest of the Creator," she noted.

"But you do have to search between the warts with a strong Osmit glass to find it," he countered reluctantly.

She was pleased he was able to see enough beyond the problems and appreciate the subtle charms of Nod City. "My point." So, they'd focused the equivalent of their own Osmit glass on Nod City to seek out the beauty.

They bought chilled strawberry cream and spooned it out of a keelit husk, then scraped the sweet fruit from the inside; as delicious a breakfast as any! A forest of bright silk streamers fluttering gently in a warm breeze turned out to be a ride on a hot air balloon to view the temple construction from a loftier perspective.

"Come, let's look, Lamech."

He rolled his eyes, but stepped in line and boarded an exact miniature of the lifting platform out on the plain of Irad. As the buildings shrank beneath them, the full extent of the temple project came into view. But Lamech was ignoring it, peering out at the sky as if pretending it wasn't there could make it go away.

Pretend if you wish, my dear.

She became aware of the chattering of the crowd about them. The floor was packed with people. Lamech's voice was wistful. "You know, Mishah, I've been told that if you climb the highest mountain and listen very carefully, you can hear the voice of the Creator." He looked at her and smiled. "Not really his voice, of course."

"Then what?" Her eyes had found the sloping temple walls in the distance. It was easy to mistake its true size from so high up, until you noticed the behemoths working beside it were impossibly small!

"The heavens are filled with the voices of the stones of fire and the whispers of the stars."

"The singing sky above the Mountains of Olphus," she noted.

"Some call it by that name." He went silent again. "I wonder if it's something we'll ever hear? Or are far-off places meant only for the eyes and ears and noses of adventurers and writers?"

She pulled her view from the stone monument and saw disappointment in his eyes. "I never knew you wanted to see such things, Lamech." He was a farmer, prophet, and amateur stargazer, not a wanderer. Not an adventure seeker. This journey to the Mother was every bit as stressful on him as it was on her. Why had he never revealed this to her before?

"This world holds so much I'd like to see, Mishah, but I feel our time is short."

"You're a young man yet. Your father and grandfathers are still with us."

He smiled and glanced at the pressing crowd, lowering his voice so only she could hear. "I don't mean my lifetime. It's this world I speak of. We're bringing judgment down upon ourselves. There's not much time left." His gaze went to the temple construction and his voice gathered strength. "It will be beautiful, but its beauty is deceptive; a symptom of the disease devouring our world. This Oracle business will seal our doom if it isn't brought to an end."

She winced and cast about, averting her eyes from the stares suddenly directed their way.

6

Judgment

When the animal handler finally put the behemoth in motion and hauled the balloon back to ground, Mishah descended the ramp with a knot tightening between her shoulder blades. She looked around, uneasy, and not certain why.

"Let's find Grandmother and the others." She glanced over her shoulder. A green-cloaked guard stood nearby, looking casually at the sky, at the balloon, at the children scampering in play. At everything but her and Lamech.

The market at the end of Barter Road, nearly a quarter league to a side, was a vast field of butterfly-bright tents and striped canopies fluttering in the soft, warm breeze; a daunting place to search out her family from among the thousands. The crunch underfoot of finely-chipped granite radiated midday heat. A lightweight dress is what she should have worn. The stretching skin of her belly itched.

Everywhere, voices filled the air, blending with a distant thum-boom-thum-shee-thrum of a bronze-drum band. In an arena, two tall, broad-shouldered men with swords and shields put on a mock battle. Their movements were swift, powerful, intricate; nearly as beautiful as a dance.

The odor of people, the stench of animals, the spicy aroma of roasted vegetables, and the sharp tang of brewer's yeast combined with the noise in an all-pervasive assault on her senses. A part of her brain retreated to thoughts of their farm and the peaceful forest land, the way the Creator had intended.

They found Amolikah and Kleg'l at a pannier's stand admiring the intricate designs in a pounded reed sewing basket. Kleg'l was examining the hinge, but Amolikah appeared distracted.

"You and Lamech have a good time?" Although her grandmother's question was innocent enough, Mishah sensed something else in it.

"It was … interesting."

"What do you think of this one, Mistress Mishah?" Kleg'l held the basket to the sunlight, moving it in a way that made the colorful pattern swirl.

"The design is very nice." She looked back at Amolikah. "What is it?"

"I think we should be leaving here."

But Amolikah had been the one who had wanted to come. Mishah cast a wary glance, but saw nothing out of place except for the worried look in her grandmother's eyes. "What's wrong?"

"My spirit is troubled." She nodded at a green-cloak not far off at a glazier's booth, his back toward them as he examined a mirror, turning it this way and that.

A sudden concern filled Lamech's face, too, as he took stock of them. "Where's Kenock?"

Amolikah glanced about the crowded marketplace, the lines about her eyes deepening. "He was here a moment while ago."

"Master Kenock went that way." Kleg'l's long finger pointed toward a huge pen with animals for sale.

"He's looking at livestock?" Lamech attached a note of surprise to his voice.

Kenock and livestock? She smiled, recalling even as a little boy Kenock would declare, "They stink, and they eat too much, and they might step on you!" Animals were a necessity around the farm, but away from it, he had little use for them.

Kleg'l cleared his throat and seemed to be slightly embarrassed. "I don't think it's livestock. I noticed a soothsayer's booth nearby."

"Soothsayer?" Lamech scowled and started off.

Mishah hurried to keep at his side. "Don't assume too much, Lamech. Hear what he has to say, first."

"Your brother craves the sins of this world."

"He's young."

"Then this is the time for correction."

"Perhaps, but not from you, Lamech."

He looked at her, his sense of righteousness clearly at war with his love for her, not wishing to hurt her. She spotted another green-cloaked guard mingling with the crowd. The knot between her shoulders formed again. Peering among the vendors' stands, she noted a third green-cloak, examining a sword and nodding toward a chuckling, big-bellied armorer who looked quite pleased. Had these men nothing better to do than browse the booths of the marketplace?

"There he is." Lamech made his way past a row of stalls with a determined stride.

Kenock was bent over a tray of cards as a man wearing a fortune-teller's collar and hat turned them over one at a time. At the sight of his brother-in-law, Kenock's face went slack. "Lamech!" he croaked. "I thought you and Mishah were—"

"It's plain what you thought. I let you out of my sight for a few hours and you sneak off to whore with the world."

"Whore with the world?" The accusation stunned him. "I didn't *sneak* off."

"This city is sinking its claws into you, and you are willingly letting it!"

"Lamech!" Mishah cast about, finding annoyed faces turned their way. "Let's leave."

"It has not," Kenock came back in his own defense. "And anyway, what's wrong with Nod City? Everyone here is friendly." He glanced at the soothsayer who appeared to be perplexed at Lamech's outburst, anxious not to be drawn into the argument. "He's friendly."

"Nod City is a dung heap of sin, Kenock. The serpent's very own lair, and you know it. I've told you of what goes on here."

Mishah bit her lips, her chest clenching. Their arguing was kindling the interest of the nearby green-cloaks. *Why always in crowds? Couldn't he at least keep his voice low?*

The soothsayer sent a withering stare at Lamech. "Here now, no call for harsh words. Nod City's my city! You two go take your displeasure somewhere else. I run a dignified business. I've no use for this sort of thing."

Lamech glowered at him then turned his anger back to Kenock. "I knew it was a mistake to permit you to run loose."

"I can do whatever I please!"

Her brother was normally an easygoing man, but his temper, when fired up, could be every bit as hot as her husband's.

Lamech was oblivious to the clear danger she perceived all around them. "This place is infected by the lie. We can be our own gods, the Oracle claims, so now everyone does what's right in his own eyes, forsaking—"

"*Lamech!*" Impatience rasped in her throat and his name came out as a sharp command that startled even her. It snapped Lamech from his anger and he turned to her in surprise.

She lowered her voice. "Enough of this!" Her eyes shifted purposefully, pulling his along with them. For the first time he noticed the staring crowd. Her throat constricted. "Let's get Amolikah and Kleg'l and leave this place."

He nodded and grimaced. His quick, mischievous smile, like a boy caught in some small offense, melted her heart. "I said I wasn't going to do it again. I'm sorry."

She took his arm in a firm grip. "Let's get away from here." They turned to leave. Her heart lurched. Six green-cloaked men of the Lodath's guard barred their way. Where had they come from, all at once like that? The guard at the balloon, and those strolling among the booths ... they must have been stalking them, waiting for an excuse to close in. And Lamech, in his zeal, had given them one. She swallowed hard, her palms suddenly clammy.

The officer was of medium height, broad of shoulders and stout waisted. His bare arms beyond the short sleeves of his green tunic rippled with thick cords of muscles. His bronze helmet caught the sunlight, the insignia that of a captain in Lodath's Guards, the plume the deep purple of the House of Cain. Mishah remembered Amolikah telling her how, in the land of Nod, the religious realm and the kingly line had been merging for years. Before her stood the results of that coming together.

"I am Da-gore, of the House of Cain, captain of the Lodath's Guard. You and your people will come with us."

Lamech gripped her hand upon his arm. "What is it you want with us?"

He regarded each of them before speaking. "There have been complaints filed."

"What complaints?"

"Attempted proselytization, stirring the people to violence, sedition against the holy representative of the Oracle on earth—to name a few."

Mishah stepped forward, licking her dry lips. "Sir, may I speak?" He nodded. "If we've offended anyone, we apologize." She shot a narrow glance at Lamech. "Allow us to go on our way and there will be no further trouble. We leave here tomorrow."

For the briefest instant, she thought his expression had softened, then he motioned to his men. "You will come with us." The guards encircled them. Amolikah and Kleg'l were taken too. The guards marched them through the market grounds and into a wagon enclosed in thick ironwood bars.

Mishah sat on a hard wooden bench, her knees quaking, the world seeming to move in slow motion. Amolikah and Kenock sat across from them, Lamech close at her side, Kleg'l at the far end. The guards mounted foot loops and grabbed a bar to steady themselves. Da-gore climbed aboard the high seat with the driver. Her stomach clenched and clenched again until she worried for the new life growing inside her. With the crack of a whip, the driver got the three-point moving.

Mishah fought off the shakes, wanting to vomit, but resisting the urge. This journey to the Mother was doomed from the start!

❀

The chamber was stone, windowless, with a sturdy wooden door. A single wedge of moonglass mounted high up the wall provided illumination. By the long, steep decline they'd been marched down, Mishah suspected they were far underground. But there was no way of knowing for sure. Stories had been told of people lost forever in the vaults beneath Government House. She shivered and prayed. At her side, Lamech's gloomy eyes were cast down, and deep lines of concern cut his face. But what was done was done. She gave his hand a squeeze, receiving no response. If they got out of here, she was going right home. She'd had enough adventuring to last her a lifetime!

The click of a key in the lock startled her. The door opened and three guards entered the holding cell.

"Follow us," one said.

Lamech stood first. "Let my family go. They have done nothing wrong. It's me you want."

"That is not for us to decide." The guards escorted them all out the door, all except Amolikah who remained sitting upon the stone bench. "Young man," her voice wavered in an uncharacteristic timidity, "old bones don't move like they once did." She sighed, "Do you mind?" and extended a hand toward one of the guards.

He stared at it. Her smile widened gently as only a grandmother's smile could to someone four hundred years her junior. She was up to something. Mishah tried to catch her eye, but Amolikah purposefully avoided it, peering up at the burly guard. He stared. She smiled. He stared some more, then reluctantly took her hand and helped her to her feet.

"Thank you, dear. I have a grandson about your age. He's a farmer."

He smiled briefly—in spite of himself.

Shuffling with an old woman's gait, Amolikah followed them into a narrow corridor reeking from the musty odor of animals and dung, illuminated at wide intervals by pale, pearly white rectangles of moonglass. Mishah took her arm as if to help her.

"What was that all about?" she whispered.

Amolikah spoke softly through smiling lips. "It never hurts to cultivate a little sympathy now and again. Age has its advantages." Past the smile, her darting eyes were fiercely taking in every detail as they ascended the long corridor.

They reached street level where dusky light fell softly through a row of windows. It was the end of the fourth quartering and soon night would be upon them. Would they be kept there overnight? Would they miss their boat in the morning? *Miss their boat!* What was she thinking? What did it matter? She'd already decided she wasn't going to complete the journey. Once out of here and away from Nod City, she was going straight home! A hundred Lamechs and Amolikahs could not make her continue on.

The corridors became wider, ceilings higher, walls decorated with tapestries and pierced with tall narrow windows. In the daylight this place would be bright and delightful. At the moment, however, gloomy with shadows, it was just one more burden to weigh her down. They passed through a heavy door into a wide shaft and up a flight of spiraling stairs. High overhead, a stained-glass cupola glowed dully with the last fading rays of the sun, but earlier it must have filled this shaft with color.

The stairway continued upward, but they debarked into a third-floor corridor. It was a short walk to a pair of tall doors, flanked on either side by four guards. Off to one side, a smaller door stood open. As they passed by it, Mishah caught a glimpse of people standing inside the room. They seemed to be speaking amongst themselves, but she couldn't hear their words, and she had been escorted past too swiftly to see their faces.

"They're waiting for you," one of the green-cloaks said as the guards halted them by the double doors.

A guard who had escorted them up from the prison nodded. The door guard shoved a bronze lever over and from somewhere beneath their feet came a hushed whisper and the door swung slowly open. As they passed through into a huge gallery, two more guards took up the rear of their party.

A sense of reverence instantly overwhelmed Mishah here. Tapestries and plaques of bronze decorated the walls beneath a crystalline ceiling that shone like the sky at midday. Evidently, the source of light was from some mineral other than moonglass. Much of the stonework that decorated the plaques glowed softly. The windows were darkening; beyond a set of them she could see the Plain of Irad where the work never ceased. The lights of the temple construction illuminated the site and the balloon, which blocked most of the sky from view.

The sound of their footsteps echoing off the polished stone floor magnified the size of this gallery beyond what the eye showed. A curious phenomenon, one she didn't understand. But before she could ponder it, a tall spire of pearly rock in the center of the gallery seized her eye. She inhaled sharply and a sudden chill brought her feet to a halt.

The obelisk was of some type of pale crystal, twice the height of a man and somewhat wider. But what held her eye was the slowly pulsing crimson glow deep within it—almost as if it were a living being! A shrinking dread urged her to flee the gallery. That slow, organic pulsing held her attention to the exclusion of all else, burning into her. The air went foul in her lungs until she reflexively drew in a deep, clearing breath. A ripple of light caught the corner of Mishah's eye, but when she looked, nothing was there.

A guard nudged her from behind. She began to move again, looking away from the crystal and toward three men on a platform elevated about half a span above the floor. Two of them were seated. The third, Da-gore, the captain of the Guard, stood off to one side.

Lamech's eyes were fixed upon the spire, his head turning to keep it in view as the guards advanced them to one side of the gallery toward the men in the chairs.

At her side, Amolikah warned, "Don't look at it." Amolikah grabbed her hand.

Mishah nudged closer to her grandmother. "I feel a churning in my spirit, Grandmother." It wasn't an affliction in her body, but as if she had encountered something foul.

"There are others here," Amolikah said.

Others? What did that mean?

Kleg'l's eyes had rounded at the crystal as well. Only Kenock appeared unaffected by its nearness, looking around the room, more curious than intimidated.

One of the seated men wore a blue coat with a resplendent gold collar. Though she'd never seen even a picture of the Lodath of the Oracle, she was certain this must be he.

The man beside him wore the purple robes of the House of Cain. A thick jumble of black curls piled atop his face with great spiraling loops falling down the side of his head and chin. His green eyes narrowed beneath bushy brows. His mouth seemed set permanently in a heavy, petulant frown. He clearly had better things to occupy his time and this was an intrusion upon them.

The Lodath leaned close and whispered. The black curls bounced as the man nodded in reply. This was clearly someone of importance. A thought suddenly came to her.

"I am Irad, Ruler of the Land of Nod."

Irad, Son of Cain! She swallowed down a lump in her throat. The dreaded warrior king. Her brain reeled at the thought. Lamech had done nothing so terrible to warrant the intervention of the mighty Irad! Her knees went to jelly. She stole a glance at Lamech. He stood unflinching, straight of spine and square of shoulders, chin thrust forward in defiance. These men did not intimidate him. *Now was not the time to kick against the goad!*

"This is Sol-Ra-Luce, Lodath of the Oracle."

Her eyes transfixed upon the scowling face of the warrior king who conquered all the Land of Nod more than five hundred years earlier. It was said he'd waged the final battle right out there beyond those darkening windows on the plain where the temple was being built. On that very ground, now called the Plain of Irad, King Sef had met his doom. Children today still cringe at their mother's skirts when the story is told how Irad had ordered the corpses of five thousand of Sef-ereck's warriors impaled upon their own spear shafts!

This was Irad the Dreaded, who afterward enthroned his famous father as king over the Land of Nod, and then according to legend, had him deposed and banished. The very same murderer who had six of his brothers trampled to death in order to seize the throne for himself. And she was standing before him! She broke out in a cold sweat.

Please, Lamech, bite your tongue.

Irad snatched a suntracer from his pocket and glanced impatiently at it, then at Da-gore. "What are the charges against these people? Hurry up, man. It's already five of the fourth quartering and I have pressing business elsewhere!"

The captain of the Guard read off a list of offenses. Mishah gasped. The litany of complaints might have contained a few grains of truth, but the embellishments were monumental. Kleg'l developed nervous feet, and Amolikah's fingernails dug hard into Mishah's hand. Even Kenock had begun to fidget.

To her relief, Lamech remained silent to the charges until the captain had finished, then he said, "May I speak?"

The Lodath nodded.

"These charges are against me, and me alone. My wife and family have done nothing wrong."

Irad shot out of his chair and strode around it, grasping the back in both hands. He was a surpassingly short man for all his fierce reputation, but his arms and shoulders were those of a man who'd cut his teeth wielding battle-axes and broadswords. The muscles of his thick neck not hidden by the beard stood out like tightly twisted ropes. "You required me for this?" His scowl burned toward the Lodath for a change. "These are religious charges, not civil! I have no time for this."

Sol-Ra-Luce merely smiled beneath the glare of the most powerful man in this part of the world. "It's a matter of formality. I do not wish to supersede my authority nor offend my most high lord and ruler."

Did she detect a derisive tone? If so, only she must have heard it for Irad continued as though he had not. "You have full authority where matters of faith are concerned, so long as they remain matters of faith. Other than a minor disturbance on the Meeting Floor, nothing here is of a civil matter, and I have any number of more important things to attend to. See to this yourself."

"Yes, my lord."

Irad flung his glare back at Mishah and her family, then strode away, purple cape fluttering in his wake. The tall doors opened and he disappeared. When Sol-Ra-Luce returned his attention to them he appeared to be holding back a small smile. What sort of man was this to be completely immune to the wrath of a warrior like Irad?

He rubbed his hands together, pressing them tight, palm to palm, putting fingertips to his mouth. He stood and for an agonizingly long moment; his gaze touched each of them in silent contemplation. His eyes widened all at once at Kenock. Something changed in the Lodath's expression. "You are different from these others."

"I am not," Kenock protested.

The Lodath's smile widened. "Oh, but you are."

Lamech was watching him and Kenock closely.

Sol-Ra-Luce turned to Lamech. "We run an orderly society here. We put few restrictions upon the people, and those that we do are light. Nodinites are generally free to do as they will. Other than loyalty to our king, and the tariffs we place on trade goods to finance our city and the projects, we rule with an easy hand. We ask only that they treat everyone else with respect and tolerance." He smiled indulgently. "Is that too much?" He'd spoken to all of them, but his view had remained upon Lamech.

"If tolerance means I must accept behavior our Creator condemns, then I will have none of it."

Mishah cringed.

The Lodath spread his hands. "You see the position you put me in?"

She saw the direction this inquiry was taking and rushed to make peace. "We are leaving your city tomorrow." Lamech held up a hand to silence her, but she went on anyway. "If we have caused a problem here, I am sorry."

"Ah, but can I allow a precedence to go unanswered? No, this matter must be dealt with. This talk of the Creator, this stuff of old legends, fills the people's heads with foolish notions. We've outgrown the need for fables. The Oracle has made the truth clear." He glanced at the ceiling as if viewing the starry heavens. "It's a new revelation from the gods. The old stories were meant merely to instruct, and so they did, but now it is time to move on. The essence of the Oracle is love. He wishes not to burden his people with harsh commands. And if he doesn't burden us, then by what right should we burden our fellow travelers on this journey called life?" His words were condescending, outwardly gracious, but laced with venom.

"Someday," he went on, "we will all be as the Oracle; gods of our own worlds. Think what a glorious age that will be. But we begin the long learning process here, and we will remain here as long as it takes us to get it right."

"We will all be gods?" Lamech's eyes rounded and he drew in a sharp breath, then he glanced at Mishah. Her eyes pleaded with him. He released his breath as if willing the fire within him to go out. When he spoke his voice was even, calm, but firm. "These lies have been told before, and believed before, and we bear the curse of them today."

The Lodath merely smiled sadly; Lamech had proven his case.

Lamech said, "You have evidence of what I've done? Of all you've accused me of?"

"Of course." He glanced at a guard and nodded. The man left the room and returned a few minutes later with the people Mishah had glimpsed from the hallway. Now that she really saw them her heart sank. The soothsayer looked uneasy being there. The women from the market stared at her from beneath lowered eyebrows.

The Lodath questioned each of them, and each gave the same story. Lamech had spoken blasphemy against the Oracle, had stirred the people with talk of lies and deception.

"By deception, he was referring to this government and my revelation as given to me by the Oracle?" Sol-Ra-Luce carefully clarified with each of them. When confirmed, the Lodath frowned and shook his head. "Sedition as well as blasphemy. It appears, in essence, the charges are all true." Further questioning gleaned from the witnesses indicated that it had been only Lamech who had instigated the trouble.

When he'd finished with them, the Lodath held all the proof he required. Somehow she suspected he'd made up his mind long before the proceedings ever started. He dismissed the witnesses then returned to his chair where Da-gore had silently remained the whole time. The king's vacated place seemed to only enhance Sol-Ra-Luce's ultimate authority in this matter—and maybe that was the reason Sol-Ra-Luce had orchestrated the scene with Irad in the first place. *You have full authority where matters of faith are concerned.* The king's words had pointedly confirmed what he'd wanted them all to hear.

This was a dangerous man. She feared him more now than she had in the beginning. Beyond scheming, he emanated evil ... this whole room radiated a malignancy that touched her in a way she couldn't describe!

"It seems the matter is clear. But I am a fair man." His smiling, infuriating eyes held hers a moment. "I appreciate that you will be leaving our land in the morning. I will not stop you."

Warning hairs shot off the nape of her neck, prickling the skin around her jaw. "You're letting us go?"

"You are all free to leave ... except for him." A finger extended at Lamech.

Her anger exploded. She wanted to claw the smug smile from his face. Lamech stopped her advance. "Trust the Creator," he said quietly.

Trust the Creator! He was being held while they were to be let free? *Trust the Creator?*

"Yes, trust your Creator. Trust him to see you through the next fifteen years while you're building the Oracle's temple."

"No!" Mishah cried. He couldn't do that to her, to them. Lamech was her strength, the father of her unborn child! How could she manage without him at her side?

7

The River

A guard grabbed her arms. It would take the whole of the Lodath's Guards to hold her back. "I'll never leave without my husband."

"Then I shall have you in chains as well."

"Mishah, no," her grandmother warned.

Mishah struggled against her guard. A second guard latched onto her.

Lamech's attending guard permitted him to approach her. He cupped her face in his large, strong hands. "My sweet."

She stilled at his touch and looked deep into his eyes.

"Even in this the Creator's purpose will be accomplished. I have peace, but not if you are held as well. You must go on your journey."

Tears welled in her eyes. She shook her head. "Not without you."

Lamech put his cheek against hers, his lips next to her ear. "Go to the Mother. Take my son far away from here."

Why did he keep saying that? Had the Creator *told* him? Or was he only guessing ... wishing? "Lamech, no, not without—"

"As your husband, I am telling you to go. Please, my sweet, do not defy me in this." Lamech pulled back and pinned her with his gaze. "Promise me you will go."

A tear slid down one cheek, and then the other. "Please don't …"

Lamech caressed away her tears with his callused thumb. She nodded. He pressed his lips to hers. Suddenly he was jerked away. The guards at her sides tightened their grip as Lamech was escorted away. His face was filled with pain, but he went with them without a struggle, resigned to the Creator's will. *Without a word!*

With no further ceremony, the Lodath's guards led them down a labyrinth of corridors and shoved them out onto the dark street. Amolikah wrapped an arm over her shoulder. Mishah buried her face against her grandmother, grief racking her body. Amolikah held her and looked nervously about. "We must get back to the inn."

"I can't leave him." Mishah said between trembling sobs. She pushed herself from Amolikah's arms, tears streaking her cheeks, salty in the corners of her mouth.

"We could free Lamech from the vaults somehow." Kenock's eyes burned with determination. "Steal him away tonight, hide him aboard the *Osar Messenger,* and in the morning be far away from here. What do you think?"

Kleg'l stared, his mouth dropping in disbelief.

Mishah stood dumfounded by Kenock's proposal, and for an instant, she even considered the proposition. But she wasn't thinking straight; her brain reeled in a torrent of anger, despair, and grief.

Amolikah put a quick end to any notion. "You'll be piling one trouble atop another," she said emphatically.

Back at the inn, Kenock wasn't prepared to give up so easily and paced the room, his forehead furrowed in thought, his mouth set in determination. Kleg'l sat in a chair shaking his head slowly from time to time, staring at his long hands.

Amolikah busied herself with her needlework and advised Mishah to do the same. But Mishah could only cry, unable to bear up under the crushing stone in her chest. Her grandmother spoke little, her fingers moving deftly, automatically, as if sewing was only a means to an end. What was she thinking? Sleep eventually stole over Mishah and mercifully snuffed out the grief—at least for a while.

Mishah awoke the next morning instantly aware that Lamech wasn't at her side. She lurched up and looked around. The crushing pain returned. Suddenly she realized Amolikah wasn't there either. Throwing off the covers, she shook her brother awake. "Where's Grandmother?"

"Humm?" Kenock stirred groggily.

"Grandmother is gone." What had happened during the night? Had the guards come and taken her away too?

Kenock and Kleg'l both rose at once, and just then the door opened.

"Grandmother!"

Amolikah rushed in and shut the door behind her. "Quick, get dressed. We haven't much time."

Mishah's heart froze. Had something even more horrible befallen Lamech? "What happened? Where did you go?" She grabbed up her dress and stepped behind the screen, stripping off her nightgown.

"I've made arrangements, but we have to hurry before the night guard leaves."

"Arrangements?" She was aware that her brother and Kleg'l were tumbling into their clothes. She struggled with the buttons. Amolikah came around and lent a hand.

"I told you it never hurts to cultivate a little sympathy."

"That guard?"

"I've arranged for us to see Lamech before they move him."

Mishah's heart leaped. She finished dressing then stood before the mirror. "I look awful."

"Lamech won't care." Amolikah hustled her to the door.

Mishah looked back at their luggage and her healing case on the table by the window.

"We'll come back for them," Amolikah said urging Mishah and the two men out the door. They hurried back to Government House. The door was bolted, but it opened at Amolikah's knock.

The guard who'd brought them up from the vaults let them in. "I managed to wangle permission from the night guard. He owed me a favor, but just for a moment. We must make haste." They hurried through the deserted corridors and into a wide hallway where four narrow tunnels ran off in different directions.

This would be her last time to see Lamech. If she could have frozen the moment and made it last forever, she would have.

She heard the distant clatter of chains and then spied Lamech coming down one of the low, dark tunnels, a guard on either side of him, iron shackles on his ankles. It tore her heart to see him this way. They'd taken away his clothes and given him the gray trousers and shirt of the temple gang to wear—the garb of a common criminal! The symbol of the House of Cain encircled by the Oracle's pentagram was stenciled upon the shirt above his heart. Oh, how it must repulse him! His face was drawn, his eyelids heavy as if he hadn't slept well, but he was smiling, strangely at ease in spite of all that had happened.

He hugged her. She clung to him, greedily absorbing his smell, the sound of his heartbeat against her ear, the feel of his arms around her. These sensations were all that mattered; they had to last for the next fifteen years. It was all of him she'd be able to take away from here.

"Oh, Lamech." She choked, strangled by her own tears.

He kissed the top of her head. "I'm so sorry, my sweet."

"What are we to do?"

He held her tight, her face buried against his chest. "We do the task the Creator sets before us, and we trust him."

The sobs rose in her throat. His arms tightened. "It will be over and then we'll have the rest of our lives."

"Over?" She sniffed. "Fifteen years! How will I stand it? How will you? Our child?"

"Our son." He smiled and wiped a tear with his thumb. "We will make the best of it. What other choice is there?"

She nodded, not understanding, desperately clinging to his every word.

"Take solace in our families."

She nodded again. Where else would she find comfort and hope? She'd lean on them until this was over. "I'll try." She drew on her reserves, what little strength there was inside her, and looked up into his face. "I'll be waiting for you. I'm going home."

He held her suddenly at arm's length. "No, you mustn't go home. I've already told you, you must go on."

His words stung her. "I can't. Not now."

"Mishah, you must. There is more to this than just the pilgrimage. It's the Creator's will that you go."

"How can it be? How can all this be part of the Creator's will? You're in chains and I'm alone. Our child will be born without your instruction and love."

"The Creator will provide."

The sobs burst again. "Oh, Lamech. I need to be back with our families. I can't go on."

"You must. You promised you would."

But she hadn't promised. "How can you ask me to continue the pilgrimage without you?"

"Mishah. Trust me."

"You ask too much."

He glanced at the nearby guards and lowered his voice. "The word of the Creator came to me. The Mother has a blessing and a word of prophecy."

"Prophecy? For our child?" She sniffed, blinking the tears from her eyes.

He nodded. "You see why it is so important you finish what we have started?"

"How long have you known this?"

"Since the beginning.

"Why didn't you tell me?" How could he have kept something like this a secret, leaving her to believe she was only fulfilling a family tradition?

"I should have. I … I was hoping to surprise you. Mishah, we *will* have a son."

A son. Like in her dream. No! Not like that! She didn't need this new wrinkle to further complicate an already untenable situation. The Mother … a prophecy … Lamech taken from her … it was all too much!

"Please, my love. Continue with the journey, then go home and wait for me. Once my sentence is over, I'll come to you."

She pushed away from him about to burst from all the emotions exploding within her. "No you won't. You'll never come home. You'll clash with everyone you meet, you'll talk yourself into a new sentence, then an extension of that one. Sentence upon sentence will pile up because you'll not keep your mouth shut." She slashed down with the side of her hand upon her open palm, emphasizing each point. "I will never, never, never see you again!"

In an instant, her anger evaporated and she threw herself back into his arms, tears erupting, gasping, spasmodic sobs wrenching her body.

He whispered near her ear, "The evil one intends only harm for us, but the Creator will use it for his good."

The guards moved in and Amolikah took her gently by the shoulders.

Kenock said, "Until we see each other again, Lamech, my thoughts and prayers."

Lamech nodded. "You and Kleg'l must see to it that Mishah

completes this journey in safety. I put her and Amolikah in your hands now." He said it to both of them, but he was looking at Kleg'l.

"I understand." Kleg'l was on the verge of tears, his throat pulsing, eyes glistening as he took Lamech's hand.

Amolikah gave him a kiss on the cheek. "My love, my prayers, my hopes will be with you, Lamech." She forced a smile. "Be wise as the serpent, and gentle as the lamb."

He seemed to understand her warning in a way Mishah could not in her unbridled emotions.

Mishah kissed him hard and long, then buried her face into his chest until the guards and Amolikah separated them. Lamech moved back a couple steps, touched the moist spot on his shirt, and brought his fingertips to his lips. "I love you all, and I'll love you forever, Mishah."

❦

"Be watchful for them mansnatchers," Captain Berg advised. He spoke with a thoughtful cadence, an accent Mishah was not familiar with. She watched his eyes lift skyward. His dark face, etched like the bark of an old oak tree, turned up with eyes narrowed against the glare of the sun. He spent a moment searching the sky, puffing his kalewood pipe, then glanced at her. "They're becoming bolder these days, they are. Particularly along this stretch of the river. And smart. Come swooping out of the sun they do. Snatch you off the deck of this here river thumper pretty as picking ants off a twig. You keep an eye out."

She hardly heard his warning. Her thoughts were elsewhere. The smell of vera-logia had swept her back to home, to the gently rolling farmland of Morg'Seth, the densely forested hills, the seemingly endless verdant crop of vera-logia standing in ruler straight, vanishingly long rows. Home seemed so far away now. She closed her eyes, grabbed the handrailing to steady herself, and imagined standing in the middle of the vast, green fields curving beyond the horizon in every direction, except north where the purpled haze of Mount Hope rose like a marker stone at the edge of the farm.

The wind tousled her hair about her shoulders while the deck beneath her feet vibrated with the steady *thump, thump, thump* of a heavy one-lung cycler. The boat thudded off of rough water beneath its hull. Here at the stern rails of the *Osar Messenger,* downwind from the 'gia tanks, the faint odor of the fuel was strongest. It brought back memories of the pressing barns beyond their village where the farms from all around had brought in their crops. At pressing time, all the men would lend a hand and the work would continue throughout the Arc of Deli, the water urn.

A rare smile came to her lips. She could almost hear Lamech expounding on the Creator's story written in the night sky as he pointed out each of the stars. And afterward, with the 'gia distilled and sent away to distant commonwealths throughout the Settled Lands of Hope and beyond, the village would celebrate the festival Dagim, the bound fish. Life had a rhythm and a flow, and she longed for that simple, predictable time again.

Fifteen years! How could it ever be the same again? He'd miss the birth of their child, the first years of its life—those very important years when a father and child bond.

Her eyes welled, as they did with almost every thought. In the last two days they'd hardly been dry half a quartering. Even asleep she dreamed of Lamech, and when she awoke alone her pillow would be damp, and the pain in her heart almost too much to bear.

Tears had clouded her last view of him being taken back down the dark tunnel. But she remembered his head, how he had held it high.

Afterward, she was vaguely aware of packing her bags and carrying them down to the *Osar Messenger.* She remembered nothing of the river steamer departing Nod City, and hardly anything of that day, or the next. Now two days out with the river narrowing, its water growing choppy, the impenetrable forests hugging and over-hanging the banks, she was at least resigned. Life would never be normal until Lamech was back in it, but she had to cope, to make the best of it, if not for herself, then ... she looked down and put a hand to her stomach.

A son. A prophecy? Let the prophecy have something to do with Lamech's safe return!

The water foaming in their wake held her eye. It frightened her to think the Creator might have singled her out for ... for what? A wide, slow moving shadow passed over her. She was only half aware of it, but a warning thought nudged its way past the grief that so con-sumed her. What was it Captain Berg had been trying to tell her?

Something grabbed her arm.

She jumped.

"What's wrong, Mi?"

"Kenock." She let go of a breath. "You startled me."

"Good thing me and not that." He stabbed a finger at the sky. The mansnatcher's narrow wings, twenty spans wide and sculpted back to points, swept down once and lifted the huge creature above the treetops where sunlight shone off the short, yellow-gray hairs, flattened tight against its body. It banked away and tilted toward the river ahead of the boat, gliding low over the water as it came back. The umber head at the end of its long neck carried an immense chisel-pointed beak. A short crest running along the skull swung side to side as the mansnatcher searched for prey. Its body appeared sur-passingly small and compact, dwarfed by the size of the rest of it. Long, yellow-scaled legs shot straight back ending in massive feet with claws nearly half a span long.

"Captain Berg says it's best we get under cover. This part of the river is untamed, and some of the animals have become danger-ous." He took her by the arm, guiding her toward the low cabin mid-deck. They passed Berg standing nearby with a proj-lance in both his hands, pipe clenched in his teeth, and his eyes following the mansnatcher.

Some of the animals have become dangerous. Turnlings, some called them. It hadn't always been so. Mansnatchers had grown notorious in the last one hundred years, but they weren't the only ones. Many beasts of the field were turning against the humans.

She could almost hear Lamech expounding on how it was the curse of creation that was causing the world to grow bloody in fang and talon. *Oh, Lamech. Everything makes me think of you.* Would she never have a moment when his face didn't suddenly swim before her eyes to fill them with tears?

She ducked under the low cabin door and went inside.

❧

Lamech's eyes snapped open. The clatter of a distant door opening had echoed down the long hallway, and now footsteps approached on the paving stones in the hallway beyond the bolted door. His eyes, accustomed to the dim light, shifted around the dark holding room. Through a slit high up in the wall, the constant glow from the temple site showed the shadowed forms of six other sleeping men.

The footsteps grew louder and stopped outside the locked door. With the rattle of levers, the moonglass shutters were flung open. His unprepared eyes squinted against the light. Men stirred and grumbled. Some groaned, hooding their eyes, others simply rolled over and pulled blankets up over their heads. A latch rasped and the door swung in.

Four green-cloaks came in and braced the door two-by-two. Next came a young lieutenant Lamech had seen in the guard room, and by his side was En'tuboc, the quort whip. En'tuboc wore the impatient scowl of a man taken away from something much more important.

Sleep, perhaps? His hair stood in all directions, his beard unbraided, half a wrinkled shirttail hanging at his left hip, angled shirtfront misaligned by one fastener.

"That's the one." En'tuboc held a coiled whip in his right hand and thrust it out at Lamech.

Lamech hitched himself up on one elbow as the officer took two steps then stopped. "You will come with us."

"Me?" Whatever grogginess remained fell away almost at once.

"On your feet."

He grabbed up his clothes and hurried into them, stomped into his boots and followed the officer out. En'tuboc scowled and worked his jaw as if devising galling tasks for his morning rotation to pay him back for being the cause of his being hustled out of a comfortable bed. They paused in the dim hallway while the door was relocked and the moonglass shutters closed. Then with green-cloaks on either side of him, they marched from the stockades, through a guarded gate.

8

The Oracle of the Crystal

Government House sat shrouded in darkness, its hallways dimly quiet, and except for the occasional heavy-eyed guard who'd snap briefly to attention as they passed, glaringly deserted. Lamech marched between two green-cloaks up to the third floor. The usual retinue of guards stood before the doors to the grand gallery. The tall double portals opened and they strode inside. Except for the Lodath and Captain Da-gore, the darkened gallery was deserted.

Sol-Ra-Luce stood alone before the crystal spire as if mesmerised by the crimson pulse deep within it. Da-gore was near him. The Lodath did not stir as they approached, didn't turn as the heavy-stepping men halted six spans behind him. The officer in charge advanced two paces more, stopped and set his spine like a weaver's shuttle, and waited in a forced pose that couldn't have been comfortable.

The cavernous gallery was different than Lamech remembered it. A smothering gloominess like a sour blanket drenched in morning dew filled the room as if the gallery, too, appeared to have been asleep. The deep shadows at the corners almost seemed annoyed now at being disturbed at this late hour. Here and there wall plaques cut through the shadows with flashes of muted colors while the ceiling glowed softly from the dim light of moonglass, arranged in sinuous bands snaking around crystal lenses no longer shining with the brilliance of daylight. A wavering in the shadows caught his eye but when he looked, nothing was there.

Sol-Ra-Luce drew in a sudden breath and his head gave a small shake. He cleared his throat and came about, a little unsteady. Captain Da-gore seemed poised to assist him if he needed it, but he gathered himself almost at once and peered a moment at them. The Lodath had that same vaguely disheveled look and that groggy gray slack about his eyes that Lamech had noted in the quort whip, En'tuboc. "You may leave," the Lodath said to the accompanying guards, flicking a hand toward the doors. "Lieutenant, stay."

The officer nodded, relaxing almost imperceptibly. Lamech could almost feel an easing in his own spine. Sol-Ra-Luce stood before Lamech. "It's time we have a little talk."

"Three of the second quartering seems an odd time to *have a talk*."

Sol-Ra-Luce smiled. "I couldn't sleep."

"You must have been the only one then." That sour blanket had begun to bunch at his nostrils. Something here was taunting him, troubling his spirit.

"Watch your tongue," the lieutenant growled.

Sol-Ra-Luce put up a hand. "It's all right, lieutenant." He turned toward Lamech. "I couldn't sleep because I was thinking of you, and the others who were traveling with you."

The others? Mishah? Concern for himself fell away. "What of them? They're all right, aren't they?"

Sol-Ra-Luce shrugged. "As far as I know. They left the city the day before yesterday as they said they would."

A wave of relief washed over him, but it left behind a frothy wariness.

"I was curious why people who so openly disapprove of the way we run our lives would bother coming to Nod City at all."

A fleeting shimmer to his left pulled his eyes. Nothing. He looked back at the Lodath, still trying to identify that vexing undercurrent, unable to get a grip on it. "We already told you we were only passing through. We'd have gone on immediately if we could have arranged passage sooner."

"Yes, so you said. You booked passage aboard a freight hauler named the *Osar Messenger* bound for Far Port."

"Yes." He almost spoke more, but caught himself.

"And your reason for traveling to a distant location where few go?"

Reason? His hackles raised in warning. He didn't know he had needed one. "We were to visit with family." He fought down an unfamiliar urge to explain further.

"Ah! Family. Of course. So simple an explanation."

Lamech shivered as something brushed his cheek. He put a hand to his face but found nothing. Sol-Ra-Luce's eyes suddenly compressed and his head cocked attentively to the left. Lamech heard nothing. Then Sol-Ra-Luce gave a shake and the smile flickered on again.

"This family member you were to visit, could you tell me something of him?"

Be wise as the serpent, gentle as the lamb. "Very old and frail. This may be our last opportunity." What was the Lodath looking for? Why was he struggling against the urge to tell all that he knew?

"It's a pity you won't make it."

Lamech shrugged. Was his evasiveness obvious? "If it is the Creator's will, then there is still a chance. The Creator counts the number of our days."

The Lodath shook his head. "This Creator business is becoming wearisome." Sol-Ra-Luce paced a few steps, glanced at the smoldering, pulsing crystal, then returned. "Tell me of the others who traveled with you."

"How could five travelers from a distant land be of interest to the Lodath of the Oracle?" He sensed the Lodath was playing a very dangerous game with him. He had to play along without jeopardizing his wife and the others. *Be wise as the serpent.* If only he knew why this man was probing, what he was looking to glean from him. Keeping his wits about him had become a battle.

"I'm interested in all that happens in my realm—mine and King Irad's, that is."

"So you are inquiring on his behalf as well?"

Sol-Ra-Luce gave a thin, knowing smile. Lamech's evasiveness must have been a challenge he'd anticipated. "If there is something of interest to Irad, he will be told. But I don't think the business of five sojourners would be of great concern to someone as busy as the Great Warrior King." His voice hardened ever so slightly. "Now, tell me of the others."

"Kenock is my brother-in-law. He'd liked to have seen more of your city. Kleg'l is our good-man, pierced into the tree of my wife's family. Amolikah is my wife's grandmother. A wise and honest lady who sits on the family counsel. And then there is my wife, Mishah." The thought of her made the words catch in his throat. "She's a healer, and happiest when home working with her sisters and I'm in the fields keeping my opinions to myself." He smiled. Had he given away too much?

Sol-Ra-Luce nodded. "How long have you two been joined?"

How could that be of interest to the Lodath? "Three years."

He went strangely silent a moment. "And what of children?"

He'd asked it casually, but it stirred something deep inside Lamech to caution. Hadn't he noticed his wife's condition? Did Mishah's full dress hide her pregnancy from him? "So far no children have been born to us. But we are hopeful."

Sol-Ra-Luce's view narrowed. Had he heard something in that? He had to be very careful. Fighting this battle was wearing him down.

The questions lasted until dawn, with Captain Da-gore silently observing. By the interrogation's end, Lamech's energy had been completely sapped away. The Lodath had not been overly hard with him, yet it was as if something in the gallery was wicking the vitality from his soul.

Almost as soon as the tall doors had closed behind him, he'd begun to feel better, and by time the guards returned him to his cell, with the dawn pink on the horizon and the air moist with the morning mist, a vast reserve of energy had sprung alive within him. Most fortunate if En'tuboc's earlier glowering had been a foreshadowing of the workday to come.

❧

Concern sliced across the Lodath's brow as he watched the heavy doors whisper shut behind the guards returning Lamech to his cell. For a long moment, Sol-Ra-Luce stared at the door. "What did you glean, Captain Da-gore?"

"He was wary, but who wouldn't be in his position?" A faint humming filled the air and Da-gore's view shifted around the gallery. A sheet of trembling pale gray light rippled like pebbles tossed into a pool of still water. All at once, the warrior emissaries of the Oracle, the unshackled-ones as they called themselves, stepped through rifts of light into the realm of man. They appeared battle weary, speaking among themselves in a tongue he did not understand. Their forms solidified out of the wavering light and they stood about the gallery in disarray.

Their tousled clothes, streaked in black, smoldered. A few of the warriors leaned heavily upon their battle-staffs. There had been a clash of arms beyond that thin veil that separates the world of men from the Oracle's realm—that promised land where all eventually arrive, be it at the end of this lifetime or a thousand lifetimes to come. Da-gore was determined to make the grade the first time around. Working out the inadequacies of his life over and over again held no appeal. A thought caught him by surprise and a slender sardonic line altered the shape of his mouth. How could he be certain this *was* his first time around—how could anyone know?

So, there had been a battle … A flicker of light caught his eye and he shifted toward the tall crystal. The spire of rock had changed, the pulsing, crimson spot beginning to snake like a globule of oil rising up slowly through water, congealing into the shape of a man. With a burst of fiery brilliance that stung Da-gore's eyes, the Oracle stepped formidably from the crystal into the room. The rock went pale and the warriors' murmurings ceased as an overwhelming energy engulfed the gallery.

Every eye riveted on the pearly glow that enveloped the tall figure; startling blue eyes, smooth, pearlescent skin, a straight, handsome nose, and a hard smile. The face was perfectly symmetrical and the eyes radiated love. The Oracle folded his hands in front of him, and gazed around at the warriors. Da-gore had seen the star-being before, and each time was stunned by his splendor.

"Another victory, my friends." His voice resonated with the power of a mighty river, like the Idikla. Da-gore imagined it shaking the very foundations of Government House. "The Tyrant's warriors are powerful, but our cause is just and we prevailed."

"We will prevail," the warriors said with a single voice.

The taut smile hitched up at the corners and the blue eyes glistened. The Oracle turned to Sol-Ra-Luce. "What do you make of this situation with the Lee-lander?"

"I sensed he was holding back, My Lord. But then Lee-landers are known to be a tight-lipped bunch—except when speaking out for the Tyrant of Old."

"They are a stubborn people, but not unreachable. Let's not give up on them just yet." The radiant smile thinned a bit. "Why do you think he was holding back?"

"Trying to protect his family, I suspect. But I don't see how a wandering band of Lee-landers passing through our land could be of concern to you, My Lord."

"There are many who wish to bury the precious knowledge of old beneath the refuse pile of their myths. Protecting his family was certainly in his thoughts, but I noticed something else, something in his face. You didn't see it?"

"No, My Lord."

Da-gore's attention was riveted. A momentary panic touched the Lodath's face. What had Sol-Ra-Luce missed? Had he missed it too? Would it even matter to the Oracle?

"You are familiar with the ancient prophecies?" As he spoke, the Oracle strode before the warrior emissaries then peered at Da-gore. The gentle probing of his thoughts almost went unnoticed, but not quite. Da-gore filled his brain with other things; memorized lists, old battle formations and strategies. It was said these beings could not actually get inside a human's mind, but they had ways of ferreting out their thoughts just the same. He refused to give his over easily.

The Lodath was saying, "There are many legends from earlier times. I know a good deal of them. What is it you saw in the Lee-lander, My Lord?"

The Oracle frowned and turned his attention suddenly back upon Sol-Ra-Luce. "We have many enemies of old. Some intend to stop us from bringing the forbidden knowledge to my children. We have a most fearsome adversary; a tyrant fraught with deceit.

"In the beginning, when man first clawed his way up from the lowly savage beasts and that spark of humanness had finally ignited within his breast and flamed to life, I came to him. I came to give him the gift of wisdom, to aid him on his long journey ... a journey that has eventually led to where you find yourself now, Sol-Ra-Luce. The pinnacle of growth and change, the conquering struggle from bestial to spiritual. Man in all his glory. But the Tyrant of Old had other ideas. He wanted to use man for his own purposes."

The Oracle shook his head as if the memory pained him. "Many of my warriors defected, shackling themselves to his will. He called himself the Creator, although it was I who planted the first seeds upon a young world. He stole that honor from me and blinded the first children of man to their true origins." The Oracle's voice hardened and the wall plaques seemed to tremble at his words. "He's a selfish creature who feeds on the worship of man. Even so, he is powerful. It has taken me all these years to rebuild my realm, and he has been fortifying his. But the children of the ages have grown in wisdom on their own. They begin now to see through his lies, and our hand is strengthening!"

Da-gore saw concern fill the Lodath's face.

The Oracle's voice took a flinty edge. "This *Creator*, this Tyrant of Old, still holds the world in a closed fist. His grasp is tightest in the Lee-lands of Morg'Seth."

The air tingled with a malevolence that seemed to turn Da-gore's blood cold.

"I know this man, Lamech. I know his father, I knew his grandfather." His eyes darkened. "I've watched the family grow stronger from father to son ... watched and wondered. Could it be from this generation—this line of zealots—that the Tyrant will attempt to bring to pass the prophecy?"

"Which prophecy? There are so many." Sol-Ra-Luce's voice trembled.

"You still don't fully understand."

"Forgive the ignorance of your servant, My Lord."

The Oracle strode before his warriors again, turned, and considered the Lodath a moment, his face suddenly heavy with a memory.

"The War of the Ages was fought over a thousand years ago, here, on your world." He grimaced. "We were victorious, but the cost was heavy. As I've already told you, I had underestimated his strength, and the tyrannical hold he had on certain warriors whom I believed to be true to me, to our cause.

"We fought hard and we fought with valor. We had our victories and we suffered our loses. Then one small triumph came into my hands. I reached one of your fathers and planted in him the seed of wisdom. That seed was the spark that finally severed him from his animal past—and from the Tyrant's stranglehold! In one glorious moment, I was able to impart knowledge, and his eyes opened and man saw evil for what it was, and he saw goodness as well. The wisdom I gave him severed him from the shackles of the Tyrant of Old once and for all. It set his feet inexorably upon the path of finding his own way, his own truths, his own righteousness in this world."

Da-gore sifted his memory for the legends, fitting this new piece of information into it.

"The Tyrant, knowing I'd unshackled the man, flung the full force of his anger against me, but we repelled his warriors." His eyes lifted toward the ceiling. "It was then the prophecy was given. The Tyrant swore to raise up a human in his name, one who will attempt to crush me in final victory. He moves even now among his faithful though deceived servants to nurture a people to fully believe his lies. He gathers his strength. He intends to possess a human to bring to pass the prophecy. This human will be from the generations of one family. And that line is those people who settled the lands of Morg'Seth."

The Oracle's magnetism pulled at Da-gore. He was a fighting man himself. He understood the Oracle's distress over a war measured not in years, but in eons!

"The Tyrant isn't blind to our efforts, although he's yet to stir from the secret vaults of his throne room to openly confront us. But that is only a matter of time. And time is short. He is gathering his forces again and I must move swiftly."

"But these sojourners, My Lord?" The Lodath spread his hands with the question. "Thousands have come before them and no doubt thousands will follow. Why these five? And what of this prisoner we just saw?"

"Why indeed?" His eyes burned with fierce heat, his jaw taking a firm set. "You did not perceive what this Lamech was keeping from you, yet it shouted plainly from his eyes. *His child!*"

The Lodath stood there, stunned. "He has none. He said so."

Da-gore saw fury blaze in the Oracle's eyes. Sol-Ra-Luce had made a grave mistake.

"'So far no children have been born to my wife or myself' was what he said. And therein lay his deceit through carefully crafted words. He has no children *yet*, but he will have soon. Even now, his wife carries their child. She stood before you and still you didn't perceive it."

Da-gore thought back, recalling the woman had been pregnant. How did such an obvious oversight occur?

Sol-Ra-Luce shrank from the star-being's sudden anger. "But what makes you think this child is the prophesied one?"

"Why else would the Tyrant protect the woman? Why did he blind your eyes ... and his." He stabbed a finger at Da-gore. "It is because of the child she carries. That is why they take the journey to the Mother."

The Mother? So, that was the relative they sought.

Sol-Ra-Luce stammered, "I've heard of this pilgrimage. It in itself is not uncommon among those people."

"A journey to the Mother would not be uncommon, nor would it have aroused my suspicions. But one escorted by a Royal Legion of shackled-ones raises suspicion."

"Your warriors?"

"They cannot intervene!"

Can't intervene? Da-gore frowned.

The Oracle's brow furrowed and he strode resolutely toward the spire of crystal then whirled on his heels and came back. "But, there is no forbiddance over human intervention." He went silent a moment, then his eyes widened as though he'd come upon a solution. "There is another. He is involved in this, yet in a way still unclear to me. He is not one of the Tyrant's servants, but the Tyrant uses him." The Oracle considered the problem. "Perhaps he is someone I can turn to my will, someone who can be useful to me."

"Who is this man? I will have him brought here at once."

"Yes." The Oracle glanced at the window, graying with the first light of dawn. "Bring him here today. Get him to accept my pledge and I can bend him to my will"

"Name the man, My Lord."

"He was the one who stood for the Lee-landers on the Meeting Floor. The one who humiliated your guards. His name is Rhone."

9

The Pledge

*T*he noise, the odors, the bustle of people assailed Rhone from every direction. The open-air market at the end of Barter Road sold nearly everything a person could want to buy. With the enthusiasm of a kitten after a ball of twine, Bar'ack trailed after him from one canopied vender to the next, stopping at all the usual places.

Food was never a concern while in the Wild Lands; everything a man could want to eat grew in abundance. Some trees produced tart fruits in the first half of the year, following it with sweet fruits the latter half. Root crops, mushrooms, keelits, orfin, legumittes grew all year long. The only extras Rhone carried were his cooking vessels and an assortment of spices. Spices could be had in the Wild Lands with a little effort, but it was easier just to bring what he needed.

Rhone advised his young protégé on a pair of boots, shaped for easy walking, yet with tall, sturdy tops to protect against tough underbrush and the occasional poisonous serpent. There had been a time when such considerations never entered his mind, but reports of people being bitten and dying had made him wary of the once-shy creatures. Serpents, it seems, were some of the first turnlings. Ancient stories gave a fanciful reason for the change, but

Rhone gave them little credence. He was a practical man. But if serpents had become aggressive, then he'd take measures to protect himself against them.

"Look, Master Rhone." Bar'ack pointed toward the makeshift arena where two warriors were engaged in mock battle. "Makir Warriors. They put on a show twice a day. See that one, the bigger of the two? His name is Klesc. They say no man can defeat him." Bar'ack started toward the arena, but Rhone caught him by the sleeve.

"We don't need to go there." He eyed the two combatants, feeling the rhythm of their practiced movements resonate in his own muscles. The one named Klesc seemed to move like the wind, never remaining in one place long enough for his opponent to lay his blunted sword on him.

"But—"

"They've taken the Usito, Makir oath, yet they peddle their training for a few glecks." His jaw tightened until his teeth hurt and the tendons in his neck went hard.

"The Usito? What's that?"

"Never mind." He pulled Bar'ack after him.

"You said the Makir were no more, yet look at those two. Look how they move!"

"The Makir have no leader since their Pyir was driven from Atlan. They are unbound." Rhone sent him a cold stare. "The Makir are no more. Men like those two are all that's left of them—men who sell themselves as though a common afaleigh."

Rhone spied the line of green-cloaks threading its way through the crowd. They advanced with an air of determination that instantly put him on alert. He hauled Bar'ack between the rippling sheets of a candy vendor and a bakery booth. The sharp odor of boiling sugar blended oddly with the aroma of yeasty bread and baking Berber-wheat biscuits.

"What?"

Rhone put a finger to his lips.

Bar'ack stiffened and looked around, craning his neck.

Rhone peered around the bright-striped back corner of the booth. The green-cloaks had stopped. A man wearing a cobbler's apron was speaking to the leader and pointing. Rhone grimaced and hurried back to Bar'ack. With a flick of his head, he led Bar'ack off in the opposite direction.

Passing a booth selling cloaks, Rhone grabbed one up and slapped two glecks into the startled seller's palm. "Keep the change." He pulled it over his shoulders, ducked his head, and bent his knees until he wasn't much taller than Bar'ack.

"What's this all about?" Bar'ack craned over his shoulder.

"Keep your eyes straight. I'll tell you later." What had alerted him? Old training? Skills honed to a keen edge at an early age, now safely tucked away in some back recess of his brain? Maybe it was seeing those Makir Warriors performing their practiced moves. Maybe it was nothing at all. Maybe everything. The green-cloaks had been keeping an eye on him. The two guards he'd overpowered a few nights earlier had put the word out. So far, they'd kept their distance and he'd ignored them. Something was different now, and it set every nerve within him tingling.

A contingent of guards suddenly appeared from behind a fruit vendor's booth. Rhone drew up, casting left and right. Past the green and yellow stripes of a musician's stall, more green-cloaks hurried along the next lane over. The alarm inside his head had been all too real. Unfortunately, it had come too late. He straightened to his full height. Bar'ack's startled eyes leaped between him and the ranks of guards. Rhone put a hand on his shoulder. "It's me they want."

The captain of the guard, a stern-faced man, advanced as the noose tightened. Rhone gave a wry smile, glancing at the ranks of green-cloaks. These men weren't taking any chances.

"Your name is Rhone?" the captain demanded, his subordinates leveling proj-lances.

Rhone nodded. "I am he."

He glanced at Bar'ack. "You two will come with us."

A man relieved him of the webbing knife in the top of his boot, and when a quick search revealed no further weapons, they escorted Rhone and Bar'ack past the booths and gawking crowd, out onto Barter Road where a wagon and more guards waited.

❧

Only once before had Rhone been inside the ruling offices of Nod City. Government House held not only the king's offices and the Lodath's living quarters, but every other official bureau a city required to run smoothly. Not that a collection of bureaucrats could ever make even the rudest country village run smoothly, let alone a place as large and complex as Nod City. But in their own inept way, the politicians and bureaucrats managed to keep the place bumbling along. Rhone had decided long ago when applying for a permit to market web inside the city limits that Government House was inhabited by fools, and the less he had to do with them the happier his life would be.

The one time he'd been here, his business had taken place on the first floor. Government House became more spacious, more opulent as he ascended the stair, improving his earlier impression of the place. When the guards accompanying him halted before the tall, high-relief doors and waited for them to be announced, it was apparent whomever he was being taken to see was a high-ranking official.

With a low hiss from a mechanism hidden somewhere beneath the floor, the doors swung open and they marched in. A man sitting in a golden, carved chair, one of two upon a slightly raised platform, watched as they approached. Rhone was aware of the twinge behind his left ear and an uncustomary dryness of his mouth. This was the Lodath of the Oracle. The second most powerful man in all the land of Nod.

The air seemed to tingle as they drew to a halt. In a glance, he took in the decor of the place and just as quickly dismissed it all—all except the pearly finger of rock in its center. The curious dull red glow held his eye a moment. A sudden closeness, like a narrow tunnel where walls pressed his shoulders, brought a shiver up his spine. The expansive gallery gave no clue why he ought to feel such ... his eyes went back to the crystal.

"The man Rhone, Your Eminence. The other is called Bar'ack."

"Put two guards by the door and send the rest away."

Da-gore gave the order, but he remained near Rhone.

The Lodath steepled his fingers and pressed them to his lips, giving a long, careful stare. "Rhone."

Rhone nodded.

The Lodath rose and stood at the edge of the platform where the extra height put him precisely at eye level. A calculated move. The Lodath of the Oracle was not a man who looked up to anyone, if anything of what Rhone had heard about was true. "You are not from the Land of Nod, are you, Rhone?"

"I make my home here, when I'm not away."

"You are a gatherer, are you not?"

"I gather web. Much of what I collect ends up on the temple project." He inclined his head toward the window.

"A most admirable occupation."

A cloud of unseen hornets bristled around him. Unable to identify the sensation, he tried to ignore it. Something kept tugging his eyes back to that crystal. He cleared his brain, drawing upon old lessons once learned but never forgotten, rusty as they might be. His attention sharpened.

"Where is your homeland, Rhone."

"Here."

A thin smile touched the Lodath's face. "I mean your family line. Tell me your father's name."

His chest squeezed and his father's face momentarily swam before his eyes. A sharp breath brought him back in control. "Why have I been brought before you?"

The Lodath's eyes took on an odd glaze. He blinked and smiled. "You stand before *me*. I ask the questions."

"Some memories bring pain."

"Pain comes in many flavors. It would serve you well to keep in mind whom you stand before, Rhone-who-hides-his-past."

"I don't hide it. I just prefer not to speak of it. Who my father was has no bearing today on who I am. I am Rhone."

The Lodath strode along the edge of the platform and stared a moment at the orange balloon far beyond the window. "For the present, I'll accept that." He looked to Bar'ack. "And you, young man?"

"I am Bar'ack, youngest of Ker'ack, a web merchant."

"I will tell you why you have been brought before me. A few days ago you were involved with a confrontation on the Meeting Floor. You came to the defense of a man and woman."

That caught him unprepared. He was expecting to hear charges for his rough handling of the Lodath's Guards, not this. He scrambled to catch up. He'd put the couple out of mind almost as soon as the incident was over. "Yes. I recall the incident."

"Recall?" The Lodath had sensed his surprise as well. "Then you do not know these people?"

"I have no idea who they are. Lee-landers, I gathered by their dress." How did those two figure into his being here before the Lodath of the Oracle?

"Yet, you aided them."

"I did."

"Why?"

Why, indeed? "I—" he hesitated. What was it he'd felt back then?

Something in the air. An urging softly spoken? "I don't know. I just stepped in. They seemed to need help."

The Lodath struck that curious pose again, holding it longer this time. Captain Da-gore advanced a step closer, looking as if prepared to move quickly. The high priest of the Oracle gave a hitch of his head and blinked and said as if no time at all had passed, "Then you know nothing of their subversive behavior?"

"Subversive?" Rhone felt the smile steal onto his face. "Curious charge, from what little I know of Lee-landers. It's common knowledge that folks from the Lee-lands of Morg'Seth are a stiff-necked, opinionated people. And it is also common knowledge they oppose the Oracle and the new challenges he represents to their beliefs. But beyond spouting hotly held opinions, I've never heard that any Lee-lander has ever made threats against any people or government." He relaxed a little. This line of questioning didn't seem to pose a serious threat to his leaving Nod City as planned.

The Lodath looked pleased with his answer. "You don't sympathize with these people, then?"

"Their opinions are their own and they are welcome to them. It must have been danger I sensed the other day. And I'd help most anyone in danger, regardless of their religious beliefs."

"You seem like a reasonable man, Rhone." The Lodath returned to his chair. "I see now that your loyalties were simply misplaced." He removed a hand from his pocket and dangled two crystalline pledge pendants before Rhone. "Accept these and I will forget all this ever happened."

"I do not wish to be pledged to the Oracle." That warning horn blared again, those unseen hornets swarming closer to his ear. He brushed at his thick mane, but there was nothing there.

The Lodath sighed and glanced at the captain of the Guard. "Captain Da-gore, what are the complaints we have against this man?"

"Disturbance on the Meeting Floor and attacking two of your guards, Your Eminence."

The Lodath nodded slightly. "The first is a minor charge, easily overlooked. The second one, however, is most serious."

Blackmail!

"You look surprised. Did you expect to get away with a flagrant attack on two warders in the service of King Irad and myself?" The Lodath drummed his fingers on the arm of the chair, waiting.

What was so important about a simple pledge pendant that he'd go to such lengths to have him accept it? "If I take the pledge, the charges against me would … ?"

"Go away."

Rhone liked the sound of that. What harm could come from accepting the foolish thing anyway? A twinge, like a small knot forming in his gut, grabbed at his stomach.

"This is all?"

"This is all." The Lodath held out the crystal pendants. Their faceted planes caught the light from the crystal ceiling and showered colors like the finest prism. There seemed to be a curious crimson pulse from deep within them.

"You need not pledge now. I merely require that you possess it." The Lodath's smile spread innocently across his crafty face. "And think about it. Put it among your belongings."

Bar'ack took a pendant, and reluctantly Rhone accepted the other. At its touch, a comforting warmth coursed through him, taking the edge off all his concerns. Rhone gazed at the colors that shot from it as he rotated it in the light.

"Captivating, isn't it?" the Lodath said.

The room blurred.

"You will have plenty of time to experience its power, Rhone. All of its power. Savor but a moment of it now."

Rhone struggled against his desire to hold it, to stare at it, and the desire to be away from its intoxication. The draw was stronger than any spell an afaleigh could weave with her perfume. It might have easily carried him away, but that is not what he wanted. He shoved the crystal into his pocket.

Almost at once his head cleared.

Mishah's heavy heart colored her world gray. She wished it wasn't so. She must shake herself free of this burdensome depression. This trip was set, cast in lime-sand, inevitable. Even if she insisted on terminating it, neither her grandmother, nor her brother, nor Kleg'l would permit it. She shifted on the hard bench, propped her elbows upon the rough table, and stared at her leather healer's bag on the table. The monotonous rocking, the incessant background thumping, the stuffy, humid air all pulled at her eyelids and brought on a heavy drowsiness. Perhaps she should take something for it?

It wasn't only she who was suffering anguish. Across the table from her, Kenock worried a strip of leather, twisting it about his finger, unraveling it, then winding it again.

All at once, he slammed the thong to the table and stared at her with troubled eyes. "What did he mean by that anyway? How could he say I'm different from you, or Lamech or any of us? I'm not."

So, that's what had been troubling him. The Lodath's accusation had been eating at him. Mishah had been so consumed with her own grief she'd failed to see the turmoil in her brother until now. She reached across the table for his hand.

"He meant nothing. He was only trying to stir us up against each other. We must not forget who he is, whom he represents."

Kenock's eyes lowered and fixed upon her hand and she felt the faint tightening of his fingers. "Lamech believed him. I saw it in his face." He glanced suddenly at Kleg'l, across the room, slumped in a chair, long legs stretched out, narrow shoulders shrunken. He lowered his voice. "He doesn't trust me. Has he ever really trusted me?"

"Of course he trusts you, Kenock." Were those only empty words? Did Lamech really trust his young brother-in-law? Passing on the responsibility of leadership should rightly have gone to Kenock as the natural heir to the family line. Yet Lamech had seen a need to divide the authority. "He was worried for our safety—worried for himself too. He had so much to consider and so little time to think it through." She lowered her voice to match his and carefully measured her words. "Two of you sharing the responsibility just seemed right to him. It gave him confidence that Amolikah and I would be safe."

"You don't have to speak to me as if I'm a child. I am different, Mi, and Lamech sees it. I've always sensed his disapproval, as if I will never live up to his standards." A lame smile abruptly tempered his earnestness. "I want to see things and do things. Lamech thinks that's wrong. But I don't see it that way. I just want—" emotion erupted in his voice, his fingers suddenly crushing hers. "I just want to experience life."

Amolikah looked over from the window where she was standing, watching the tangled shoreline slipping past. The good-man stirred in his chair. No one said anything for a moment. In the midst of their silence, the muffled *thump, thump, thump* swelled within the confines of the small cabin.

Mishah worked her hand from his grasp and smiled, trying to understand. He *was* different, but not how the Lodath meant. He had a young man's thirst for adventure, but he was a true believer. She knew it in her heart, and so did Lamech. "I know you will take care of us, Kenock."

Kenock shoved the thong into his pocket and stood. She watched him through the door window as he climbed the stairs to the deck and disappeared beyond a crate labeled: SCYTHE BLADES, TUBAL-CAIN IRONWORKS, NOD CITY.

Amolikah took the bench across the table from her. "He's angry and hurt, dear, but once he sees how much we all need him, he'll feel better."

"I know he will."

"And you will too. Time helps the wounded heart heal. As a healer, you can appreciate that. When we've finished this pilgrimage and return home, you'll settle into the routine of life again and await Lamech's return."

"Have I any other choice, Grandmother?"

"You see, you've already taken the first step."

"Have I?"

"Acceptance, my dear. Acceptance of those things we cannot change will put your feet on the right road."

Acceptance and strength, the sort only the Creator could supply, Lamech would certainly have added. Her throat constricted. She was doing it again. Everything brought her thoughts back to him. Amolikah's faith was perhaps the strongest of the four of them, yet the events of the past few days had plainly tested even it.

Hurried footsteps pounded the deck somewhere beyond the cabin. Mishah came around as Kenock pulled the door open. "Come! Look."

Kleg'l, Amolikah, and Mishah exchanged glances then followed Kenock up onto the cargo-packed deck and to the stern rail. He pointed skyward. "There. See?"

As they bent back their necks and shaded their eyes to the sun, Captain Berg came from the pilothouse and peered up from beneath a wide-brimmed grass hat. He swung the tube of a long, leather bound glass from under his arm and put it to his eye.

"I've not seen anything like it," Kenock said.

Neither had Mishah. The Lee-lands of Morg'Seth was an agrarian society, not steeped in the latest contrivances as folks were in this part of the world. But they weren't an isolated band either. They had books, and good communication, and the travelers who frequently passed through their land always had stories to tell, and never lacked for a ready ear to tell them to. What she saw high overhead, a mere thumbnail in size, had been described to her before.

The long reed basket was tapered at both ends and draped in the fluttering banner. Above the basket, looking like two elongated conch shells fitted end to end with their spiraling points facing forward and backwards, was the envelope. It glinted silver and purple above while its underside looked to be black and unadorned. The conch shells, woven of the finest spider silk, dwarfed the basket beneath. She couldn't make out the cables connecting the two, but they were there. Something that appeared to be an array of mirrors extended like paddles around the sides of the machine. From the forward prow-point of the basket, three arching arms cantilevered forward, and harnessed into them were three giant condors, their wings flapping in unison. It was a slow, easy, powerful pace, and it pulled the machine swiftly through the sky.

"What is it?" Kleg'l asked.

Amolikah said, "It is called a sky-barge. I saw one once before, many years ago. Mirrors heat a gas inside the balloon by focusing sunlight onto its dark underbelly."

Captain Berg lowered his glass. "That's a sky-barge, all right. That one makes the trip between Nod City and Far Port more or less on a regular schedule."

"Might I have a look?" Kenock asked and was given the glass. He stared through it briefly before putting it into Mishah's anxious hand.

The distant image expanded before her eye and the three big birds flapping stoically came into sharp view in front of a high seat where a speck of a man sat, presumably controlling them through lines too thin to be visible from this distance. The other men aboard were specks as well. At least two of them stood at the side rails. Some moved about the barge, but what they were doing was too distant to make out. The mirrors rotated like paddles, this way and that, catching the sun to warm the air inside the silken sack. It was a curious and fascinating glimpse of a land removed from the Lee-lands of Morg'Seth; one of many interesting and odd sights she'd been promised the farther they traveled from home and the deeper they pushed into the Wild Lands where Chevel-ee, the Mother's village, lay far off the main thoroughfares of trade. The barge altered its course slightly. A flash of sunlight filled the telescope and stung her eye. She turned away and blinked.

"Oh, oh, there be trouble," Berg thrust a finger skyward.

At first Mishah thought he was pointing at the sky-barge. But the next moment she spotted them. She swung the glass and picked out six winged creatures circling slowly above the balloon. "Mansnatchers?"

"Crafty beasts, they are. Turnlings," Berg said. "Two adults and four fledglings."

"Can they harm a sky-barge?" she asked, lowering the telescope.

Berg nodded. "No telling what those creatures will do. An unpredictable lot, too. Looks like that bunch is out hunting." A low growl rumbled in his throat. "Mansnatchers are smart enough to know if they stay above 'em with the sun to their backs, they won't be spotted."

Amolikah shaded her eyes toward the sky-barge. "Is there some way to warn the people?"

The wide-brimmed grass hat shook. "Not from here. Let's just hope someone aboard her catches sight of 'em before they snatch a man off the deck or rip a hole in that balloon.

Mishah whispered a plea of protection to the Creator for the people aboard the barge, then put the glass back to her eye hoping to spot some indication her appeal had been answered.

10

Mansnatchers

Rhone leaned on the hand rail, fingers wrapped around the thick, woven fibers, feet planted wide upon the reed deck to steady himself against the sway of the balloon and forward lunge at each measured wing beat from the three giant birds in harness. Even at this altitude, the smell of the forest reached him on the upwelling of warm air. The familiar and comforting aroma of moist earth and pungent tree bark conjured up colors and textures in his brain.

"The forests are so vast," Bar'ack said, his grasp tight as iron hammered in a forge, his eyes wide with wonderment. "I mean, they just go on forever." Bar'ack was getting his first taste of adventure, and relishing every morsel of it.

The fare had been expensive, but Ker'ack had insisted on paying it. The view almost made it worth the money. Rhone stretched an arm toward the vast forests. "The Wild Lands stretch a thousand leagues north, west, and east of the Settled Lands of Hope. Clear to the Border Seas to the west and the remote mining camps of the Ugmot District isolated among the Ugmot Mountains in the far northwest. I know of no one who has explored them to the east, but your friend, Frobin, writes of the Kenimites who supposedly live beyond the Morning Light Mountains."

"And of Atlan, the island kingdom of the Hodinites. I've read of it." Bar'ack peered down at the river that cut a slash through the green trees like a wide band of beaten silver, glistening in the sunlight. "The river is narrower than it was only last quartering."

"It will continue to narrow and grow more dangerous as we near the mountains. Once past Far Point, the Idikla enters the Ara Gorge where it becomes unfit for travel. Some say its headwaters are in the mythical Cradleland." Rhone gave a short laugh. "Your friend Frobin writes something of that as well."

"He must have traveled all over the world to have seen so much."

"Or have a vivid imagination."

Bar'ack gave him a sharp glance. "You don't believe his stories, do you?" His voice held a slight edge.

Rhone's wide shoulders gave a small heave. "Anything is possible, but you said it yourself, he must have traveled all over the world to come up with some of the things he writes about. I know something of travel in the Wild Lands. Let's just say I'm skeptical."

Rhone scanned the carpet of greenery below them, his view coming around to the three birds harnessed to their perches. The driver on his high seat expertly handled them with a fistful of reins and a colorful vocabulary that would shock the faint of heart. To the east, a herd of sten-gordons lumbered lazily across a clearing. Were these turnlings too? Rhone pointed them out to Bar'ack who hurried across the barge to the opposite railing for a better look. Birds, like fly specks, flew above the treetops. A flock of flamingos waltzed toward a clearing in perfect unison, like a rose-colored shoal of fish.

Rhone strolled along the deck, his legs stabbing this way and that as he battled the motion of the sky-barge. He steered clear of the bronze pedestals where mirror-men expertly worked levers to keep the polished reflectors aligned and sunlight focused upon the underside of the balloon. He turned his eyes from the glare off its black underbelly, preferring a view of the forest passing beneath the sky-barge, and grasped the railing at Bar'ack's side. The trees stretching endlessly away in this new direction looked no different than they had from the other side of the barge.

The driver gave a cluck and a shout, and heaved at his reins. The sky-barge lurched to the right, taking a new tack that cut across the course of the river far below. Mirror-men scrambled at their levers and in a moment they'd adjusted the mirrors' angles and brought them back into focus.

The captain of the sky-barge joined them at the railing. He was a tall, young man; slim of body and face, and wore a neatly trimmed black beard. He'd been both friendly and helpful the whole trip, and seemed not at all affected by the importance of his job. "It's not far now, Master Rhone. Another quartering should have us over Far Port. We'll make land just beyond the village." He carried a polished bronze tube under his left arm and lifted it to his eye, directing it forward, past the draft birds' immense flapping wings.

"You make this trip often, Captain Jakl?" A shadow passing briefly over the treetops caught Rhone's eye, then it was gone.

"Maybe once a month. Not much call for passage to Far Port." He lowered the glass and gave an easygoing smile that crinkled the sunburned skin at the corners of his green eyes. Jakl looked to be even younger than Bar'ack, and must have excelled in what he did to have attained his high rank at such an early age.

Bar'ack pointed at the distant boat pushing its way up the river. Both men leaned over the railing for a better look. River traffic had been heavy the previous afternoon when they'd lifted off the tethers. Much of it had been temple barges being pulled up the river against the current by teams of three-points along the river road. But at the Hawk Mountain canal, they'd all left the main channel and headed inland. What shipping remained upon the broad choppy Idikla had slowly diminished as the scattered villages became fewer and the water rougher, until finally traffic had disappeared altogether. For the last half quartering, Rhone had not seen a single boat.

He squinted and tightened his grip on the handrail as the sky-barge came about again, completing its maneuver and settling in on its new heading. Mirror-men scrambled to readjust their reflectors while the bird handler sawed at the reins and stabbed a foot down on a pedal and shouted, "Kia-kia-kia, whoo-a tee-kia."

Rhone stiffened suddenly and cocked his head. Something had brought a tingle to the back of his neck. He'd spent enough time in the Wilds to know he shouldn't ignore those small signals. He tried to filter out the sounds of the barge and the powerful *whoosh* from the giant birds, searching for that *something*.

Bar'ack started along the railing toward the bow where the bird driver worked his pedals and reins. Rhone studied the treetops below; the long undulating shadow of the barge drifting across them. He recalled the shadow he'd glimpsed earlier—seen and dismissed. Maybe it was nothing … but that feeling had begun to ripple along his spine. Here and there another shadow poked beyond the edges of the barge's shadow, flitting briefly into view before disappearing again. There had been something familiar in them … and then it came to him! *Mansnatchers!*

Rhone glanced up, squinting against the blinding glare, feeling the heat full on his face. "Captain Jakl!"

The captain came about with a start.

"Mansnatchers!" Rhone stabbed a finger at the balloon.

Jakl glanced up just as one of the winged predators swooped beneath the balloon. "Men to arms!"

Rhone spun as an ear-piercing screech rent the air. The mansnatcher dove under the immense shadow of the lifting envelope, its color shifting from a pale yellowish-gray to nearly black. Claws extended, it snatched one of Jakl's crew off the deck and winged skyward with the doomed man's arms flailing the air, his guttural screams muffled by the pounding of the giant wings. Two more came in. One latched onto the lead draft bird and with a burst of feathers and a shower of blood, ripped it from its traces leaving the bird's feet still clutching its perch, the lower body still caught in the harness.

Rhone dove to the deck wiping the splattered blood from his eyes as the rush of wings passed over him. In an instant, mansnatchers were diving in from every direction. Men rushed to the railings, weapons jumping to their shoulders.

Bar'ack stood at the railing, his feet riveted there, his eyes and mouth wide open. One of the beasts swooped under the edge of the balloon, reaching claws extended for Bar'ack.

Rhone slammed Bar'ack to the deck. Razor claws raked Rhone's back, ripping his vest and sending needles of fire down his spine. The mansnatcher swooped through the barge, dodging cables and guys, grabbed a crewman, and shattered an array of reflecting mirrors as it fought its way free of the barge and climbed skyward. Caught in its sharp death-grip, the guard struggled against the piercing claws until the beast's long, horned beak snipped the man's head off.

"Stay down!" Rhone shoved Bar'ack toward a narrow space under the high seat where the driver was fighting for control of the two terrified birds that remained.

Proj-lances filled the air with acrid fumes, but the mansnatchers seemed to have an uncanny sense about avoiding the darts. Rhone rushed to the center of the barge, ducked and swung his sword at deadly talons streaking his way. With a thud and the crunch of bone, a severed foot thumped to the deck and the mansnatcher careened into a cable, wings flapping like tent sheets. It righted itself on one leg, the stump gushing, making the deck slick with blood. Snapping in ferocious anger, its bony beak severed one of the suspension cables.

The barge tilted with a jolt. Men lurched over the side. Rhone sliced his way past the deadly wings and thrust deep into its heart. Giving forth a death-screech, the mansnatcher tumbled over the edge and plummeted into the treetops far below. A mansnatcher screeched behind him. Rhone threw himself behind a bronze regulator pedestal as eight razor claws stabbed out, missed, and caught the pylon instead. Levers, mountings, and cables running out to the mirrors ripped from the deck. The barge shuddered. Rhone grabbed for an ironwood cleat. A crewman hurdled into the air and clawed at nothing all the way down to the forest below. The foundering sky-barge lurched wildly.

The frantic draft birds had abandoned any semblance of synchronized flight. The driver, himself in near panic, shouted and wrestled with the reins. Rhone noted this in a glance, and then a pair of gigantic wings blotted out his view. When they passed, the bird handler was gone and the reins fluttered momentarily in the air then fell straight down between the two terrified condors.

Rhone looked around for Bar'ack. The young man had both arms folded around a support, trying desperately to keep beneath the high seat, out of reach of the barrage of deadly claws. Jakl's men fought valiantly. Swords flashed in the sunlight, Proj-lances hissed as dart after dart rocketed through the smoky air. Out beyond the silken envelope, one of the darts found its mark. At the explosion of fur and blood, another mansnatcher folded its wings and plummeted from the sky.

Jakl stood his ground in the middle of the barge half obscured in the shadows of the lifting balloon. He wielded a lance, thrusting and ducking, managing to keep just out of reach of a determined mansnatcher. The battle attracted the eye of a small mansnatcher who suddenly swooped in from the other side. Its wings batted aside one of the guards as if he'd been a toy soldier, and it banked for the captain, stretching its spikes for Jakl's unprotected back.

Rhone leaped to his feet, and bracing against the tilting deck, hurled his sword. It rotated once, twice, and its broad blade sank deep into the mansnatcher's side. With a wild shriek, the beast arched back and lurched upward, its span-long beak snapping like harvesting shears, ripping open the underside of the balloon. The beast crashed back to the deck, its wings convulsing in the throes of dying, ravaging the compass binnacle and venting controls.

Rhone darted past the spasming wings and wrenched his sword from muscle and bone, turning to lend a hand to Jakl's desperate plight. In a moment, the two men dispatched another mansnatcher.

Breathing hard, Jakl took in the situation in a glance. Another poof of feathers and the second of their draft birds disappeared. "We're going down!" Jakl grabbed a stanchion and cast about. Those of his crew who hadn't been thrown overboard or snatched away hung to the foundering craft like leeches. Rhone had the impression most of the men were missing. He shot a glance forward. Bar'ack was still huddled under the driver's seat, apparently unharmed.

"If we go down in the treetops not one in five among us will make it to the ground alive, Captain."

"I know." He was already scanning the ground, his view coming back to the rip and the rush of warm air from it. "The river then." But they had already veered more than a league off its course.

"We'll never make it." A screech brought Rhone about and a flash of his sword fended off the diving claws. "There." He shoved the point of his blade at a clearing that had just come into view.

"Yes." Then Jakl frowned at the empty driver's seat and the single bird flapping in wild desperation, but with no direction.

"How long have we?"

Jakl glanced again at the ragged hole and shook his head. "Not long enough." He shouted orders to lighten the vessel.

Rhone shoved his sword under his belt and grabbed his way along the tilting deck to the empty driver's seat.

"What are you going to do?" Bar'ack croaked, still huddled beneath it.

"Hold tight." Rhone pulled himself up into the seat and eyed the lone bird far out on its cantilevered perch, the reins dangling from its harness. The forest seemed to loom closer now. He hesitated, but the choice had already been made for him. Some might call it the hand of the Creator. He preferred to think of it as just plain, unfortunate luck. Taking a breath, he calculated the distance, tensed his muscles, and leaped. The woven beams rushed toward him, his fingers locked into the weave, and with a sudden yank on his arms, he stopped, swinging out over the forest.

Muscles bunching, he hauled himself up, swung a leg over the beam and pulled himself on top of it. The barge lurched and his fingers dug in tighter, his legs squeezing the beam like a vice. Slowly he dragged himself forward. Reaching the perch, he straddled the forked relief slot where two arms of the cantilever branched and went forward, ending at the perch. The basketwork here was crusted in the bird's dried, white excrement. He clambered over it, feeling the rush of wings, grabbed hold of a harness strap and spoke in a soothing tone. These animals were bred to this life and used to human handlers. Taking a second firm grip, Rhone stood, braced himself, timed the wing beat, and leaped to the bird's back.

Startled, the condor turned with snapping beak. Rhone jerked back and twisted aside. Apparently realizing Rhone wasn't a mansnatcher, or a threat, the giant bird stopped snapping and rotated its head all around. No doubt searching for mansnatchers. Rhone was searching, too, as he settled himself in place, wrapped his left hand into the straps, and grabbed up the dangling reins in his right.

He stroked the smooth neck feathers and tried to imitate the sounds he recalled the driver making as he heaved on the reins, fighting the bird's natural impulse to fly straight ahead. He tried a few more remembered phrases, slowly managing to calm and turn the frightened bird. The bird banked, the horizon tilted, and the clearing slanted up into his field of view.

The leafy tops became more distinct, each individual tree an undulating topography in terrifying exactness. Here and there a break showed the floor far below. These trees rose two and three hundred spans, more than half of that distance sheer, naked trunk where sunlight seldom struck. Impossible to climb down without ropes. Rhone momentarily lost sight of the clearing.

Bar'ack's voice rang out over the flap of wings. "Rhone! Behind you!"

The booming of wings signaled a renewed attack. His sword streaked from his belt and he swung out and felt the blade bite into the scaly leg. The beast shrieked and tucked its injured foot, red eyes flashing, bony beak snapping at the sword. It rose out of reach, wheeled overhead, and dove again. Rhone readied himself. Then a sharp hiss whistled past his ears. The explosion rocked the man-snatcher over and its wings rippled skyward as it fell, crashing through the treetops. Rhone glanced over his shoulder as Bar'ack was lowering the proj-lance. A tight grin pulled at Rhone's face. Maybe Ker'ack's youngest son had the makings of a wildlander after all.

The clearing came into sight again, but the dangling guide ropes of the lopsided sky-barge were already dragging the treetops, catching, pulling the barge lower.

"Kia-kia-kia." Rhone shouted, the only phrase he could remember clearly. Draft birds provided no lift to a sky-barge, but merely pulled it through the sky, and what he was asking of this single bird was more than any driver ought rightly to have expected. But he had no choice. Still five hundred spans of treetops stood between the faltering barge and the clearing, and the forest was already reaching up its leafy fingers and grabbing at them. He flicked the reins and shouted again.

"Cut those lines," Jakl ordered. "Everything not bolted down over the sides." In the midst of the confusion and the destruction, Jakl kept a clear head. "Adjust those mirrors. Get some heat on that bag!"

Rhone put the captain out of mind and concentrated on managing the flagging bird. A small lurch told him they'd gained a few spans of altitude; hardly enough to sustain them more than an extra few moments.

"Kia-kia-kia." The treetops parted and the clearing loomed suddenly in sight again. "Kia-kia-kia!" Grassy, wide, and welcoming, but yet too far. The barge lurched again with a crack and snapping fibers and a bronze mirror pod went crashing through the nearby trees. The sky-barge's bow passed over the edge of the forest, then its middle … and then the stern snagged a branch. The deck leaped up and tilted steeply. Rhone glimpsed two or three bodies careening overboard. Men hung from the sides, feet dangling over the abyss. Another jolt ripped the basket free of the tree and it slipped with gathering speed toward the grassy floor.

Rhone dropped the reins, grabbed the harness, pressed his head hard against the bird's feathered back, and waited for the impact.

❧

Although the aerial battle seemed to stretch on for a long time, she knew it hadn't lasted more than a few moments before the sky-barge suddenly listed hard to one side and began a long, slow slide toward the forest. By now the doomed barge was far off from the river where Kenock had first spotted it.

Mishah gasped and flung a hand to her mouth as it disappeared from view. A rush of birds bursting skyward marked the spot; the only indication the sky-barge had crashed. No sounds reached them from what must have been a far distance now. For a moment, no one aboard the *Osar Messenger* said a word; each struck silent with awe and shock at what they'd just witnessed.

With a clack, Captain Berg's teeth grabbed resolutely onto the stem of a pipe. The old river captain was shaking his head. "Cursed blights is what they are. Ought to hunt down ever' one of them mansnatchers."

"Those poor souls." Amolikah's fists clenched the railing, her face lined with concern, her eyes wide as they turned and settled upon the captain. "Is there anything we can do for them, Captain Berg?"

Scowling at the dark cloud of distant birds, he shook his head. "I wouldn't know how to begin to search for them, mistress. There's a hundred square leagues of forest out there, some of it too thick to pass through, and all of it filled with things that'd make a mansnatcher look like the main attraction at a child's petting park."

"We have to try." Kenock stepped forward, eyes burning with sudden zeal. "We've got to help them."

It would be Kenock who'd insist on a rescue. Her brother's motives were pure, but his impulsiveness needed to be held in check. It was his heart telling him what to do now, not his head. Yet, if there was a way ... "Captain Berg."

He glanced at her.

"I'm a healer. Perhaps we could put ashore for a quartering and see how the land lies off in that direction. If there is anything we can do to help, then shouldn't we at least try?"

"Mi's right." Kenock stepped through the breech she'd opened for him. "We ought to try before saying it can't be done."

Berg considered that as a wreath of smoke rose from his pipe. "If we did, who would go? I can't leave the *Osar Messenger* unattended."

"Your engineer and first mate. Me and Kleg'l."

"And me," Mishah put in. "I am the healer."

The captain's view shifted between them. "Couldn't send the engineer. The cycler needs constant looking after."

"All right then, you and the first mate. With, Kleg'l and me, that's four. We have proj-lances and swords aboard, and if it proves too dangerous or impassable, we'll break off the attempt. At least we'll have the satisfaction of knowing we tried to help."

"And me," she reminded them.

"Mishah." She could tell he was about to become patronizing and fatherly. "It's better if you stay here with Grandmother."

She'd opened the way for him and now he wasn't letting her walk through. "I'm not a child anymore to be told what I can or cannot do. And I'm not an adventure seeker either, so it's not for that reason I want to go along. There might be people there who need my training."

Kenock frowned. She'd showed him a point that made sense.

"Well," he hesitated.

"No one is going," Kleg'l announced, taking a tentative step away from the railing. His throat bobbed and he tried to look square at Kenock, but was having difficulty. "Master Lamech said we are to see Mistress Mishah and Mistress Amolikah safely to the Mother and back. This diversion into these wilds is anything but safe." He swallowed and licked his lips, his view bouncing between all of them there. "The plight of those poor people calls to me as well, but Master Lamech gave us clear orders, Master Kenock. He would not at all approve of this. You heard Captain Berg. There're dangerous beasts roaming these wilds. Turnlings! He said they made mansnatchers look tame by comparison. I cannot go against Master Lamech's wishes. I will not put my Mistresses in such peril."

The mention of Lamech's name brought the pain rushing back into her heart. Their arguments blurred around the edges. She fought against being overwhelmed again.

"I make the decisions here, Kleg'l," Kenock shot back.

Amolikah stepped forward and gave each of them a stern look. "As much as I wish to help those poor souls, I'm afraid Kleg'l is right. We can't let anything distract us from the journey."

"Grandmother, Lamech put me in charge—."

"You and Kleg'l. And right now, Kleg'l is showing the most sense."

Pain showed in his face.

"I'm sorry, dear," Amolikah's tone softened, but Mishah could see the wound had already been opened. "We have a more important task at hand. You heard Lamech's words." Her view shifted warily. Mishah sensed she was reluctant to speak further of the matter in front of strangers.

She pushed the pain back into a locked compartment in her brain. "Grandmother is right. We need to go on." Going on was the last thing she wanted to do, yet a part of her had been pondering Lamech's words. Curiosity had taken root and was slowly growing. What was this prophecy the Creator had told him to expect from the Mother?

"Lamech would be the first one ashore to help," Kenock argued.

"You are right." Amolikah placed a gentle hand on Kenock's shoulder. "But not this time. Not with Mishah and the child she carries."

Berg cleared his throat, took his pipe in hand, and stabbed its stem at them. "You all seem to have forgotten who's in charge here. This being my boat, I have the final say-so." He paused to consider each of them. "I got me a schedule to keep to, and supplies to deliver. We'll not be stopping. We'll make Far Port by morning and I'll tell folks there what we saw. Maybe some of the wildlanders there will mount a rescue." He shrugged his meaty shoulders. "And maybe not." He shoved the stem of his pipe back into his mouth. "And that's the final word on the matter."

Kenock had been overridden on every front. Mishah put a hand on his arm. He'd wanted to do the right thing in spite of the impossibility of it. He jerked away from her touch and strode to the front of the boat, out of sight behind a crate bound for Far Port. She looked at their good-man and saw his worry.

As their eyes met, Kleg'l winced. "I truly did not wish to go against Master Kenock."

"I know."

Amolikah took her by the arm and started her toward the cabin. "We ought to stay indoors, dear. No telling when those dreadful creatures might return."

She offered no resistance. In spite of her resolve not to encourage her grief, she was thinking of Lamech again. It ripped a hole in her heart not to be with him.

11

A Narrow Escape

A blackness deep and palpable, and somehow comforting, enveloped Rhone. He floated dreamily within it, relishing the silence and the weightlessness. But at the very moment he had become aware of blackness, an annoying little imp wormed its way into it; an imp with a wicked little sword and a penchant for dancing about his left shoulder, prodding it with its sharp point.

This annoyed Rhone in a vague, detached way. The more he thought about the imp, the more the silence gave way to a faint hiss then a far-off commotion like a flutter of sheets in a wind. Staying within the comfortable oblivion was suddenly impossible, yet the thought of leaving it irritated him. He clung to the blackness. That imp danced harder and faster and pricked some more, and the commotion swelled in his ears until finally his eyes popped open.

Grass stood green and stiff before his eyes and pricked his cheek; the smell of it strong. Without moving, he listened for sounds of danger, immediately identifying the squawking and flapping to his right and dismissing it. Not hearing anything else, he pushed himself up from the grass and winced. The first rotation of his arm sent a fiery needle up his neck.

He looked around. The wreckage of the sky-barge lay nearby,

half enveloped in the deflated bag that had once buoyed them up. The three cantilevered traces had snapped at their base, two of them lying off to one side, their fibers ripped and split, their perches still holding bloodied feet, legs, and a few clinging feathers. The third condor had somehow survived the crash, although broken by it. It lay caught up in its harness, flapping and hissing, snapping this way and that with its sharp beak.

Rhone stood, shaky on his feet. His head cleared. He tested his arm and found that it still worked in spite of the pain. Scattered about the clearing were lumps twisted into shapes men were never designed to take.

The huge silken bag draped over half the clearing, one of its points still stuck in the treetops at the far end. The sun had dropped far down the horizon and shadows filled the edge of the clearing. How long had he been unconscious? It was hard to know for certain. The bird squawked horribly. Rhone would have put it out of its misery, but its snapping beak did not let him get close enough.

"Bar'ack! Captain Jakl!"

He bent under an edge of the deflated balloon where it sagged over the barge, climbed up over the gunwale, and stood on the tilting deck grasping a reflector pylon to steady himself. Deep shadows lay everywhere beneath the silken sheets. Nothing moved. The high driver's seat had been crushed backwards with the impact, its woven fibers snapped and needlelike splinters shooting out in every direction. The cabin amidships had folded in on itself on one corner, and the far side reflectors had all been flung across the deck as the barge had crashed down first on that side. A man sprawled beneath one of the twisted mechanical arms, his cloak rusty red. Rhone lurched down the deck, grasped the compass binnacle that seemed still firmly rooted in place, and called again.

No reply.

He worked his away across the deck and stopped suddenly, his ears alerted by the faintest of sounds. He wheeled around and strained to catch it again. The settling barge had developed creaks and groans along its length, but this was something different. Leaping over the far side, his legs taking up the impact like springs, he slashed through the silk with his webbing knife, parting it as he moved toward the faint muffled call.

The man was wound up in the fabric of the balloon, bound tight as a caterpillar inside its cocoon, and just as secure. Rhone severed the cocoon and caught Jakl as he tumbled from the sheets. Jakl had apparently been thrown from the barge moments before impact and gotten himself twisted up in the sheets. The deflated balloon had saved his life.

"Rhone! Creator be praised, you're all right." Jakl looked quickly all around. "The others?"

From where they were standing, draped in spans and spans of murky, limp spider silk, they could see no others. "You're the only one so far."

Concern deepened in Jakl young face. "Your friend?"

Bar'ack had been at the front of his thoughts. "I'm still looking. So far everyone but you is dead. But some may have survived the crash."

Jakl batted at the shreds of silk dangling before him. "We'll need to get rid of this. We can cut the main stays and drag it aside."

The captain's decisiveness was a trait Rhone was growing to admire. "Here." He thrust the hilt of his webbing knife into Jakl's hand. "I'll fetch a sword." Batting his way from under the balloon, Rhone found his sword where it had fallen and set about attacking the tethers. One by one the braided strands that held the barge to the balloon gave. It took Rhone ten more strikes with his honed blade to do what a mansnatcher's beak had accomplished in a single snip.

Although tough as ironwood spikes, the finely woven spider silk fluttered lightly in the faint evening breeze. Rhone and Jakl dissected the useless gasbag from the wreckage, then straining beneath the sheer volume of it, dragged the tattered balloon off to one side, uncovering four more bodies, and one survivor—a mirror mate named O'tev. Like Jakl and Rhone, the mirror mate had not been thrown off the sky-barge, but had ridden it down, his final tumble cushioned by the deflating balloon. But O'tev fared a mite worse, suffering a broken arm. Bar'ack wasn't among the dead, so where was he? Rhone glanced to the forest.

By the time they helped O'tev to the barge and bound his damaged arm it was dark. Rhone refused to wait until morning to resume the search. Jakl said, "I'll fetch a lamp."

Rhone studied the forest as the moon crept up over the treetops. The stars sharpened and filled the blue-black bowl overhead. His last glimpse of Bar'ack had been of him clutching a cable just before the sky-barge cleared the treetops.

Jakl reappeared swinging a couple of shuttered moonglass lanterns; pale light magnified in faceted lenses cast a soft beam out in front of the captain. He handed Rhone a lantern, and slipped a proj-lance from off his shoulder. "We might want to have these too."

Rhone hefted the weapon, checked the loads in the box beneath the long tube, and started off.

Their lights glanced off the tall grass. The condor, Rhone noted, was now quite still. Once inside the looming black wall, beneath the canopy of that nearly impenetrable forest, there'd be no moonlight to guide them. The weight of impending doom settled over Rhone. Bar'ack had not stayed with the sky-barge, riding it down as he and the captain and O'tev had. That meant he'd been lost over the forest; a plunge to certain death.

Any hope Rhone held out for his young friend vanished. He steeled himself for what he knew he'd find—if he found anything at all. These lands were filled with scavengers. He recalled another trip made years earlier to find a friend. The same helplessness had gripped him then; that slow, creeping despair as time passed and the lost man's fate became more certain. When Rhone finally found his friend, it was not in a forest as he knew he'd find Bar'ack, but in the far corner of a barn, his bloodied sword still in his hand, the bodies of thirteen Amlik-ites strewn before him. He'd not died easily, and his death had not come cheap to the Amlik-ites. Even so, the loss had wrenched Rhone's heart leaving a stone in its place, and it had taken what seemed like forever for that lump to dissolve. Remembering it now, more than 118 years later, still sent a bolt of pain, and sketched a grimace upon his face. He forced the memory from his head.

They came to a pile of branches at the forest's edge, snapped off when the sky-barge had snagged the treetops. They circled the jumble, lanterns held high, showing the tangle of growth beyond. Wielding his sword, Rhone cleared the way into the forest. Dark tree trunks loomed before them and familiar odors filled his nose: Cedarwood bark, the sharp tang of oily gopherwood, the rich aroma of deep, black earth, mushrooms, molds ... he sniffed ... and web.

"Javian spiders," he said softly.

Jakl gave him a questioning look.

"I can smell them." Rhone caught a greenish-golden eyeshine in his lamplight. The eyes stared long and unblinking, then disappeared.

"What's that?"

"Hooked-tooth." He could almost see the big cat crouched in the shadows, watching them.

"How do you know?" Captain Jakl's voice wavered slightly, his light darting about as if trying to cover every direction at once.

"The color of the shine."

Jakl swallowed hard. "Have they turned?"

That was the big question on everyone's mind when they entered the Wild Lands. Which animals had turned, and which had not. "I've not heard any accounts of hooked-tooth tigers turning to meat. But it's hard to know for sure."

"I've heard some javians have." Jakl's light caught a red monkey as it scampered up a tree and disappeared into shadows.

"Some have." Rhone had found it more and more of a challenge to deal with the javian spiders. They had a rudimentary intellect, but functioned mainly on instinct—an instinct that seemed to be slowly swallowing up the thinking side of their being. Still, there were a few left who had the ability to communicate with humans. Rhone had heard stories of the beginning-time—the Cradleland time as some called it—when humans and beasts lived together and spoke freely. According to the legends something terrible had happened in that world of the far past, severing the bond between man and beast. But that was only myth.

The Oracle claimed time was endless, that the world had existed for millions of years and the sun, moon, and stars had shined on many reincarnations of it. The Lodath declared this with religious fervor, and perhaps he was right. No people survived today from that beginning-time. A few ancient folks insisted the legends were true, but theirs were faded memories at best, and as the Oracle has said, not to be trusted.

Rhone tried not to get involved in the religious controversies. He'd encountered a sample of it on the Meeting Floor, and in a moment of weakness gotten in the middle of it. Look where that had taken him.

His thoughts came back around to Bar'ack. The lad might have lived to a ripe old age of seven or eight hundred years. Instead he'd been struck down in his youth. He dreaded breaking the news to Ker'ack and Sarsee.

He came to a sudden halt, cocking his head. The snapping of twigs and leaves beneath his feet, the twang of steel slashing against the vines and branches had so filled his hearing, he'd almost missed it.

"What?" Jakl glanced around, his proj-lance leveled and ready.

Rhone's eyes compressed slightly in concentration. "That way." He thrust his sword in the direction and charged off, his blade swiping vines and the undergrowth aside with a sudden burst of energy.

Jakl scrambled along at Rhone's heels like a man dreading the thought of being left behind in this tangled, black world filled with spiders, hooked-tooth tigers, and who knew what else!

Could someone have survived such a fall? It seemed impossible, yet Rhone was certain he'd heard the faint cry for help. Bar'ack, or someone, was either alive, or his mind was playing a taunting game with him.

"Here! I'm over here!" came a distant shout.

"I hear him," Jakl said.

Rhone set off on a new bearing and drew up in a small clearing, the ground softly bathed in moonlight showed a jumble of fallen trees. A javian clearing. Jakl came huffing to a stop beside him.

"Rhone!"

Suspended upside-down halfway between treetops and earth with his arms and legs flung wide, Bar'ack seemed to be floating in the air.

"What's all this?" Captain Jakl shined his lamp upward. The light caught other items up there with him, and glinted off long, translucent rays.

"Web!" Rhone circled beneath Bar'ack, tracing the fine strands with the weak beam of his light. "Javian."

"Get me down from here!"

"Are you hurt?"

"No! Not yet!

Rhone found the anchor lines stretching down to six trees bordering the clearing. The location and design was typical of javians; a funnel-shaped web constructed in a clearing with a wide mouth at the bottom, narrowing to a chimney near the treetops. In the daytime, sunlight heats the upper reaches of the web causing a natural convection current that sweeps in the balls of puff-pollen to be snagged on the sticky filaments. Puff-pollen being the spider's preferred food, the javian spiders collected them and bound them in web cocoons, then stashed them in long pearl-like strands along the outside of the web to be eaten during the seasons between puff-pollen eruptions.

"Quickly! Before the spider comes back!"

The web was in a poor state of repair and rapidly deteriorating. Large holes gaped where a captive bird or frenzied dragonfly had fought its way free of the clinging fibers. The long strands of silk had lost their liquid shine so characteristic of a well-maintained javian web.

"It's not coming back." Rhone shifted the light around the silken trap that filled the clearing fifteen spans above him. This web had a nice strand of pollen beads in place along one of the outside arches … but no spider. Like so many others he'd encountered lately, it had been abandoned. Besides Bar'ack, the web held a collection of leaf litter, giant dragonflies, and elephant moths.

"Get me down anyway!"

Rhone grinned. Bar'ack was alive! By some capricious quirk of fate, he'd tumbled through the forest to land on the only spot able to break his fall and spare his neck. An abandoned spider web. How lucky could one man be? Rhone's grin wavered for an instant. It had to be luck. What else could account for it?

Jakl's head craned up at the man sprawled in a spider's web sixty spans above the ground. Rhone handed him his lamp.

"Where are you going?"

"To cut him out of that thing."

"You're climbing up there?"

"You know of another way?"

Jakl just looked at him.

"You want to do it?"

"No!"

Rhone smiled, testing his weight on one of the anchor lines. "I didn't think so."

"You'll get stuck too."

"If I do, you can come up after me."

Jakl looked horror-stricken at the thought.

A javian's web was made up of several different components; anchor strands, walking strands, and the capture strands all went into its design. So long as he avoided the later, he'd be in no more danger than climbing a tall, rather unstable ladder. Rhone worked his way up the anchor line to the first course of web, which in a javian web was a walking strand. It's what the spiders used to move about on, otherwise they'd all be stuck in their own webs. Using the anchor strand for balance and a walking strand to stand on, Rhone worked his way up to Bar'ack.

"I was starting to think I'd be stuck here forever. I've been trying to cut myself free." He had a knife out and all the strands across his back had been severed.

"You'd have cut your way loose eventually—that is if a mansnatcher didn't spot you first."

Bar'ack shivered. "Why didn't you tell me about things like mansnatchers before we left?"

"Frobin didn't mention them?"

Bar'ack sighed with exaggerated patience and rolled his eyes. "Just get me out of here."

Rhone laughed and worked his webbing knife through the strands that held Bar'ack's arms, freeing them first. After making sure Bar'ack had a firm grip on one of the walking strands, he set about severing the capture strands that glued him firmly in place on the web's sloping side. When he'd finished, the abandoned web had acquired a new hole in its tattered fibers, and Bar'ack was once again on solid ground.

They returned to the sky-barge where O'tev had discovered some extracts in a healer's chest. They'd worked marvels on his pain and he had managed to start a fire in spite of his broken arm. Bar'ack was plainly shaken by the whole experience. As the night wore on, he mumbled about how narrowly he'd escaped death, declared praise for the Creator for having spared him, and from time to time lapsed into unintelligible babbling to himself. Rhone caught snatches of it—phrases like *never again ... smashed flat ... Frobin said nothing ...*

Rhone had seen warriors returning from war react the same way. Sometimes it took days for them to come to grips with their own mortality and their great good fortune of having survived one more battle.

After a while, Rhone tuned Bar'ack out, his thoughts divided between the practical problem of finding their way to civilization and the more perplexing question of why the spiders were abandoning their traditional webbing grounds. They'd left whole strands of puff-pollen behind in their flight. Whatever had compelled the spiders to move away must have come upon them quickly.

12

Earth-Born

Da-gore hesitated a moment outside the tall doors, then assuming the bearing and stature of his office, advanced to learn what was so important for the Lodath to summoned him this late in the evening. The door opened and he grimaced. The Oracle and two of his emissaries were here as well.

The Oracle's blue eyes found him and held him as he approached.

He bowed formally at the waist then glanced at Sol-Ra-Luce. "Your summons ... surprised me."

"A matter of grave concern has come up. A matter that you must attend to at once." No perfunctory greetings. This was serious.

"What has happened?"

"The sky-barge carrying Rhone went down in the Wild Lands." The Lodath glanced to one of the emissaries. "Ekalon watched it happen. It was the doing of the shackled-ones. He managed to intervene in spite of their resistance, keeping Rhone and young Bar'ack alive."

"That is most fortunate."

"It is of little consequences now." Irritation rose in the Oracle's voice. "I needed him to use against the woman."

Use him against the woman? "We know they were heading to Far Port, My Lord." How could something like this so greatly trouble the lord and ruler of the world? There was more here than the Oracle was letting on.

"Captain Da-gore can mount a company of men and follow her, My Lord," Sol-Ra-Luce suggested.

"No. I no longer need to have her followed. I have determine the reason why this woman is being protected by the Tyrant's shackled-ones." The Oracle's eyes narrowed, the pearl aura about him taking on a faint shade of pink. "The matter has taken a more serious turn. The woman must not be allowed to fulfill her mission. She must be killed. I want no mishaps this time, Sol-Ra-Luce."

"Killed?" Da-gore had no qualms with executions—official or unofficial—but this coming from the Oracle was a surprise he'd not been prepared for. "Yes, My Lord." He glanced at Sol-Ra-Luce. "I will make it so."

"And just to insure nothing goes awry, Captain Da-gore, I will send my own warriors."

His own? Da-gore inclined his head at Ekalon. "Him?"

"My emissaries are limited in what they can accomplish in the world of men. I will be sending the Earth Born."

"The Earth-Born?"

"Children of men, but of a different seed."

Da-gore searched his memory, recalling sketchy stories of giants; half-human, half—? Half—? Half whatever it was that creatures like Ekalon and the other emissaries of the Oracle were. *Gods?* The Earth-Born were reputed to be frightening creatures, invincible in battle and in possession of a cunning and a wisdom far beyond man.

"They will see to it nothing goes wrong this time," the Oracle continued.

Da-gore nodded. "As you command, My Lord." *This should be interesting.*

"Prepare to leave immediately!" The pink was fading back to a pearly white.

"All will be ready by dawn, My Lord."

"The Earth-Born will be sent directly to the Guard's Sanctuary."

"Very well, My Lord." Da-gore pulled his eyes back to the Lodath. "I'll begin the preparations immediately."

"Yes. See to them."

Da-gore turned sharply, gave an authoritative stomp of a heel, and strode out the tall doors.

※

Da-gore's duty and desire was to carry out the Lodath's orders. He'd not risen to captain of the Guard by questioning those in authority above him. For 262 years, he'd been a warrior in King Irad's army, and he'd liked it. The training and discipline fit his temperament perfectly. The excitement of battle was food for his soul.

Then this new religion sprang up, one backed by a god who could be touched and heard, not one rooted in old beliefs and legends of people long dead. The Oracle had chosen his spokesman on earth from among King Irad's most trusted advisers, a man named Baal-moloch. He'd set him up as head of this new religion, changed his name to Sol-Ra-Luce, bestowed the title of Lodath of the Oracle upon him, and immediately began to forge a close alliance between this man and the king.

To enforce the Oracle's new religious rules, and to collect the taxes to build the Oracle's temple, Sol-Ra-Luce culled an army of his own out of King Irad's regulars. Irad was only too happy to go along with the plan once it was made clear to him that the temple taxes would be funneled through *his* finance ministers. The bond between state and religion had been firmly cemented.

When the call went out for army volunteers, Da-gore was determined not to be one of them. He had attained rank, a nice home,

women whenever he wanted them … a lifestyle completely compat-
ible with his nature. But when offered the position of captain of the
Lodath's Guard, he saw opportunity far beyond what was available to
him if he remained in King Irad's army. Although the battlefield
would be gone from his life, the prestige would more than offset the
lack of action.

Although he'd remained impassive throughout the meeting with
the Oracle and the Lodath, inwardly his heart leaped for an opportunity to bear arms again, even if the object of his arms was nothing
more than a helpless woman and her unsuspecting companions. To
be away from Nod City, to be on the march, to hear the ringing of
clashing weapons—even for just the few moments he was certain any
battle with these travelers would last—was something his soul
craved.

He would have preferred to choose his own men, men he trusted
and personally enjoyed being around. He had no idea what sort of
soldiers the Oracle's Earth-Born might be.

It was dawning when the heavy, enclosed wagon rolled through
the gate. He was shocked to see what climbed out of it. The Earth-
Born were built like no warrior he'd ever seen; six spans, maybe six-
and-a-half spans tall, with shoulders a span-and-a-half wide. Who
short of a Makir Warrior could defeat men like this?

The Earth-Born wore leather and iron armor that covered their
shoulders leaving most of their massive chest bare, except for a band
of iron scale across their hearts. Their stomachs were ripples of hard
muscle. The muscles of their legs stood in long taut cords from feet
to thighs, then disappeared beneath short leather and iron skirts.
From a braided leather belt hung a sword nearly three spans long.
Sharp features sculpted their faces and leant a strangely handsome
air to these Earth-Born. Their thick hair, ranging in color from jet
black, to red, to a glossy auburn, was cropped close and curled over
pronounced foreheads. Their jaws seemed overlarge.

Any man might easily be intimidated by these *man-god* creatures, but a leader of men could not afford to be, or at least not show it. Da-gore advanced and his gaze steadied on them. They were especially young, and young men could be hard to handle. He immediately sensed their resistance to him, but apparently they'd been given strict orders to obey. How long would that last? He picked the biggest and fiercest looking of the six. "What are you known by?"

"Herc of Ulex." The commanding tone matched his size.

"Ulex? What name is that?"

"My father's," came the rumble from deep in his chest.

"I am Ulex," An emissary who stood amongst the giants stepped forward. He was one of the star-beings. Some called them gods.

The other five were called Atala of Entes, Per of Seus, Pose of Doon, Plut of Ott, and Hepha of Astus. Da-gore remembered them simply as Herc, Atala, Per, Pose, Plut, and Hepha.

"Are there more like yourselves?"

Hepha answered, "Yes. Many." His voice was pitched half an octave higher than Herc's, but still sounded as if it had begun as an explosion deep within the god-man's chest.

"Where are you from?"

"The Mountain of the Singing Sky—," Hepha began to say.

Ulex interrupted him. "The Oracle has prepared a special place for our offspring to be raised and trained. Its location is not important."

Although their size and bearing were impressive, Da-gore sensed he was dealing with children. Not one of them could have been more than thirty years old. Is that why an emissary was assigned to accompany them? Someone to keep an eye on the boys? Was this their first trial in the field?

"Very well." *Singing Sky*. He filed the information away to be mulled over and examined later. He strode before the god-men. "You will follow my orders, is that understood?"

They all nodded except Plut. Ulex sent the Earth-Born a scowl. The giant reluctantly grunted his loyalty. Da-gore turned away and grimaced as his stomach plunged. He'd have to work doubly hard to maintain his authority among these Earth-Born. Give them another fifty or one hundred years and he was certain they would become completely unmanageable, unless kept under a very tight rein from the beginning. Yes, he'd have to hold the reins exceptionally tight. For the first time since accepting the commission as captain of the Guard, he questioned his decision. Life had been so much less complicated under Irad's regime. He hadn't joined the Lodath's Guard to play nursemaid to overgrown children.

He assembled his troops; Lieutenant Err-nor at his side. The Lodath's staff bearer, Gai-lek, before them, and behind them the six Earth-Born the Oracle had sent. Taking up the rear were the animal handlers, a dispatch rider and his mount, the healer and her equipment, and two three-points, draped in the Lodath's banner. The tips of the three-points' horns wore golden caps, and golden chains hung around their necks and down under their broad bellies, hitched to heavy freight packs carrying all the supplies the company would require for the expedition.

When all was ready, Da-gore adjusted the chin strap on his helmet, nodded to the staff bearer to raise the colors, and signaled his lieutenant to shout the order to move out. With the drumming of feet and the lumbering rumble of the three-points, the company left the Guard's Sanctuary. Far Port would be a march of almost three days. The Lodath's orders were to make haste, and Da-gore intended to do just that.

❦

A pair of fish leaped alongside the boat leaving a fluorescent trail in their wake. Mishah sighed and looked away. Her spirit had never been lower. Mansnatchers had devastated a sky-barge. She'd watched men plucked up, impaled on iron-tough talons, and decapitated. And worst of all, she'd lost Lamech. It was all too much. How much more could she take?

The glimmer fish veered off and shot leaping across the river as Far Port came into view around a bend; a sparse, dilapidated town clinging to a muddy riverbank, its wharves and piers sticking out into the churning water.

Amolikah gave Mishah's hand a reassuring squeeze. "It's not as bad as it looks. Truly, it is not. I know where we can find decent lodging for the night. Then we will hire a wagon and horse to take us the rest of the way."

"Why me? Why us? Lamech said the Creator is using us. Why couldn't he leave us alone to our farm, our family? Why this trial?"

"Oh, my dear. It's a wonderful thing to be used by the Creator. I don't know what awaits us, but you can be assured it is something wonderful."

"Lamech in prison? Wonderful?"

Amolikah's smile radiated patience. "We see things only in pieces, and only what is immediately happening to us."

"Isn't that what matters right now?"

Amolikah took a slow breath. "We cannot see the whole pattern, but someday from eternity's doorstep, when the veil is lifted from our eyes, it will become clear and will be beautiful beyond words. Then we will rejoice in our part in it."

Amolikah's faith was as strong as Lamech's. If only she could borrow some of it.

"Move sharply now! Get those bow lines ready." Captain Berg hustled his crew into action as the *Osar Messenger* chugged toward a long pier sticking far out into the swift river current. He took the helm and called for more revolutions. "Make ready, men." He glanced at Mishah and Amolikah standing at the bow railings. "Better take a firm grip, mistresses. We'll be cutting across some mighty rough water."

The boat rocked and plunged through the chop, Captain Berg wrestling the big wheel while his men stood fore and aft with stout ropes, looped and ready to toss. The cycler chugged and strained, spewing the odor of unburned 'gia into the air as the experienced crew brought the boat alongside the pier. Men tossed out ropes with the precision of herders, spun the ends about windlasses, and drew the boat safely into the fenders.

Kenock and Kleg'l came from the stern where they'd watched the landing. Kenock made no effort to hide his excitement. He'd apparently dealt with his disappointment and put the matter to rest. "Here we are, Mi. Look at this village. Have you ever seen anything like it?"

She hadn't, except in books and artists' renditions of far-flung outposts. Beyond all the boats moored at the pier, Far Port meandered along the banks of the Idikla like a brown smear against the verdant green forests, forever encroaching and forever being hacked back—just far enough. A single road ran along the docks, paved in crushed stone. An open gutter running alongside the road flowed with the stench of sewage funneled into a culvert and dumped into the river. The boat made secure, she stepped off the gangplank onto the pier.

The crew carried off their bags first, depositing them on the decking. Through the gaps in the planks, Mishah could see the Idikla's rushing waters. The roar of the river filled her ears, and the pier seemed to sway in the buffeting current.

A narrow footbridge bore them over the ditch. On the other side of the street stood flimsy board and batten buildings on river-rock foundations, dripping moisture and growing green slime at the corners. A raised boardwalk ran along the front of the buildings—some canopied, but most of them not.

A bright, hot sun glared in the clear sky, and everywhere she looked—land, streets, or buildings—Far Port seemed to be smoking.

She loosened her collar another button and mopped the perspiration from her forehead with a handkerchief. They moved to the board-walk and paused under a faded shiverthorn canopy, enduring the curious and sometimes leering stares of men wearing the rude clothes of wildlanders or teamsters. For anyone heading into the wilds, this was be their point of departure. Most everything one needed to take on a jaunt to distant lands could be purchased in Far Port.

"We should get off the street." Kleg'l glanced toward the busy wharf traffic and the big-shouldered stevedores already busy hauling freight off the *Osar Messenger*. "This looks to be a place where trouble might find you."

Amolikah gathered her bag from the boardwalk. "This way."

The main road led away from the busy wharf and past a fist of shabby festival halls all within a few hundred spans of each other. The gravel beneath their feet gave way to miry mud. They walked along the grassy shoulder, toward a cluster of log, stone, and board and batten homes near the forest's edge. Each dwelling had a large garden and barns for their animals. Sheep dotted the landscape, grazing the verdant hillside.

Mishah kept looking skyward, but nothing dangerous dove out of a blinding sun at them. Grinning, Kenock walked with an unfamiliar swagger, but Kleg'l's showed none of the younger man's buoyancy. His long face remained impassive, and she knew he was fretting. Lamech had made a wise decision placing him in charge with her brother.

"Tell me again how far it is to the Mother?" Kenock asked as they passed through a gate and started up the walk toward one of the houses.

"Not far from here. Two days, and there is an inn along the way."

"Why doesn't she move closer to her children?" He plucked a green stalk of sweet grass and stuck it between his teeth.

"Her children live across the face of the Known World now."

He grinned. "I mean us. We're special to her somehow. It would be so much easier if she'd move down to Morg'Seth."

Mishah said, "The Mother is far too old to be moving."

"She is today, but she could've easily come five hundred years ago, when Grandfather Seth brought his family down."

Amolikah shook her head. "The Mother will never leave Chevel-ee. Too many memories. Too much sadness in her heart." She looked at Kenock. "The Mother's life has been a wearisome burden. She's watched her children grow up to misery and move away only to find suffering." Amolikah frowned. "Now that the Father is gone, she'd never leave Chevel-ee. The Mother found her happiness in him, for there has never been, nor ever will be, a more perfect relationship than those two had."

Kenock grinned. "Yeah, they were made for each other." They chuckled at the quip they'd heard a thousand times before.

The house was a rambling stone building with long a wing off to one side. They climbed two steps to a porch and Amolikah knocked. A woman appeared and looked at them a moment. "Amolikah?"

"Leahia!"

Leahia threw open the door and the two women hugged. "How long it has been?"

"Fifty years and then some. You look just as you did that day I left you."

"You're too kind. Come, come honor my house." She tugged Amolikah through the door.

"May your servant find favor in your eyes."

Leahia's bright pink pudgy cheeks puffed, her green eyes bright and wide. "Your presence always gladdens my heart, Amolikah."

Amolikah introduced each in her party. Leahia beamed at Mishah and took both of her hands. "So, you're going to the Mother! The last time you were here, you were growing strong and healthy inside *your* mother's womb. I remember Emeiah as if it was only yesterday, her happy face, so pretty. Her excitement at the thought of being a mother. How is she?"

Mishah wasn't prepared for it. It hadn't been all that long ago and the pain still lingered near the surface. A lump caught in her throat and her eyes glazed. Leahia glanced to Amolikah where tears had begun to well in her eyes too.

"She's not … ?"

Amolikah nodded. "Almost three years ago."

"I'm so sorry."

Mishah forced a smile past her grief, feeling the wet streak down her cheek. "She fell through the cover of an old well. It had become overgrown, the wood had gone bad over the years, and we'd forgotten it was there."

"She is with her father now," Amolikah said.

Leahia hugged them both. "Sit down. I'll bring tea. I have it hot on the stove."

They found deep, leather chairs and soft couches, and dropped their luggage on the floor beside them. Mishah dabbed her eyes dry and focused on the paintings on the wall, the bright rugs, the knick-knacks and mementos from far-off places, and frilly touches that made a visitor feel immediately at home.

Her thoughts turned again to Lamech and what he faced. Had she done the right thing leaving him behind, alone? If she'd stayed, how could she have helped? No, he'd told her to go, had practically begged her to do so. She was doing the right thing.

Leahia returned with the tea, and she and Amolikah traded old memories and recent news. Amolikah told about the ordeal they'd had in Nod City, the adventures on the river freighter, and the attack of the mansnatchers. Leahia smiled and nodded in the appropriate places and looked concerned and frowned when the story called for it. Her mood seemed in lockstep with Amolikah's.

Later she showed them to their rooms, Amolikah and Mishah together, Kenock and Kleg'l in another. She had lunch ready by the beginning of the fourth quartering, and afterward told them that Master El-weel was a man they could trust to hire a horse and wagon from, to complete their trip.

Afterward, Mishah stood on the porch looking up the hill toward the rambling buildings of Far Port. Leahia's home was a comfortable reprieve, exactly what she needed right then. For a moment she forgot her troubles, relishing the wild beauty of the country and the smell and sound of rough water. Tomorrow they would be on their way again. Two days, the visit, then home. She smiled until she remembered she was going home alone. She winced, determined not to cry again ... and was successful this time, but the bright beauty of the landscape had faded, and the sound of rushing white water dimmed in her ears.

13

A Purveyor of Magnetics and Moonglass

Kenock and Kleg'l walked back into town later that day, scraping their muddy soles upon the grassy edge as they went. "These roads are in an awful state," Kenock grumbled. This adventure was wearing him thin. No wonder, considering all that had happened.

"I expect they will be getting worse before improving." Nothing seemed to shake Kleg'l.

The first person they met gave them directions to El-weel's livery on the other side of Far Port. Kenock absorbed the atmosphere of this rugged outpost on the edge of nowhere, the leaping-off point for everywhere. "I want to visit some of these shops before we head back." He waited for the rebuff and was surprised when Kleg'l, who had no imagination at all, said he wouldn't mind poking around a bit too.

The gray-and-brown riverfront buildings gave way to a thick grass hillside where sheep grazed. El-weel's place was up a plank road about two hundred spans, backed against the forest.

They found him leading a pair of chestnut horses to a paddock alongside one of his three barns. He was a short man with a thick chest, narrow waist, and a square, solid face. His arms were big, his hands rough as tree bark, and his grip solid and sincere. He wore coarse shiverthorn trousers, a leather jerkin over a dingy gray shirt, and heavy boots.

"Mistress Leahia sent you to me?" El-weel's eyebrows hitched up with the question. He went on without waiting for a response. "Well, that's as good a recommendation as any. What can I do for you two?" Beneath the wide brim of a grass hat his dark brown eyes studied them.

"We wish to hire a horse and cart," Kleg'l said. "We are journeying to Chevel-ee and will be away for seven or eight days."

El-weel's eyes compressed slightly. "Chevel-ee? That's a quite a ways. On what business would my equipment be engaged?"

"Just transporting Master Kenock, myself, and my two mistresses."

His eyes narrowed further. "And what business are you on at Chevel-ee?"

Kenock thought it none of the liveryman's business what their business might be, but Kleg'l remained imperturbable. Like Amolikah, he was a person with a mission, and its successful completion was all that mattered. "We are making the pilgrimage. My mistress is with child, you see."

His eyes widened and a broad grin moved across his face. "Ah. Sethites, are you?"

"They are. I'm a Jalekite."

"No matter, you're all welcome at El-weel's livery." He nodded toward one of the barns. "Come along. I can fix you up with a rig straightaway." They started walking. "Been traveling a while, have you?"

"Almost three weeks," Kenock said.

"I remember years ago, before boats got them new cycler engines, it would take a week of paddling just to get from Nod City to here. Pilgrimages used to take two, three months. Back then most young ladies never bothered making them because of the difficulty. Only those truly devoted to the Mother—those mainly from among the

Sethite people—bothered." He laughed. "But listen to me telling you something you already know!"

"You've met the Mother?" Kenock asked.

He shook his head. "Never did. She used to travel about the Settled Lands in the early days, visiting her children here and there, but that was before my time. After her sons and daughters had spread to the far reaches, she couldn't make it to all of them anymore. That's when they started this pilgrimage thing, you see. At first, it was any excuse to visit her." He frowned and chewed his lip a moment as if remembering. "Now it's only the Sethites who come. She just stays in Chevel-ee—her keep, her last bastion ... her prison." He grimaced. "Once the Father fell asleep, she faded quickly. Some say she's near the end and anxious to join him. Better for her, but a loss for us. The Mother has lived a long full life, longer than anyone else."

He drew a breath and went on in a lighter tone. "Must be some good reason why the Creator filled her up with so many years."

"How old is she?" Kenock had heard various accounts on her alleged age. He wanted to see if El-weel's story jibed with the incredible claims his family had made.

"Don't know the actual count—since the beginning is all I know for sure, and how many years has that been? You get different tellings." He huffed. "Course, *some* folks out of Nod City claim all that is foolishness. This Oracle fellow says there never was a beginning, only cycles after cycles, and we're just in one of those cycles. But I still hold to the old way, Creator be praised." He gave a sly smile, "Until someone proves to me the Oracle is right. My mother and father believed, and that's good enough for me. They even knew some of the First Children personally."

Kenock folded his arms across his chest and slowly shook his head. "It's hard to know what to believe these days." He glimpsed momentary disapproval in Kleg'l's face. He didn't care. What if the Oracle was right? What if the world did run in cycles—man coming, man going, and just cold darkness in between, and then things starting all over again. Was it wisdom to accept stories as true just because your parents or your grandparents believe them? Kenock wanted evidence, not hearsay.

El-weel shrugged and continued toward the barn. "The Creator don't always make it clear to our eyes. Sometimes we need to look deeper into the matter. Sometimes we just know what's true because we feel it in here." His knuckles tapped his chest. "Anyway, I think it's our believing in things we can't see or feel, but made plain by what we see all around us, that pleases the Creator the most."

Made plain? Nothing so far had been made plain to Kenock. How could some men and women—Lamech, Amolikah, El-weel—be so certain of their beliefs as to never question them?

They stepped into the darkened barn and El-weel went to a small, lightly sprung cart painted a startling yellow with a bright green-and-yellow striped canopy. "Here we go." He ran a hand along the box. "This will get you up to Chevel-ee and back again in good stead. Sturdy, lightweight, but stout enough to handle those rough roads ahead. It'll carry the four of you and your luggage, and keep the hot sun off of your necks. I can rent it and a horse for two glecks a day. Plus, I'll be wanting twelve glecks as a deposit, but you'll get it back when you return the horse and cart in good shape."

Kenock looked the cart over, staring at the gaudy canopy. "We'll look like fruit peddlers."

El-weel gave a short laugh. "It's not as if you're going to see many folks on the road to Chevel-ee who'll care." His smile turned to a frown. "Except for country rogues and highwaymen. You keep an eye out for those kinds of snakes." The smile returned. "It's a good rig, and I'll give you a good horse to pull it."

The livery man spoke the truth, but Kenock wished for something more stylish.

Kleg'l said, "We'll take it. Have it ready for us in the morning." He untied the strings on the family's purse and paid the deposit and seven days' rent. As he refastened the purse to his belt, El-weel slanted an eye toward the purse and shook his head.

Kleg'l's fingers stopped working. "What is wrong?"

"This here is Far Port, friend. Not part of the Settled Lands of Hope. We're not a well-ordered and peaceful place like Morg'Seth. You wear that money pouch on your keeper like that for folks to see, someone's gonna take it away from you. You can almost count on it."

Kleg'l slipped the pouch from his belt and hid it away in a pocket beneath his vest. "Thank you for the warning."

El-weel nodded. "That's more like it. Better safe than sorry here in Far Port."

On their way back to town, Kenock said, "One thing is certain, we'll be seen coming for leagues around in that fruit peddler's cart."

Kleg'l blinked and rolled his narrow shoulders. "Like Master El-weel said, we're not likely to meet many travelers going to Chevel-ee. It's transportation we require, and it need not be fancy."

The main street of Far Port smelled of fish and sewage and the strong odor of burning trash. The festival halls lent their own peculiar pungency to the ambiance—sweet ale, roasted nuts, and pickled keelit rinds.

A shadow flitted across the street. Kenock ducked and glanced up, but it was only a small red pocket dragon winging its way through the hot sky toward the fringe of forest. He let go of the breath and followed Kleg'l through the open doorway of an outfitter's shop.

They found nothing there they needed and continued on, stopping in a bakery for a round of dark bread and a wedge of cheese. Farther down the street, Kenock convinced Kleg'l to turn into The Boom and Anchor Festival Hall for a mug of ale before returning to Mistress Leahia's house. Kleg'l resisted, but agreed after it became clear Kenock intended to have his ale with or without him. They sat at a table by themselves, sipping a watered-down brew and listening to snatches of conversations all around them. It was mostly talk of the river, of the Great Falls just north of here, or of boats and fishing. There was talk of the forests too, where wildlanders slip away for months at a time and come back with tales of adventure and danger. Wondrous stuff to stir up a young man's soul, but Kenock's soul was reaching its full measure of adventure. Like Mi, he was anxious to be back in the comfort of his own home in his own village, even if life in the Lee-lands of Morg'Seth was about as exciting as watching rocks grow moss!

❧

Night wore itself out against the flat gray anvil of dawn. The fire had burned to embers and the shadow-creatures retreated back to the forest's deep umbra before the growing morning light. Ekalon stepped through a sliver of light and stopped to sniff the air. A shackled-one was about somewhere. A snarl curled his lips and he stalked toward the twisted wreckage, leaped aboard, and started along the gunwale.

To his left, a low groan drew his attention. He moved in that direction and peered at the sleeping man whose arm was bound tight. Ekalon's mouth hitched toward a grin. He found Captain Jakl curled up in a blanket looking uncomfortable, and Bar'ack crouched against the twisted high-seat, softly purring in his dew-drenched blanket.

Rhone was asleep too, sitting upright against a wrecked mirror pylon, a proj-lance across his legs, fingers wrapped tightly about it. Ekalon glanced around for Sari'el. With the shackled-one nowhere in sight, he stepped toward the big man. This human was curious, and somehow different from the others. There was an alertness about him evident even while he slept. If Ekalon had been fully within the four-dimensional realm in which humans were imprisoned, he was certain the sleeping man wouldn't have let him get this close.

He lowered his battle-staff toward Rhone's forehead …

"Up to more mischief, Ekalon?"

The voice from behind didn't really startle him. He'd known Sari'el was somewhere nearby. Ekalon withdrew the staff, turned, and looked up. Perched upon the roof's corner, Sari'el gripped his battle-staff in his right hand, one end resting upon his right thigh, the other pointing up at the pinkening sky. The shackled-one's casualness told Ekalon a hedge of protection had already been set up around Rhone.

"I told you he was not to be marked or in any way touched from our realm." Sari'el's ruddy face pinched into a scowl.

"Just seeing if you meant it, Sari'el."

"When have you ever known me to say something I didn't mean?"

"So true. You were always so serious. You never enjoyed yourself, Sari'el, even in the before-time."

"That's where you are wrong ... once again. You just didn't understand the nature of my joy. There will come an age when this struggle is forgotten. Until then, I see nothing humorous in it."

Ekalon scoffed. "It's a struggle you can't win, Sari'el. Come, join us. It's not too late." They were the *unshackled-ones*! They'd thrown off the Tyrant's yoke ages ago. It was the Oracle they served now.

"It is already later than you think, Ekalon."

Ekalon shrugged. "Why is this human special? What does the Tyrant want with him?"

"It is not my place to question the Creator. He sees far beyond what we ever will."

Ekalon's view slid toward the sleeping figure. "You said he may not be marked, but he may be tempted as a man."

Sari'el nodded.

Rhone stirred, coming awake.

"So be it, then." A plan began to form in the back of his mind. He would draw this human into the service of the Oracle one way or another. Humans were an easy lot to tempt. Hadn't his master already reached the man with the pledge crystal? Rhone was obviously worldly, and worldly pleasures were simple things with which to entice such humans.

※

Rhone awoke, stretched, and walked through the wrecked barge waking the others. Captain Jakl arose immediately without a word. Bar'ack moaned, complaining his shoulders and his back ached.

"Frobin must have forgotten to mention the joys of sleeping in a blanket."

Bar'ack only scowled at Rhone.

O'tev was in pain. A packet of powder from the healer's chest soon eased his agony to a bearable level.

Rhone shrugged a heavy pack onto his shoulder.

Jakl looked across the clearing, then at Rhone. "You're the wild-lander. Which way out?"

Rhone glanced at the sun. "That way is east. The river is to the west. The River Road follows the Idikla all the way to Far Port. All we have to do is find the River Road." He pointed. "That way."

The captain said, "I wonder how many leagues we drifted from the river."

Rhone checked the proj in the chamber of his proj-lance and snapped the breech shut. "Let's find out."

Jakl looked back at him, then beckoned toward the forest. "After you."

They packed what they could carry and might need, nearly empty-ing the healer's chest of pain medicine. Bar'ack seemed to have worked out the kinks in his shoulders as they started for the forest. At least he quit complaining about them.

The climbing sun warmed the land, evaporated the morning mist, and drew out the perfume of the trees, flowers, grasses, and deep, rich earth. Rhone set a westerly course and held it mainly by dead reckon-ing, occasionally glancing toward the sun, always mindful of the lay of the shadows. That was the only compass he needed, though he carried a small bronze pointer in the pocket of his vest. The land was mostly level and the hike would have been easy except for the dense growth that barred their way and resisted their swords.

The beasts they encountered were more curious than dangerous. Most had not yet turned, as the mansnatchers had. They shared a clear spring pool with a herd of deer, lingering a while to watch a red-and-yellow sten-gordon grazing. If it was a turnling too, it ignored them as it held its long, heavy tail straight out with its towering body tilted slightly forward to balance itself on its two enormous hind legs. Pebbly skin rippled as its massive head reached and ripped off a branch filled with ripe keelits. Holding the branch in the claws of its tiny forearms, it picked off each of the tough-husked fruits.

"If that one should ever turn ...," Bar'ack shook his head leaving the thought unfinished as the ground trembled and the sten-gordon lumbered away.

"Some already have," Rhone whispered.

Bar'ack and Jakl glanced at each other. O'tev was in too much pain to pay the foraging beast any attention.

Rhone held his course and a full quartering later they emerged onto the wide, hard-packed track of the River Road.

"That wasn't so difficult." Jakl looked back the way they had come, clearly relieved to be out of the forest in spite of the cavalier remark.

"Not when we have a wildlander like Rhone to lead us!" Bar'ack's enthusiasm had returned now that they were on the road to Far Port.

O'tev endured without complaining, but his suffering showed. Jakl opened another packet of powder and climbed down the steep, tangled embankment to the Idikla River to dip out a bottle of water and mixed it up for him.

O'tev sat in the shade with his back against a tree and his head on his chest, eyes closed, cradling the damaged arm to himself, and waiting for the pain medicine to take effect.

Rhone scanned the sky, squinting against its brightness. Bar'ack strode over. "Looking for mansnatchers?"

"No sign of any about."

"Thank the powers that be for that!" He dug through his pack for a cake of compressed nuts and fruit. "Want some?"

Rhone shook his head and Bar'ack drifted off and shared some of the food with the captain and O'tev.

A hard march would have them in Far Port by morning. Rhone glanced at O'tev. He wasn't up for much more marching. The trip from the sky-barge had all but done him in. He needed rest, and a healer. Both could be had at Far Port. Rhone heard a sound. His head snapped around, his view compressing warily down the road.

"What is it?" Jakl asked.

A faint, distant tinkling, like the ringing of a hundred tiny bells, was growing steadily louder. "Someone's coming." Rhone glanced at Bar'ack, pointed to the proj-lance, and hooked a thumb toward the forest. "Sounds like a wagon."

Bar'ack grabbed up the weapon and scurried off the road, into the trees. O'tev dragged another proj-lance to his side, within reach of his good arm but discretely out of sight.

Jakl glanced toward his proj-lance, leaning against a tree. "I don't hear anything."

"You will in a moment." The tinkling became louder, more distinct. Then a wagon rounded a bend in the road, two black buffaloes in harness. It was a moonglass merchant. The wagon was painted glaring yellow and trimmed in a glossy black, with walls flaring up and out over the tall wheels toward a roofline that peaked a span and a half above the driver's head. The driver sat in a box halfway up the side of the wagon, covered in its own peak matching the slope of the main roof. The contraption appeared to be a small country house on wheels including the driver's box, which doubled as a front porch. A shake-shingled roof with a glazed chimney poked up out of it, and shards of moonglass dangled from the eaves, swaying and clattering against each other with the rocking of the wagon. Come nightfall, his wagon would be a dazzling display of colored light; a rolling advertisement for his wares.

Rhone's concern eased, but didn't go away. Clever ambushes had been staged before. "Hold your place a while longer," he said softly toward where Bar'ack lay in wait.

As the wagon rattled closer, the driver became clear. Tucked back in the shadows of the front box as he was, he'd been hard to make out at first. He was a slight-built man wearing a cloak of bright purple as if he were a royal dignitary instead of a purveyor of moonglass.

He hauled back on the reins and brought the buffaloes to a halt, a worried look on his face. Finding three strangers on a lonely road in the Wild Lands would make any prudent man suspicious. Rhone put up a hand and fixed a smile in place. "Peace, friend. May your servant find favor in your eyes."

The merchant hesitated and glanced toward O'tev, plainly disconcerted over seeing the bedraggled figure bound up and obviously in pain. His view came back to Rhone, and although Rhone tried to be friendly and nonthreatening, his size, and the size of the sword at his side, was enough to give the merchant pause. The merchant cleared his throat. "Your presence gladdens my heart ... I think," he added more softly.

"We had a mishap aboard a sky-barge on our way to Far Port."

Suspicion clouded the merchant's eyes. He glanced around. "Where is the sky-barge now?"

Rhone pointed toward the forest.

"Hum. And you have only now reached this road?"

"Just a few moments before you arrived. I am Rhone, and this is Captain Jakl." Rhone indicated their injured companion. "That unlucky fellow over there with the broken arm is O'tev, one of the barge's mates."

The merchant nodded. "I'm Elfin'ron of Morg'Lavin. Supplier of fine magnetic implements and moonglass."

"A worthy business. Moonglass is in high demand these days."

Elfin'ron gave a nervous laugh. "Somedays. Profits have been poor of late." His glance slid toward O'tev and the proj-lance at his side.

A cautious peddler, this one, and no highwayman. Rhone called to Bar'ack. Seeing Bar'ack emerge from the forest holding a proj-lance seemed to unsettle Elfin'ron more than finding Rhone and Jakl in the middle of the road.

"This is Bar'ack."

Elfin'ron recovered from his alarm, nodded, then squared his shoulders as if to show he was not intimidated. "Well, if it was Far Port you were bound for, you've at least happened upon the only road there."

Rhone heard his hesitancy. Elfin'ron was not going to volunteer to carry this bedraggled troop aboard his wagon.

"We've suspected as much. We've fought our way for many leagues through the forest to this road. Captain Jakl, Bar'ack and I would find no difficulty in continuing on to Far Port. But O'tev is in a bad way."

The man was stuck. There could be no gracious way out of taking them all aboard, and hospitality was still a point of honor with most men. Elfin'ron pouted a moment, then accepting the predicament, his face brightened. "But of course you are all welcome to travel with me."

He set the brake, secured the reins, then climbed from his high box and opened the back door to his rolling cottage. Rhone helped O'tev into the tiny building that, except for a narrow aisle down one side, was packed tight with sheets of moonglass and boxes of magnetic implements held down with ropes.

Jakl and Bar'ack crowded onto a little covered porch off the rear of the wagon while Rhone squeezed into the driver's box with Elfin'ron who was clearly regretting this encounter, but trying not to show it. He released the brake and flicked the reins.

14

The Boom and Anchor

I still think we should have tried to helped those people." Kenock plucked a pickled keelit rind from the bowl on the table and shoved it into his mouth. "How dangerous could it have been anyway? We'd have been well armed." His lips tightened in renewed frustration. Had anyone survived the crash? It seemed unlikely, with those brutal creatures attacking the sky-barge as it plummeted. Still, if he could have lent aid he would have, had the others been willing.

"Have you forgotten your promise to Master Lamech? Our first duty is to see Mistress Mishah safely to the Mother, and to watch over Mistress Amolikah. I know it's hard to ignore the sufferings of others, but we have a duty, and we mustn't forget it."

Of course he hadn't forgotten. Kenock tasted his ale and made a face. But Kleg'l was right and it rankled. "They serve up the dregs here in Far Port." He fished through a bowl of nuts. The tough, salty flesh only made him more thirsty and he called for two more mugs of ale. It was better than water, and this might be the last festival hall they saw until they came back this way.

The hall keeper brought the drinks over to their table and collected a coin from Kenock. Kleg'l looked at the mugs, his lean face impassive. "We should be getting back, Master Kenock." He glanced to the window. "It's getting dark."

"Go back now and we'll have to listen to women's talk." Kenock took a sip and wrinkled his nose. The festival hall was crowded with men, and several different conversations might be listened to, if he concentrated; any one of them would be more interesting than listening to Amolikah and Leahia catching up on times past.

"Mistress Mishah will be concerned." Kleg'l took a small sip, then set the mug back onto the table.

Kenock's view drifted languidly toward the lowering sun, bathing Far Port in a deep orange light. The hall keeper was busily lighting lamps and candles. He didn't see a pane of moonglass anywhere. This far from civilization, people clung to the old ways, even though Far Port was the funnel for most goods moving out of the Wild Lands.

Kleg'l leaned forward and said quietly, "I am uneasy here. We should leave now."

Kenock was not aware of anything unusual. "Why?"

He glanced around the room. "Some of these men are watching us with too much interest. And they don't look the type to be wanting to strike up a friendly conversation."

Kenock tipped up his mug. "You're imagining things, Kleg'l. Drink your ale."

He pushed it aside, his mouth taking a stubborn slant.

Kenock sighed. How could he enjoy his ale—even cheap ale like this—with Kleg'l clucking nervously and trying to gather him under his wings? "All right, we'll go listen to the women talk."

Kleg'l stood. Kenock took a long swallow and left his half drunk mug on the table. He eyed the men as they left and still didn't see a cause for Kleg'l's concern. A couple of unkempt, lantern-jawed rivermen watched them leave, but once past their table, the men went back to their mugs.

The street was nearly empty, the once-bustling wharf now

practically deserted. A couple of men sat among crates holding fishing poles. Boats moored along the dock cast long shadows over the land. Somewhere, a cycler sputtered and coughed. Overhead, a flock of dark birds winged toward the setting sun. The air had cooled and smelled clean and earthy. The nearby forest now lay dark beneath a leafy canopy, the low sunlight torching their tops with a final burst of green.

In an alleyway, three men huddled over lines scratched in the dirt. One rattled stones in his fists and tossed them out onto the lines. As the stones rolled to a stop, cheers and groans erupted and money was exchanged.

Kenock listened to the muffled thumps of their footsteps upon the boardwalk, imagining himself bigger and bolder, and tougher. Far Port had a magic about it. It was the kind of place that brought out the manliness in men. He swelled his chest … then deflated. The big feeling couldn't sustain itself. He winced at the memory of the sky-barge disappearing into the forest. Had anyone survived? Couldn't he have helped them? If only he could have convinced the others!

The burden weighed on him. Someday, somehow, *he'd* be the one making the decisions, setting down the rules! Perhaps if he'd tried harder, he could have convinced them … that's what men did, after all, wasn't it?

He slid a glance at Kleg'l; long, lean and stiff-gaited, doggedly pursuing one goal—and that alone. Men were supposed to be flexible, willing to make snap decisions and then act on them. Not unbending like Kleg'l and Lamech. He scowled, surprised at his sudden bitterness, and forced it back into its dark den. There was too much here to revel in. He would not let Kleg'l's single-mindedness ruin it.

The foreign smells and sights and sounds of Far Port stirred his soul. He could almost imagine hearing the distant roar of the Great Falls just beyond the bend in the river, although the falls were still too distant for that. In spite of the trouble they had at Nod City, he thrilled at what lay ahead. Taking in a deep breath, he drew himself up a little taller as they pointed their feet up the muddy track toward Leahia's house.

❦

Mishah sat in a cane chair, sipping her tea, listening to Amolikah and Leahia's "catching up." Their reminiscing keenly interested her, especially when they spoke of her mother. Movement beyond the window drew her eye to the darkening road. Kenock and Kleg'l appeared amongst the lengthening shadows, striding unhurriedly toward the house. Had they any luck in securing transportation? Or was Far Port going to be another Nod City, another forced delay?

Holy Creator, if this pilgrimage is really of your will, why have you allowed so many obstacles? Why have you removed Lamech from us?

She listened for the answer and gave a wry smile. Was Lamech the only one to whom the Creator spoke so clearly? Or was his imagination more vivid than hers?

They stepped to the porch and she heard them scraping their shoes on the iron blade and scrubbing them on the woven mat outside the door.

"We've located transportation," Kenock announced as he and Kleg'l entered the house.

"Wonderful." So, this wouldn't be like Nod City. The news encouraged her. Kenock had a curious look on his face. "What's wrong?"

"Nothing, my dear sister, so long as you don't mind looking like a vegetable peddler." He grinned, but his words held an edge.

Kleg'l was unperturbed. "It's a fine wagon, Mistress Mishah. Sturdy and reliable. It might be a bit colorful, but it will serve our purposes."

"Colorful? It's blinding yellow with a yellow-and-green canopy!" He was still grinning.

Amolikah set her teacup on the table at her elbow. "It sounds lovely to me."

Leahia glanced at the kitchen door and seeming to remember something, disappeared through it. Kleg'l wandered down the hallway toward his and Kenock's room. Her brother stood there a moment, his eyes staring but lifeless, his lips tight and turned down. Falling heavily into a chair, he stretched out his legs, his fingers rapping an impatient beat on the arm.

Mishah tasted her tea. "Is something wrong?"

He looked at her. "Thinking."

"Brooding is more like it, dear boy," Amolikah said gently.

He shifted his eyes toward her. "I am not brooding, Grandmother."

"Something has put a hook into your mind, Kenock." Mishah set her cup aside and stood.

"It … it's nothing."

She waited. Whenever Kenock said that, in just that way, it was almost certainly a prelude to a venting of emotion.

"Well, maybe there is something." He leaned suddenly forward, drawing his legs back, his hands grasping his knees. "We could have helped those people, Mi. We could have made a difference. It would have taken only a little time out of Captain Berg's precious schedule. There had to have been injured people on that sky-barge. Some might even have died because people like us didn't take the time to help them. You can appreciate that, being a healer. I'd have thought Kleg'l would have backed me up. Instead, he remained in Berg's camp, and we passed them by as if their lives were meaningless."

His earnestness touched her, his words striking a tender spot in her heart. "I *am* a healer, and I *could* have helped, it's true—and I wanted to. But Captain Berg had made the decision to leave, not Grandmother, not I … and not Kleg'l. Kleg'l was only following Lamech's wishes to keep us safe. He would have resisted a rescue attempt even if Captain Berg had agreed to it. That's just Kleg'l's nature—to carry out his master's orders." It was that unbending devotion that had lifted him from an indentured servant into their family in all but blood. "He could have acted no other way." She took Kenock's hand. He stiffened at her touch, stood, and walked to the door.

"Where are you going?"

"Back into town."

"Now?" It was already dark.

"Evening meal's on the table," Leahia called from the kitchen.

Amolikah glanced to the open kitchen doorway then back at Kenock.

Mishah took a step closer to him. The thought of Kenock wandering about Far Port after dark sent a chill through her. "The evening meal is being served." Her hand lifted toward the kitchen. "Don't go, Kenock. Have the evening meal with us." She almost swayed him, then he caught himself and his face tightened again.

"I'm not hungry."

"We'll have a long day of traveling tomorrow, and the next. You need to keep up your strength."

"At least take Kleg'l with you," Amolikah said.

"No." His face softened slightly. "I'll be all right, Grandmother."

Mishah's lips tightened. "All right. If you must go, go. But be wise. Be careful." In some ways, her young brother was as stubborn as Lamech!

He looked at her a moment, then nodded and left.

She stood at the window watching his tall form fade into the darkness. Amolikah came up behind her and put a hand to her shoulder. "He's angry. Pray the Creator will keep him safe."

"Why are all the men in my life such mules?"

Amolikah patted her shoulder.

Leahia came out of the kitchen with a burning brand to light the candles and a lamp. A circle of moonglass in a frame of copper cast its pale light about the room. "Evening meal is ready. Tell the men."

"Kenock won't be joining us," Mishah said.

Leahia's surprised look turned puzzled. Mishah glanced out the window. "He went to Far Port."

"Oh," was all she said, but her concern had suddenly drawn shadowed lines across her face.

❧

"A webmaster?" Elfin'ron's bushy eyebrows arched upward. Rhone noted the expression of interest in spite of the gathering gloom of nightfall. The ceiling above Elfin'ron's head was paneled in moonglass of a soft bluish hue. A cluster of levers at Elfin'ron's right hand controlled how much or how little light showed on the seat and foot box. He'd opened just enough of the shutters so he and Rhone could see each other. "Interesting occupation. I've met some men in your line of work. I once even considered doing it myself, but I like a soft bed and a roof over my head too much." Elfin'ron smiled amiably.

In the hours Rhone had ridden with Elfin'ron up on the driver's seat, the peddler's wariness had given way to genuine curiosity. Rhone had discovered an underlying bitterness as bits and pieces of Elfin'ron's life came out in conversation. This was a man who'd once had large plans, but circumstance had played against him. He'd never married and boasted too forcefully that bachelorhood had been to his good fortune. He was a man stuck in an ordinary life, like almost everyone.

Wasn't Bar'ack running from the same trap that had ensnared Elfin'ron and Ker'ack, and most of the ordinary people who live ordinary lives? Rhone frowned. Here was a man longing for the extraordinary while he himself had wished for only the *ordinary* on more than one occasion.

"Where have you traveled?" Elfin'ron shot him a sideways glance.

"Mostly east." They did share one similarity. They both led largely solitary lives. The difference was Rhone had grown comfortable with his solitude while Elfin'ron had not. He longed for conversation. Rhone tried to accommodate, but his answers were almost always curt.

"Heard there's been some problems over east."

Rhone's curiosity was piqued. "What have you heard?"

"Talk from travelers, from folks in villages and peddlers I see from time to time. You probably know about it—if the rumors are true. The spiders, isn't it? Moving deeper into the wilds. Least that's what I hear."

"What you hear is true."

"Know what's causing the change?" He fiddled with the levers to shift the angle of the light off their eyes.

"I have my suspicions." And Rhone suspected the peddler had his, too. With so much time on lonely roads between far-flung villages, peddlers had time to think about things. "Do you?"

"They're turnlings."

Rhone looked back at the dark, unfolding road, disappointed at the shallowness of Elfin'ron's answer. He'd hoped the peddler would have had a fresh idea. It was plain the spiders were turnlings. That didn't explain …

"But not just turnlings." Elfin'ron's sudden grin said he'd fed him that lame answer first, holding back the meat of the nut for effect.

"They're sensitives."

Rhone's eyebrows hitched toward the bridge of his nose. "I've never heard that word used to describe an animal."

"Neither have I until a few weeks ago on the village green over at Aml-ee. Some of the men there were talking about it. One of them is a webmaster like yourself. He's of the opinion there is something hereabouts the spiders have become sensitive to, and they are moving away from it."

The theory was interesting, but flawed. "Spiders don't leave their food behind unless something drives them from it."

"Ah, but not if the thing or things have affected the food. They'd leave it behind, wouldn't they?"

"What kinds of *things*?"

Elfin'ron shrugged. "I thought you, being a webmaster, might have some notion what's causing it."

Sensitives? Could that be the answer? Here was a new idea to explore. Elfin'ron's wagon crested a hill. He hauled back on his reins, bringing his animals to a halt. "There it is." He pointed at the scattering of lights in the distance. "Far Port." He craned his neck from under the little peaked roof and studied the stars. "And I judge it to be a little after the first quartering. Won't be long now. Got a place to stay?"

"No."

He got the team moving again. "Far Port never shuts down. The festival halls keep busy all night. You'll find food and drink at one of them. Send someone to awaken the healer and bring her to see to your friend back there." He hooked a thumb over his shoulder at the wall to their backs.

❦

Although the ale was not the most flavorful, after two mugs Kenock didn't care. His head had begun to buzz pleasantly and the edge to his anger had blunted. But he didn't stop after two. The third and fourth that followed further dulled his senses. The festival hall had grown vaguely out of focus and the sounds a low roar in his ears. If he tried really hard, he could pick out bits and pieces of conversation around him, but the effort wasn't really worth it. What did it matter what others were saying?

He stared at the mug on the table until it stopped moving and guided his hand for the handle. The Boom and Anchor was less crowded than it had been earlier. The few knots of men occupying a scattering of tables appeared as happily involved with their ale as he was with his, except for two men across the room who kept glancing at him. They looked vaguely familiar. With a smirk, Kenock lifted his mug to them. They ducked their heads. Kenock tilted it to his lips and took a deep pull, dribbling down his chin, then wiped his sleeve across it and tried again.

He'd already used up the money in his pocket and the night was still early, but he was happy. He hadn't let thoughts of the sky-barge bother him for—he'd forgotten how long. He'd stopped worrying about it right after he resolved that one day he'd have the power to decide life-and-death issues. And that decision had come just moments before he'd happened on a second startling discovery. If he *could* wield such power, he could command the world! The notion had made him giddy and he'd immediately ordered his third mug of ale … and that was … how long ago now? He couldn't remember.

He lifted his mug and frowned when he found only the empty bottom. He searched his pockets again, hoping he'd overlooked a coin or two the last time, but he hadn't. A wave of desperation washed over him. No more ale. He'd have no excuse to stay. He'd have to leave. He'd have to face Mi and … he shuddered … Grandmother. His logic came to a halt and he chuckled. "The soon-to-be-ruler-of-the-world, cowering at the skirts of his sister and grandmother!"

The door to the festival hall opened and a long, cautious face peeked in and looked around.

"Kleg'l!" Kenock beamed and waved him over. The men in the festival hall glanced up as the lean man slipped through the doorway and came tentatively to his table.

"I was afraid I'd find you like this, Master Kenock," he said in a hushed but reproving tone.

"Like what?" Kenock blinked then gleefully stabbed a finger at the chair across the table from him. "I'm glad you've come. I can use a little company and conversation." He glanced side to side then lowered his voice a little. "You brought the purse, didn't you?"

Kleg'l folded his long body into the chair. "Mistress Mishah and Amolikah are worried about you."

"And they sent you to find me?"

"We ought to be getting back to Mistress Leahia's boarding house."

Kenock waved a hand in the air. "Not yet. I like it here. Say, why don't you order us each a mug of ale, hmm?"

Kleg'l glanced around the room. "And I wish you'd lower your voice. You're attracting attention. Let's be away from here."

"No one here cares anything about you or me." Kenock leaned forward. "Someday I'm gonna be ruler of the world. Whatcha think of that, Kleg'l?"

"I think you've had too much ale."

Kenock grinned. "Well, you just wait and see." He lifted his mug then remembered it was empty. "Did you bring the family purse?"

"It's safely tucked out of sight as Master El-weel suggested." He glanced around with a worried look. "And you should keep your voice down."

"My voice is down."

"You're yowling like a cat with its tale stuck in a 'gia press."

"And you're fretting like a hen over her chicks."

"Am not."

"Am too."

Kleg'l readied another response then caught himself. "This is not the time or place for this, Master Kenock."

"Then open those purse strings and give me some money."

Kleg'l glared stubbornly.

Kenock scowled. Kleg'l was going to be difficult. "Kleg'l. Tell me your name."

The long face stared incredulously a moment. "It's Kleg'l, of course."

He smiled. "Now tell me my name."

He spied the trap and his expression pinched. "*Master* Kenock."

"What is the difference between the two, other than the obvious?"

Kleg'l clamped his lips together and glared.

Kenock was proud of his logic. He opened a palm to Kleg'l and waited.

Kleg'l's eyes grew dark and his nostrils flared. He stood, bony knuckles grinding into the tabletop as he leaned forward. In spite of the anger in his face, his voice remained low and controlled. "I'll tell Mistress Mishah of your whereabouts, and that you won't be returning soon." He wheeled and strode for the door.

"Kleg'l! Kleg'l, come back here." Kenock stood, knocking over his chair. "Kleg'l, give me my money!" He lurched across the room, grabbing Kleg'l by the collar, his free hand balling into a fist.

The two men glared at each other. The room went quiet. The ale-induced fog parted and suddenly Kenock felt the eyes staring at him. Aware of what he almost did, knowing how he would have regretted it in the morning, his fingers relaxed and he stepped back. "Kleg'l, I'm," his voice faltered, "I'm sorry."

"Are you coming home with me, Master Kenock?"

Did nothing ever disturb that controlled exterior? "No. Not just yet." He started back to the table, reeled and stabbed out a foot to catch himself. By the time he'd reached his chair, uprighted it, and collapsed into it, Kleg'l was gone. He glared at the patrons. "Well, what are you all staring at?"

Slowly they went back to their business. He purposefully shot an angry look at the two men who'd been watching him. They were gone. He stared a moment, recalling the words he'd shouted at Kleg'l, then looked to the door.

His view shot back to the empty table. "Oh, no!" He groaned to his feet and staggered toward the door.

15

The Healer's Task

Rhone studied the dark lay of the village as Elfin'ron's heavy wagon—glowing like a festival hall on wheels, its driver's box bathed in a soft blue glow, and multicolored icicles of moonglass dangling from the eaves swaying and clinking together—rumbled into Far Port. Real icicles were a rare sight. Few folks ever had a chance to see them form into long daggers then drip, and melt away. Ephemeral things, icicles, never lasting very long. Rhone had been to the heights of the Illackin Mountains several times and had seen icicles. Elfin'ron's dangling shards reminded him of them in all but color. The icicles Rhone had observed had all been as clear as glass.

Men stepped from festival halls and stared as they rolled past. "There's the Last Port, the Leaky Hull over there, Boom and Anchor across from it."

One was as good as another for the business at hand. "Just let us off anywhere."

Elfin'ron hauled back on the reins. "Good luck finding the healer. I hope she isn't away on some other business. Might I recommend the Gopher Keg up the street? The owner is an honest man, still holding to the old ways. Keeps a sharp eye on his establishment. Hardly ever hear of any trouble over at the Gopher Keg.

And if you plan to stay a while, you can find boarding houses just outside of town at the end of this road."

"Thank you, Elfin'ron. You've done us a great service." Rhone pressed a shaved gleck into the peddler's hand.

Elfin'ron looked at the silver coin with surprise. "No need to pay me, Master Rhone. Was coming here anyway." He tried to return the coin, but Rhone climbed down off the wagon, leaving Elfin'ron showering thanks and well wishes down upon him and the others.

The wagon rolled up the street and turned a corner, the clinking of moonglass and the rumble of wheels fading; a blob of light moving slowly toward a row of dark buildings in the distance.

Rhone turned to O'tev. "How are you doing?"

"Ask me in the morning," he groaned, and Bar'ack lent him support.

Jakl slung the healer's bag over his shoulder. "He needs something stronger for the pain. I've given him the last of the birch extract powder, but even that isn't helping any longer."

"Elfin'ron recommended the Gopher Keg." Rhone pointed to the festival hall up the street and they started walking. Something not quite as subtle as a feeling, but more substantial, like a thought, brought him to an abrupt halt. He looked up the dark street, then across at an even darker alleyway.

"What is it?" Bar'ack glanced nervously about.

It hadn't been a voice, more like a whispered thought that had momentarily touched as lightly as eiderdown upon the convolutions of his brain, and then had been blown away with a breath. Rhone shook his head. "Nothing." Indeed, it had been nothing ... or had it? He started walking again.

Rhone ... the alley.

He jerked to a stop and turned. This had been more than a feathery touch. The thought had the sharp edge of a command.

"Now what?" Jakl cast about worriedly.

"Did you hear it?" No, of course he hadn't. It had been inside his head, or spoken next to his ear. What had made him think of that?

Bearing O'tev's weight on his shoulder, Bar'ack moved past them and toward the festival hall. "Let's get off the street."

"A moment." Rhone peered into the dark slash between two buildings. A sound reached his ears that was real, not imagined. He moved to the mouth of the alley, hearing the faint scraping at its far end. His eyes probed the darkness. All at once, a shape turned and a second shape separated from the blacker shadows.

Rhone's fist tightened about the proj-lance.

"Away with you, if you know what's good for you!" a warning voice growled from the darkness.

He stood his ground, trying to make sense of it all. What had alerted him? Had he heard them on some level lower than the conscious?

"I said be away with you," the surly voice grated.

Rhone's eyes grew accustomed to the fainter light. Something lay upon the ground. He might have mistaken it for a pile of rubbish if not for a small movement and muffled groan.

"Men who prowl about dark alleys almost always are up to no good." Rhone advanced a step.

"This is none of your business."

Make it your business, Rhone.

The thought startled him, and he remembered a similar feeling back in Nod City on the Meeting Floor when he'd helped the Leelanders. What was going on with him?

Almost on the heels of that thought came another. *This is none of your concern. O'tev is your concern.*

The two conflicting notions held him momentarily in a fist of indecision. The quick movement of a blade catching a stray ray of light made any doubt evaporate. With a cat's reflex, he sprang aside as the first man lunged. He brought the butt of the proj-lance up, felt it connect and heard the crack of teeth slamming together. Wheeling with a precision that had once been second nature, he saw in his mind what was impossible to see with his eyes. He'd already marked the second man's locations, his speed and direction. His brain made the calculations. Ducking low, Rhone thrust the proj-lance into the darkness and found muscle and flesh. With an explosion of breath, the second man folded in half. Grabbing him by the collar, Rhone drove him into the timbered wall, rattling the building with the impact.

It was over almost before it started. Rhone straightened up, glanced at the two crumpled shapes at his feet, then at Bar'ack. Jaw unlatched, Bar'ack's eyes had grown big as hen's eggs. Men from the festival hall came drifting out the door, curious what had crashed into the side of the building.

A groan reached him from the far end of the alley. Rhone went to a young man trying to push himself into a sitting position, smelling of ale. A drunken brawl was all it had been. The man's mouth was bleeding, his clothes disheveled. He looked at Rhone with what seemed to be a surge of soberness.

"Kleg'l!" He began feeling around in the dark.

Rhone spied the shape in the shadows. He knelt beside the body and his hand found a warm wetness soaking the shirt. He checked for a pulse and breath. There was still life in the man. He scooped him up in his arms and carried him out of the alley.

The young man staggered behind them but stopped when he reached the two unconscious assailants. He stooped to retrieve something and hurriedly shove it into his pocket.

Out on the main street, the light of the festival hall's window showed Rhone a thin puncture below the man's rib cage. He laid the man gently on the street and put pressure to the wound, feeling warm blood pulse through his fingers, rapidly draining this body of its life force. Onlookers gathered around him. "Someone go for a healer," Rhone barked, tearing open the shirt. One of the big vessels had been severed and he needed to get pressure on it.

"The healer's not here."

"She's gone off to Longrun, on her usual circuit," another added.

Rhone probed the wound for the artery and stemmed the flow temporarily, but it would take a healer's touch, a healer's knowledge of powders and tinctures to keep the man from bleeding to death.

The young man dropped to his knees by their sides and put a hand to the man's head. His face went pale in the weak light, his wide eyes showed fear. "Is he dying?"

"He will if we don't find him a healer."

"My sister, she's a healer," he slurred.

"Where is she?" He pressed harder, slowing pulsing flow to a trickle.

"She's staying with Mistress Leahia."

"I've got a cart just around the corner," someone offered. "I know the place."

Rhone carried the man around to the far side of the Boom and Anchor to a two-wheeled delivery cart hitched to a horse. "Someone run ahead and tell the healer we're on our way," he said, lifting the man into the cart. It started off with a lurch. He concentrated on the thick vessel beneath his finger, reassured by the still strong pulse, although Kleg'l's breathing had slowed to a soft wheeze. It seemed as if the wagon had just started moving when it rocked to a stop and the brake ratcheted in place. The wagon box dipped then lifted as the driver leaped from the seat and came around to lend a hand. They carried the man into the house.

"This way," a woman said leading them down a hallway into a room. Rhone laid the man upon the bed. The woman gasped.

"Kleg'l!"

Rhone looked up. He knew this woman. Where had they met? "You are the healer?"

"Yes." She pealed back blood-soaked material.

"You know him?"

"He's our good-man."

Her shock had lasted but a moment. Her eyes compressed, her mouth taking a hard set. In a glance, she took in the wound and Rhone's finger thrust into it up to the second knuckle. "Severed vessel?"

"Feels like it might be." He saw an older woman who had come in with them place the healer's bag on a table.

The healer reached for the pulse in his neck with one hand while with the other lifted his eyelids. Turning to a leather case, she pulled out and opened a moonglass that gave off an unusually bright light. She removed a vial and a packet of powder and mixed the two.

"There was another man." She held the concoction to the light.

"The young one?"

"Yes. Kenock. My brother." Her eyes lingered upon his face, then widened perceptibly. "Do I know you?"

She was startling pretty, and now that he saw her in the better light and noted her dress, her eyes, and even the timbre of her voice, and he remembered. "The Meeting Floor in Nod City."

"You. Of course." Confusion momentarily darkened her eyes. She blinked, then turned back to Kleg'l. The liquid bubbled in the wound around his finger, turning from brown to yellow, then pure white.

"My brother? Where is he?"

"I thought he was with us. He must be on his way. We were in a hurry and he was ...," he hesitated.

Her eyes hitched up. They were golden brown. "Was what?" She reached for another paper packet, tore it open then dipped a slim knife into an open jar of some bitter-smelling liquid.

"Drunk."

Her mouth tightened. In spite of that, it was still a pretty face and he found it impossible to take his eyes off of it as her expression shifted from anger to concern.

"He'll be here soon." He had no way of knowing that for sure, but somehow he wanted to reassure her. "There was no room in the cart for him."

She turned her attention back to Kleg'l. "I must slow his heart." With deft fingers she positioned the knife, made a fine slit in Kleg'l's forearm, and sprinkled a gray powder into the wound. "There. Grandmother?" She glanced around the room.

"I'm right here, Mishah." She, like the healer, was dressed in the manner of Lee-landers, and there was that customary wariness in those green eyes so common to folks of that tribe.

"Prepare a flask of quintin root. Then have Mistress Leahia bring me hot water."

"It's on the way!" A shorter, heavyset woman who'd been standing out of their way dashed out the door.

"I'll need the dasmin thread and a needle."

"Number three?" The older woman was already unpacking boxes and pouches from the healer's bag.

"That will do." She cut away the remaining shreds of Kleg'l's shirt and poured more of the brown liquid into the wound. As it bubbled to clear, she wiped the skin around it. "A spade probe, a claw ... no, two claws, and the gin leaf."

"Red or yellow?"

"Yellow."

The grandmother's hands moved swiftly and expertly among the contents of the healer's bag, finding just the right items and laying them out in order.

The healer glanced up at him again. "Grandmother will help now." She looked over her shoulder. "Take Master—"

"Rhone."

The older woman came around to his side of the bed and as he extracted his finger, hers entered and probed a moment. "I have it."

Rhone backed out to the door to where a crowd had gathered. "If you need me for anything—," he started to say, but it was plain the healer and her grandmother knew what they were doing. He went back into the welcoming room.

The door burst open and the healer's brother came through, looking wildly around.

"Where is he? Is he …?" The question caught in his throat, as if to ask it would be the same as confirming it.

"The healer is tending to him now," Rhone said. Three other men came through the door, one of them wearing the golden shoulder braid of a Gate Warden. Right behind him were six or seven other men. Captain Jakl helped O'tev into a chair. A groan slipped out as he settled in place.

Mistress Leahia, hurrying past with a pot of steaming water in her mittened hands, broke stride long enough to scowl at the crowd gathering in her welcoming room, then charged down the hallway.

Kenock took off after her.

Rhone snagged him by the arm and hauled him back. "The healer is doing what needs to be done. I don't think she requires any help from us." The last thing she needed was a panicked, drunken brother leaning over her shoulder.

Kenock stared at the smear of blood on his shirt from Rhone's hand and attempted to wrench free. He tightened his grip and guided him into a chair.

The man with the gold braid turned to the men who'd come with him, and those standing about. "Close the door on your way out." He said to Rhone, "Let's all sit down and have us a talk."

Rhone nodded, looked at his hands and went to the kitchen to wash them. When he returned, Kenock and the Gate Warden were in chairs across from each other. Jakl stood by the window, staring out. O'tev leaned in a chair with his legs extended, his head tilted back, his eyes closed, his mouth stretched in a grimace. Bar'ack was perched on the edge of another chair, leaning forward with his arms upon his knees. His eyes shifted around the room as if looking for danger, but careful not to make eye contact with anyone there. His glances most often were directed at the man with the gold braid.

"I am Capak, Chief Gate Warden for the Longrun district." He sounded tired and Rhone sensed this sort of violence was not uncommon here in Far Port. Capak's view shifted to O'tev. "What's wrong with him?"

"He was injured in an accident." Jakl spoke to the darkened window where the lights of Far Port showed in the distance. He turned. "The healer needs to tend to him, as soon as she is free."

Capak nodded and looked to Rhone. "You're the one who broke up the fight?" He seemed to be appraising him, his size, his bearing.

"I am. It appears to have been more serious than just a fight. You did take those men into custody?"

"Not yet. By the time I was summoned, they'd regained consciousness and run off. But they will be found. I got the story from several of the men who were there. Now I want to hear it from you."

Rhone took the only vacant chair left in the room. "There's not much to tell. We got into Far Port in time to stop what was happening in the alley, and here we are."

"How did you arrive? No boat has put in since this morning."

"We came with a peddler."

"A dealer in moonglass and magnetics?"

"The same."

"I know the man. He comes through here regularly."

"Bar'ack and I were traveling from Nod City. The sky-barge carrying us crashed in the wilds."

Capak's eyes widened. "So, you're the ones. A boat captain

reported witnessing a sky-barge go down in the wilds. Mansnatchers, was it?"

Rhone nodded. "The four of us were the only survivors. We found the River Road and Elfin'ron found us."

"Humm. And what business brings you to Far Port?"

"Is that important?" How much of his personal life did Gate Warden Capak expect him to hand over without good reason?

Capak frowned and his eyes took on that appraising look again. "No, I suppose not. Where are you from, Master Rhone?"

"Nod City."

"I mean before Nod City."

Rhone stiffened. Like the earlier question, how much was he prepared to give? His past was a closed book, one he had no intention opening again. "I've traveled much."

"Then to what ruler do you pledge allegiance?"

"To none but myself."

The frown lengthened noticeably. "I see." He considered his next question a moment. "In all your travels, have you ever been to the land of the Hodinites?"

Bar'ack's eyes stopped their shifting and bore uncomfortably upon Rhone.

"I have seen the country of the Makir. Why do you ask?"

"You have the look and the bearing of a Hodinite, but you wear the rude garb of a wildlander. Which is it?"

Rhone carefully culled the emotion from his voice. "I'm a web-master. That makes me a wildlander."

Capak nodded. "Very well. I will put in my report you were in Far Port to depart for the Wild Lands to conduct business." He looked to Bar'ack. "You two are traveling together?"

"Yes, sir. I am apprenticing to Master Rhone."

"Have you anything to add to what Master Rhone has said?"

"No, sir."

"The man who is wounded. Can you tell me anything of him?"

The young man whom the woman had called Kenock spoke up. "His name is Kleg'l. He's our good-man." The experience was sobering him. His voice was stronger, his words no longer as slurred as when Rhone first spoke with him.

"And your business here in Far Port?"

"It is just a stopping-off place."

"For?" Capak's eyebrows lifted with the question.

"We—my family, that is—are traveling north."

"There is not much north of here."

Kenock opened his mouth, then closed it, hesitating. Rhone could see that through the drunken haze, the young man was thinking, weighing his words. "We are visiting family."

Capak stood, looked at Rhone, then Kenock. "Do you two know each other?"

"No." Their answers came almost as a single word. "We never met until this night," Rhone added.

The Gate Warden chewed his lower lip a moment. "Curious. You are both being evasive. But since neither of you has done anything against the rules of this district, I see no reason to pursue this interview further."

"I know nothing more about this incident than what I've told you," Rhone said.

Capak nodded, his view shifted to Kenock.

"Nor I, other than the motive was robbery. They wanted our traveling money."

For the first time, Capak smiled. "And that, young man, is a common crime in a place like Far Port where we have too many travelers passing through. Did they get it?"

"No, thanks to Master Rhone."

Kenock's admission seemed to go further to satisfy the Gate Warden than anything they'd told that evening. Here, at least, was a motive to a crime he was familiar with. The Gate Warden walked to the door, then turned back with a hand upon the latch. "I hope your good-man recovers. I will be looking for his attackers. Evening peace."

"Evening peace," they muttered as he left.

16

A Protector Is Sought

N ow we will close the wound." Praise the Creator, the knife had only nicked the vessel. Mishah sealed the deep gash with a gin leaf wrap and packed medicine moss into the wound. Amolikah handed her the dasmin thread already fastened to a needle. As usual, she always seemed to know exactly what Mishah needed next. Mishah worked with an extra measure of confidence whenever her grandmother assisted. Kleg'l was healthy, and if the medicine moss did its job, there'd be no infection and the body would absorb it in a week or two. The healing combination of leaf and moss should put Kleg'l back on his feet in a few days. At least she prayed so.

As she worked, she struggled with her gratefulness that Kleg'l was alive and her anger toward Kenock's immaturity, his impulsiveness and rebellion! Outwardly, she worked with skill and patience, drawing the inflamed flesh together, tying off a stitch, then repeating the process. Inwardly, she could have screamed! At least she'd been near to help him.

By the time they'd finished, Kleg'l had regained consciousness. To assuage his pain she gave him a dose of scarlet poppy extract.

"Mistress Mishah? Mistress Amolikah?" Confusion showed in his eyes. "Where ... why ..." He looked around him and his view came upon the inflamed gash, closed now with catlike whiskers running along its length. His eyes rounded and his hands felt up and down his sides. "My vest!"

"It's over there."

"Our money."

Mishah hadn't taken the time to consider why Kleg'l had been attacked until just then. She grabbed up the vest and felt for the pouch. "It's gone."

Kleg'l's eyes welled, his voice cracked. "I'm sorry. I failed you, Mistress Mishah. Now whatever will we do?"

Whatever, indeed? *How can this trip be your will when so much evil has happened?* "We'll figure something out, Kleg'l. For now, you need not concern yourself with it. You must rest, you must give your body time to heal. I'll get you something to drink now."

Amolikah sat in a chair by his bed and took his hand. "Don't worry about it, Kleg'l. The Creator will provide a way."

Mishah stepped out the door and leaned against the wall. The hallway was empty and for the moment she was alone. She didn't have to be strong for anyone else's sake. She could let down her guard, and she did. Her eyes stung. She brushed away the tears. A ragged breath tore at her lungs.

The moment passed and she straightened up, brushed at her stained dress, tugged at the bright vest. She'd not let this curve in the road throw her off course. What would Lamech say if he were here? *Be strong. The Creator's ways are not our ways. He will take care of his children.* The thought sent a shiver through her. She stood away from the wall, pulling herself tall. There was still Kenock to face, and she didn't want to do it wallowing in self-pity.

In the welcoming room, she was surprised to discover so many different faces. Kenock was slouched in a chair. When he spied her, he drew himself together and stood.

"How is he, Mi?" His face cleaved with worry.

"I think Kleg'l will be all right," she said flatly. Any more than that and she would have exploded.

He grimaced. "You're mad, aren't you?"

"Kenock! Look what has happened! Kleg'l was almost killed. You're drunk! And now we've lost all of our traveling money." She would have gone on, but didn't want to air her dirty laundry in front of strangers.

Kenock shoved a hand into his pocket. "We didn't loose the money, Mi," and he placed the heavy pouch in her hand, closing her fingers around it. He left her standing there and strode down the hallway. Maybe he was retreating to his room. Maybe looking in on Kleg'l. She didn't know. Her eyes were wet again.

"Mistress?" Rhone stood before her. She patted her eyes and looked up into a strong and handsome face; skin darkened by the sun, eyes filled with concern. "I know you're tired, but could you have a look at another man?"

"Another?" What more could happen tonight?

He pointed.

"What happened to him?" Her control was back, her professional concern shouldering out her personal ones.

"A broken arm."

"When?"

"Yesterday. We've been treating the pain but ran out of the powder a quartering or two ago."

She drew in a breath, sent Mistress Leahia to prepare a cup of tea for Kleg'l, then went to fetch her case of remedies.

❦

In the glaring, unbounded blaze of a naked sun, the planets burned before Mishah's eyes as stones of fire: Pulcra and Malik the Swift, incandescent like burning diamonds. The bluish Earth radiated with a sapphire's luminescence. Oric burned scarlet, her vast shallow seas as motionless as molten ruby upon her surface. Then there was the one beyond. The fifth one. The one called Rahab, burning yellowish white beneath the distant sun's fire.

"Behold the place of the Rebellion."

Mishah glanced with surprise at the tall creature standing beside her, as diaphanous as gauze, as ephemeral as the morning fog. Although she hadn't been aware of him before, his sudden presence neither startled nor frightened her. Somehow, she had expected him.

"I don't understand."

"All of this was once the realm of the Son of Light." The being's arm made a great, sweeping arc. "He walked up and down among the Stones of Fire. He strolled amongst the greensward of the Garden of the Creator."

In an instant, the shimmering being swept her past the burning stones and showed her the pale pearl called Rahab. To Mishah's surprise, the luminous body wasn't hot at all. There was a cool harshness about Rahab; a brittleness that sent a bolt of dread through Mishah. The surface bore a great, ugly crack, circling from pole to pole: she lay in ruin, except for here and there where Mishah caught glimpses of a glittering city shining as if shaking a defiant fist at the destruction all around it.

Most of the cities were in a heap. Bridges of ruby and emerald, fashioned as if by the hand of a master jeweler, lay in disrepair, fallen into the rivers they once spanned. But amongst the ruins, Mishah saw a past glory that even now stole her breath. She wanted to see the still-standing cities but the being of light drew her away from them.

"What happened here?" she asked.

"He was a child of perfection in all his ways … until iniquity was found in him."

"Iniquity?" She thought the being's eyes had saddened, but how could she be sure?

"This was the place of the Rebellion." His awed tone spoke more clearly to her heart than did his words. "It began here. The Son of Light led his legions of rebels to the very throne room of the Creator. There was war in the heavenly places. The Creator cast him down and this is the result of the war."

She stared at the pearly globe now ten thousand leagues beneath her feet. From here, its fragile nature was still evident. The crack snaking across its surface moved and rumbled. "This cleft? What does it mean?" She searched the being's face for an answer.

"It formed at the time the Son of Light and his rebels were cast back from the Holy Mountain. The weight of his sin was so great, Rahab could not contain it. It is only by the Creator's grace that Rahab still exists." As if to make this perfectly clear, the faint form of a hand materialized out of nothing to wrap about Rahab, holding it as one might carry a fragile egg with a cracked shell.

"But why?"

"Rahab is reserved for judgment."

"Judgment?" The word reverberated in her ears as the worlds spun away in their orbits. Suddenly Mishah was back on earth and strolling amongst tall forests. Not the forests of home, but of a strange place, a deadly place. An odor of decay lay thick in the air and made her nauseated. The child stirred within her womb. A deeper shadow passed overhead. Her heart raced for she knew what must come next.

※

"The first time you see a javian, its size may surprise you. Judging from the web, you might expect a much larger spider." Rhone sipped his mug of tea and studied the forest that lay not far beyond Mistress Leahia's window. At his side, Bar'ack listened with the studious attention an apprentice gives the master.

"I've seen pictures."

Rhone looked down at his young protégé and grinned. "From one of Master Frobin's books, no doubt."

Bar'ack gave a smile in return. "Actually, it was in a book Father has at the shop."

A sound made Rhone glance across the room. The healer was mumbling in her sleep, turning fitfully upon the couch.

"She dreams," Bar'ack noted.

He nodded. "They appear to be troubling dreams." The three of them were the only ones in the room. The healer's brother, Kenock, had gone to bed to sleep off his intoxication. The grandmother had taken up a watch at the bedside her good-man, Kleg'l. And O'tev and Captain Jakl had disappeared into their respective rooms. Mistress Leahia had suddenly acquired a houseful of guests, and she was busy in the kitchen preparing a late morning meal for when they would all arrive at her table. The strong odor of baking bread was pleasant and reminded Rhone how hungry he was.

Rhone's view came back to the healer, curled up under a light blanket Mistress Leahia had tucked about her. She'd had a husband with her on the Meeting Floor, but he had seen no sign of him here. As his view rested upon the sleeping woman, an unbidden longing stirred to life within him.

Bar'ack's voice was an unwanted intrusion. "When do we find the spiders, Master Rhone?"

Rhone drew in a sudden breath. The air had gone stagnant within his lungs, and he hadn't even realized it. He pulled his eyes off the sleeping woman and focused back on the ragged edge of forest, brilliant green in the bright morning light. "Soon, I hope." His purse was nearly empty. If he didn't find web soon, he'd have to resort to another way of keeping bread in his stomach. He'd been collecting web for over ninety years and he liked the work. But sometimes circumstances force a man to move on.

The Lee-landers have money.

Maybe the spiders' sudden migration was a sign for him to move on too. But what could he do? What kind of work was he good at? He immediately dismissed the first thought that entered his head, but considered the one that followed it. He knew the Wild Lands and understood how to survive with ease within them. Perhaps he could become an outfitter? A guide? Maybe folks like these Lee-landers, traveling to some far reaches for who knows what reason, might want to hire on a guide. The Lee-landers had money.

What had made him think that? The taste of disgust filled his mouth. He wasn't a mercenary. His sword was not for hire. He'd sworn an oath to a code of living once, and that oath was still important to him, even if it wasn't to others. His thoughts went back to Nod City, to those two warriors putting on their mock battle in the marketplace.

"How do you speak to them, exactly?"

"Hmm?" Rhone forced himself to refocus his thoughts.

"The spiders. I know a webmaster speaks to them, cajoles them somehow to give up their web. But whenever I've asked, the answer is always the same. In some vague way, a webmaster and a spider just understand each other. How is that possible, Master Rhone?" Bar'ack's wide, earnest expression held a hint of concern.

"Legend has it, in the beginning-time humans and the creatures understood each other, but for some reason, the ability died off. Today, only a few men have inherited the skill, and then only with certain creatures."

"I've heard the legends." Bar'ack's fingers absentmindedly rolled the Oracle's crystal pendant that hung around his neck.

"Through the writings of your favorite author?"

"He believed the legend is true. What do you believe?"

The crystal that hung beneath Rhone's shirt seemed suddenly to burn against his chest. "There are many things we don't understand. I cannot say whether men spoke with animals in days past. All I know for sure is that in some way that I do not understand, I touch minds with the spiders. All successful webmasters do. It becomes a challenge of wills. I urge the spider from its web, and it in turn resists. In the end, if I'm successful, the spider complies. Some days I cannot reach them, and I leave empty-handed. When I am successful, I harvest their web and leave a gift."

"Could you not just kill the spider and take its web?"

Bar'ack's suggestion disturbed Rhone. "That's not done, any more than you would kill a weaver to acquire his cloth."

"But it's only a spider."

Rhone frowned. "The forest is full of turnlings. Why they are changing, no one knows. Could it be because men have begun to kill them for food? Or convenience? The world used to be in balance. Something is working to disrupt that balance."

"The Oracle says he will set it all right again once his temple is built and he returns to dwell within it." Bar'ack had stopped worrying the crystal and was gripping it tightly now in his fist.

"No! ... No!"

Rhone and Bar'ack turned at the sounds of Mishah's muffled cries, her thrashing upon the couch. Rhone went to her and placed a hand upon her shoulder. She startled awake at his touch and looked wildly about.

"It's all right. A dream only," he said.

She calmed as she came fully awake. "I'm sorry if I disturbed you." She appeared embarrassed and tugged her vest around and straightened it. Her hand went suddenly to her stomach and she appeared momentarily to be ill, then it seemed to pass.

She was pregnant. How could he have missed it before? "No. You didn't."

"We were just talking of the forest, and of its mysteries." Bar'ack grinned at her.

She was young, perhaps Bar'ack's age. She did not smile too widely but maintained a properly aloof manner. Precisely as she should, being a married woman and in the presence of strange men. A prim Leelander, this one was. Rhone reminded himself how he'd never cared much for them as a tribe, but something about this woman was different.

She can be yours, if you want her.

What was she like when she wasn't being prim and proper? She was certainly attractive. Could he, if he wanted to, win her heart? He frowned. He should not be thinking such things.

Her eyes narrowed with a Lee-lander's suspicion. "This is the second time we've met, Master Rhone. And both times you have helped us." She stared at him. "Don't you find that odd?"

"Simply a coincidence."

She smiled. "My husband says, 'In the Creator's world, there is no such thing as coincidence.'"

She'd opened the door to the question that had been foremost on his mind. "Where is your husband? I haven't seen him."

Her smile dimmed. "Lamech's still in Nod City." She drew in a breath, but the renewed strength in her voice was forced and tenuous. "He was arrested on several charges, none of which should have brought him the punishment he received at the hands of the Lodath."

"What was his sentence?"

"Fifteen years. Fifteen years building that temple he loathes so much!" Her eyes glistened. She sniffed and wiped them abruptly.

"What was he charged with?"

"The Lodath called it sedition."

"Was Lamech being seditious?"

"Of course not. He had no interest in overthrowing the government of King Irad. He's a farmer and a preacher. He only spoke out against what he saw as spiritual wickedness. If he was seditious at all, it was against the Oracle. And can it be seditious to speak out against a being no one has ever seen, or a kingdom not yet established? So far he's just some cosmic god who speaks through his earthly representatives. No one even knows if he is real or some elaborate deception. Lamech saw the evil in that."

So, even the healer was infected with a Lee-lander's zeal. He decided he did not want her even if he could have her.

She inhaled sharply, anger in her face. "Fifteen years!"

Bar'ack was listening with interest, a corner of his mouth hitched up as if trying to ferret out the error in her premise.

She stood, "I need to look in on Kleg'l, and O'tev." She started away, then turned back. "Will you and Master Bar'ack be staying in Far Port?"

Rhone shook his head. "We'll be traveling north. We'll likely be leaving later today, after I've spoken with Captain Jakl."

"I see." She appeared to have something else on her mind, but then dismissed it and padded stocking-footed down the hallway.

"She doesn't understand what the Oracle says." Bar'ack sat on the arm of the couch, shaking his head, looking down the hall where she'd disappeared.

"And you do?"

"I grew up in Nod City." He said it as if that explained everything. "I've heard the Oracle's message for years now. And first off, he's trying to set the world straight on this whole Creator business. The Oracle is an ascendant being, and so are we—only, he's more ascended than we are." He grinned. "But we all started out the same, and our ultimate goal is to be like the Oracle and establish worlds of our own, but that's only after we achieve the status of godhood ourselves. And that could take millions of years, and thousands of lifetimes." Bar'ack's eyes grew big. "But here is the point, Master Rhone. We won't have to go through all those lives, to make all those mistakes. The Oracle is coming back to Earth, to teach us what we need to learn—and that's not all. He is bringing helpers with him."

"Helpers?" So far everything Bar'ack had told him was well known. Some people accepted it, others, like Lamech and Mishah, rejected it.

Bar'ack sprang to his feet and strode to the window, turned, and strode back. "Yes, helpers. Other ascendant beings like himself." He was getting into his subject, his hands moving nearly as fast as the words tumbling from his mouth. "You see, it's like this. If these beings—these helpers—were to marry human women, then soon their children would populate the world. The gods' life forces would mingle with human life forces, bypassing millions of years of slow change. In just a handful of generations, we can achieve all that the Oracle promises! Why wait for the natural development of the human animal to continue at the snail's pace it's unfolding now?"

Rhone stopped him. "You mean the Oracle's plan is to breed us into gods? To change the natural course of human development?" Here was a fable pure and simple. He laughed and shook his head. "It's a good thing I got you out of Nod City when I did. That place is filling your head with fantasy."

Bar'ack laughed too. "Well, who knows, there might even be something to it. I don't know that I believe all of it myself. But you can see how little the healer comprehends what's really going on. It is much bigger than just which god to worship. It's which god can help us. So far, the Oracle wins."

"And how do you judge winning?"

Bar'ack thought a moment and shrugged, grinning. "I don't know. But at least he has a plan."

It was a plan all right. A scheme so grand it had to be fantasy. Yet, if true, what did it mean for mankind? Could mere men become gods? Could it happen in the course of only a few generations? Would it be a good thing if they did? He wasn't buying it, not yet at least. But ... it was an intriguing notion.

In a chair at Kleg'l's side, Amolikah huddled beneath a light blanket, her head against the tall caned back, her eyes closed. Mishah padded softly into the room, careful not to disturb either of them. She'd given Kleg'l a tonic to help him rest and he seemed to be sleeping peacefully enough. His breathing was shallow but even, his color healthy. She carefully lifted back the sheet. The wound was redder than the surrounding skin, but showed no sign of infection. That was good. The medicine moss was doing its job, slowly dispensing strong protectorants into his system.

She started for the door to check in on her other patient.

"I'm not asleep, dear." Amolikah's voice came soft and drowsy. She didn't open her eyes right away.

"You should be."

The older woman drew in a breath that seemed to invigorate her. Her eyes opened and she straightened up in the chair, wincing at the resistance of joints, bent too long in one position. "I think I slept on and off."

"I can give you something."

"No, no. It's daylight. The night is for sleeping, dear. The day is for working. I hear Leahia knocking about the kitchen. I should be helping her." Amolikah glanced at Kleg'l. "He slept restfully all night."

"The wound looks good."

"He had a fine healer."

Mishah smiled. The compliment wasn't necessary, but appreciated. "Healing is always in the hands of the Creator, Grandmother."

"Yes, dear, but last night it was *your* hands that he used to accomplish the work of *his* hands."

And whose other hands does he use? Mishah glanced out into the hallway, looked around, then closed the door and lowered her voice. "I need to talk to you about something, Grandmother."

"What is it?" Amolikah leaned forward.

Mishah crouched, gripping the arm of the chair for balance. The growing life inside her restricted her breathing. Her pregnancy had yet to be much of a burden, now that the morning misery was past, but other changes were taking place. She tired easily. She was always uncomfortable. Her full-cut dress hardly hid her thickening girth. She hadn't wanted to be away from home when she became large and clumsy and waddled like a duck, but the pilgrimage had been delayed until she was seven months along. Now she was stuck with it.

"It might be a couple weeks before Kleg'l is strong enough to help Kenock protect us on the road to Chevel-ee."

"If we must wait, we will. We've brought enough money to see us through this. Lamech was quite thorough in his preparations. And I have a little money of my own, if we should need it."

"It's not the money that concerns me, Grandmother. But the delay ... I'm," she gave a defeated smile. "It's becoming more and more difficult for me."

Amolikah touched Mishah's hand. "You'll be fine. I know you're farther along than you planned to be. You'll do what you must, and you'll get through it. Others have."

"I'm still not convinced of the 'must' part. This is more Lamech's quest than mine. And he's not even here to take part in it!" She winced. "I'm sorry. That sounded selfish, didn't it?"

"Don't berate yourself for it. What is it that's really on your mind, Mishah?"

Sometimes her grandmother's perception was frightening. She'd tried to work into it slowly, and here Amolikah had seen it coming all along. "I had an idea. No, it was more than an idea. It was almost as if a voice had spoken inside my head." She smiled at that. "I'm beginning to sound like Lamech."

"And that's such a bad thing?"

"No. Of course not."

"And what did this voice in your head say to you?"

Mishah gave a wry smile. "Well, you might think this crazy, but it said we should offer Master Rhone the job of guide and protector—at least until Kleg'l is fit to stand by Kenock's side if danger should come again."

Amolikah widened her eyes. "Did it, now?"

"He and his young friend are traveling north. There is only one road leading north, as far as I know. And it goes to Chevel-ee. If we were to convince them to wait a couple days until Kleg'l is fit to ride in the wagon, and pay them a fair wage, perhaps they would agree to it. Master

Rhone has already helped us two different times. Has the Creator placed him in our path for this purpose?"

Her grandmother's green eyes narrowed sharply. "We know nothing about this man, dear."

"Other than he has been right there to help us when we needed him. Once in Nod City, and again here, last night. He seems to be an honorable man. He saved Kleg'l at his own risk."

"But is he a man of faith?"

"Does it matter? We need his help, and he has a proj-lance."

Amolikah's eyebrows arched. "I'll think the matter over. What would Kleg'l advise?"

"He'd say hire the man and let's get this pilgrimage over." Kleg'l's gravely voice startled them both.

"I thought you were asleep." Amolikah said.

He opened one eye and slanted it at the two of them. "I *was* asleep."

"How do you feel?" Mishah leaned over and stared into that single pupil.

"I am in much pain, and my strength is not what I'm used to. Other than that, I feel good. You are a superb healer, Mistress Mishah."

It gladdened her to see him so alert, and to hear his subtle humor. "And I am surprised at you, getting in a fight and allowing someone to put a knife into you."

"It was not intentional, I assure you."

She smiled and ran her fingers through his tangled hair. "Thank you for going after Kenock. I'm sorry it came to this."

"And Master Kenock?"

"He's sorry too. He disappeared into his room and I haven't seen him since last night, but I'm sure he'll be looking in on you soon." She stood. "Well, I must look in on Master O'tev."

"Who?"

Amolikah patted his hand. "I'll explain it to you, Kleg'l."

17

Wandering Path Inn

Kenock awoke to a hammer inside in his head pounding needles into the back of his eyes. His tongue had swelled two sizes too large and filled his mouth like an old leather strap—a mouth too parched to moisten it even a little. He rolled out of bed and thumped to the floor and clasped his head to keep it from exploding. Sitting there, he caught sight of himself in the mirror. He'd slept in his clothes and looked as bad as some of those derelict humans he once laughed at, sleeping off too much ale behind the festival halls back home in Morg'Seth. His face wore knuckle bruises, and his chin was scraped and caked with dried blood. His ribs ached when he breathed—but nothing hurt as badly as the throbbing between his temples!

He turned away from the mirror and squeezed his eyes at the glare of the morning sunlight coming through the window. Standing, grabbing the bedstead for support, he lurched to the door, pulled it open, and wandered out into the hallway. The door to Kleg'l's room stood open, and the temptation to walk past without stopping was strong. But his concern for their good-man won out. In spite of what he might find inside there, he had to know. He rapped lightly on the door jamb and stepped inside.

What he saw encouraged him. Kleg'l appeared alert, reading a small book. He set the book upon the side table, giving a soft grunt and a twitch of his mouth at an apparent stab of pain. "You look terrible, Master Kenock."

He winced and peered down at himself. At least he hadn't vomited all over himself during the night. "I know. I caught a glimpse of myself in the mirror." He forced a smile. "You, on the other hand, look well."

"I'm doing well. Mistress Mishah's a skillful healer." He imitated one of Mishah's frequent explanations of the miracle of healing. "'Gin'enet leaf will speed the body's natural healing, and the medicine moss will stop any infection. And don't forget the air, or I should say the air pressure. The Creator has given us a world designed to heal. The remedies grow all around us, if only we have an eye to see them and the knowledge to use them.'"

Kenock smiled at Kleg'l's passable performance. It had been his sister's fascination with things like leaves, moss, roots, and air that had led her to take the training of a healer. Kenock moved to the foot of the bed, his head pounding with each step. "I ... should have listened to you and Mi. Sometimes it takes a robber's fists to pound sense into my thick head. It gladdens me to see you are going to be all right, Kleg'l."

"The Creator was with us."

Kenock winced again. Had he been? How could Kleg'l be so sure? Did he really believe it, or was it just words to say?

"Have you spoken with your sister?"

"Not yet." He tucked his shirt into his pants. "Is she still angry with me?"

"Most probably, but her anger never lasts long. You should know that."

"I do. Mishah is a remarkable woman." He shoved his fingers through his hair, knowing he'd have to face her sooner or later. Might as well be sooner. "I'll stop back in a little while."

Kleg'l nodded, and with a soft groan, took up his book.

Kenock did not find Mishah in the welcoming room. She wasn't in the kitchen either where Leahia was slicing apples into a bowl. At her elbow was a pile of carrots and levin roots waiting to be shredded. She looked up and her eyebrows pinched. He'd momentarily forgotten his disreputable appearance.

"Where is Mishah?"

"The side porch. Would you care for tea?"

"No, thank you. Just some water, if you please."

She filled a wooden cup from a water bucket on the counter. He guzzled it down and took a breath. The water was a welcome relief to his parched mouth, but did little to slake the horrible thirst. He sheepishly held the empty cup out. She refilled it, and he carried it through the graceful oval of the kitchen door out onto a porch of neatly fitted fieldstone. The view from here was toward the forest a few hundred spans beyond—perhaps it was even a lovely view. But at the moment nothing pleasant registered in his aching head. The porch extended the length of the house, and at its far end, in chairs of woven cane set around a table of a similar construction, his sister, that large man named Rhone, and a third man—he'd recalled him from the night before but didn't remember ever hearing his name—sat over mugs of tea, in earnest discussion.

Each step was a hammer's blow to his head. By the time he reached them, he had to grab for one of the carved roof support posts to steady himself.

"Kenock, come sit here." Mishah's gentle voice held concern, not reproach. This was encouraging. She took his arm and helped him into the chair she'd abandoned. "You don't look well."

"It was stupid of me to have had so much ale." He shielded his eyes with a hand and drank more water, then set the mug on the table.

"You're not the first man to discover that." Rhone's voice held an edge of amusement, but not a trace of condemnation.

Mishah stood behind him with her hand lightly upon his shoulder and gave an understanding squeeze. "It's past. Forget it."

"I know exactly how you feel." The unnamed man gave a short laugh and a shake of his head. Kenock reckoned him to be a few years younger than himself. His face beamed a friendly smile. His wide-set eyes seemingly laughing at Kenock's sorry condition.

Mishah said, "This is Master Rhone, and his friend Master Bar'ack." She explained their coincidental meeting back in Nod City and again last light, and concluded with, "and Master Rhone has agreed to accompany us as far as Chevel-ee. He and his friend are heading that way anyway."

In spite of the throbbing in his skull, Kenock wrenched his head around with a start and stared at her. Mishah smiled and gave his shoulder another light squeeze. "This way we can continue the pilgrimage without having to wait until Kleg'l is fully recovered. I've been informed that the road between here and Chevel-ee can be a dangerous place."

"I'm able to safeguard us on the road." He tried not to allow his feelings to show, but knew they must.

"No doubt you are." Rhone possessed a deep, easygoing voice. Yet, there was no mistaking his confidence. "But since we are all traveling the same road, perhaps your sword will come to our help as readily as ours to yours?"

Was it really for mutual protection that they would be traveling together? Kenock studied the big man, noting his easy poise and wide shoulders. He couldn't picture his sword ever coming to Rhone's aid. But Rhone's diplomacy had skillfully drowned the sudden fire that had sprung up within him.

"Perhaps." Kenock looked back at his sister. "And you think this is wise?"

"I do, and so does Kleg'l."

So, she'd consulted with Kleg'l before she'd consulted with him. "And Grandmother?"

Mishah frowned slightly. "Grandmother has her reservations, but has agreed to the arrangements."

Kenock didn't know what he thought about it. His head throbbed and his mouth was gritty as sand. All he really wanted to think about was going back to his room and sleeping. He'd worry about it later.

"I know what will make you feel better," Bar'ack said, standing suddenly.

"What?"

"Come with me." Bar'ack took his arm.

He held back. "Where to?"

"Mistress Leahia's kitchen. I'll put something together that will set you right."

He didn't want to be bothered with this fellow's home-brewed remedy. He wanted to go back to bed and die. But Bar'ack had him firmly by the arm, and he went with him anyway. His willpower seemed as weak as his general thinking process.

In the kitchen, Bar'ack guided him into a chair. "Mistress Leahia, have you ..." Kenock didn't listen to the list of ingredients. He cradled his head in his hands with his elbows on the table, trying to stop the pounding inside his skull. Distantly, he was aware of Bar'ack busying himself in the background.

"Here, drink this down." He shoved a thick, red concoction under Kenock's nose. It smelled as if it might dissolve nails.

"Are you sure?"

Bar'ack laughed. "I've been in your shoes more times than I care to remember. And every time, when I thought I wanted to die, this has taken care of the problem."

Kenock eyed the thick, bubbling liquid then looked at Leahia. She was watching with a curious expression.

"Why not. How much more can this harm me now?"

"Drink it all down in one go. Pinch you nose if you don't want to taste it. If you stop long enough to get a taste of it, you'll never finish it."

Kenock prepared himself for the worst, then guzzled the potion. Afterward, he couldn't remember it having any taste at all. It went down smooth, quick, and without pain, leaving only a slightly peppery tang in his mouth, and that was all. His belly gurgled some and he laid his head upon his folded arms and heard Leahia ask, "Is he all right?"

"He'll be just fine in no time at all."

And in a few moments his head began clearing, his thoughts sharpened, the drumming stopped, and his tongue no longer felt as if it belonged in a sten-gordon's mouth instead of his own.

Bar'ack gave a laugh. "See, told you so."

Kenock grinned, cautiously waiting for the pain to return, and was pleasantly surprised by its complete absence. "Amazing."

"I'll teach you how it's made. Then next time you can take care of it yourself."

"There won't be a next time."

Bar'ack looked amused. "There'll be a next time. There always is."

The trees had changed. It was an unfamiliar forest, yet somehow eerily familiar. These trees grew taller than Mishah could ever imagine, and were packed more tightly together than forests back home in Morg'Seth. Their branches arched in a solid canopy far overhead, and in places daylight turned into twilight and the road disappeared up ahead in murky shadows even though it was only the fourth quartering and the sun was high in the sky.

At times she was awed by the quiet of the forest, and at other times she wanted to drive her fingers into her ears because of the crickets and birds and choruses of frogs. Sometimes a distant growl rolled ominously from the shadows. One moment the road would be gloomy, and then suddenly it would leave the forest and stretch out over green rolling hills, filled with flowers and golden butterflies nearly the size of their little rented cart. But the most curious of all were the waterfall trees.

Kenock had stopped the cart at Rhone's bidding, and the web-master took them across a grassy field to show them one of the curious trees, growing alone in the midst of a vast green plain. Amolikah stayed with the cart and Kleg'l.

Mishah's gaze traveled up the stubby trunk. It was more than twelve spans tall, and it spread out into a perfect umbrella of green leaves. Dangling from the canopy were hundreds of fine, leathery tendrils. Another time she might have thought it beautiful. Now it reminded her of pencil-thin vipers. They hung clear to the ground, where a thousand tiny suckers drank in the morning dew from the tips of the grass.

Though curious, it made her shudder. "What other surprises can come from the Creator's mind?" she wondered aloud. Bar'ack had turned away, and snickered.

Rhone said simply, "This world holds many wonders, most we've yet to discover."

Did he believe as they did, or was he like his young friend, one of the Oracle's converts? Mishah had not heard Rhone mention his faith. Had he any? She'd already gleaned from some of Bar'ack's comments where his allegiance lay. If Lamech were here—she cut off that line of thinking as soon as she realized where it would take her.

The road gradually deteriorated into a double-rut track, and their progress slowed so as not to jostle Kleg'l who was stretched out in the cart upon a blanket and a mattress of straw. As the day drew on toward evening, Amolikah assured them that before nightfall they'd come to an inn. Before the last light had left the sky, they rolled through a towering gate and into the stone-walled courtyard of the Wandering Path Inn. The proprietor was in the doorway with a broom in hand when Kenock pulled to a stop.

"Welcome, welcome. Welcome to the Wandering Path! Ah, you folks look weary. A long road behind you?" The innkeeper had a broad, bald head, small eyes, and a great, black beard. He appeared pleased to see them, and as there were no other animals or carts tethered to the rail or in the lean-to barn off to the side, Mishah decided they were to be his only guests for the night.

"We left Far Port with the rising of the sun," Mishah said, climbing down off the wagon seat. It seemed much longer than only one day since setting off in their bright yellow "vegetable cart" as Kenock insisted on calling it. How many leagues had Rhone and Bar'ack walked, as there was not enough room on the little cart for all six of them? Bar'ack leaned wearily against the tall wheel and massaged his toes through his boot. Rhone seemed hardly affected at all by the daylong march.

The proprietor nodded. "I suspected as much." He grinned, his teeth a flash of white behind a tangle of black beard. She couldn't tell the color of his eyes in the long shadows filling the courtyard, but the smile was friendly, and his apron appeared clean. Always a good sign.

"We will be needing three rooms, with comfortable beds," Amolikah said, accepting Rhone's hand and dropping off the back of the wagon. "There is an injured man here who will need his rest."

The proprietor's wide welcoming face took on a worried cast. "How badly injured?"

Mishah slung her healer's bag over her shoulder. "He's in no danger, Master ... ?"

"Dorn-ek."

"Master Dorn-ek. He's in my care, but as my grandmother said, he will need his rest."

"Ah. You're a healer?"

"I am."

Dorn-ek stepped down from his porch and came around the wagon, poking his black beard over the side.

Kleg'l grinned at him. "I will not die in your bed."

"Humph. I should hope not." Dorn-ek grinned. "Well, welcome one and all! Come on inside and I'll get you settled in your rooms."

Mishah made the introductions. When she got to Amolikah, Dorn-ek studied her and asked if they'd ever met before.

"Yes, indeed. It was more than fifty years ago. My daughter's pilgrimage. Now it's my granddaughter's."

"I thought I'd seen you before." He tapped his head. "Don't usually forget the face of someone who's lodged with me. Been at this business nearly three hundred years now, and I've got a bunch of faces stored up here—some of them I'd *like* to forget." He laughed, then frowned. "Not as many folks coming through here as there used to be. The old ways are dying off."

"Yes, indeed they are, Master Dorn-ek." Amolikah took up her bags and followed the proprietor inside. Kleg'l, buoyed up between Rhone and Kenock, came slowly behind them. Bar'ack took up his and Rhone's bags and wandered in after them.

Mishah stood a moment all alone in the deepening gloom, staring at the solid forest encroaching nearly to the rock wall. The coming night made the looming trees more foreboding. "Someday you'll march right over this inn and swallow it up, won't you. That's you're intention, isn't it?" She grinned to herself. She was speaking to the trees. It had been a long day.

She looked at the inn; its heavy stone walls more than ample to support the sturdy, timbered second story and thickly thatched roof. As she considered the building, she couldn't shake the disturbing feeling that someday there would be nothing left of this for anyone to find.

Words from her dream came to her. *Behold the place of the Rebellion.* She jolted. Why had she remembered the dream just then? She shivered and hurried after the others.

The tidy welcoming room immediately boosted her spirits. A double fist of lamps mounted around the walls and overhead drove back the night and filled the room with a comforting glow. The floors were scrubbed and polished, their heavy planks, although scuffed and darkened, in fine repair after three hundred years of foot traffic. Four tables and twenty chairs sat neatly arranged. A huge hearth against the back wall held what was a tiny fire for its size; just enough to keep an iron kettle of water steaming.

Rhone and Kenock eased Kleg'l into a chair. Mishah peeked under his bandages. The extra two days spent with Leahia had been rest well needed for all of them.

Dorn-ek introduced his wife who'd just come in through a door that might have led to their living quarters or the kitchen area. Mistress Eleen was a tall, thin woman with black hair and dusky skin. Her dress was brightly colored and of a finer material than Mishah's practical shiverthorn dress. But then Mistress Eleen wasn't traveling.

Mishah sighed. Travel required something sturdier than the exquisite cloth woven from the silk of the shimmer caterpillar, or even practical cotton. In truth, she wore the same coarse clothing even when at home and not traveling. Life on a 'gia farm did not lend itself to cotton and silk. But at least when she'd been home, her dress had draped gracefully over her curves. Now it was too snug and uncomfortable.

"I'll move a comfortable bed down here onto the main floor for Master Kleg'l," Dorn-ek said. "The rest of you come with me and I'll show you to your rooms." He started toward a staircase along the wall. "By the time you're all settled in, Eleen will have food on the table." He hesitated with a foot on the first step and turned back to them. "I expect you eat traditional?"

"Traditional," Mishah said and everyone nodded in agreement except Bar'ack.

"I will eat meat, if you have any."

They looked at him. Dorn-ek smiled. "We usually only cook traditional here, Master Bar'ack. But since we have so many guests of different beliefs coming through our door, we do have meat available for those travelers who ask for it. If you wish, I will have Eleen prepare some."

Bar'ack seemed suddenly aware of their eyes on him. "No. It isn't important." He grinned. "I'll just eat what everyone else eats."

"What does meat taste like?" Kenock asked.

"It has a good flavor."

Amolikah shot Kenock a sharp look. "If men were meant to eat animal flesh, the Creator would not have provided such a bounty of fruits and vegetables and grains."

Mishah scowled unexpectedly.

Kenock rolled his eyes. "I was just asking, Grandmother, that's all."

Rhone stepped aside as Kenock pushed past and clumped up the stairs. He turned his dark gaze toward Mishah. Why did he look at her that way? She averted her eyes.

"Didn't mean to cause trouble." But Bar'ack seemed more humored by the incident than contrite.

They followed Dorn-ek to their rooms. Like the welcoming room, the sleeping quarters were spotless, if not a little old-fashioned.

"I've yet to pipe water up here," Dorn-ek apologized, "but there is always plenty of hot water down on the hearth." Dorn-ek left her and Amolikah, and took the men to their rooms.

Mishah glanced around: two beds, a couple simple forest land paintings, and a thick carpet. Simple and cozy. She sat on one of the beds and bounced. "This is perfect. I won't sink in and never get out."

Amolikah tested her bed with little interest, then stood at the window, staring at her own reflection in the lamplight. "I saw your look a moment ago. You think I was mistaken for correcting Kenock?" She remained staring out the window, but Mishah saw that she was watching her in the reflection as well.

Mishah dropped the healing bag off her shoulder and set it on the bed. "In spite of his youth, he is an adult. He should be allowed to make his own choices."

Amolikah turned from the window. "Even if they are the wrong choices? You saw what that could mean. Kleg'l almost paid for Kenock's wrong decision with his life."

"He's learned his lesson. It won't happen again."

"Perhaps not that exactly. He may be an adult, Mishah, but your brother still harbors the wild notions of youth."

"Is that so wrong?"

"He has responsibilities. He's next in line to take over the farm—now that Lamech is not here."

Lamech. He was never far way from her thoughts. Tears stung her eyes.

"I'm sorry."

"He might take some wrong turns, but haven't we all? The Creator will guide him back onto the correct path. Don't you believe that?" Here she was instructing Amolikah in faith when it was she who so often needed encouragement in that area. Amolikah and Lamech were the two strongest people she knew.

"It is our duty to keep him from that wrong path, dear."

"How do you purpose to do that? Lamech tried and only succeeded in alienating himself from Kenock."

Amolikah started to speak, then shook her head. "I don't know. Keeping an eye on the company he keeps might be one way."

So, that was what was bothering her. "You mean that young man with Master Rhone."

"I mean both of them."

"You still do not approve of them accompanying us?"

"No."

"Why?"

"They're worldly men. Especially that young one. He's a product of Nod City and all that it represents. What would Lamech have said had he been here?"

"Had Lamech been here, I wouldn't have felt the need to ask strangers to help us." Her anger shocked her and she struggled against the tears, but they burst forth in great, gasping sobs.

Amolikah put her arms around her. "It's all right, dear. Cry it all out." She stroked Mishah's head and held her tight. "Cry it all out, my darling."

18

A Rebel Spirit

After dinner, Rhone helped Dorn-ek light a fire in the courtyard in front of the inn. The fire ring of soot-blackened stone was circled by a second ring of gray granite benches, polished smooth by generations of travelers.

They'd hauled Kleg'l's bed outside and propped the good-man's head up so that he could join in as much as he was able. Eleen brought out a bowl of large, chewy goreberries and a bundle of skewers made of willow branches. The fire burned hot and high at first, casting wild, dancing shadows across the courtyard and stone walls. After a while, it dwindled to a bed of hot embers, perfect for roasting goreberries. They all sat around turning their skewers above the embers and singing choruses of "Mist in the Valley" and "The Ladies at Ka-a-kak's Well."

Rhone enjoyed listening to the songs, the fire, and the company. The big gate was closed and barred, and the stone wall stood tall enough to keep most creatures outside. It was one of those rare moments when he could relax and let his guard down—a little.

Between the songs, Dorn-ek entranced them with tales of old. Rhone imagined him honing his skill entertaining visitors from one generation to the next, as he was doing here with Mistress Amolikah and her granddaughter and grandson. Bar'ack leaned forward with absorbed attention, listening to the tales as if they were stories out of the pages of *Frobin's World Travels*.

The healer kept one eye on Kleg'l and the other on the fire, singing with the rest of them, but Rhone sensed it was an effort for her. And he could understand why. It was in the middle of the nostalgic "Memories of Paradise" that she rose quietly from her place, bent over Kleg'l and spoke softly to him, then wandered back to the inn.

She climbed the steps of the porch and paused a moment in a shaft of light before the open doorway. She appeared to be debating something, and, coming to a decision, turned from the doorway and strolled along the porch, around the corner, and out of sight. Rhone waited for her to return. When she didn't, he became curious.

Dorn-ek was now leading a stirring rendition of the "Serpent Song," waving his arms and bellowing, "The serpent's head will rise no more, rise no more, rise no more . . ." They were all clapping their hands and singing along, and Rhone saw his opportunity to slip away unnoticed.

He spied her in the shadows near the stable wall, standing alone, staring up at the starry sky. He hesitated, lingering in the shadows of the inn himself, and almost turned back. The healer obviously wished solitude, but something seemed to be urging him on. Stepping away from the corner of the inn, he strode across the dark yard.

He was almost to her when she became aware of him and turned with a start. "Oh. Master Rhone. It's you."

"I didn't mean to startle you. I ..." He'd almost claimed to have found her by accident, but he abhorred lying. "I noticed you were gone and came to see if you were all right."

"Your concern is appreciated, but I'm well." She looked up at the stars and drew in a weary breath. "It's been a long day and I'm tired. When I get tired, nostalgia makes me sad."

"The songs brought back memories?"

She nodded. "I used to sing them as a child with my parents, sitting around fires like that one. The words of that last tune touched me."

"Memories of Paradise"? He'd heard the song before but had never paid the words much attention. It was the tune he enjoyed.

"It normally wouldn't have bothered me."

"What does it mean?"

She gave him a wide look. "You don't know?"

Her surprise irritated him. How could he know every culture's fables? He'd been raised far from the Lee-landers' myths and traditions. "I know only that it has something to do with a very old legend."

"Yes, very old. It's a song about the beginning-time, when mankind was driven out of the Cradleland. You know something of the story, don't you?"

"Everyone has heard versions of it, but with so many different tellings, who could ever be certain of the truth?"

She looked back at the sky, seeing what? "It was a time of great sadness. A time of deception. Of loss."

"So the song says."

"But not without hope."

"Ah, yes. Hope. A necessary element in all fables. The song speaks of that as well."

Her eyes narrowed. "You don't believe it, do you?"

"I believe what I can see and touch, healer. Fables may be built on the foundations of truth, but over the years those foundations become lost beneath the brambles of retelling."

"If Lamech were here he'd have a ready answer for your claim, Master Rhone."

"What would your husband tell me?"

She thought a moment, and then her view went back to the stars. "He'd say the story of hope is written in the stars, Master Rhone. It's there for anyone to see, if he has a willing eye and an ear to hear the truth." She smiled at him. "And now I'm sounding exactly like my husband."

He stared at the points of light. Stars were merely tools. He knew their names, of course—Ha-ga-t's water ladle, the three bright stars of Oar's sword belt, and a hundred others—and their paths through the night sky. Stars were useful for telling time and seasons and directions. Some people with overwrought imaginations even saw shapes in them, but that was the occupation for dreamers. "Show me the hope you speak of."

Her head tilted back. "My husband knows it better than I, but I will try. In the heavens are twelve signs, and each tells part of the story of man's coming redemption and the end of all evil. It begins there, with the sign of Beth-ulah." She pointed. "Beth-ulah is the sign of the virgin. She holds a branch in one hand and an ear of corn in the other."

He peered at the cluster of stars. Where was there even a hint of a woman among them, let alone any of the rest of what the healer was telling him?

"The brightest star in the sign of Beth-ulah is called Ts-mech," she continued. "It's located in the ear of corn in the virgin's left hand. See? Ts-mech means 'the branch' and speaks of a Child who will someday be born of the virgin and will reclaim fallen mankind. He is shown in the constellation called Comah. It's all part of the sign of Beth-ulah. See?" She pointed again and drew an imaginary line with her finger.

"A child being born to a virgin?" He gave a short laugh. "Now we *are* speaking of fables. I see nothing up there but stars. How can you see pictures in them?" Why did he play along with this lesson when the teacher was so lovely, so near, and they were alone? He eased closer and lowered his head next to hers, pretending an interest in the sky. "Show me how to see this sign."

She looked at him and took a single step to open the distance between them. "Master Rhone, if you only think of it as a child's mystery drawing that emerges from connecting the dots, you will never see it. The dots of heaven can be connected in a hundred different ways to make any picture one wishes. The names of the signs—Beth-ulah, Mo'zanaim, Akrab, and the others—they are given as story points only. The signs describe a certain group of stars. The names of those stars inside that group further elaborate on the story."

"A clever fiction constructed by men with too much time on their hands."

"This is not of man's contrivance. The pattern has been given by the Creator as a prophecy. But it takes instruction to read it."

"Given to whom? Why is this the first I've heard of this prophecy in the stars?"

"The story was told by the Creator to my husband's grandfather. He wrote it in a book. My husband, Lamech, helped with the writing when he was a child."

"So, that explains your husband's zeal. He inherited it from an equally zealous grandparent. You say the Creator actually was here on earth, and he spoke to a man?"

"Yes, Enoch walked with the Creator and spoke to him."

She was emphatic, and seemed to truly believe it. Were all Leelanders so gullible? No wonder they were such a stiff-necked people. "The Lodath says the Oracle will soon return to earth and walk with mankind and instruct him as well. How is your belief so different from that which the Lodath teaches?"

"One is of truth. The other is a lie."

Her confidence bordered on smugness. How could anyone put a

crack in such resolute conviction? "And how do you determine which is which?" He had her there.

But she merely smiled as if he were naive. "The Creator sends his Spirit to those who believe. It's his Spirit who separates truth from lie."

"You have an answer for every challenge, don't you?"

"No. I wish I did, but I don't. My husband, on the other hand …"

"Mi? Mi, are you back here?" Kenock's voice came from around the corner of the inn, and a moment later so did he.

"I'm over here."

Rhone stepped back from her as Kenock homed in on her voice.

"Oh, there you are." Then he saw Rhone. He gave him a look of surprise before glancing back to the healer. "Kleg'l said you were going up to your room."

"I was. But I changed my mind and came back here to be away from the crowd and to look at the stars."

"Your sister was just showing me the signs in the heavens and the stories they represent. I'm sure she told it as well as Lamech could have, and she's given me something to think about."

In the darkness, a quick grin flashed across Kenock's face. "And what do you think?"

"I think your sister believes it, and that you're not sure."

Kenock's eyes hardened ever so slightly.

Rhone bent slightly at the waist. "I'll see you later. Evening peace."

❦

Mishah watched the tall man stroll around the inn and out of sight. She looked back at Kenock. Rhone was more perceptive than she'd given him credit for.

"I'm not sure I like that man very much." Kenock crossed his arms and scowled at the darkness.

"I think Master Rhone can be reached."

"Reached? Oh please, Mi. Not you now. You're not Lamech. Don't even try."

But I did tell it every bit as well as Lamech could have! The revelation startled her.

"Besides, you should know better than to allow yourself to be alone with a man who's not your husband."

That snapped her head around. "*I* should know better?"

His lips tightened and hitched to one side. "All right, so I haven't exactly been a paragon of wisdom myself lately. Still, there is the matter of propriety."

"Give it up, Kenock. We're all traveling together, and we're hundreds of leagues from any place that would hold propriety of any importance. And besides, Master Rhone was just concerned about my safety. That *is* why we asked him along."

"And I'll say it again, Mi. I can see to your safety as well as that man."

She stiffened. It was useless to argue with him. "What is it you wanted?"

"Grandmother asked me to find you."

"Why?"

"I don't know."

Mishah started for the inn.

"She's up in your room."

Mishah looked back at him. "Are you going to remain out here?"

He hesitated, then kicked at the dark turf and came along. She wondered at the strife between them, and even between Amolikah and herself. It had never been like this before. This pilgrimage was taking its toll on all of them. Even Kleg'l had butted heads with Kenock. How could something so disastrous be of the Creator's will? It made no sense ... but she'd promised Lamech, and it was a promise she intended to keep in spite of all her misgivings.

❧

The fire burned bright, washing the stars from the black sky and ruining his night vision. Da-gore turned his face from the flames and stepped beyond the ring of firelight. Being incapacitated in any way grated against his warrior's training. He may have grown soft in flesh and muscle in the years spent serving as captain of the Guard, but he hadn't lost the warrior's edge—that suspicious nature that kept him always on the alert.

The Earth-Born didn't like him. That was unimportant. Leadership wasn't a popularity contest. So long as they obeyed him, Da-gore was satisfied—and so far they had, in spite of the undercurrent of disdain he'd sensed. It wasn't him personally. It was his humanness. They, being half human and half god, were a new and superior race. Or so they believed. Da-gore compressed his mouth into a tight line.

He stole a glance, risking more damage to his night vision. There they sat, giants spaced around the fire, unconcerned. Perhaps their eyes didn't dim to the flames as human eyes did? One thing was certain, their appetite for meat matched their size. Between the six of them they'd consumed a full-grown hart. Herc had caught the fleeing animal on the run, snapping its neck as if it had been a hen. Their strength and their speed were truly awesome, but their self-discipline was notably lacking. Children, that's what they were. He was in command of children! But what sort of children? If the Oracle's emissary had not been present, could he have controlled them? This wasn't the first time he'd wondered, and that nagging doubt was a growing chink in his self-confidence—a breach he had to close.

His lieutenant, standard bearer, dispatch rider, healer, and animal handlers sat apart from the giants. Most, like himself, kept their backs to the blinding blaze.

Pose was reaching for another log.

"No more." Da-gore strode back into camp and stopped across the flames from the giant. "Let the fire burn down."

"I like a big fire," Pose rumbled.

"You've had your big fire." Compared to these god-men, Da-gore was puny in their sight, but he stood his ground. Authority flows from determination and steadfastness. Emissary Ulex watched from nearby.

Rebellion grew in Pose's eyes while on the faces of the other five giants smiles blossomed. They'd been looking for a chance to test him. The giant glanced at the log in his hand and then, with a defiant grin, tossed it into the fire.

Da-gore reached for a nearby bucket of water and doused the fire.

Pose leaped to his feet, his shoulders snapping off the lower branch of the tree above him as if it had been a dry twig.

"You are under my command," Da-gore said evenly. "Disobedience will not be tolerated."

A wicked grin contorted Pose's face. His dark eyes narrowed and a growl rattled deep in his throat as he stepped over the sizzling wood where flames fought back to life.

Across the way, Emissary Ulex rose to his feet as well.

Da-gore anticipated this. His proj-lance was within reach and he snapped it up, leveling it at the giant's broad chest.

Pose came to a halt, staring down at the weapon, his huge fingers flexing at his side. Pose could snap his neck as easily as Herc had the hart's, and he plainly wanted to. Hate smoldered in the giant's eyes.

"Captain Da-gore." Ulex advanced a step. "I will handle this."

"You stay out of this." Da-gore's eyes locked onto the giant's. Pose wasn't about to take orders from anyone, be it this emissary overseer or his commanding officer. Discipline must be swift and certain if the others were ever going to accept his authority.

Da-gore saw it coming. Pose lunged, fingers reaching. The captain of the Guard pulled the trigger. The proj-lance flashed, but Emissary Ulex materialized between them and snatched the proj in mid-flight. At the same instant Pose, already in motion, slammed into Ulex and was flung backward onto the fire as if Ulex had grown the roots of mountains and a skin of granite. With a roar of pain Pose rolled off the hot coals, beating them from his skin.

Ulex stood with the proj in his hand spitting flames. What nature of beings were these creatures from the stars? Creatures who moved swifter than the eye could see? Beings able to snatch up a proj in flight? He'd stopped breathing and now drew in a long breath and slowly lowered the weapon.

Pose sat on the ground, brushing embers from his arm. He rotated his shoulder, winced, and glared up at him.

Ulex tossed it far into the forest. A flash and an explosion shook the air and for an instant the trees stood in sharp contrast. Then all was darkness again. "I said I would handle it."

The smell of burning hair wafted from the giant.

"You should have handled it *before* he chose to disobey my orders, Emissary Ulex." He couldn't afford to show fear. His view narrowed toward the giants. "Any further insubordination will be grounds for immediate execution." His view shot back to the emissary. "And I will expect no further interference from you."

"I cannot allow you to harm them, Captain Da-gore."

He scowled. "If you can't instruct them to obey my orders, you will remove them immediately." His heart was pounding, his forehead cold as ice with fear. Yet, he held Ulex in an unwavering stare. "Do you understand me?"

The emissary's face remained expressionless, his wide eyes unblinking. What was he thinking? Sometimes these creatures were so human-like, and then at other times … . Their true nature was completely alien to Da-gore's understanding. "You will have no further problems, Captain Da-gore."

Ulex flicked a hand and Pose rose to his feet and slunk into the shadows. A disaster had been averted, yet Da-gore couldn't stop thinking the reins of control had slipped in his tight grasp, and he was dangerously at the end of them. The humans with him mumbled softly in the background while the other giants gathered together by the emissary.

He took a deep, quieting breath, his heartbeat slowed, and a chill sent a shiver through him. He'd known there would be trouble. The Earth-Born were not going to easily be controlled by humans. He'd managed to prevent this disaster, but in the future ... ? He'd deal with it when the time came.

The company decamped and moved out early the next morning. Captain Da-gore took the lead as usual with his lieutenant and the Lodath's standard bearer on either side of him. The company seemed more fractured than ever, the humans and the Earth-Born distancing themselves by a wider margin today than they had the day before. The giants lagged at the rear near the pack animals while Emissary Ulex kept apart from both humans and Earth-Born.

Bringing these giants along made no sense at all. Why had the Oracle ordered it? Da-gore and his soldiers were fully capable of running down four travelers. The tremendous power of the Earth-Born was unnecessary for such a simple assignment. He recalled the urgency in the Oracle's voice. Was that why these half-gods were sent along? To ensure he carried out the executions? Or was this a test of some kind? What plans did the Oracle and the Lodath have for these creatures? Could a future army be made up of such half-breeds? If so, it would truly be an invincible force!

Da-gore shook his head. There could be no army where its soldiers couldn't be controlled. If indeed the Earth-Born were being bred to fill the ranks of King Irad's army, or the Oracle's, in short time there would be no place in that army for humans. Humans would soon become slaves to these creatures! They must, if this cross-kind breeding was permitted to continue!

"Far Port ahead, Captain," Lieutenant Err-nor said when they crested a rise in the road.

"Not much of a village to speak of, is it?"

"Easily turned inside out. We'll have no trouble finding the fugitives."

"No, no trouble at all." Da-gore looked back at the six giants. At least he sincerely hoped not.

19

First Blood

Activity along the wharf abruptly stopped when they marched into Far Port. Feet seized in midstride, and the boardwalks seemed momentarily lined with statues. A few folks managed to keep about their business, but their eyes remained fixed upon the six giants.

"The big ones make a big impression," Err-nor said.

Da-gore cast about the village, spying a group of men perched upon some crates at the end of the wharf. "Let's see how big. Herc, come with me." Da-gore and Err-nor strode out onto the wharf, with the giant lumbering behind them.

Da-gore appraised the men in a glance. Stevedores. Strong in the shoulders and probably weak in the head. Their suddenly circumspect glances shifted from the giant to him as they advanced. "I'm looking for the captain of the river-runner *Osar Messenger*."

"That ... that would be Captain Berg." One of them hooked a thumb over his shoulders at the squat freighter, his view jolting nervously between the giant and Da-gore. "That's his boat over there."

The dock trembled beneath Herc's weight as they continued past the men. At the *Osar Messenger*, Da-gore and his lieutenant tramped across the gangplank. The boat tilted steeply when Herc's great, leather-shod feet boomed onto the deck planks.

A voice from inside the cabin shouted, "Here, now! What's going on with my boat?" and the next instant, a stout man with a bearded face and a pipe clenched in its mouth appeared in the doorway. He froze there, his eyes widening and the pipe drooping.

Da-gore recalled the man from interviewing him in Nod City, when the Lodath had first given him orders to follow the Leelanders.

Berg recovered his pipe before it slipped from his lips. "Captain Da-gore, is it not?"

So, he remembered him as well. A second man lingered in the shadows behind the captain. Da-gore nodded and stabbed his finger at the deck in front of him and waited.

With a hard swallow, Captain Berg left the cabin and came out onto the deck, his view welded to the giant with his arms folded across his expansive chest. Berg forced his eyes off the giant. "A long way from home, aren't you? What is it I can do for you, Captain?"

"The other man too."

Berg glanced back at the doorway. "Petra."

Petra emerged hesitantly and stood by his captain; a slight man with thin black hair slicked to one side. His face was gaunt and weathered, and his wide mouth twitched at the corner.

"Is there anyone else aboard?"

"Rest of my crew is in town."

"You transported a group of fugitives up from Nod City a few days ago."

"I've hauled no fugitives. I carried a family, but you already know that."

"Where are they now?"

"I don't know. I just got paid to haul them, not babysit them." An undercurrent of rebellion edged his voice.

Here was a man who didn't like to be ordered about. Da-gore took delight in squelching rebellion. "Herc. Encourage him."

The giant was swift for his size. He grabbed Berg about the chest in two immense fists, slammed the captain back against the wall of the cabin, and held him there, a span and a half off the deck.

"I don't have any patience for games, Captain. The fugitives. Where are they?"

"I—I don't know. They left my boat with all their luggage. I haven't seen them since." The captain's face blanched.

He was holding back. A stubborn, proud man, this one, and Da-gore would break him. "Herc."

The giant's thumbs contracted, pressing into Berg's chest, slowly squeezing the breath from his lungs. "I ... I ..." His voice went weak, disappearing deep in his throat as his eyes bulged, and a scarlet pall began to creep up his neck. His mouth gulped like a fish out of water. "I think they took a room in town. All ... all I know."

Petra's face was ashen. "They took a room at Mistress Leahia's boardinghouse," he blurted. "I heard there was some trouble there the other evening. Please, let the captain go. That's all we know. Honest. I'd tell you if there was more. Those people didn't mean nothing to us."

That had been almost too easy. He'd gotten as much information as he needed here—enough to put him on the trail at least. Perhaps these giants were good for something after all. He considered continuing the punishment, but he had no real interest in it. Berg would have confessed himself, had he an opportunity to draw breath. "Let him down, Herc."

The giant's mouth contorted into a broad, ugly smile and his huge thumbs pressed harder.

Berg squirmed on the edge of losing consciousness.

"Herc!"

The Earth-Born glared at Da-gore with the snarl of a child being deprived of a favorite toy.

Captain Berg's face crimsoned, his eyes popping like egg whites about to burst. Da-gore drew his sword. "Insubordination will not be—"

Throwing his head back with a growl of rage, Herc flung Berg far out into the choppy river. The captain came up for a gulp of air, bobbed once, twice, and then was swept along by the current and disappeared. Fury burned in the giant's eyes. He turned on Da-gore, and Da-gore readied his sword. Out of the corner of his eye, he saw Ulex materializing on the pier. Some force, some unseen hand seemed to reach out and restrain the furious creature. Seized in a frenzy, Herc wheeled around and snatched up a beam of ironwood from the cargo hoist and swung it at the cabin, splintering the corner.

Petra, up until now frozen with fear, leaped over the side of the boat and fought the current for the shore. Herc demolished the cabin and then began heaving barrels of distilled sap into the river.

Da-gore and his lieutenant crossed over the gangplank. Da-gore paused long enough to give Emissary Ulex a narrow glare of disgust before marching back to his company.

With the *Osar Messenger* still rocking side to side, timbers groaning and splintering, Da-gore got his company moving, leaving Herc to his emissary father. He wanted nothing more to do with any of these volatile creatures.

His first inquiry as to the location of Mistress Leahia's boardinghouse brought an instant response from a man whose face had gone suddenly gray at being spotted and called over by the captain of the Guard.

His men marched to the end of the road and halted outside the low, stone wall. A woman came out onto the porch. Da-gore and his lieutenant met her on the flower-bordered pathway.

"Are you Mistress Leahia?"

"I am." Her green eyes darted to the troops gathered just beyond her aspedaza plants. "What is this about?"

"You are harboring fugitives."

Her pudgy cheeks flamed. "I have no fugitives here. Just two men, and one of them injured."

Da-gore's hand dipped into a pocket of his green cloak and drew out a paper. "The fugitives names are Mishah, Kenock, Amolikah, and Kleg'l."

Her bright cheeks paled. "Fugitives? But they—" she looked back at the soldiers, but Da-gore knew it was only the Earth-Borns that held her eyes. "There is no one else here."

"You admit they were here?"

"I take in many boarders. Far Point is the gateway to the Wild Lands."

Her evasiveness irritated him. "Where did they go?"

Mistress Leahia's eyes shifted and her tongue flicked across her glossy lips. "I don't know."

"Why are you protecting these fugitives?"

"They aren't fugitives. They're just travelers."

Da-gore signaled Lieutenant Err-nor into the house, holding the Earth-Born outside. He came out with the two men.

"These are the only ones," he reported.

"Your names?"

"Captain Jakl."

"O'tev," said the man with an arm in a sling.

"You own one of those boats, Captain Jakl?"

"I captained a sky-barge."

Da-gore glanced around the rolling hills hemmed in by dense forests.

"It wrecked in the Wild Lands. Mansnatchers. My man, O'tev, broke his arm in the crash."

"What do you know of these fugitives?"

"I didn't know they were fleeing the law. They were here when we arrived. One's a healer." Jakl inclined his head at the other man. "She set O'tev's arm."

"And where are they now?"

"They left. Three days ago."

"Where are they going?"

"They didn't confide in me. All I know is they hired a wagon. One of them, the good-man, was injured."

Da-gore looked back at Mistress Leahia. "You know where they went, don't you?"

"N—no, they never said."

"She is lying," Plut rumbled. "I see it in her."

"Where have they gone?" His patience was thinning, but of a more immediate concern was the ripple of expectation coming from the Earth-Born. These were men—no, children—of action. Standing around waiting for him to draw the information out of her was not their method.

Mistress Leahia clamped her mouth and scowled.

Captain Jakl shot her a tense look, his voice strained. "Tell the captain what he wants to know, Mistress Leahia."

"He gives worthy advice. What reason could you have for protecting them?"

"They are very old friends. They're not criminals to be arrested by the Lodath's green cloaks and ... and ..." She stared at the giants.

"That's your final word?"

"Mistress Leahia!" Captain Jakl implored.

"I'm going to send for the Gate Warden!" She put on a stubborn face and attempted to sound brave, but her voice wavered, and her eyes had begun to glisten. She stepped around Da-gore.

"Hold her."

Lieutenant Err-nor took her by the arms. She struggled hopelessly against the green cloak as the ripple of excitement amongst the Earth Born swelled.

"Burn the building," he ordered.

What little bravery remained collapsed in a look of horror and a flood of tears. "No, please! Not my house."

"You've reconsidered?" He knew she would.

She uttered a word through her tears he didn't quite catch.

"Chevel-ee." She repeated, fighting for control, her wide, wet eyes staring at the rambling house. "Chevel-ee. That's where they've gone to."

"What business takes them there?" He tried to place where he'd heard the name before, but like Hepha's Singing Skies a few days earlier, this, too, was one of those vague recollections. How was he expected to remember every geographical location in the Known World? It irked him, just the same.

Her sobs lessened. "They make a pilgrimage to the Mother—"

The Earth-Born roared as if with sudden pain, throwing hands to their heads. Something was happening, something terrifying, yet completely incomprehensible to human understanding. Da-gore looked toward the sky and then the forest. Nothing! What was it these god-men felt that he did not? Err-nor glanced at him with blank confusion.

Pose and Atala stuffed fingers into their ears and shook their heads, stomping their feet until the ground shook. Per, Plut, and Hepha staggered like drunkards, holding their heads as if they might explode.

From down the road, a roar cracked the air. Whatever was happening here, Herc felt it on the pier too.

All at once, the god-men went absolutely still. Suddenly Plut gave a warrior's cry and heaved back his spear, as long as a weaver's beam and as thick around as Da-gore's forearm. He hurled it, impaling Captain Jakl to the porch upright.

The sight of first blood snapped something inside their brains and the rampage began. Mistress Leahia's house went up in flames, the woman flung alive into the inferno. O'tev fell beneath Plut's slashing sword, as broad as a harvester's blade. Da-gore shouted for order, but his words fell on deaf ears. With the homestead engulfed in roaring flames, they turned their rage toward the town of Far Port.

He had lost control. Completely and utterly, it had crumbled. His thought now was to save his own men. He hurried them out of the path of destruction as voracious flames chewed through the wooden buildings, past the giants mangling and killing and setting fire to piles of cargo waiting on the pier. Herc, having sunk the *Osar Messenger*, joined in on the destruction. Following the citizens fleeing Far Port, they escaped into the forest to a place of safety where they watched the town disappear in flames.

By evening, with the sky thick with smoke and the sun a pool of molten copper lowering into the treetops, the fury of the Earth-Born finally burned itself out. Like drunks after a binge, they staggered out of town and onto the road toward Chevel-ee. Darkness was upon the land when they fell to the ground and appeared as dead.

Warily, Da-gore approached the sleeping giants and ordered his men to make camp. Emissary Ulex prepared a fire for them. Da-gore stood before it, watching the being a moment.

"What happened back there?"

Ulex considered him with big, oval eyes. Did these beings ever blink? As if in answer, Ulex blinked.

"The Oracle ordered it."

"The Oracle? You were in communication with the Oracle?"

"We are always in communication with the Oracle. We are his eyes and his ears. It is through us, and many others like us, unseen to your eyes, that he shapes events and controls his servants."

"Who are his servants?"

"We are—you, all who have accepted his token, and countless others who haven't yet—are his servants."

Da-gore's hand went to the pendent beneath his tunic. For a moment it seemed to burn hot against his skin.

Ulex's large eyes peered curiously at him. "Yes. You feel his presence. You neither hear the Oracle's voice nor see his form, but you feel him."

I'll keep my affairs from his prying eyes, Da-gore vowed.

Ulex showed a rare smile. "I know you believe your thoughts are hidden from us, Captain Da-gore." He gave a small, acquiescent nod. "They are. But we need not enter your mind to know what you think. Humans wear their thoughts like clothing outside their bodies. We have but to observe to know what is hidden in your mind. You think you are still your own man? You are not. It is only a matter of a word whispered in your ear. If you are one of the Oracle's servants, you will obey. You must obey."

Da-gore stiffened.

"Believe as you will, Captain Da-gore."

Da-gore rebelled at this notion of being controlled by some unseen being. It was the last thing he wanted to hear right now. He brought the conversation back around to where it needed to be. "What happened to them back there?"

"The Oracle was angry."

Anger was all too human a trait, and it reassured Da-gore to know that the gods suffered from it as well. "What brought it on so suddenly?" He thought back, trying to recall what might have triggered it.

"The Oracle has been watching the woman, Mishah, and her family. These are set-apart humans. There are other beings, like us, who have taken a keen interest in them. The Oracle wants to know why."

"Others?" Da-gore didn't understand.

"You're a soldier and you fight wars against your own kind. We are soldiers as well, and our battles are against our kind. This world that you see," his arm swept in an arc, "is only a shadow of what exists on the other side. You have no knowledge of the battles won and lost all around you."

"Right here, right now?" Da-gore probed the deep shadows and cocked an ear, hearing nothing.

"Not at the moment, but yes, there are other battles."

"Against other beings like yourself?"

He nodded.

"And these people we pursue, they have companions like yourselves?"

Again, he nodded. Da-gore got a glimmer of the scope of the Oracle's power and reach.

"The travelers are not aware that the enemy has assigned his own emissaries—the shackled-ones—to guard them."

"Shackled-ones?"

"Beings like us, still enslaved, who did not break the Tyrant's shackles, as we did long ago. Because of the shackled-ones, we cannot touch these sojourners."

Can't touch them? He'd seen the power Ulex had over the Earth-Born. How could humans be untouchable?

"That is why the Oracle needs you. You are not forbidden."

"What affected them earlier?"

"The woman speaking their destination. Suddenly it was clear about the one called Mishah."

"Why is she so important? The Lee-landers seem harmless enough. Or does the Oracle fear the words they speak?"

"It is much more than that. It is not the woman herself, but the child she carries."

"What is the importance of this child?"

"He will be a servant of the Tyrant of Old. His very existence endangers the Oracle's realm."

"A mere human child worries the Oracle?"

"I cannot say more than this."

"Cannot or will not?"

"It is all the same."

Da-gore stood, scowling. Information was being kept from him. He was in command, yet it mattered not to this creature. In command? That was a joke. He was a pawn. If he were smart, he'd take his men out of there at once. The Oracle didn't need him, not with beings like the Earth-Born at his disposal.

Da-gore made a wry smile. But he wouldn't leave. He was a soldier, and a soldier followed orders—up to a point.

20

A Shy Spider

"Tonight we will sleep in Chevel-ee," Amolikah said without prelude the next morning, once they left the Wandering Path Inn.

Tonight. This plagued journey is almost over! Tonight Chevel-ee, tomorrow the Mother, and the next day it's home for us. Mishah put a hand to her belly as a tiny knee—or was it an elbow?—nudged her. *And none too soon.* But a home without Lamech would not be the same.

Too many delays had already hindered the pilgrimage. She was further along than she wanted to be at this point. She'd hoped to be home by now, but the 'gia harvest had come just as she'd become pregnant, and Lamech had to tarry for that. And then there was the morning misery, when the smell—even the thought—of some foods made her ill. She'd wisely delayed until that stage had passed, but now she was almost eight months along, showing, and unable to move as gracefully or efficiently as she once had.

And what of Rhone's plans? He'd remained tight-lipped, always guarding his thoughts, but not as careful with his eyes. They revealed a subtle interest in her. Sometimes she'd catch his gaze when he didn't realize she was watching. Her feelings toward him wavered constantly between appreciation, reliance, and concern.

"Once we reach Chevel-ee will you go on ahead, Master Rhone?" She looked up at the tall man striding silently at her side. She'd begun the day riding alongside Kenock, but the hard seat and the cart's stiff springs, jostling her for hours upon hours, had gotten too much, and she'd abandoned the seat. The exercise felt good—at least for a little while.

"Bar'ack and I will continue into the northern Wild Lands."

"Oh." Her disappointment both surprised and frightened her.

"But perhaps not right away." He grinned. Had he read her mind? "I'm curious about this creation legend—the Cradleland—spoken of in song and story."

"Like last night around the fire?"

"Yes."

"You expect to learn about it in Chevel-ee?"

"Isn't the woman you go to see, the one you call the Mother, from the beginning-time, from this Cradleland?"

"She is."

"Then she can tell me of the place."

"Would you believe her if she did?" Mishah pressed a palm into her aching back.

He shook his head, his brow glistened from the heat and humidity, his dark brown mane catching the sunlight as it moved across his shoulders. "It depends on what's in her eyes as well as her words." He levered the proj-lance over his shoulder, walking with an easy pace. She sensed he held back to keep in step with her. His long strides could have easily put him far out ahead of the party and in Chevel-ee hours before them.

"You can read people that way?"

"Most often."

"Do you read their minds as well?"

His brown eyes shifted down at her, amused at the question. "To interpret an expression is one thing, Mistress Mishah. That's simply a matter of training. What's in the mind is something else entirely. Often the eyes reveal more truth than the lips.

> "'Deception conceals in a blackened heart,
> But the windows of the soul are unshuttered to the wise.'"

Bar'ack snapped from his reverie and stared at Rhone. "That's a verse from *An Elegy to a Fallen Warrior*. You know it well enough to quote from it, Master Rhone?"

He shrugged. "I must have read it at some time." His lips twitched with a quick smile.

Not only was he confident enough to face a crowd of belligerent men single-handedly, he was well-read too. Could he and Lamech have been friends, given a chance? Rhone appeared an educated man, and that would have appealed to Lamech. What other mysteries did the quiet man harbor?

Suddenly Rhone stopped and sniffed the air. The wagon rolled on a little way before Kenock realized he'd left them behind. The big man stared at the forest. His eyes narrowed and he sniffed again like a dog on a scent trail. He left he road and entered the forest.

"Where are you going?" Bar'ack dove after Rhone, in hot pursuit.

Mishah stood there, dumbfounded. "What is it?" she called.

Rhone shouted back, "Javian."

"Javian?" Excitedly, Bar'ack began sniffing the air, batting away branches to keep up. "I don't smell it. What does it smell like?"

Kenock jumped down from the cart. "I'm going too."

"Master Rhone!" Mishah called. She glanced at Amolikah and Kleg'l still in the cart.

Amolikah looked surprised and annoyed.

Mishah shook her head, caught up her dress, and went after them. "Master Rhone, we're paying you to see us to Chevel-ee, not to take a field trip."

Kenock came back for her and took her by the elbow, helping her along.

"Why are we delaying here?" she asked. "To look at spiders?" She had never seen a javian spider, only heard of them. The undergrowth was thick and crawling with insects, some the size of small dogs. She lifted her dress higher to keep it from snagging.

"I expect we will learn that in a moment," Kenock said.

She wished she could move faster, but she was doing her best. An amber worm as big around as her arm scurried past on what seemed to be a thousand tiny legs, shuttling in perfect synchronization. "Oh!"

Kenock kicked it aside. "Harmless."

"I know." She began breathing again. "But I can do without surprises like that, harmless or not."

Up ahead the forest thinned and Rhone and Bar'ack had stopped where it opened up onto a clearing. A bitter smell tinged the air. By the time she and Kenock reached them, Rhone was in the middle of explaining something to the younger man.

" ... make their own clearing when none is available."

"How do they do that, Master Rhone? How does a spider fell a tree?"

The clearing was strewn with deadfalls, most appearing to have been downed only a few days earlier. She peered at them a moment, seeing nothing else.

"Do you smell it now?" Master Rhone asked.

Bar'ack nodded. "How can I help but smell it?"

The powerful odor vaguely reminded Mishah of the gum resin from the roots of some varieties of parsley plants used to treat stomach gas and arrest spasms. She had some in her healer's bag. "It smells like serpent's dung root."

Rhone nodded. "A good description."

"Why are we delaying here, Master Rhone?" She was breathless, and she didn't much enjoy crashing through jungles. He pointed skyward. Mishah tilted her head back and caught sight of the great funnel of silk reaching skyward. "Oh my." She spied a dark shape far up the funnel near its narrow opening. "It's so large." The sight of the web awed her and cooled her anger. She stared at the shiny black orb, like a polished ebony bead, high up the web. "Is that the spider?"

"Yes. You might think a spider that spins such a funnel would be larger."

"It looks plenty large to me."

His face beamed at her wonderment.

"What you smell," Rhone glanced at Bar'ack, "what Mistress Mishah likens to serpent's dung root, is a strong poison the javians secrete around the base of trees. In a few days, it soaks into the roots, dissolving the tough fibers until they can no longer bear weight, and the tree falls. In this way, javians make their own clearings, the proper size for spinning their webs."

Kenock murmured quietly, "It's said a webmaster can speak the language of the javians."

"It's not exactly speech Master Kenock—at least not the way we think of speech." He stepped around the clearing, viewing the web from a different angle.

"Then what is it?"

He looked back at him. "Sounds, posturing, gesturing—it's a contest of thought where our minds touch and I try to persuade the spider to give me the silk."

Mishah remembered the stories of old, of a time when what Rhone was describing was a common ability amongst men and animals. "And if he does permit you, what do you give the spider in return?"

He showed surprise, then appreciation. "You know something of this, do you?"

"I've heard it spoken by the elders of our tribe."

Bar'ack strode around the perimeter of the clearing and came back with an excited gleam in his eyes. "Master Rhone, how do I begin?"

"What do the elders tell you, Mistress Mishah?"

His eyes boldly held hers. A rush of excitement tingled her skin, and she knew it should not be. She broke the contact and stared at the thick leaf litter amongst fallen branches green with moss and damp with the humidity of the forest. The bitter javian odor over-powered the tangy smells of trees and flowers and herbs. "The sto-ries of the beginning-time have been carefully preserved, Master Rhone. They are taught to children who then teach them to their children. In the beginning-time, man and animals communicated freely. If it were not so, the Mother would not have been so easily deceived by the serpent."

"The serpent from the song?"

"The very one." She glanced up, relieved that his stare had lost its sharp edge. "In the beginning-time, it was not uncommon for the Mother and the Father to communicate with animals, to learn their wisdom, to touch their minds as well. But after the Mother was deceived, and then the Father, and they were cast from the Cradleland, nature began to change. Men and animals lost the abil-ity to speak. Then slowly, some of the animals began to change, to become dangerous, even deadly."

His mouth took on a humorous slant. "So, am I a throwback because I can speak to the spiders?"

"Show me how it's done," Bar'ack implored.

She took in a long breath and felt her mouth lock into a deter-mined line. Why did he always take her so lightly? Did he think she didn't know what she was talking about? "You make it sound negative, Master Rhone. If you are a *throwback*, you are blessed. The gift must have been important for the Creator to have given it in the begin-ning." Maybe he and Lamech wouldn't have been friends, after all.

Bar'ack pointed. "The spider climbs higher up its web."

Rhone glanced at him, then back at her and withdrew a greasy lump wrapped in oilcloth from his pack. "Spider balm. They can't resist the smell of it. This is what I offer in exchange." He sliced a wedge from the lump with his webbing knife. "Just a small amount is all it takes."

Mishah came nearer for a better look. "It's such a trifling thing. Why do the spiders value it so?"

Bar'ack peered at the golden yellow slice in Rhone's hand. "How is it made?"

"A concoction of lotus gum and honey, mixed with puff-pollen. I will show you later." His eyes went back to hers and that look had returned to them. She shivered in spite of the heat. "To the javian it is delightful, like strong drink to some men, or the smoke from the dried leaves and flowers of the sawleaf rope plant."

"Show me how it's done!" Bar'ack's enthusiasm was consuming him.

He held her in his gaze a moment longer, then glanced at Bar'ack. "Watch." He stepped into the clearing and stood beneath the wide opening of the web's funnel, Bar'ack right on his heels. Rhone motioned him back, stooped, and opened his pack again. This time he took out of it two polished sticks, scored round about with concentric ridges. Mishah moved along the edge of the clearing to see better.

He tapped the sticks three times, slid them together with a rattling rasp. Kenock's footsteps crackled the leaves near her. "What's that suppose to do?" he whispered.

She shook her head and gave him a mystified look.

They waited.

Again, Rhone tapped the sticks and rasped them together. What response was he expecting? The only reply to his effort was the spider scurrying farther up his web until its legs found the upper rim of the narrow opening.

Bar'ack whispered, "What's wrong?"

Rhone scratched the back of his neck, rolled his shoulders, and worked the sticks together again. The rasping filled the clearing, but this time as it died away, the spider rubbed two of its legs together, repeating the sound.

Mishah glanced at Kenock. "So that's it."

Rhone glanced back at them. "Something is making the spider uneasy. Perhaps too many people. Retreat a few paces. You too, Bar'ack."

Hesitating, Bar'ack backed out of the clearing, joining them. Rhone attempted again. The spider bobbed up and down once. Rhone went to hands and knees and mimicked the movement. The spider crept tentatively down the side of his funnel and stopped again. It clicked its legs, this time rapidly, and in no pattern Mishah could discern.

But Rhone apparently had, for suddenly he was frowning.

She bent close to Kenock's ear, "Is there something I'm missing here?"

"How would I know? Bar'ack?"

"I've never seen it done before."

She folded her arms across her stomach, which was becoming a convenient ledge to rest them upon. Rhone attempted the sticks again. The spider pumped violently and the whole web swayed.

He held out the spider balm, but the creature refused to come any closer. Suddenly it shot back up to the top of its web and hunkered down, pulling its legs in until all that was left was a glistening black orb, streaked bright red in the sunlight.

Rhone stood, looking perplexed, and walked back to them, shaking his head.

Mishah unfolded her arms. "What happened?" She kept her voice low.

"Something has frightened it."

"Was it us?" Bar'ack shoved his fingers through his dark hair, hugged his arms, and strode to the clearing. He stared up a moment, came back, then stalked to the clearing again. "Were there too many of us? Is that what frightened it?"

"I don't think so. Something else. I sensed not just wariness, but panic, and a deep, terrible dread. Even now …," he looked up at the black orb clutching to the very edge of its web. "I sense desperation. If we stay here much longer, it may abandon the web."

Bar'ack came back, fingers clenching and unclenching. "Aren't you going to try again?"

"No."

"Why not?"

"You heard him." Kenock turned away from the clearing. "That creature is terrified of us. Let's get back to the wagon."

Mishah nodded. "Yes. We've been away from Grandmother and Kleg'l too long."

"But … but …"

"Another time, Bar'ack." Rhone carefully rewrapped the spider balm and returned it to his pack.

Mishah picked her way cautiously across the tangled ground, wary of things that crept and things that slithered, and creatures that clung to trees just waiting to drop unexpectedly into her hair. She now understood why this vast, mostly uncharted region beyond Far Port was called the Wild Lands. Rhone didn't speak, his face stern, his eyes focused, his mouth describing the tight line of a man deep in thought.

When they reached the road, Amolikah was standing alongside the cart, arms folded, face pinched. Kleg'l sat against the side boards, his long legs hanging off the tailgate. She stepped away from the cart and pointed at the sky. "We're losing the sun. What could possibly be so interesting about a spider's web? We'll never make Chevel-ee before nightfall now."

It hadn't felt like a long time, but then beneath the forest canopy, one tends to lose track of the sun. Still, they couldn't have been more than an hour. Her grandmother was just miffed at being left alone, that's all. In hindsight, it hadn't been a smart thing to do, detouring to examine a spiderweb. El-weel had warned of highwaymen along this road—a lane once well traveled and secure, but in these latter days, one that had fallen into disuse, and was haunted by rogues and turnlings.

Instinctively, she looked to the sky and rubbed her arms at sudden gooseflesh. The turnlings frightened her more than the rogues.

Rhone dropped his pack into the wagon. "We'll arrive after dark then."

Amolikah stiffened, her features sharpening.

He levered his proj-lance over his shoulder and started ahead with long strides. Amolikah glanced a question at Mishah.

"It was interesting, but I know you were worried." She climbed onto the seat beside Kenock.

Amolikah boarded the wagon box and leaned into a corner. "All I could see were mansnatchers and brigands swooping in on us."

"I know, Grandmother."

Bar'ack hopped up on the tailgate, helped Kleg'l arrange the pillows at his back, then slouched against the sideboard, dangling his left leg off the back. "Brigands and mansnatchers are the reason you've got Master Rhone and me along." He grinned.

Kenock cast over his shoulder, a scowl darkening his face as the wagon gave a small lurch and moved ahead.

21

A Giant Challenge

Da-gore studied the stone wall with the careful eye of a tactician. In any other circumstance, he'd have sent men back around the inn and approached it from two directions. But this road was little traveled, and the inn's gates stood wide open. The innkeeper was expecting no trouble. He moved the giants through the gate, keeping the three-points outside with their handlers.

Da-gore climbed the porch. The giants spread out, looking the place over, nodding to each other and grinning in a way Da-gore didn't like. He clanged the big bronze knocker three times.

"Welcome, welcome. Welcome to the Wandering Path Inn." The innkeeper smiled and drew his door wide for him, then froze, seeing the giants beyond his porch steps. His smile crashed and his face blanched—what little Da-gore could see of it behind the charcoal-pile beard.

"Your name."

"Ah, it's Dorn-ek."

"Dorn-ek. Four travelers, fugitives from the king and Lodath stayed at your inn."

His eyes shifted between the giants in his yard and Da-gore. "King Irad?"

"You know of another?"

"Nod City is a long way off. I've not seen any of his soldiers in many years." He seemed to be recovering from his shock. "We, ah, we have many travelers spend the night with us. Perhaps you can describe these pilgrims?" The innkeeper's meek smile wasn't very convincing. Why did everyone try to protect these people? Da-gore ground his teeth. "Two women, two men."

"Two women and two men? No. No, no, no. No party like that has passed by here. Err, what did these two women and two men do?"

He was lying. Da-gore grabbed him by the shirtfront and hauled him down the steps. "Ulex."

The emissary came over, face bland, large eyes unblinking, uninterested. "Captain?"

"You say you can read us as easily as a book. Read him."

Ulex studied the innkeeper. "You say the humans we seek were not here?"

"I, ah, I … err, yes … that is, no. Not two women, two men." Dorn-ek's left eye developed a twitch, his bald head suddenly glistening in the low sun.

"He is not lying to you, Captain Da-gore. Yet he is being deceptive. Perhaps some persuasion will bring out the truth here." The emissary glanced to the giants. "Pose."

Pose lumbered across the yard, standing over them. He was a full two heads taller than any of the humans, and a head above the emissary. His deep-set eyes narrowed dangerously at the innkeeper.

Dorn-ek shrank back into Da-gore's grasp.

"Going somewhere?"

The innkeeper turned with eyes twice as large as when he first greeted Da-gore at the door. "Actually, there were four men. Not two." The admission tumbled out. His lips tried to smile, but shaped a tight, pale line instead.

"Four men?" Da-gore shot a look at Ulex.

The emissary nodded. "Now he tells the complete truth."

Pose looked disappointed.

"When did they leave?"

"This morning. Very early. They wished to reach Chevel-ee by nightfall." His frightened view leaped to each of them, then stopped, riveted upon the inn. A woman stood there. "M—my wife. Eleen," he said in answer to Da-gore's questioning glance.

"Bring her here."

One of his men brought the woman down and placed her at Dorn-ek's side. She snapped indignantly out of his grasp and glared at Da-gore. Da-gore stood before the two of them, enduring her frowning eyes, sensing a hot spirit and a strong will. The question still burned in his brain. "Why is it people want to protect these fugitives? You just tried, the woman in Far Port tried. What is it with these four—or now it appears to be six?"

Eleen opened her mouth, but Dorn-ek spoke first. "They're just sojourners. They are taking the traditional pilgrimage to the Mother. They're harmless." The innkeeper spread his hands and lifted his shoulders. "What have they done?"

"You risk your life for sojourners?"

"They're—they're brethren also. In the days of the migration, they moved further south than we. That's all."

"You know them then?"

"No. We never met until yesterday evening."

Da-gore shook his head, perplexed. "It doesn't answer my question."

Eleen said, "We share a kindred Spirit. The Spirit of the Creator."

Ulex grimaced and backed away. The giants became restless. Rampaging giants were not something he wanted to deal with—he didn't want to lose control again, and ordered everyone out of the compound except his lieutenant. Alone now, Da-gore breathed a little easier.

He'd caught a glimmer of what might be behind this loyalty among people who didn't even know each other, but he still didn't understand it. It had religious connections. Some fools will die for hotly held philosophies. But then, he was willing to die for his king and his commander, the Lodath. Didn't that put him in the same category?

Da-gore dismissed the thought, but the bitter aftertaste of it lingered. The innkeeper's worried face contrasted sharply with his wife's scowl. She would indeed be a challenge … perhaps had it been another time … he dismissed that thought as well. He had a job to do, but what to do with these two?

"I could have you both arrested for withholding information from an officer of the Lodath's Guards." But then he'd be burdened with them.

"We told you all we know," Dorn-ek pleaded.

"After I dragged it from you. For willfully hiding information, I could have your place burned." Yet the destruction of Far Port hadn't pleased him.

Eleen's scowl darkened. Fire burned in this one. The woman's appeal grew more and more. Perhaps on his way back? Now, that was a possibility.

"But to show you mercy, in the name of the Lodath, I will spare you and your property—this time. In the future, consider well whom you befriend. Enemies of the realm abound, and they make for costly bedfellows, innkeeper." His burning stare softened slightly for Eleen. He turned on his heels and strode out the wide gates.

He'd maintained command here. He'd succeeded where in Far Port he'd failed. A soldier was never too old to learn new tricks. Outside the gates, he faced a new challenge. God-men, nearly five spans tall, anticipating another free-for-all as they had in Far Port.

He'd snatched the opportunity from them, and like a drunkard kept from his ale, these god-men were short-tempered. He had to defuse them.

As the giants sulked around, Da-gore came to a decision. But which one should he choose? Herc had lost control of himself on the *Osar Messenger*, ignoring his orders and destroying the boat. Pose had challenged him the first night by the fire, and defied him every chance he could since. Plut likewise had challenged his authority from the very beginning. It had been Plut who'd initiated the rampage in Far Port. That left Atala, Per, and Hepha. So far these three had been the most compliant. Hepha had even offered to tell him about the Mountain of the Singing Sky—before Emissary Ulex had stopped him.

Da-gore drew in a breath and pulled himself up to his full height. "Hepha."

The giant, shoulder-bouncing with Herc to see who could topple the other, looked up with a start. Herc slammed into him, knocking him aside a step. Hepha wheeled on him, snarling.

"Hepha!"

He looked at Da-gore, rubbing his bruised shoulder. "What?"

"I have a job for you."

"What job?" He seemed annoyed at being distracted from his game, but curious too.

"The fugitives are a day's march ahead of us. I weary of this pursuit." He glanced through the gate. Eleen still stood by her husband's side. "I suspect you're fleet of foot?"

"I am faster than any of my cousins."

A barrage of insults pummeled him, and he grinned as if relishing them.

"I wonder." Da-gore nicked Hepha's pride.

"You doubt my abilities?"

"Apparently your cousins do."

The giants laughed, and no longer seemed agitated at not being allowed to have their way with the innkeeper and his property. "We'll see. I want you to run ahead and seize the fugitives for me. Think you can handle that? Six humans won't be too much for you, will they?" Another nick at the giant's pride.

"I'll wring them out like dirty wash rags."

He had his attention now. Good. "Wring them if you like, only just be sure it's the young woman who gets wrung first. Is that clear?"

Hepha snarled a smile while his cousins looked disappointed that they hadn't been chosen for the task.

"Away with you, as swift as you can."

Ulex started off with Hepha.

Da-gore pulled in a deep breath and raised his voice. "Where are you going?"

Ulex looked irritated at the tone in his voice. "I accompany him."

"There comes a time when they must be on their own, emissary Ulex. Do you not trust him to do this simple task?"

"I am capable," Hepha growled.

Ulex peered blankly at Da-gore. Da-gore was certain the Emissary understood what he was doing. It was dangerous challenging one of these star-beings, but he'd lost face back in Far Port, and now it would require a certain amount of bravado to regain it.

"Very well." Emissary Ulex's flat voice hid any trace of his true feelings. "I don't see what harm can come of it."

"None at all." Da-gore forced his breathing back to normal. He'd won this round.

Hepha started down the road, long strides carrying him out of sight in a few moments. Da-gore put his troops into formation and with the forest's lengthening shadows before him, resumed his march.

Amolikah poked the flames of their cook fire with a stick. Her normal patience had given way to frustration. This delay was unnecessary, and Mishah knew her grandmother was wearying of the pilgrimage just as she was. It hadn't gone right from the start.

"I don't like this either, Grandmother, but we need to eat."

"That's not what I mean, dear, and you know it."

Mishah glanced at Kenock and Bar'ack sitting off to one side, quietly discussing something. Rhone was away in the forest somewhere nearby. She could hear him chopping with his sword.

"Where are the dangerous highwaymen? Where is the need to have asked those two along in the first place?" Amolikah whispered.

"I, for one, don't lament the lack of danger, but thank the Creator for his provision."

The firelight sculpted frowning shadows on her grandmother's face. "You are right, dear. But this is more than a traditional pilgrimage. I believe the Creator is working all around us. We'll rest easier once—" Her words broke off and her head swung around.

Mishah's voice lowered. "What is it?"

Amolikah shook her head. "A feeling, like … like … like a shiver deep inside me."

"Danger?" Mishah looked around.

"I'm not sure."

The crunch of Rhone's footsteps grew louder. A moment later he stepped into the light and dropped an armful of wood near the fire. "That will keep us until we've finished dinner."

Her grandmother seemed to shake off the feeling, and Mishah tried not to let it bother her either. "The fire is comforting, Master Rhone." She peered into the nearby shadows. "What sort of creatures inhabit these forests?"

"All kinds. Some harmless, and others not so."

"The turnlings," Amolikah said.

Rhone nodded.

"Do you know what has caused them to turn, Master Rhone?" Mishah asked. Was he perceptive as well as handsome?

"No. Perhaps the same thing that's frightening the spiders. A peddler I met recently thinks they might be sensitives. But I've only heard of humans with that ability."

"You mean like those who speak to spiders?"

He nodded again. "It is all part of the same ability—what you say was lost when the first parents fell. The legends you teach children so that they can teach their children." He held her a moment in his stare.

He was showing an interest, though coming around to it cautiously. How to broach the subject? Lamech would know. "Not only do we teach it, the story is written in the stars."

"Ah, that again."

"It's true." She looked up past the treetops at the frosting of white across the blue-black bowl of heaven and gave him a smile. "The Creator writes his plan in the stars for all to see, Master Rhone, and so that none will be ignorant of it."

❧

There was that annoying, contented confidence again, but this time she'd added a hint of playfulness that she'd kept hidden from him until now. What was it about this woman that drew him? Was that fire he'd seen in her eyes? Was he a mere moth to those flames? He put away the thought. She was another man's wife and carrying his child.

"Tell me of this 'fall,' Mistress Mishah. The legends are too incredible to believe."

A smile brightened her face. "You, a man who speaks to spiders, finds it hard to believe?" What an opportunity for Lamech, if he were here. She willed her smile not to falter at the sudden pang in her heart.

He laughed. "I yield to your point."

Rhone.

"But it does sound fanciful, don't you think?"

She shook her head.

Mistress Amolikah said, "No one questioned it even as late as two hundred years ago, for most of the First Children were still with us. But as they went to be with the Creator, all began to change. The spirit of deceit crept into the Learning Halls and the Worship Circles. The yearly sacrifices became mere rituals, performed by men who glorify themselves with pious words and spotless robes of silk and gold and precious stones, but whose hearts were far from the Creator. Believing the simple truths became naive." Mistress Amolikah shook her head. "But man's beliefs will never change truth, no matter how far they stray from it." She paused suddenly and looked around.

"What is it?" Mishah asked her.

"I'm not sure."

The eiderdown stroked his brain again. *Rhone, heed my voice.* He looked up with a start.

Mishah stared at him. "You hear something too?"

He was certain a voice had spoken his name! Suddenly the thought came clear, as if it had been whispered in his ear. *Leave this place immediately.*

"Now?"

"Now, what, Master Rhone?" Mishah's eyes held concern. "What do you mean?"

Was this the same voice, the one he'd heard moments before the sten-gordon had attacked, the one he'd heard on the Meeting Floor? Each time it had given a warning or a command ... he shook his head to dislodge the notion, but it wouldn't move.

"We need to leave." He stood and started hitching the horse into its traces.

"Leave now?" Mishah stood too. "But why?"

"I don't know."

Mistress Amolikah stared off into the blackness, in the direction of the road. "Someone's coming."

Bar'ack and Kenock came over. "What's going on, Master Rhone?" Bar'ack asked.

"Gather everything. We're leaving." He grabbed up his proj-lance and tossed it into the cart with his pack.

Bar'ack looked around then sniffed the air. "What is it?"

"I don't know. I just know we need to leave." Why weren't they heeding his words?

They quickly loaded the cart and helped Kleg'l into it. Rhone hurried Bar'ack and the women into it, tossed their bags after them and instructed Kenock to drive without stopping until he reached Chevel-ee. The sudden sense of urgency was overpowering. He couldn't explain it. He led the horse to the road and gave it a slap on the rump.

"Master Rhone, what about you?" Mishah called as the wagon rattled away.

"I'll catch up." He stood peering down the dark road, tuning out the normal night sounds and listening. "All right," he whispered to himself, "I got the Lee-landers on their way. What am I looking for?"

But the voice inside his head was silent. Rhone drew in a breath and listened a moment longer. Nothing. He turned to jog after the cart, but drew back and looked down the road when the faint sound reached his ears. A distant thump, and then another, as if something was running. He glanced over his shoulder at the cart, fading from sight, then back toward the sound. Someone—no—some*thing*, was following them.

He sprinted to the cart and leaped aboard. "We're being followed. Let's see what sort of legs this horse has."

"Followed!" Kenock gave a shout and snapped the reins. The horse moved into a half-hearted canter.

"Who?" Mishah asked, worry in her eyes.

"I don't know. It sounds like a large animal ... two legged ... long strides. A man riding a horn-crown, perhaps, or a gerup."

"I had a feeling," Mistress Amolikah said.

"Highwayman?" Kleg'l noted ominously.

"No, not highwaymen," Mistress Amolikah said, her wide eyes fixed upon the dark road behind them.

Kenock snapped the reins again harder. "We'll know soon enough if I can't coax more speed out of this lazy plug!"

A shape appeared far behind them, a shadow rounding a bend in the road. It wasn't a horn-crown or a gerup. It was a man. But what kind of man? "There!" Rhone thrust a finger at their pursuer.

Mishah gasped. "What is it?"

"I don't know." Instinctively, Rhone's hand went to his sword.

"I can't get this sack of bones to go any faster," Kenock shouted.

"It won't make any difference," Rhone replied. "It's going to catch up with us in any event. I'll have to delay it." Rhone leaped off the rushing cart.

"Master Rhone!" Mishah called.

"I'll meet you in Chevel-ee."

The cart clattered away, and as the giant sprinted toward him, sounds blurred in his ears and the forest seemed to fade away. For an instant, the approaching giant disappeared. In his mind's eye Rhone saw high, umber stone walls, a bright, sandy arena, a thousand faces peering down at him from the rising galleries. He was back in the Pit of Ramor. His blood ran hot, a sword was in his hand, and there from the arced tunnel strode three Makir executioners. A cheer from the crowd ...

But the vision wasn't real. A ghost from the past. Another life. Another world. He inhaled sharply and the painful memory of gallery cries dimmed, the phantom stone walls melted away.

This *was* real. A being, the likes of which he'd never encountered before, was slowing to a stop before him.

Rhone gripped his sword two handed, realizing he'd chosen the weapon out of instinct instead of clear thinking. His proj-lance would have been a far more practical defense against this being.

The giant stopped ten spans from him. The moonlight glinted off narrowed eyes and drew a silver line along thick, snarling lips. Rhone rarely had to look up to any man. This one stood at least a head taller than he, and his shoulders spread half a span wider. Massive muscles rippled and great biceps bulged as the giant slowly drew a sword from his belt. The huge man had strength and reach over Rhone, and a weapon twice as thick and half again as long.

Rhone grimaced and emptied his lungs. *Center yourself. Remember.* He drew in a calming breath, fingers tightening about his own sword as his brain raced to collect half forgotten bits and pieces. He'd had training, a warrior's training, but it was rusty from years of disuse. "Who are you?" *And what are you?*

"Hepha. You stand between me and the fugitives." His words rumbled away in the darkness.

"Fugitives?" He couldn't mean Mishah and her family. "I know of no fugitives."

"Then stand aside."

"Who are these fugitives you look for?"

"A woman, and others."

Fugitives? From what? He didn't have time to think about it now. He had to stall. "From what tribe are you, Hepha? I've never met anyone your size."

"I am of Hepha of Astus. I am not of any human tribe. I am Earth-Born."

"Earth-Born?" He had heard the rumors of these giants. The Nephilim, some called them. "Where do the Earth-Born come from?"

"The Mountains of the Singing Sky. Now move aside, human."

He filled his lungs and emptied them again. "No."

The immense sword shot up and circled the giant's head, making an angry whir like a teased nest of hornets. With a glint of moonlight, it struck downward.

Rhone sprang to the left, ducking, his reflexes a tad slow. The whoosh of steel sliced the air just above his head. It was a clumsy attempt, all power, no skill. Hepha was a novice with the blade. The knowledge emboldened him.

Rhone parried a second strike, managing to hold onto his sword in spite of the blow that rang his sword like a bell. He instinctively leaped up, drawing his legs in tight. Hepha's broad sword skimmed beneath Rhone's heels. As it did, Rhone struck downward. His blade skittering along Hepha's leather forearm cuirass, biting into the giant's hand as it glanced off.

With a yelp, Hepha backed off a step. He peered at his bleeding hand, concern showing in his broad face. He looked at Rhone, gave a roar, and charged, swinging the sword like a harvester blade. Rhone could do nothing but try to keep out of its path, dodging, feigning, finally diving behind a tree.

The tree trembled from the blow, but stopped the rampaging blade and held it briefly in its tough fibers. Like the armor-plated club-tail, this giant had a soft underbelly. The giant's leather corslet parted just above the sword belt. Ducking low, Rhone sprang around the other side of the tree and struck with the speed of a serpent. The sword encountered flesh, then hard muscle, then drove deep and twisted.

Hepha threw back his head with a deafening bellow. His arms flew wide and he staggered from the tree, staring at the half span of steel protruding from its belly. He took three faltering steps backwards and stumbled. The ground shook when he fell, writhing and lurching. Then he went still and stiff.

Rhone staggered onto the road, the tremors of battle radiating from his body. The sound of pounding feet at his back spun him around. Bar'ack drew to a halt, a proj-lance in his fist. He stood there, staring. But it wasn't the giant that held his eyes. It was Rhone.

22

Chevel-ee

*U*lex insisted on marching at the head of the column. Da-gore would have rather the emissary remained to the rear with the others of his kind, but Ulex was determined to stay out front. Perhaps in doing so, he hoped to urge the company of soldiers along at a faster pace.

Suddenly Ulex gave a jolt, stopped in his tracks and went rigid.

"What's wrong?" Da-gore asked. The emissary looked as if locked in some sort of a trance.

As suddenly as the trance had grasped him, it released him. "Hepha. I must go to him." All at once the air shimmered, and a rift opened in the pale wavering light. Ulex stepped through the tear and the vision winked out, leaving only spots before his eyes. Da-gore caught his breath and the air settled heavily in his lungs, as if a foul vapor had escaped from the opening. Then he thrust a hand through the space where the emissary had stood.

The giants looked at each other, concern darkening their faces.

Da-gore turned on them. "Do you know anything about this?"

Per nodded. "Hepha is lost."

"Lost?" Da-gore scowled. "How could the gia—the Earth-Born get lost following the road ..." suddenly he understood. "Dead?"

"His body is dead. But his spirit is lost."

"What?"

Plut turned his eyes on the captain of the Guard. "His body has been killed, forcing the spirit to leave it. When one of us dies, there is no place of rest for our spirit. Our spirit is not like yours. It is …," he thought a moment, "without hope. When we die, our spirits are denied peace. We are doomed to wander, searching for other bodies to cloth ourselves."

Without hope. Forever searching. Da-gore shuddered. If there was any truth in that, he wanted no part of it. The Lodath never mentioned this unpleasant side of the Oracle's love. At least in the legends of these Lee-landers, their Creator cared for the spirits of those who'd died believing in Him.

Da-gore considered this and all that it meant, then shook off the cold shiver tingling his spine. He ordered the small company ahead. Whatever had happened, he'd learn the full truth soon enough.

Rhone spun around at the sound of feet pounding up behind him. *Bar'ack!* For some reason, he wasn't surprised to him coming back. "I told you to make haste for Chevel-ee."

He stared at the giant, then at Rhone. "You could have gotten yourself killed."

"It's a risk a protector takes. What are you doing here?"

"You left your proj-lance in the cart."

Rhone exhaled sharply, turned back to the giant's body, and wrenched his sword free. "This was sufficient."

Bar'ack's wide stare returned to the dead giant. The question was plain on his face. How much could he, should he, tell? "Let's get out of here. There might be more of these beings around."

They'd started after the cart when a flash of pale light flickered at their backs. A jagged rift opened in the air, leaving a man standing there—but not quite a man. He had the form, but the face was different. The eyes were too large. This was something else entirely. The being peered at them, then looked down at the fallen giant and went to his knees by the giant's side. "Which one of you did this?"

Rhone placed himself in front of Bar'ack. "I did."

"Do you know what you've done?"

"I've defended myself."

"You've condemned Hepha to endless wandering, to endless seeking."

Rhone had no idea what that meant, but he didn't like the look in the being's eyes, or the way it leveled the black staff that up until now it had been holding upright in one hand.

The night flashed bright again. A seam in the darkness opened like a book, spilling a golden light across the shadowed landscape. When it closed, a second being stood between Rhone and the first.

"Sari'el," the first creature hissed, backing up a step.

Rhone grasped to make sense of this. Where were these beings coming from? Who were they?

"You are beyond your limits, Ulex," the second being said.

Some quality of tone in his voice transfixed Rhone.

"Be gone from here and take that foul thing with you."

"Hepha wanders."

"You knew the consequences when you abandoned your first estate and chose to dwell in different habitations. Now you have fallen twice. Hepha will wander until all things are fulfilled. And then there will come an end for you, and for him."

"You assume much, Sari'el."

"It is ordained."

"Nothing is certain." Ulex maneuvered away from the giant's body, warily keeping his staff pointed at Sari'el. "All I must do is take the human woman."

"She is beyond your touch."

Ulex nodded. "Perhaps, but not beyond his!" He pointed at Rhone. Instantly a fire kindled in Rhone's chest, as if a burning coal had been placed there. His thoughts filled with violence, and in his mind's eye Mishah fell beneath his slashing blade. Rhone fought the images. These weren't his thoughts, but something from outside him!

Suddenly his head cleared.

Another flash blinded the night as the two beings locked in combat. Fire leaped from their staves, exploding in fireballs of red and gold, deflected or avoided somehow by each opponent. They moved faster than any warrior Rhone had ever encountered. If the giant had moved as they, Rhone would have had no chance of defeating him.

In a fountain of golden sparks, the combat ended. Sari'el stood a moment peering down at a pile of gray ash at his feet. He straightened up, looking haggard and flushed, his clothes scorched and disarrayed.

"Master Rhone."

Stunned, Rhone glanced up from the smoldering remains. He and the being were about the same height, and although Sari'el gave the impression of being of slighter build, Rhone sensed a strength unimaginable.

"Who are you?"

"I am Sari'el, a guardian and messenger of the Creator."

"Who was that?" He pointed to the pile of ashes.

"A watcher of the Fallen One." Sari'el leveled a slim finger. "Your soul is being contested for. Consider well your allegiance." Sari'el stepped backward into a wavering sheet of light and disappeared. The faint odor of lilac lingered in the air.

"What did he mean, 'you're being contested for?'" Bar'ack asked.

Rhone shook his head. The experience had shaken him. What *had* Sari'el meant? And why was his voice so familiar … ? Rhone grabbed Bar'ack's arm. "Let's catch up with the cart before any more of those creatures show up."

They jogged along the dark road, and a long while later, spied the rest of the party far up ahead. When they finally reached them, Rhone took over the reins up on the driver's seat beside Mishah.

The moon was now low in the west. Soon the sky would brighten. He gave a brief account of what had transpired, then looked at Mishah. "He said you were fugitives."

"Fugitives? We are running from no one. We've broken no laws that I'm aware of."

He consider her confused and terrified expression, the deep worry lines forming suddenly around her mouth. She was, indeed, quiet lovely. Wholesomeness was a thing too easily brushed aside these days, but the Lee-landers still valued it, and Mishah radiated goodness, if not more than just a smattering of naiveté. His earlier thoughts of violence drifted back. How could such notions have ever entered his brain, even fleetingly as they had? What had put them there?

"Someone wants you dead." *And they tried to get me to do it.* The memory made him shiver.

"How can that be? What threat am I? To whom?" She searched his face with fear in her eyes. Protectively, she wrapped her arms around her expanding belly.

He shook his head. "I was hoping you might shed some light on that."

"I have no answer."

He believed her. Should he say more? It would be unfair not to. "I don't think we've seen the last of those … those beings."

She hugged her arms, rubbing them. "The Creator will protect us if that is so."

"Mistress Amolikah, do you know anything of creatures like Sari'el?"

"I have an idea. There are beings that do the Creator's bidding. We simply think of them as messengers. The faithful messengers are here to help us, the fallen ones to harm us. Beyond all that which we see," she stretched an arm, "there is another unseen world that touches ours. We are prisoners here, but those beyond are not so constrained." She considered him narrowly. "I believe Sari'el was a messenger of the Creator."

He shivered from a sudden chill. "And the other?"

"A servant of the serpent." Her words were brittle, her eyes compressing to thin slits.

"What of the giant?"

"I don't know, but I fear it portends a new evil in the world."

As they drew near to the gate of Chevel-ee, two low walls of dressed stone rose up on either side of the road. In the rising sun, a mosaic of colored glass cast a kaleidoscope of colors across the paving stones. The village gate stood eight spans tall and five wide. Its double doors of wood, carved in woodland scenes and strapped in bronze, were closed. The stonework surrounding them had been skillfully crafted, but the details were mostly lost on Rhone as the cart clattered to a halt before them. The single thought that had consumed him since his battle with the giant was to get them safely within the stone walls of Chevel-ee.

Bar'ack cast nervously about as Rhone leaped to the pavement and pulled a chain at one side of the doors. Inside the walls came the muffled reply of a bell. It seemed a long time before a small door at eye level slid open.

The face that peered out the hatch looked them over a moment. "State your business." He sounded as if holding back a yawn.

Mistress Amolikah said, "We wish to meet with the Mother."

The guard's face took on sudden interest. "Lee-landers?"

"Yes."

"The Mother awaits your arrival." He disappeared and a moment later one half of the gate swung inward.

"Awaits our arrival? How could she know?" Mishah asked.

The gate warden said, "She knows many things."

Rhone climbed up onto the wagon seat and moved the cart inside. The solid walls were only a marginal reassurance. Not even stone walls could keep the giants out if they truly wanted inside. And what of those other beings? What had Sari'el had called himself? A guardian. And the other, a watcher? The two beings had known each other, yet they fought to the death. Rhone was confident in matters concerning men, beasts, and the Wild Land, but this encounter with aliens was something he didn't know how to fight.

Inside the walls, a man took their horse and cart to the stables while the gate warden who'd let them in escorted them to the stone warden tower and told them they would be summoned shortly.

He didn't want to be here. He wanted to be atop the wall where he could watch for his enemies. He circled the little room once then dropped heavily on a wooden bench, beside Bar'ack, and fixed his view upon the glassless window opening onto the village where Mishah stood, staring into the golden morning, worrying her fingers and shifting from foot to foot.

Mistress Amolikah came over to him. "I owe you an apology, Master Rhone. I doubted you. I didn't trust you fully because you were ...," she hesitated.

"Not a Lee-lander?"

She nodded. "Yes. But I see I was wrong. I am indeed thankful you chose to accompany us here to Chevel-ee. If we'd been on that road alone, and that creature had attacked us—" she shivered.

"Why does someone want Mistress Mishah dead?"

"I don't know," but her tone said something else.

"If I am to help you, I need to know."

"Help? We have arrived at our destination, Master Rhone. You and Master Bar'ack will be going your own way now. You've already helped us."

Continuing on to locate spiders had been his plan. Then why was there that uncertainty now? "You're right."

She turned away, spoke to Kleg'l, and a moment later the good-man came over with the money pouch and paid Rhone the agreed-upon fee.

Bar'ack leaned forward slightly. "I'm glad we're done with these people. Master Rhone, can I ask you a question?"

But Rhone's thoughts were still back on that dark road. A messenger of the Creator, coming to him? It made no sense.

"Master Rhone?"

He glanced at the young man. "What would you like to know?"

"When I came back to help you ... well, I saw the fight—most of it."

He'd known it wouldn't be long before Bar'ack's curiosity became too much to contain.

"I was lucky."

"There was more to it than luck. I've seen men fight as you did—in the contests put on in the marketplace. Warriors from different parts of the known world, paid to entertain the marketgoers. You saw them too, remember? You said the skill of a Makir Warrior was not a thing to be sold, or a thing to be displayed for sport."

Rhone looked at him. "I said that?"

"You did. And then the other day, you quoted from memory a verse from the *Song of the Makir*."

"I can quote from memory Lasay's *Sorrows of Yesterday*, and Ser'ike's *Morning's Mists, Evening's Calm*." Rhone didn't want to remember the past, but his encounter with the giant had brought it all too clearly into focus again.

Bar'ack held him in a steady gaze. "What were you before you became a webmaster?"

He filled his lungs and emptied them slowly. "I was a searcher and a wanderer."

"And that's all?"

Bar'ack's prodding suddenly irritated him. "Does reciting Lasay make me a cleric?"

"No."

"Does reading Ser'ike make me a philosopher?"

"Again, no."

"Then how does quoting from the song Pyir Turck wrote make me a Makir Warrior?"

Bar'ack stiffened and drew back. "It's just that you seem to know so much of them. You speak of the Makir code of honor as if it is something burned in your own heart. You have the size of a Hodinite, and when you walk, your bearing is that of a man not to be trifled with. It doesn't take much imagination to picture you as one of those legendary warriors from the Island of Atlan. And then last night, the way you handled yourself against that giant—"

Rhone scowled at his apprentice.

Bar'ack broke off and stared sullenly across the room. "I've angered you, and I apologize. I will not pry where you don't want me."

Rhone considered the young man a moment then said gently, "I've seen many things in my travels, Bar'ack." His friend's son was only showing honest curiosity, and an exuberance that characterized youth. "I have strength and a natural ability." He paused, casting a glance at Mishah. "Some might call that a blessing from the Creator."

Past her, he saw the town through the oval window. Chevel-ee appeared an ancient village. Low stone shops and houses lined the wandering streets laid out in an age before folks were concerned with ruler-straightness. Some of the paving stones had dips and ruts worn into them from years of foot and wheel traffic. The windows on the shops had no shutters, and in some cases no glass. Many of the buildings still lacked proper doors. Apparently, thieves were rare here.

Rhone knew a little of the history of Chevel-ee. It had begun as a family compound centuries ago, and had remained close-knit ever since. Many kingdoms and lands claimed one or more ancestors from Chevel-ee. The Lee-landers insisted this place had been the wellspring of all civilization, and that the Mother—the mother of all who ever lived—still resided within its walls.

He wasn't prepared to believe that, any more than he was prepared to believe messengers of the Creator had visited him the night before, though he had no better explanation.

23

The Mother

The door opened and the young woman entered. "Morning peace. Day springs new," she frowned, "but I fear all is not well."

"Morning peace." Kenock rose swiftly. He felt as if he were smiling foolishly, but for some reason couldn't help himself. "This is my sister, Mishah, and this is Amolikah, our grandmother ... and Kleg'l, over there, our good-man. Oh, and Master Rhone and Bar'ack over there."

She wore a brown jumper of hemp cloth over a white cotton shirt. The jumper was wonderfully embroidered over the shoulders, about the cuffs of her sleeves, which ended just below her elbows, and around the hem in a wide band of color. She remained in the doorway where the morning mist beaded upon the frame and sunlight gleamed off her red hair. She nodded to each of them. "My name is Cerah. The Mother awaits you. We must hurry."

They gathered their belongings, bade farewell to Rhone and Bar'ack, and left the gatehouse. Kenock strode alongside Cerah, hardly noticing the birds that sang and hopped along the ground, gleaning bits of food. He wanted to say something, but his tongue tied and his wits faltered at her beauty. They turned a corner and hurried down another deserted street. Green-and-red parrots perched along roof edges, preening in the morning sun, while the butterflies clung to eastern walls flexing gold and black wings, warming themselves in the golden light.

"You live in a beautiful village." Almost as soon as the words were out, he realized it was a lame thing to say in light of the urgency of the situation.

She merely looked at him and nodded.

❧

Mishah paced the room. The antechamber wasn't large, but it was curiously decorated. Its stone floor bore serpent heads in mosaic. The walls were of stones so precisely fitted, she was certain the joints would not permit even the finest sheet of rice paper to slip between them. But would they hold up against a giant? She chilled, and burnished her arms to drive it from her.

A window looked out onto a garden that had been tended by a skilled gardener. A path of some small-leafed, deep green ground cover led to a curiously carved portal of white stone. A stream issuing from a fountain in the center of the garden branched into four tiny, rippling rills and meandered toward the four points of a compass.

She stood at the window a moment, then looked at Kenock studying two ancient garments of animal skins behind glass. Why would anyone display such worn items? Her view shifted to Amolikah in one of the chairs, leaning into a cushion, hands folded, eyelids shut. Every now and again, her lids crawled from movement behind them. Her lips formed soundless words. How could she be so relaxed after what had happened last night? Kleg'l occupied a bench against another wall.

Kenock was about to take a seat when the room gave a shake. He grabbed for the chair. "What's that?"

Amolikah came out of her contemplation and looked around. "The earth moves."

Mishah glanced nervously about. The earth moving ... giant footsteps, perhaps? *Relax. Do you want to frighten this baby into the world here and now?* She put an arm around her large belly and drew in a breath, suddenly wishing that Rhone had remained with them. "Grandmother, what if they come looking for us here? How could we leave?"

"The Creator saw to it that we arrived here safely. He will protect our going as well ... if it be his will."

Surely he would. She had to trust, as Grandmother trusted ... as Lamech would have. If it were only herself she had to worry about, and not the baby, or the others.

The door opened and Cerah stepped in. "Is everyone all right?" She looked at each of them, "The earth is unsettled." When her view found Kenock, it lingered a moment. Her eyes seemed to brighten and her smile spread a bit wider. "The Mother is ready to receive you now. She has been expecting Mistress Mishah for a very long time."

"Expecting me?" Mishah stiffened. "Why?"

Amolikah moved beside her and took her arm. "We will know soon enough."

Entering the room was like stepping into an oven. She broke out in a sweat. A good, strong blaze burned in the large fireplace. Upon the hearth stood a single chair, and upon it a thin woman, old as time itself and frail as the brittle leaves that crushed beneath Mishah's feet at the season of the falling. The Mother stared at the fire and did not immediately turn at the sound of their footsteps on the stone floor.

Cerah motioned them to stop, then she went to the old woman. "Grandmother," she spoke softly, touching her shoulder lightly.

"Yes, I know," came a reply so low, Mishah nearly missed it.

Cerah helped the Mother rise, adjusted a shawl over her thin shoulders, and put a short, straight walking stick into her hand. She turned shakily and came to them with Cerah at her side. Pale eyes buried in a face of deep lines and ancient crevices studied each of them. Her hair, white as bleached cotton, contrasted sharply against her olive skin. But it was the eyes, dark and large in their sunken sockets that struck Mishah; intelligent, with a sharpness unaffected by the years—windows of great wisdom, and of overwhelming sadness. To look into the old woman's face was to look into the heart of torment.

"Amolikah." She weakly. "We see each other again."

Amolikah gently took the delicate shoulders and pressed her cheek against the ancient flesh. "I've prayed often for this day. This is my granddaughter, Mishah."

The Mother considered her in a manner that made Mishah wonder if the ancient woman weren't looking inside her. After a moment, the Mother nodded and smiled. "You are a blessing for these sad eyes, my child."

Blessing? What could be blessed about her? Lamech had said their child would receive a prophecy and a blessing. That the Creator was using them in some mighty way. But why? Mishah shivered in spite of the heat and the heaviness of air.

Amolikah went on, "And this is my grandson, Kenock."

The Mother shifted her smile and clutched his hand in both of hers. "My children grow so straight and tall," she frowned. "You are so like I was." Her voice wavered and filled with sadness. "Resist the rebellion. It will come to no good end."

Kenock flinched at that.

"And our good-man, Kleg'l," Amolikah finished.

"Kleg'l." The mother's expression widened with sudden surprise. "You have Jalek's eyes."

"Have I? I never knew my great, great grandfather."

"Jalek was my twelfth son. Always the quiet one, and so introspective. You have many of his features."

"I am pleased."

The Mother indicated a long table. "Cerah, will you bring the tea?"

She helped the ancient woman into a chair and hurried out of the room. "Please sit, all of you." Mother Eve motioned to the chairs. "Cerah will bring the tea."

These pleasantries were killing Mishah. "Mother Eve, why are we being pursued?"

Eve's lips compressed, her white head shook. "Your journey has been long and troubled, and you are filled with much fear."

"I fear for my husband and my unborn child."

"Yes. But there is another fear that burdens your heart, my precious child."

"What is happening?"

Mother Eve's eyes narrowed. "Evil seeks you."

Her dream! The room's heat was suddenly unbearable. She caught a ripple of light near the fire—only the heat playing tricks with her eyes. Her heart pounded her ribs. "Why does it pursue me?" Could this old woman really know what was happening? Did she have an explanation for the dream that had haunted her for months?

Cerah shouldered open the door, carrying an oval tray with a teapot and mugs. Kenock rushed to help her. Cerah's smile engendered a giddy look from her brother's face.

Cerah set the tray on the table and poured the tea for each of them. "Is there anything else I can get, Grandmother?"

"No, my dear. Leave us now for a little while."

Kenock frowned. His sudden infatuation with this pretty young granddaughter of the Mother might have amused Mishah if her worries hadn't been so great.

"Cerah is of the line of Seth," Mother Eve said.

So, she had noticed Kenock's interest.

"Cerah is too attentive. I worry about her. She spends too much time with me. She's sat at my side since she was old enough to walk."

Kenock sighed, "She's quite lovely."

"Lovely, yes, and wise for her years, but far too young to spend so much time with someone whose years are all used up."

Amolikah touched the ancient woman's gnarled hand. "I pray for many more years, dear Eve."

"After 1,056, who needs more? This tent of mine is cracked and dried up. Like the first clothes the Creator made for Adam and me." Her view shifted briefly to the closed door. "Why do I keep those old things around? A shell of their former beauty. Like me."

Amolikah said, "Yet so exquisitely made by the hand of the Creator. Like us all."

"Maybe that's why I've held onto them." She drew in a breath. "I've been 126 years a widow. I am so ready to go home to be with Adam. To walk with the Creator as we once did, in the beginning-time."

Amolikah nodded. "I can understand your loneliness."

And so can I. Mishah's heart ached for Lamech. The Mother's words had opened the still-fresh wound.

"But the Creator has given me a task to do, and until it is completed, I can not leave." Her view shifted suddenly to Mishah. "My little one, events are moving quickly." She gathered the shawl with bony fingers. "I know of the encounter on the road."

Her heart pounded. "How could you? It just happened last night."

"A messenger visited me. He told me you'd be coming today."

No one spoke for a moment. Lamech had told her his grandfather had spoken to messengers of the Creator, even the Creator himself, but she'd suspected those stories may have become somewhat embellished over the years.

Kenock said, "Do messengers visit you often?"

"Not anymore. Before the exile his messengers would frequently visit us, and we thought it not strange. We were very much as they were ... in the beginning. We wore the same clothes." Her voice faltered, her eyes glistened.

Kenock pointed to the closed door. "Those in the antechamber?"

Eve smiled and shook her head. "You do not understand. Those were rags even when new, compared to the clothes the Creator had provided for Adam and me. Before I listened to the serpent's voice, we wore the Creator's glory. Like his messengers, we shone with a radiance unmatched. Even the Greater Light did not shine with the glory the Creator gave us for our covering. After we disobeyed, that glory fled from us. We saw how naked we were and we hid ourselves. The Creator found us hiding among the laurels and sewed crude garments of animal skins to cover our nakedness." She looked down at herself and plucked at her silken dress. "There is no glory that compares to that which the Creator gives freely. Someday we will receive it again. But first the serpent's head must be crushed."

"The prophecies are clear on that," Amolikah said. "But when will it happen? We see the world around us falling away from the Creator's ways. People listen to every new philosophy that comes along. This Oracle is only the latest."

"It breaks Lamech's heart to see the people flocking to him," Mishah added.

Eve nodded. "Lamech is very much like his grandfather."

How could she know that as well? An emptiness shriveled Mishah's heart. She forced her thoughts off her husband and back onto the Mother's words.

Eve's eyes grew intense. "When will it happen? We see the beginning even now." Her view closed on Mishah like a fist. "You, my precious daughter, you bear the beginning."

"Me!" Mishah heaved in a sudden breath, holding it as if frightened there might never be another.

"Your son."

She put a protective hand to her stomach. Mother Eve had said it too. A son! The dream of a son fleeing before the Evil came back to her with frightening clarity.

Eve leaned forward, her eyes paralyzing Mishah with their intense fire. The stifling air around her turned icy, like a breath off a mountain summit. But before the old woman could speak, the door burst open and Cerah hurried to the table.

"What is it, daughter?"

"Grandmother, they're at the gate!"

"So soon?"

"Boseth just brought word."

Eve's face hardened. "Are the warders holding them?"

"They haven't tried the gates. Chief Gate Warden Goret has them bolted, as you'd requested."

"Then we still have time." Eve looked back at Mishah with an urgency tempered with … what was it? Then she knew. Lamech often wore that same look when faced with a dilemma, yet confident the Creator's hand was in it, and that He would work out the details. "Soon you must flee, my precious daughter."

"Flee? Back to Morg'Seth?"

Eve's head shook. "You cannot return to Morg'Seth."

Kleg'l stood with a jolt. "If there is danger here I must get my mistress safely home."

"There is danger," Eve said severely. "Beyond what you can imagine." She looked at each of them. "The time has come for the prophecy." She turned toward Cerah. "Bring me the Hodinite, Rhone."

"What has Master Rhone to do with this?" Mishah demanded. They'd asked him to escort them, that was all. He'd been in the right place at the right time. He needed the money and they had paid him. He'd touched her heart and made her feel guilty for it. Why was the Mother asking for him now?

Eve studied Mishah, her sunken eyes two deep pools within the crisscrossing valleys of her face. "He is part of this. You are the weft and he is the warp. You are of one piece."

Part of it?

"Hodinite," Kenock breathed. It was plain he'd not heard the rest. His view shot back to the Mother. "Then Bar'ack was right. Rhone is—"

"A Makir Warrior," Eve said. "Now hurry, my daughter, and fetch him."

"Yes, Grandmother."

"I'll go with you." Kenock sprang to Cerah's side.

"Quickly," Mother Eve urged.

When they'd gone, the Mother looked at Kleg'l. "This is a private thing. Please wait in the antechamber. Her eyes moved briefly to Amolikah. "I wish you to stay. You will need to have the knowledge I have for Mishah."

Amolikah looked at Mishah. Mishah gave a small nod. She wanted her grandmother at her side. Her heart raced as the door to the antechamber swung shut leaving only the three of them in the oppressively hot room. An open window to her back overlooked the garden and allowed in the rippling of falling water from the fountain, and a faint breeze scented with flowers. It was all that kept her from becoming ill. Grandmother seemed to be taking all this better than she; at ease, yet attentive.

Eve looked to Mishah. "You have come to me as the women of your tribe have done for hundreds of years."

Mishah watched her with a fixed stare and a lower lip caught in her teeth.

Eve sat a moment looking at both. "I had a visitor some months back. He told me a daughter of Seth had conceived a son."

A son. It must be true. But what did it mean? Was the dream true as well? A frightening shadow of things to come?

Eve fixed her eyes upon Mishah. "Seth's tribe has always been faithful to instruct the children in the true knowledge. You remember the first prophecy spoken by the Creator?"

Mishah hurriedly reviewed her childhood lessons. "The first prophecy was spoken in the Cradleland, after Mother E … I mean after you, ate from the Tree of Knowledge."

She winced and nodded.

Mishah hesitated. Apparently Mother Eve wanted to hear it from her lips. "The Creator cursed the serpent, then said he would place an aversion between the serpent and the woman, between its seed and her seed—" Mishah suddenly understood. "—You will bruise his heel, but he will crush your head. The mosaic on the floor in the antechamber. The pattern of serpent heads."

Mother Eve nodded again. "It reminds me of the promise whenever I stand there."

Mishah's hand began to shake. She buried it in her lap and gripped it tight with the other. "What does this have to do with me? That prophecy hearkens unto a coming Redeemer."

"You are correct, my daughter."

"It can't involve my child."

Amolikah placed a hand on her shoulder and must have felt the tremble that had shaken her just then. "Fear not, dear. Whom he ordains, he will empower."

Was that supposed to comfort her? She wanted Lamech. She wanted his arms around her, his strength … his understanding. She wanted to hear him say everything was going to be all right. That she was merely fulfilling a family tradition making this pilgrimage. She wanted nothing to do with prophecies, with giants!

Eve cupped her hands about the warm mug as if relishing the heat. "No, Daughter, your son is not the promised Redeemer. That time is still future; the days and the quarterings of his coming are known only to the Creator. But the son you carry will preserve the generation of the coming Redeemer. He will bring comfort to mankind." She paused, her eyes growing cloudy. "The Creator has not told me how he will use your son, only that he will be the first of a new generation."

Mother Eve tilted her head back and closed her eyes as if trying to remember something exactly. "The world waxes evil and a shadow settles over creation. Evil pursues good, and generations flow through a polluted land, mixed with unclean blood. By his grace alone, your son will remain unstained. The pure seed. The Creator will split the heavens and purify the land."

Split the heavens? Purify the land? Mishah trapped the breath in her lungs.

"But the Evil pursues your son, Mishah."

"Will the Creator save my son?" The words slipped from her lips before she realized it. Words taken from a nightmare!

"He will, and your son will save all."

Mishah inhaled. The very words from the dream! She gripped her grandmother's hand.

Mother Eve's throat bobbed. She looked exhausted, but her voice remained strong. "You must flee to the Wild Lands, you must seek the Sanctuary."

"The Sanctuary?" Mishah whispered.

"The Cradleland," Amolikah said softly.

"But I want to go home to Morg'Seth."

Amolikah's grip tightened within hers.

"You cannot. Flee to the Cradle where he will comfort you."

She couldn't go home? What was Mother Eve saying? The Cradleland? Going home was all she'd thought of since starting this pilgrimage. It wasn't her idea to come. Lamech and Grandmother had urged her to it. She'd fulfilled her family obligation, but she'd lost Lamech. And now this! How could she possibly go on?

The room began to shake. Mishah gripped the arms of her

chair as a lamp suspended from the ceiling made ever widening gyrations overhead. The teapot crept for the edge of the table. Amolikah rescued it at the last moment. The tremor passed and no one moved for a moment.

Mother Eve opened her eyes. "Another. They come more frequently now. You haven't a moment to loose." Her expression softened. "I don't understand the Creator's purpose, Mishah, but I learned long ago to do his will. Someday you will understand."

24

A Secret Beneath the Wall

*D*o you know where he is?" Kenock asked as Cerah hurried them through the narrow streets. Vendors' booths and shops flashed past them, but he had eyes only for the pretty granddaughter of Mother Eve. A granddaughter how far removed? That was impossible to tell. Eve seemed to refer to every woman as her daughter, or her lovely daughter, or her precious child. Kenock suspected the old woman had many other endearments as well. She was, after all, *the Mother*.

"I would expect to find him on the wall, with the warders."

"Why there?"

She looked at him with wide brown eyes, fiery hair cascading to her shoulders, shining in the rays of the sun's greater light. "Master Rhone is a warrior. Where else would he be?"

A Makir Warrior no less! The discovery was still too fresh. How could the Mother have known? "The Mother seems to know a lot about us." He ducked his head as she led him under a low, dark passageway toward an egg-shaped slash of light at the far end.

"Grandmother Eve remembers everything. Mention it only once, and she will never forget. She may be very old, but her mind still soaks up knowledge like a dry sponge in a bowl of water." Cerah looked at him, her features muted by the deep shadows. "You and I, we've lost so much of that natural intelligence the Creator crafted for Eve and Father Adam. And the further we drift from the beginning-time, the more we lose. It's all part of the curse. It has left nothing untouched."

"But man is getting smarter." His feet splashed into an unseen puddle. "You should see the engineering achievements of Nod City, and the advances in engine technology—the powerful cycler aboard the *Osar Messenger* is something we didn't have even twenty years ago."

"Smarter?" She sounded amused. "Man has accumulated a body of knowledge to draw from, but that simply gives us the *appearance* of intelligence. Our brains struggle where the Mother's glides. She tries to explain concepts that to her seem simple, but to me are unfathomable. No, Master Kenock, we are not becoming smarter. Our intelligence, like everything else, is subject to the curse."

Her accusation went against almost everything he believed, although Lamech would have probably agreed with her. He grimaced. In spite of their sometimes-heated arguments, he missed his brother-in-law.

They emerged from the tunnel at the base of the village wall. Here and there, shops carried on enterprises that did not require the heavier traffic of the main thoroughfares: A cooper, a wheelwright, a tannery. It was a tight place, protected from even the slightest breeze, where every odor settled and clung. He was happy once the narrow lane opened up near a flight of stairs. Cerah sprang up them, two steps at a time, lithe as a gazelle, her hair bouncing. Kenock was right behind her.

At the top of the low wall, a narrow rampart maybe four spans wide ran below a parapet three spans high. Men rushed past them, some carrying proj-lances, but most unarmed. Only the gate warders wore uniforms. Kenock and Cerah dodged the crowd, and as they came around a corner, Kenock spied the road below upon which they had earlier arrived. He stopped and his breath caught.

Cerah stared. "What are they?"

"Giants." A knot formed in his throat. Supply wagons, three-points, and handlers waited just behind them. Two men were approaching the gate. One wore the cape and plume of an officer, and the other carried the standard of the Lodath of the Oracle.

Then Kenock spied Rhone, standing a head taller than any other man there. Bar'ack was with him. "There he is." He took her hand and wove through the crowd. "Master Rhone!"

Rhone glanced over, the set of his jaw rock solid. "What is it?"

Cerah said, "The Mother has asked to see you."

"Me?" Rhone's view narrowed.

"Both of you," she said.

A *Makir Warrior*. Men of legends; their stories told around campfires by men who longed for adventure. And here he'd been traveling with one all the while and had never known it.

Rhone shot a glance at him. "What is it?"

Kenock realized he'd been staring. He forced his eyes away. "Nothing."

"Chief Gate Warden of Chevel-ee!" the officer below called. The hubbub along the village wall went suddenly silent. Men pressed against the parapet to better see the giants farther down the road.

"I'm Chief Gate Warden Goret," a man standing nearby replied. "What do you want here?"

Kenock recognized the officer as Da-gore, the same man who had arrested them in Nod City. Da-gore sneered at Goret's demanding tone and crossed his arms. He glanced along the wall as if measuring its strength and the resolve of the men manning its ramparts. "I am Da-gore, Captain of the Lodath's Guard."

A murmur rippled along the rampart.

Captain Da-gore put authority behind his voice. "We are after six fugitives. They are within your walls."

"We harbor no fugitives, and you have no authority here."

"My authority comes from the Lodath, through the grace of King Irad."

"The Lodath holds no sway in Chevel-ee. We've never ceded our independence to King Irad, or to the Lodath."

"Villages beyond King Irad's realm retain their independence only by King Irad's benevolence, and only so long as their men of arms are able to resist invasion. Are you that strong? Be careful with your words, Chief Gate Warden."

"Invasion? Is that what you threaten? Do you intend to do here what you did in Far Port?"

This seemed to catch Da-gore by surprise. "Word travels fast. If it comes to it, I will."

"Far Port was unwalled. I see only seven of you," Goret's confidence was belied by a nervous twitch.

Rhone mumbled, "Don't stroke against the fur."

"Name these fugitives," Goret went on.

"Mishah, Amolikah, Kleg'l, and Kenock of Morg'Seth. Rhone and Bar'ack of Nod City. You have one quartering to turn them over to us."

Kenock flinched at the sound of his name. Up until now, the danger had been faceless.

The Captain paused to let that sink in. "Or we will take them from you."

"Master Rhone," Cerah said again. "The Mother waits for you."

Rhone shifted his proj-lance to his right hand and seemed reluctant to turn away from the scene below. "Lead the way."

Da-gore strode back to the Earth-Born. The Chief Gate Warden had no intentions of meeting the deadline, but he'd give him the allotted time just the same, then he'd move in. The wall, although stout, was low and easily breached. The men he noted guarding it were farmers, not soldiers.

"Per. Circle the village and tell me how many gates, their strength, their locations."

Taking shield and spear, the giant started out across the fields in an easy lope.

If his company had been at full strength, he could have easily overpowered the village. But he hadn't set out to take a village. He was only supposed to capture and execute four fugitives. He was ill prepared for the task at hand. His thoughts paused. He still had five giants and they'd proven what they were capable of back in Far Port.

"Once we enter the village, the fugitives must be found. I don't care what you do to them, but I must see their dead bodies lying at my feet. If the townspeople resist, make an example of them. We cannot let it be said that a backwater village thumbed its nose at the Great King Irad, or the Oracle's Lodath.

❦

The house in the center of Chevel-ee was larger than most dwellings that Rhone had noted as they made their way through the village. It was built of smooth stone with a high, arching roof. Cerah hurried them inside. The heat enveloped him like a wet blanket as they passed into the inner room. What manner of person builds such a fire on so warm a morning? Soaring, open-arched rafters were covered in a thatch of reeds. He looked to see if the windows were closed, but like most of the buildings in Chevel-ee, the windows had never been provided with either glass or shutters. He noted, as he entered, that the whole family was together.

Cerah moved instantly to the side of an ancient woman. "Grandmother, this is Master Rhone and Master Bar'ack." Cerah looked at them. "This is Mother Eve."

Kenock hovered near Cerah, watching his sister. Her face showed distress. "Mishah?"

"Oh, Kenock." She rushed to him and he engulfed her in his arms.

"What's wrong, Mi? You're shaking like a leaf."

"I can't go home—we can't go home."

Mistress Amolikah said, "We must move on."

Kleg'l looked concerned. "If not to Morg'Seth, then where?"

Mishah shook her head against her brother's chest then pushed away and wiped her eyes. "The Cradleland."

Ah, Rhone thought, *so that's why he'd been summoned.* The sharp thump of the butt of his proj-lance against the stone floor startled them. He leaned onto the barrel, his brow furrowing, his eyes narrowing warily.

Mishah looked momentarily to Kleg'l, then at her brother. "I don't understand any of it."

"The Cradleland is lost, Mi. And even if we should manage to find it, its gate has been sealed. We'd never get in."

"He who seals also has the key to open, if it be his will. The Cradleland is not lost, but the way is little known these days." The Mother took her walking stick and went to the book beneath the mirror. She opened it and withdrew a yellowed and brittle paper, tightly folded. "Adam and I made many pilgrimages back to the Cradleland in the early days. We had somehow hoped the gardener might take pity on us and let us back in. But to no avail. It was forbidden to us forever." She closed the book and laid the paper atop its cover. "Rhone, my son."

He stiffened. She reached for his shoulders and gripped them weakly, yet he felt every bone in her hands.

"My precious son." A small smile brightened the sad face. "You have such broad shoulders. Hodin had broad shoulders."

"You knew Hodin?" Rhone had never met the first ruler of Atlan. Hodin had died the year of his birth.

"Hodin was my fourteenth son. The biggest of my children, Hodin naturally took it upon himself to watch over his brothers and sisters while they were in the field tending the flocks or working the ground. He was bold and strong—a natural fighter like you, my son."

According to the legends, this woman and her husband had been the first humans, fashioned by the hand of the Creator. That brought up a curious question. "Who would Hodin protect his brothers and sisters from?"

The Mother's eyes pooled. "I had thirteen sons and nineteen daughters before Hodin. It was the 190th year of the world, and I'd been a great-great-great-grandmother many times over." She turned from him and taking a walking stick from Cerah, tapped back across the stifling room to the table beneath a mirror. Her hand fell upon the leather covers of a book. She looked at Rhone's reflection. "My first son, Erik, joined to his sister, Timeia. They had sons and daughters. Lavin, my second son, joined to Ayah, my first daughter, indeed, my first born, and they had sons and daughters. By the time my third son, Maleck, took Lavin's daughter, Selah, the sons of man numbered in the hundreds and had begun to spread out over the face of the earth.

"The Creator blessed the wombs of my daughters, but the hearts of my children waxed cold and bickering broke out; first over the tilled fields, then over the flocks, and finally over industry. After Maleck, I had Cain." Her words caught and in her reflection a tear streaked her ancient cheek and dampened the book beneath her hand. She sniffed back her sorrow. "After Cain was Soren. Soren was a clever man. He studied the creation to find ways to make industry of it." She turned and considered Rhone a moment. "He was the first to harvest web."

"I never knew that."

"There is so much already lost. Why are the memories of my children so short? The Creator warned us it would be so. That is why Adam put it down in a book."

Rhone crossed the room and stood over her. "That book?"

She lifted it into her arms, heavy by the appearance, but then, she was frail. The cover was worn and stained; it had drunk tears before. "This is the Book of Generations. It tells of the Creation as the Creator and his messengers revealed it to us. It tells of our children, and where they settled. It is a record of all that transpired before Adam went home to be with the Creator."

"It must be quite valuable."

"Priceless. It holds the very words of the Creator." She placed it back upon the table.

And those words were obviously of a private nature, for she didn't offer to show them to him. He dragged a hand around his neck and wiped it on his vest. "Why did you asked me here?"

"Because you are in danger. You all are in great danger."

Rhone cradled the proj-lance in his arms. "By the giants outside the gates? They are mighty warriors, but they can be defeated."

She shook her head. "That is not to be. They will be defeated, but not by your hand, my dear son."

His muscles tightened across his shoulders. Why did she keep calling him that? Even if by some queer turn of events she *was* the mother of all, she didn't know him. They were strangers.

"You are not here by accident."

"I don't believe in your Cradleland." He didn't intend to be drawn into this problem any further.

"I know." She placed a hand upon his chest and pressed against the crystal pendant beneath his shirt. Although her touch was light, he flinched as if a burning brand jabbed him. "What secret do you hide here?"

He backed from her touch. "You said I was in danger. How so?"

"In this life, we struggle not against flesh and blood, but against wickedness in the spiritual realm."

"The giant I killed was flesh and blood."

She shook her head. "This world is only a shadow of what lies beyond. The real battles are being waged all around us, but we cannot see them. Rhone, my precious son, dark forces wish to have you."

Sari'el's words almost exactly. "Why?"

"To do their bidding, of course, for they cannot do it themselves," the Mother said gently. "The Creator has placed limits. They can only work their evil through human instruments. These giants at the gate are tools, wrought by evil. Their blood is poison, and soon it will seep into all of mankind. If you are to be perfect in your generation, you must avoid these beasts at all cost." Her view moved about the room and halted on Kenock. "Keep your daughters from the poison." She looked at Mishah. "Instruct your son, for this very poison is the weapon the Evil will wield at him."

"This is none of my affair. Bar'ack and I have come to search out web." He hitched his head toward the wall in a way to mean what lay beyond. "Once in the Wild Lands, those creatures will never find me."

The Mother lifted a bony finger at him. "They will, my dear son. They will. You have accepted their mark. Through it they will find you, and eventually control you."

"I've accepted no mark." Rhone scowled. "No one controls me."

"It isn't too late. The Creator wishes to use you, but you will have to decide."

"I am a servant to no one."

"Everyone is a servant to one of two masters, and we are free to choose which. Be wise in choosing yours, Rhone."

He hefted his proj-lance, "I'm needed on the wall." He started for the door.

"Rhone." The Mother's quiet voice had the power to stop him. "You don't believe in the Cradleland. So be it. Unbelief is a growing blight upon the land. My precious daughter must flee to the Sanctuary, and she needs you to take her."

"I can take care of my sister." Kenock's back stiffened and he stared at the Mother, then shot a glance toward Rhone. "We don't need him."

Mistress Amolikah said gently, "Kenock, you are a farmer, not a warrior. Do you think it not curious that of all the men who we might have asked to help us, the Creator chose to bring Master Rhone into our lives, and at just this time?"

"You were against his coming."

"I was wrong."

Kenock's resolve crumbled at her admission. Rhone ached for Mishah's brother. It was a man's nature to want to protect his family, and here he was forced to admit he was not capable of protecting them against the dangers they faced ahead.

The Mother pressed, "You are no man's servant?"

"I am not."

"Very well. A workman is worthy of his wage, a warrior of the spoils."

Rhone scowled. What did the old woman have up her sleeve?

The Mother returned to the table beneath the mirror, opened a drawer, and lifted out a pouch. She put it in his hand, forcing his fingers about it with both of her hands. "You are being paid for your services. You are no man's servant."

Kenock took Mishah by the elbow and slipped the heavy healer's bag off her shoulder, transferring it to his own as they hurried down a narrow twisting cobblestone lane through a back portion of Chevel-ee. Maybe he wasn't a warrior like Rhone, but this was his family and he would see to their needs as best he could. "You all right?"

She nodded, but he knew she wasn't. For days, the strain of this pilgrimage had been draining her reserves. "We'll be safe once away from the village."

She just looked at him. Kenock grimaced at the pain in her face. Mishah had a vulnerability that lay near the surface, but beneath it resided a tough crust, not easily penetrated. This stress coupled with her pregnancy had been chipping away at that crust since the day Lamech was taken from her. She was too far along for this flight. He should have insisted she not attempt the pilgrimage this late in her pregnancy.

Cerah led them through the twists and turns with the innate knowledge of one born and raised in Chevel-ee. What would she do if the giants managed to gain entry? And the Mother? A part of Kenock wanted to flee while another part wanted to stay. Watching Cerah, he knew why he wanted to stay. In the short time they'd known each other, an attraction had developed between them. He was certain she felt it.

Kleg'l remained at Amolikah's side, lending a hand to the older woman on the uneven streets and steep gutters, and across wagon wheel ruts. He didn't look well.

As they hastened along, the Mother's parting warning to Rhone stuck in Kenock's brain. "You must get precious Mishah to the Cradleland before the baby is born." Mother Eve's words had struck his sister like a fist. Kenock suspected it was at that moment Mishah had finally accepted the truth. She *wasn't* going home. He remembered how the Mother had placed the map in Rhone's hand, how she held onto it until the last minute. And maybe at that moment the Mother, too, had finally accepted the truth. *She* wasn't going home either. The money purse that she'd freely pressed into Rhone's hand had meant nothing compared to that yellowed map.

"Go northward until you reach the Border Sea, then around its western tip. Be careful not to cross the sea, for Leviathan dwells in it. Continue northward, through the land of Eden, that once fair and fertile country. It is no more so. No one dwells there; it is a wasteland of thorns and brambles. The map will show you the way to the Cradleland."

Rhone had glanced at it briefly, refolded it, and slipped it into an oilskin pouch, sealing it tight against moisture. He'd handed it to Mishah who buried it deep inside her healer's bag.

"Here we are." Cerah's voice brought Kenock's thoughts back to the present.

"Where is it?" Rhone eyed the stone wall, perhaps half again as tall as he. Vines grew thick enough here that Kenock could have easily climbed to the top and slipped over the other side if he had wanted to.

Cerah pointed. "There."

Rhone drew his sword and hacked away enough of the vines to reveal a stout wooden panel, flush with the stones.

"There is a second door on the other side of the tunnel." She brushed at the lingering green tendrils that still hung about the door and tried to raise the bar, stuck from years of neglect.

Kenock dropped the bag and put a shoulder to the bar. Warrior or not, he could still open a door. The wood creaked and slowly the bar lifted from an iron slot. Rusty hinges groaned as he pulled it open. Shadowy stone steps descended into blackness. Cerah glanced at him. "The tunnel will take us under the cleared land beyond the wall and into the forest, about a thousand spans beyond. There may be water down here. The drains haven't been checked in years."

"How many years?" Did he care, or did he only want to see those wide, brown eyes attentive to him one last time?

"One hundred, maybe more. Before my time. Chevel-ee has maintained her walls only because they are there and people see them, but we've had no use for them since the days King Irad marched through the lands. This passage was built to get the Mother safely out if need be. It has never been used. The people don't see it and don't think of it anymore."

Rhone descended the first couple steps, stopped, sniffed the dank air, and listened. "There's water down here."

Cerah took a moonglass from a pouch. "I'll show the way. Come." She moved ahead and down the hewn stone steps.

Kenock took Mishah's arm.

"I can make it all right."

She sounded angry. Had he done something?

He followed behind her with Amolikah behind him, her hand upon his shoulder to steady herself. Kleg'l came next and then Bar'ack, bringing up the rear, the two extra proj-lances the Mother had given them levered over his shoulder. The echo of their footsteps off the close, slick walls made a vaguely claustrophobic sound. The air smelled of mold. A peculiar white slime clung to the steps, making them slick. Kenock picked his way down the descending passage watching Cerah's silhouette in the faint light of the moonglass. Was it his eyes, or did the light actually dim as they crept deeper underground?

The last step ended in a pool of water ... only it wasn't the last. Kenock's next step found water at mid-calf, and the next brought it to his knees. The floor leveled. Cerah waded a few spans ahead and stopped to shine the dim light back at them. "Everyone all right?"

Kleg'l, moving stiffly, helped Amolikah down the final step. For a moment, her heavy skirt floated on the water before soaking through and sinking. "We're fine back here," she said.

"What's happening to your moonglass?" Mishah asked.

Cerah tilted it first one way and then another. At certain angles it seemed to brighten, and others go dimmer. "It's the weakening of the veil."

Rhone took his moonglass from his pack. Like Cerah's, it flickered halfheartedly. He glanced at the ceiling arching less than half a span over his head. "Something must be blocking the Earth's magnetic veil."

Kenock said, "What does that mean?"

Cerah's face stood out of the shadows, her straight nose a defining, sharp line in the flickering light. "It means the veil is failing. It can no longer penetrate the iron in the rocks about us. Mother Eve has told me about it. In the beginning the veil was much stronger, but we are only now seeing the results of its slow death. Moonglass does not shine as brightly as it once did—even beneath the open sky—and the dancing lights have lost their vigor. Mother Eve says it's just one more effect of the fall."

"Lamech and I noticed it in Nod City," Mishah said.

"So have I," Bar'ack said softly.

Rhone shifted his light, making it flicker brighter then dimmer. "Interesting."

Cerah started cautiously ahead, as if feeling her way along with her feet. Kenock put a hand to Mishah's shoulder, and she did not shrug it off this time. The tunnel echoed with the *plop, plop, plop* of dripping water. Here and there, slender daggers of pale rock grew down from the ceiling. Rhone broke them off where they impeded the company's way. The water deepened to Kenock's waist. He lifted his pack upon his head and steadied Mishah's healer's bag on his shoulder.

Mishah pressed palms to the rock wall, carefully feeling her way along. Amolikah's grip tightened on Kenock's shoulder. The water climbed to his chest. Cerah held her weakened light high overhead while Rhone's feeble moonglass darted along the ceiling, illuminating the dangerous points of rock for them to see. He'd moved his own pack to his shoulder along with his proj-lance.

Cerah gave a sudden cry. Rhone's arm swept around, pressing Mishah and Kenock against the wall. Amolikah, Kleg'l, and Bar'ack instinctively followed. A slithering ripple of water passed before them, a triangular head held up, a forked tongue the length of a man's hand tasting the air. Kenock felt the long, powerful body brush against his chest. The serpent passed into the shadows. Mi released a breath.

"What was that?" Bar'ack croaked.

"A spearhead," Rhone said.

"Is it ... is it a ..."

"Turnling? Yes. But humans aren't their usual fare. If you smelled like a rat, you'd have something to worry about."

Mishah drew in a sharp breath. "Might there be more of those creatures in here?"

"Yes." Cerah moved ahead again.

Water chilled Kenock's chest. Mi was already holding her chin up as it swirled around her neck. Cerah's head, and her arm held high with the moonglass, were all he could see of the young woman leading them on.

Kleg'l said quietly, "Perhaps we should turn back. If it gets much deeper, my mistresses will not be able to make it."

Rhone said, "If it gets much deeper, we may all need gills."

"We will see," Cerah said calmly.

Kenock realized she was no longer walking, but treading water, struggling against the weight of her dress. Rhone caught her under the arm. Kenock helped Mi, while behind him Kleg'l buoyed up Grandmother. For what seemed the longest time, the water level stayed steady, then gradually began the creep down his chest. The floor had begun to angle upward. Mi found her footing and Cerah moved ahead more swiftly. Soon the water was at their knees and then suddenly the stone floor rose out of it. The moonglasses brightened showing a short flight of steps ahead. "We are here," Cerah said.

Rhone sprinted up the steps and examined the latch on the door. "This one is locked."

She climbed up beside him. "It's the outside door. The lock is a precaution in the event it was discovered." She took a slender bronze rod, notched along its length, from her pouch and slid it down a hole in the lock until it clicked in place. She pulled a lever, stubborn from so many years of neglect. Rhone braced himself and hauled back on it. The lock snapped open and the door moved enough to permit a sliver of light. Rhone shoved and the door gave way, opening to a low cave, strangled by a bramble of prickly vines.

"These were planted here to keep prying eyes away."

Rhone chopped through them, and they emerged in the forest. When Kenock looked back, nothing of Chevel-ee could be seen through the dense growth.

"Go quickly." Cerah glanced nervously about.

Kenock didn't want to say good-bye. "What about you?"

"I must return to Mother Eve. She needs me." Her wide, brown eyes held his, and seemed as if not wanting to let go. He knew he didn't want to let go. "This path will take you to the old Derbin-ee road and cut a day off your travel. Derbin-ee is a village on the south shore of the Border Sea, two days' march from here. From there, go west over Dragon Pass and around the western reach of the Border Sea."

Kenock couldn't trouble his mind with such details. He could think only of Cerah, and the danger that awaited her back in Chevel-ee. "Will you be all right? Will the men of Chevel-ee be able to hold against those creatures?"

"It is in the Creator's hands."

He took her shoulders. "Will I see you again?"

Her shoulders rolled beneath his grip. A sudden sadness shaped her pretty face. "I don't think so."

Mishah and Grandmother were wringing out their dresses as Rhone and Bar'ack adjusted the packs onto their shoulders.

"Cerah, why don't you—"

"Come with you?" She glanced at the cleft between two rocks, hidden behind the bramble except for the gash opened by Rhone's sword. "No, I must go back." With unexpected swiftness, she kissed him on the cheek, turned from his grasp, and dashed between the rocks, halting a moment. "Creator be with you all," and then she was gone.

Kenock stood there, something wrenching inside his chest. He couldn't part this way and he leaped after her. Rhone's fist caught him. "She has her place and you have yours."

Mishah slipped an arm around his waist. "Maybe we can return this way."

But the horrible fear was, when they did, Cerah would be gone.

"Kenock," Mi urged. "We must flee."

The ground shook, trees shuddered around them, and birds burst from their branches. The earth tremor pulled him from his stupor. Was Cerah in the tunnel? Would another tremor bring it down upon her? And what power did he have to stop it if it did?

He didn't want to leave Cerah, but he had to.

Creator of all, protect Cerah, he prayed. But the words left a gaping hollow in his chest, as if he knew they had fallen on deaf ears. The Lodath's accusation rang in his head. He *was* different.

25

Going Home

Cerah's steps froze when the earth shook. The walls of the tunnel groaned and bits of rubble splashed down around her. Spearheads slithered from cracks and boiled the water as they fled into the dank blackness. The earth stopped trembling and Cerah exhaled a nervous breath and continued along the dark passageway.

She couldn't get Kenock from her thoughts. They'd known each other for only a couple quarterings, yet she'd felt a stirring inside her such as no other young men of Chevel-ee had ever kindled. How she wished he could have remained for a day, or two, or even a week, so she could test the feeling.

Back within the village walls, she shut the ancient door, wrung the water from her dress, and started for the town square. As she left the back alleys, she noticed how the streets had filled with men hurrying toward the town's main gate.

"Denn-in," she called, spotting a friend.

Denn-in turned aside from his two companions. "Cerah." He stared at her.

She quirked her mouth sideways. "I came upon some water. You know me, not very graceful sometimes." It wouldn't be wise to spread word of the pilgrims' escape.

"I've never known you to be clumsy."

"What's happening?"

"Have you not heard?"

"I've been away on an errand for Mother Eve."

"A family from one of the lowland farms was seized by giants. Their leader is demanding we open the gates or he'll execute them there on the road."

"Which family?" She knew several from the outlying district who brought their surplus crops to the Chevel-ee marketplace.

"I don't know." They started moving toward the gate. "The Chief Gate Warden has ordered all men to arms."

She squeezed the water from her skirts, leaving a trail of wet footprints on the cobbles. "What sort of men would use innocent people to get what they wanted?" Men were becoming more and more evil. She knew she had been sheltered in Chevel-ee where they shunned the world, and this was beyond her understanding. She shouldered in among a throng of men filing up the stairs, then forced her way between Master Dor-tas and Master Elwoc.

"Mistress Cerah!" Elwoc looked startled at finding her suddenly at his side. "You don't belong up here. Get yourself down into the village where you'll be safe."

A farm cart stood some distance off, its single gray horse still in the traces, the family hidden behind the towering bulk of three huge men. "Who are they?"

"Master Boroos and his wife." Dor-tas frowned at her. "Elwoc is right. You belong down in the village."

Cerah's throat constricted. Boroos had eight sons and six daughters. His wife, Esliah was a chanter, and sometimes led adoration songs to the Creator and played the leolpipes for the monthly sacrifices. Cerah had worked with Esliah on last year's Creation Eve Atonement. "What can be done?"

Both men shook their heads. "We'll have to wait and see."

A man strode up the road toward the gate. At his side was one of the giants, wrapped in leather and iron battle armor. The giant's sword looked long enough to impale a fist of men with a single thrust, or fell a small tree in one blow. The lump in her throat moved to her chest.

"You'd best get down into the village now." Elwoc's words now sounding distant and unreal, holding no real urgency as the man below drew to a halt.

"Your time is up. Open your gates and turn over the fugitives or bear the blood of these farmers on your hands, then face the wrath of the Oracle's soldiers."

Cerah knew Master Goret wouldn't open the gates. "The Mother has given orders they are to remain closed." What of Boroos and Esliah? Did the Mother know of their danger? Cerah had to believe so. Somehow, she knew everything that happened in Chevel-ee, as if a myriad of unseen informants kept her apprised.

Chief Gate Warden Goret's voice boomed his reply. "Our gates will remain shut. Those people have no part in this. If murdering them is a sign of the Oracle's love we hear spoken of, then that's one more reason to keep you and those defiled creatures from our village."

The face within the polished helmet did not flinch, but the way the eyes narrowed slightly sent prickles along her arms. The captain drew his sword and held it overhead. She caught her breath. A second giant shoved Boroos and Esliah out onto the road. Cerah bit her lip as icy bands tightened about her chest.

"Your final word?" the captain asked.

The crowd along the rampart had gone silent. Cerah clutched the stone parapet. She could see the gate warden's face, the torment of the decision he was being forced to make. Goret clutched a projlance, useless in this instance. "Captain Da-gore! The Creator is not deaf to the cries of innocent blood. I beg you, not only for their sake, but for your own! Spare them!"

Now Cerah did see his countenance change; lips snarling, eyebrows pinching together. His sword quivered as if caught in a conflict between one or the other decision. Then as if suddenly resolving the conflict, it slashed downward. A moment later the giant's sword glinted in the sunlight. The thud wrenched Cerah's heart from her chest, shattering the icy bands. She gulped a breath, her nails digging into the coarse stone, then turned her head away. The vision of that massive blade slicing through both Boroos and Esliah burned into her brain. She was suddenly ill. The sensation passed with the roar of rage from the rampart. A hail of arrows arched over the wall.

The giants lifted a roof of shields that suddenly bristled with the deadly darts. Two blows from a sword severed the traces and the horse galloped across the farmlands. The giants overturned the produce cart, hoisted it overhead, and drove for the gates. Cerah moved to the other side of the rampart as the heavy panels burst inward and the giants heaved the wrecked cart into a line of men. The giants formed up in a circle, their long swords carving deadly arcs through the defenders, their shields repelling arrows and swords. Battering their way past Chevel-ee's first line of defense, they struck out in pairs, cutting a swath toward the center of town.

Cerah pushed through the rushing men, half stumbling down the stairs. Her ears rang from the sound of battle, the cries of the wounded, and the drumming of footsteps as she fought her way against the flow of bodies into an alley and rushed along the back ways to the Mother's dwelling. The alley emerged onto a lane, her way momentarily blocked by giants advancing into the city, growling and hurling their huge swords this way and that, somehow always managing to repel the defenders with skill and strength. Cerah backed against a wall as the battle shifted her way. She had the odd feeling these giants weren't alone ... for they seemed to know in advance where the next attack would come from, as if something unseen were watching over them and speaking to them.

She spied a break in the battle and dashed across the street. Taking the next intersection, she added a burst of speed. The Mother's house lay just ahead. Her feet pounded the path to the door and she rushed inside. She folded at the waist and grasping her side as she drew in a ragged breath, feeling her heart pounding her ribs. She shut the door behind her, crossed the antechamber to the Mother's sitting room, and pulled open the tall door.

"They have breached the gate, Grandmo—" She stopped, startled to discover the Mother wasn't alone. Standing near the hearth and flames was a tall man wearing a black jerkin and holding an ivory-and-gold staff. "Oh, I didn't know you had a visitor." She wanted to blurt out that the giants were in the village and seemed unstoppable, but somehow she sensed the Mother already knew. Cerah had seen Mother Eve's strange visitors before, how they came and went with hardly a sound, how solid walls melted before them, offering no more interference to their movement than the magnetic veil encircling the world presented to her. This one was different. He radiated a presence none of the others ever had.

"Come nearer, my daughter." Eve beckoned with a thin hand. Cerah had never been invited to join her when one of her *visitors* was present.

"The giants have burst the gates!"

"Yes." She indicated the tall stranger who a moment before had been speaking in earnest to her. "He has told me."

"What are we to do?" Cerah went to her, her view drawn to the visitor like flutterleaves to a moonglass. "They're heading this way. I saw two on the lane not far from here." How could she protect Mother Eve? Why weren't the villagers forming a line between those creatures and this house? What if they couldn't stop them? "The tunnel. We must get you to the tunnel, Grandmother. The giants will be here soon."

The ancient lines in Eve's face deepened, a weariness filling her voice. "Don't concern yourself about me, my precious one. For the moment, I am safe. Look." She pointed out the window where a faint blue haze stood like a wall. Cerah hadn't seen it coming into the house. "He protects you?"

"No, my dear. Not me. You."

"Me!" She stared at the being whose pulsing energy fill the room, somehow muting the edge of her concern. "Who are you?"

"I am Gabriy'el, the Warrior of Elohim. I stand in the presence of the Creator."

Cerah grabbed for Mother Eve's hand.

"Fear not, daughter of man, for I am here to comfort Eve."

"I'm going home." Her sudden smile was more peaceful than Cerah ever remembered seeing upon the tormented woman's face.

"Grandmother." Cerah hugged her neck, sudden tears stinging her eyes.

"Do not grieve. I am ready. I have lived with torment more than a thousand years. Every time I see one of my precious ones suffer, I see my own rebellion. I was the vilest of sinners, yet through all, the Creator has loved me and forgiven me. He kept me here for his purpose. Now I have completed it."

"Then let me go with you. I've been at your side since a child. You've been both mother and father to me, friend and mentor. Take me with you."

"Your time is not yet. You have still to complete his purpose for you."

"My purpose?" She wiped her eyes. "What is my purpose?"

Gabriy'el said, "Some search all their lives for the answer to that question and never find it. You are one of the Blessed Ones, oh daughter of man. Your purpose will be revealed to you."

One of the Blessed Ones? Dread mixed with wonderment. The horrible battle beyond Mother Eve's walls dimmed in her ears and fled from her thoughts. "What ... is ... my purpose?" Did she really want to know?

Mother Eve rose, and taking her arm for support, crossed to the table where the book lay. "The Deceiver will fill the world with many evils. He hates humans because of all created beings, they are the only ones who will be forgiven. He hates me because for a short time he had me in the palm of his hand, but the Creator forgave me and took me back. He hates my precious daughter, Mishah, because of the child she carries. That is why the giants, the Earth-Born, the cursed of the cursed, are upon us." Eve placed a hand upon the book. "And he hates, he hates truth." She staggered and drew in a breath. Cerah started for her, but Gabriy'el was already at her side. "This book contains truth. You know what is in it."

"I've read it many times." The world around her shifted slightly, somehow losing the sharp edge of reality. The blue haze beyond the window deepened, rimming the fighting villagers in shimmering light, making them faintly translucent. She could see amongst them other beings—beings like Gabriy'el. So, that was why the giants appeared invincible. *Their* messengers were protecting them. The vision wavered and she was back.

"It contains Adam's words," Mother Eve was saying, "but more than that it bears the very words of the Creator. The *truth* of his creation. It is this truth the Deceiver wants to eradicate from the world of men."

Gabriy'el said, "Before the coming judgment, the serpent will deceive many. Men's hearts will wax cold, and they will shout, 'When will the kinsman redeemer come? Since all the fathers of old have perished off the face of the earth, all things continue as from the beginning of creation.' These men will have come to believe the lies that lead unto death. They are willingly ignorant that by the Creator's word the heavens were of old and the earth separated from the waters." Gabriy'el's sharp, blue eyes pierced her. "And when they believe the lies, and teach them to their children, then sudden destruction will overtake them as a flood. The world will be cleansed of their defilement, and the earth will open its mouth and consume the deadly blood."

"What is my purpose?" The dread she'd first felt was gone.

Eve lifted the book and held it out. "Your purpose, my precious daughter, is to protect the Word."

Cerah took it from the old woman's trembling hands.

"And to pass it down to your daughter."

"My daughter?" Was this a prophecy for her? Cerah looked at the scuffed, stained tome. It wasn't heavy, yet she felt she was bearing a tremendous burden. "What do I do now?"

Gabriy'el pointed with the ivory staff. "You must flee into the wilderness."

"I can't leave Mother Eve alone—not now, not yet."

"You must. My path is ending, but yours is just beginning. It lies before you today."

She stared at the ancient matriarch, then to the tall, shining being at her side, his hand resting lightly upon the old woman's shoulder. Suddenly it was all so clear.

"Your eyes have been opened to the truth, daughter of man. The Daughter of Elohim has never been alone."

Never alone. The words filled her with peace in spite of her sorrow. Mother Eve was not sorrowing. She'd said she was ready, and now Cerah understood the deep truths buried in those simple words.

"You must go now," Gabriy'el said. "The time is almost here."

"I've not packed anything. I'm not prepared to leave."

The messenger bent and lifted a pack from the floor. She'd not seen it there a moment before. She stared at it, hesitated, then took it from him.

Mother Eve opened the drawer and withdrew a watertight oilskin pouch. "You will catch up to the travelers. You must help them reach the Cradleland. There you will be safe for a season."

Cerah slipped the book into it and rolled the end tight and tied the bindings. The travelers ... *Kenock!* She'd momentarily forgotten him. Everything was happening too fast.

Mother Eve hugged her. "Now go, my precious daughter. Hold my love in your heart until we meet again."

The tears flowed freely over Cerah's cheeks, along the curve of her lips and her chin. She hugged the old woman like a fragile doll. "*Will* we meet again?"

"Oh, precious, you know we will." They held each other, then Eve broke the embrace and stepped back. "Now go."

She glanced at the fighting beyond the window. The streets ran red, and smoke had begun to drift through the windows. She cast a questioning glance at Gabriy'el.

A voice behind her said, "I will guide you out of the village."

Cerah wheeled around. He was tall, like Gabriy'el, but not so powerfully built. His mouth was stern, but his green eyes tender and reassuring. "Who are you?"

"I am Ari'el."

She drew in a breath and expelled it sharply. She looked back at Mother Eve, her heart forever bound to the old woman with ropes of love that could never be severed. She didn't want to leave, but she knew she must. "Until we meet again."

Mother Eve smiled. "Remember, my precious Cerah, none of the Creator's children walks through this world alone."

❁

The first few steps were the hardest. Once out the door, the clamor of the battle filled Cerah's ears. Smoke stung her nose and a taste of sulfur clung to her lips. The blue haze still encircling Mother Eve's house was beginning to dissipate. She hurried through it, swirls of blue mist vanishing into wispy trails, and then she was amongst the fighting villagers and trying to keep up with Ari'el.

The giants, powerful as they were, were bleeding and staggering under the onslaught. Yet, still they swung their massive swords tirelessly and men lay in her path by the scores—her friend, Denn-in, among them. She stopped to stare. Ari'el gently urged her on.

Although battles raged all around them, no one paid her or Ari'el any attention. She was moving through a dream. Men charging up the street to join the fight passed through her as if she were not there. It shocked her the first time it happened, but by time she strode unharmed out the main gate and beyond the walls of Chevel-ee, she was used to it. The messenger led her into the forest and onto a footpath. They passed the briar where Kenock and the others had escaped by way of the tunnel. Her clothes were still damp from helping them.

A distant rumbling reached her. She stopped to listen. The forest went strangely silent. All at once, the footpath heaved beneath her. Birds burst from upper branches as trees bent suddenly one way and then whipsawed back the other way. Cerah pitched forward. Ari'el, seemingly unaffected by the shaking, steadied her. A sharp crack from the direction of Chevel-ee, like shattering rock, rang in the air. Her view came wildly around and found Ari'el's calm face.

"It is over," he said.

"Mother Eve?"

A radiance filled his face.

Cerah's heart wrenched, her eyes suddenly stinging.

"She is at peace, Cerah," he said gently, holding her firm in spite of the ground rumbling and trees quaking. "Now the earth measures out its vengeance upon those who murdered her."

Da-gore's nose wrinkled at the stench of burning flesh and smoldering timbers. Crumbled walls and scattered bodies littered the streets beneath a pale gray ceiling of smoke. He'd entered Chevel-ee only after Plut and Herc had emerged, battle weary but alive. The earthquake had been the final straw. When it had struck, villagers fled the gates and dropped from walls like rats abandoning a sinking grain barge.

Ordering the three-points into a lance formation, Da-gore, his lieutenant, and Herc and Plut reentered the village, keeping between the huge animals where a sniper's lance or arrow couldn't reach them. Atala staggered from the swirling smoke, dazed and wounded. He'd lost a lot of blood, but his huge body had a lot to give. Da-gore sent one of the handlers to fetch the company healer. She arrived looking vaguely dazed at the sight of all the carnage, gave Atala a look of despair, and set immediately to work on the giant.

They found Pose wedged into a corner formed by two buildings. He'd not been as fortunate as Atala. He'd killed a least fifty villagers before falling to their overwhelming numbers. Was his spirit wandering like Hepha's? Da-gore still didn't understand the true nature of these beings, these half-human half-gods from the stars.

Da-gore said, "Where is Per?"

Herc's bottomless voice rolled up from deep inside him. "He was trying to get the old woman."

Da-gore looked up at the giant. They'd been sent in after a young woman and her companions. "An old woman? Couldn't he find a more challenging adversary?"

Herc snarled. Plut said, "Our master desired her dead."

Our master? They spoke of the Oracle in the same manner as the emissaries. Why should that surprise him? They were, after all, sons of emissaries. "It seems your master has a particular lust for the blood of women." Da-gore didn't try to hide his disgust. The more he learned of this *master*, this Oracle from the stars, the less honor he felt in serving the Lodath, his human representative on earth. "What of the fugitives?"

Herc said, "They were with this woman, the one they call the Mother."

"Show me the place." Bodies. He needed bodies. Not the masses strewn about, but four specific bodies, and one in particular.

At the center of the village, the street came to a sudden end, cobblestones broken off, some outstretched over a yawning chasm filled with rubble. The building that had once stood there was gone. The earth had opened its mouth, bitten off a chunk of the village, and swallowed. Da-gore pinched the bridge of his nose, removed his helmet, and pressed a palm into his temple. How was he going to explain this? Where were the bodies, the proof the Oracle had demanded? Were they at the bottom of the chasm as well?

"Gather the survivors." He exhaled, a sudden weariness enveloping him. "Maybe someone saw a body." He grimaced. Who was he fooling? He was just going though the motions so that when he stood before the Lodath he could say he did this or he did that ... and perhaps it would not go so hard on him.

26

A Story in the Stars

A sturdy tree was all that kept Mishah from being tumbled off her feet when the ground began to heave. *Grandmother!* She cast about for the older woman. Kleg'l had caught Amolikah in one arm and a low branch in his other hand. He appeared in pain. Had his wound opened and begun to bleed again? This was much too much strain for a man who rightly still belonged in the sick bed. And what about a woman more than seven months pregnant?

Bar'ack and Kenock were flung out onto the ground like gaming cubes while Rhone, as if knowing what to expect, went to his haunches at the first shock wave, a hand thrust out behind him.

The sky erupted with startled birds while cries of frightened animals rang through the forest. A flop of dragons momentarily cast their shadows. At least it wasn't mansnatchers. Mishah's fingers clenched the bark tighter, the rough wood chafing her cheek as the quake tried to shake her loose and throw her to the ground. Slowly the tremors lessened.

When it finally ceased, Rhone stood, legs braced for a second shock, and surveyed the small party. He gave Bar'ack a hand up. Kenock got shakily to his feet. Amolikah detached herself from

Kleg'l's grasp and bent for her pack where she'd dropped it. All at once her head snapped up and she stared down the path from which they had come. Taking a couple steps, she went rigid.

"What's wrong, Grandmother?" Mishah rushed to her and grasped her arm. "You're trembling."

"Something dreadful has happened."

Mishah blurted the thought that first came to mind. "The giants are coming?"

Amolikah drew in a trembling breath. "I fear they've taken Chevel-ee." Her eyes fixed on Mishah. "My spirit is suddenly heavy, as when my husband passed on, and your mother." She shuddered. "Yes, the giants will come, but first they will have their way with Chevel-ee."

Rhone said, "We must take advantage of whatever delay Chevel-ee has given us."

Amolikah seemed to shake off the black feeling. She picked her pack up. "Our destination has been made clear. Nothing must be allowed to delay us."

Mishah's jaw tightened. Their destination *was* clear, and it was taking her away from Morg'Seth and home, and farther from Nod City and Lamech. Yet, what choice is left when the Creator's hand leads? The only way back to Morg'Seth, it appeared, was through the Cradleland.

※

Rhone set a brisk pace at first but slowed when Mishah showed signs of tiring. In her condition, she should be riding, not part of a forced march. Perhaps some means of transportation could be had somewhere along the Derbin-ee Road. He hacked away branches and brushed aside delicate fingerling spider webs.

"My mistresses need to rest," Kleg'l said finally. The good-man was not faring well either.

Bar'ack, who'd spent more time peering over his shoulder than at the trail said, "No time for rest. They can be on us any moment!"

So far there had been no indication the giants were near. "We'll rest," Rhone said.

Bar'ack's eyes darted. "Is that wise, Master Rhone?"

"Would it be wise to birth a child here and now?"

Bar'ack glanced at Mishah.

The forest spoke to those who understood its language. The buzz of cicadas and hoppers never ceased, and Rhone easily tuned them out, listening past the background noise. A clan of monkeys chattered some distance away. Some creature—a serpent or a scaled-tail shrew—burrowed amongst the leaf litter. "I'll know when they come."

"How will you know?" Bar'ack asked nervously.

"Birds are talkative creatures, but will momentarily hush when disturbed."

Bar'ack cocked his head to one side, listening.

Kenock dropped his pack and helped his sister to the ground, against a tree. "Can I get you a drink of water?"

She stifled a groan and nodded, holding her stomach. "The little one is restless."

Amolikah opened Mishah's healer's bag, sorted through the bags of powder, and mixed one with a measure of water from a water skin. "Take this."

"What is it?"

"Katale root."

"Yes. Good." Mishah drank it down and made a bitter face.

"What is katale root?" Kenock asked.

Amolikah closed the case. "It's simply a fortifier to help her blood take in more strength."

Rhone found a spring of sweet water and took a long drink. He preferred its coolness to the warm water they carried in their water skins. He kept an eye on the trail as they ate. The high sun was midway through the fourth quartering, and he hoped to reach the road Cerah had told them about before nightfall. But how far ahead was it? On a good road, they might travel most of the night. An easy but steady march would be best for Mishah's condition and Kleg'l's wound. If only he'd traveled this land before ... but this was all unknown territory to him.

He gave a short laugh at the irony of it. The Lee-landers prayed for guidance, and what had their Creator send them? A stranger to the land. If he were so concerned about his children, why didn't he send them a guide who knew his way around?

The birds suddenly went silent.

Bar'ack's head snapped around, sudden panic on his face. "Master Rhone!"

"I heard." He grabbed his proj-lance and drew back the sparker. "Off the trail."

Kenock helped Mistress Mishah and Mistress Amolikah to their feet, then Kleg'l. As the good-man and the women slipped away, he took up the extra proj-lances the Mother had provided them.

Rhone pointed to cover, and in an instant, the path was deserted, the trampled grass and ivy the only evidence they'd been there. From down the trail came the rustle of a limb and the crack of a twig. Rhone shoved his proj-lance alongside the trunk of the tree and sighted down the tube, his finger curling around the trigger.

Cerah stepped into view, stopped, looked around, and said, "Where are you?"

"Cerah!" Kenock sprang from cover.

Rhone lifted the barrel of his proj-lance and stood. She seemed mildly surprised to find weapons trained on her, but showed no sign of fright.

Kenock gave her a hug. "What are you doing here? How did you find us?"

"Ari'el brought me here."

Rhone had heard only one traveler. "Ari'el? Where is he?"

"This is Ari'el. He … " She turned, then looked around. "He's gone."

How could he have completely missed detecting her companion? Rhone stalked Cerah's back-trail a little ways, then returned. "This man Ari'el has the lightest steps of anyone I've ever seen. I found only your tracks."

Cerah smiled. "I'm not surprised. Ari'el is a messenger."

"A messenger?" Before he could ask, the women and Kleg'l returned to the path.

"What happened in Chevel-ee?" Mistress Amolikah asked. "Is the Mother all right?"

As Cerah's eyes filled, telling of the attack, Kenock put a hand on her shoulder. Rhone watched Mishah's face congeal into grim determination.

"I had a feeling," Amolikah said. "But I'd hoped I was wrong."

"How far to the Derbin-ee Road?" Rhone figured this talk of the Mother's demise was a conversation that could wait.

Cerah thought a moment. "Maybe another quartering, if we move swiftly."

"Mistress Mishah is tiring." Rhone inclined his head at Mishah. "It there any place between here and there where we might find transportation?"

"Unlikely. Nothing but Wild Lands."

"I can keep up," Mishah said with a flash of anger in her eyes. "No need to concern yourself with me, Master Rhone. You already have what you desire."

Her hostility surprised him. *What he desired?* "What does that mean?"

"You don't know?" She glanced at the Mother's money pouch hanging from his belt.

※

As in Far Port, those villagers who weren't killed by sword or earthquake had fled across the fields and into the trees. Da-gore had not the men to chase them down and bring them back. The few men and women he did manage to capture had to suffice.

"What of the fugitives within your walls?" he demanded, striding along a trembling line of frightened prisoners. Plut and Herc stood behind them, their ponderous swords conspicuous. His lieutenant stood at his side while some distance away the healer oversaw the construction of a litter to carry Atala.

The captives remained silent, their eyes turned down to paving stones streaked red.

He needed a body, whether it was the right one or not. *He needed a body!* "Not one of you knows anything?" His voice held the fracturing edge of dwindling patience. "You!" Da-gore's sword shot toward a quivering woman.

"I know nothing of them, sir."

"No. Of course not! No one knows anything of them!"

"And you?" The glinting point of steal lifted the chin of a man biting his lip, shaking like a leaf in the wind.

"I'm a cobbler. I make shoes. I'd not heard of any fugitives, sir."

Da-gore resisted the urge to thrust and make the cobbler an example for the others. But what would be the point of it? They weren't warriors or village elders. They were cobblers and innkeepers and bakers. He'd learn nothing useful from them. Examples were valueless now—or were they? "Herc, kill one of them."

The giant strode before them, delight gleaming in his eyes. He stopped in front of a man and raised his sword, but before he could strike, the man fell to his knees and blurted, "They had an audience with the Mother."

Da-gore grabbed the giant's sword hand and glared into pleading eyes, in a face drained of color. A smudged blue sash across his chest bore an embroidered red key upon it. "You are?"

"Eson, sir," the man stammered, "night keeper on the north gate." His view flicked briefly to the giant. "We got word that travelers had been allowed entrance through the main gate last night, and that they were seeking an audience with the Mother this morning." He pointed where the earth had heaved and collapsed, and pavement had crumbled away. "They must have been with her when it happened."

Da-gore suspected as much himself. His scowl darkened. A body! All he needed was a body! But the earthquake that had engulfed almost a quarter of the village had swallowed up the evidence he required. His report to the Lodath would be ill received unless he had something more to offer than the trembling words of a few survivors. Herc was slyly lifting his sword.

"Herc."

The giant glared at him. Da-gore stretched out a hand. His lieutenant put a proj-lance in it. Reluctantly, Herc lowering the heavy weapon.

Da-gore's mouth tightened in frustration. They fought him at every turn. What sort of army could exist, populated with Earth-Born such as these? "The healer needs help lifting Atala onto the litter."

Grumbling, Herc sheathed his sword and grudgingly followed orders ... for a change.

"Plut, find a place to hold these prisoners."

Keeping his feelings to himself, Plut herded them toward a building.

It was over. It ended here. He had no bodies to prove the fugitives' deaths, but he could take back assurance that they had met their end in Chevel-ee, reportedly visiting a woman known as the Mother. Would that satisfy the Lodath? Da-gore could only hope so.

※

Ekalon stood before the Oracle, although he didn't call him by that name. The one known as the Oracle to men was known to Ekalon by another name: Lucifer, the Prince of the Power of the Air. Some called him the Dragon or Serpent. He was neither, although he freely used them to do his will.

Lucifer gleamed in his own light, still retaining his former splendor in spite of his fall from grace and the rebellion he led—one in which Ekalon had freely joined. Indeed, Lucifer was the most beautiful creature to come from the hands of the Creator. One might almost confuse him for the Creator Himself; a trap even Lucifer had fallen into. But he wasn't and would never be, for like all that existed, he had been fashioned by the hand of the Creator. Ekalon wanted to believe the Rebellion had freed him, and millions like him, from the Tyrant of Old, but in truth, he suspected he'd made a dreadful mistake. Only swift action now might, in some remote way that he didn't fully understand, save him from the fires awaiting the rebels at the end of the ages.

"The humans have escaped again," Ekalon reported. "Captain Da-gore thinks they are dead."

Lucifer rose from his throne, a wispy greenish red mist trailing behind him. "Humans are fools and incompetent. If only I could reach down there and …." His fingers clenched into a fist, the glow about him taking on a deep reddish hue. "We must mount another army. Delay the humans."

Others stood with them as well; messengers like himself, and the pitiful spirits of Hepha, Pose, and Per, unclothed in their disembodied form. Of all creatures, these genetic mutants were the most miserable. They had not the nature of messengers nor that of humans. In death, there was no rest, but ceaseless wanderings, searching for a body to inhabit. They pleaded even now to be given bodies again. Lucifer ignored them.

As he pondered the problem for an instant of time, the light shimmered about him taking on a placid glow, a glorious aura of greens and blues, streaked with a golden tendrils swirled from his head as if from a crown. "Have you been able to influence Rhone?"

"The shackled-one, Sari'el, is always present. I can but only watch. My influence is small, unless Sari'el can be removed."

"We cannot remove him, but perhaps we can distract him." Lucifer considered the three miserable spirits, a violet light radiating suddenly from him. "Pose."

The spirit approached, whimpering. "What do you want of me, Master?"

"Go to the Derbin-ee Road and find a human who will let you in. Make him kill the woman. Per, you go to Derbin-ee. The humans are weak there. You may enter whichever one is the most vulnerable. Stir the people up against the travelers."

The spirits flashed away. Lucifer turned back to Ekalon. "Inform Da-gore the fugitives live. Then tell Sol-Ra-Luce to send his troops stationed in the west-lands to Dragon Pass. We will trap them against the sea and the mountains, and be done with this threat once and for all." The light enveloping him deepened to a pink then faded to a pearly mist.

Ekalon nodded and stepped through a rift in time and space and was instantly in the Lodath's presence.

❦

Shadows had begun to fill the forest when all at once the trees gave way to a narrow track, not much more than two wagon ruts wide with an island of tall grass between them. But Mishah's spirits remained as dark as the coming night. Kleg'l was not doing well, and her own body, in spite of how fervently she ordered it to behave, seemed to be conspiring against her. Her hips hurt, her back ached, and a strange cramping deep down inside of her had begun to worry her. She wanted to sleep. She wanted to stretch out on her bed at home, close her eyes, and awake the next morning with Lamech at her side. But it wasn't a dream. Would Lamech ever sleep at her side again?

Kleg'l stepped out onto the Derbin-ee Road and stared into the gloom, swaying slightly on his legs. Mishah went to him. "Let me look at your bandage."

"I'm all right, Mistress Mishah. I must get you to safety."

"You are not all right. Now, let me look."

He staggered against a tree and slid down. She peeled back the adhesive and removed a blood-soaked pad of gauze. "Just as I feared. Grandmother—" Amolikah had already anticipated her need and had the case open. "Quintin root powder, and some more bandaging."

It was dark before she had stopped the bleeding and bandaged the wound. "Kleg'l needs to rest now. There will be no more traveling tonight."

"We can't risk stopping." Bar'ack's voice seemed to rise an octave.

She silenced him with a look. "We are not going any farther tonight. If the Creator means for us to reach the Cradleland, then he's going to have to delay those giants somehow." She narrowed an eye at Rhone. "Start a fire. We can all use some tea." If he was going to accept their money like a common hired laborer, then he could take orders like one!

"No fire."

She glared at him, but he was determined. Grandmother prepared cold food. Kleg'l reclined on a blanket roll propped against a tree. Kenock and Cerah huddled shoulder to shoulder, talking too softly for Mishah to hear. What they were saying wasn't any of her business, but they did remind her of those heady days when she and Lamech were courting.

They'd known each other since her birth, being cousins on

neighboring farms. He was older than she, and they had never really noticed each other until the harvest festival seven years earlier, which just happened to coincide with her forty-fifth birthday and the final days of her eighteen year apprenticeship with Mistress Alveer. She was now a master healer, she'd reached her years of independence, and she'd met the man she was soon to fall in love with.

Lamech, whose first wife had died forty-two years earlier, was quiet and gentle in all but his zeal to serve the Creator. In that, he was explosive, with a preacher's fiery spirit and his grandfather's gift for striking the tender underbelly of his listeners. He'd grown up at Enoch's side, who had a reputation as the "Creator's torch." Enoch had been honored in the lands of Morg'Seth, Morg'Jalek, and Morg'Gark. "The Lee-lander with the words of the Creator," they'd called him. Later, when his accusations struck closer to the roots, they changed the appellation to the "Thorn of Jared."

Enoch had walked with the Creator and carefully recorded all that he learned. He'd been taught the story of man's salvation as the Creator had written it out in the stars, so that all might see, none might be ignorant of it, and none would have any excuses for disobedience. But most folks chose not to believe his warning of impending doom. Lamech, however, had been his eager student, learning all that he could, carefully transcribing Enoch's piles of scribbling into books so that the words would never perish off the face of the earth.

Mishah sat holding a cool cup of water, wishing it were warm tea. She recalled Lamech's clumsy romantic overtures, the first bundle of field lilies he'd shyly given her, the first time he'd worked up the nerve to take her hand—as though he'd never been with a woman before. She remembered the way he talked about the past and the future ... their future ... as if it had already been written out. He was fascinating. He knew all of Enoch's prophecies, and sometimes, when in a somber mood, spoke of the

"Cleaving of the World" in a way that both frightened and capti-vated her. Yet he was confident that whatever happened, their family would be preserved.

The wedding had been large—most of the village had attended—and almost all her first, second, and third cousins and aunts and uncles from beyond the Lee-lands of Morg Seth had come. Afterward, Lamech moved into her family home, built their own addition to the now-rambling structure, and began working her father's farm. He was a stickler for formalities, and although he longed for a place of his own, he was determined to give the bride's father the customary 120 years. He'd dutifully fulfilled his obligation to the father of his first wife even though she had perished before the time had been satisfied.

These memories comforted her, filling her with a warm glow; a glow that dimmed when Rhone returned from scouting the dark road. He caught her eye, and smiled.

She looked down into her water cup. Knowing the danger they faced, how could he have even considered leaving them alone in Chevel-ee? She frowned. Was it that, or was it his taking the Mother's money that had embittered her? She stopped that line of thinking. Was she being too harsh? Had it even been fair of *them* to have invited him into their troubles? She'd been so certain the Creator had sent him to help.

He pointed to the patch of open sky past the black treetops at a constellation showing clearly. "That's Taleh, the lamb. Have you a story for that one?"

Why was he asking her this? Was he genuinely interested, or had he sensed her coolness and desired to crack the ice in this manner? She had no desire to speak to him just then, but that wouldn't have been fair either, if his interest was sincere. What would Lamech have done? A smile briefly lifted her mouth. What a foolish question. Lamech never passed up an invitation to speak of his Creator, and neither should she. She put aside her unresolved feelings and tried to sound pleasant.

"All twelve of the constellations tell picture stories, Master Rhone."

"Explain it to me." He sat across from her, his high cheeks standing out of the shadows.

"As in each, there are three sign pictures here. The lamb, the Daughter of Splendor, and the sea serpent, Leviathan. The chief star in the forehead of the lamb is called El-nyth."

"Wounded? Is the lamb hurt?"

She nodded. "He will be wounded unto death. The star in its left horn is El-shr'ta."

"Bruised." What does it all mean?"

"You know how we use lambs as sacrifices to the Creator?" She waited for his acknowledgment. "Taleh is the Creator's sacrificial lamb. Bruised by the serpent and bound by death, but death will not hold him captive for long. As the star sign shows, the lamb is still very much alive."

"To whom does the Creator need to sacrifice?"

"Himself, on our behalf, for we cannot offer a sacrifice great enough to blot out the stain of the first transgression."

"Now you refer to the Mother."

"She, and the Father. It was actually Father Adam's transgression that cast mankind into darkness."

He thought a moment. "And what of the second sign?"

"The Daughter of Splendor. She is the lamb's bride. In the times when the Creator returns to redeem mankind, he will select a bride, and she will be all those people who have trusted the Creator's sacrifice to remove Adam's stain."

"How can humans born after the transgression be held liable for it?"

She shrugged. "It's a mystery, but we see it all around us."

"You mean like the moonglass in the tunnel?"

"That, yes. And the Dancing Lights growing dimmer. The turn-lings you've spoken of. It's all the result of the transgression. Someday it will all be put back in proper order." She saw the skepticism in his face.

"What of the last sign? The sea monster?"

"Its name is K-nem. The bright star in its jaw is Mn'kir, meaning 'bound.' In the tail is the star Den'b Ka'to, meaning 'thrust down.' In it's neck is Mir, the Rebel."

"What is the word picture it draws?" He crossed his legs before him.

"The serpent, who is the Rebel, and sometimes called Leviathan, cannot be bound by man, but will be bound by the lamb and made low, because of the sacrifice we couldn't make for ourselves."

Rhone sat a moment in silence, a distant look in his eyes. His fingers grasped something beneath his shirt as if to hold it away from his skin. With a sudden breath his eyes came back to her. "All very interesting." He stood. "I need to keep watch."

She nodded, neither pleased nor sorry to see him go. The telling of one of Lamech's stories had put her in a melancholy mood, and the occasional sharp cramping pain deep inside her womb was continuing to worry her.

27

Possession

The ruins of Chevel-ee still smoldered when Captain Da-gore regrouped his command and prepared to depart. He had no sooner turned back onto the road to Far Port than Ekalon stepped through a shimmering rift between their worlds. The emissary ignored the battle-weary giants and immediately took Da-gore aside. "The woman and her companions have escaped."

Escaped! They'd slipped through his fingers again! "There were witnesses!"

"They saw nothing."

A body! He should have dug up the whole village looking for the woman's body. "How do you know this?"

Ekalon's large eyes peered without blinking. "We have ways."

Da-gore scowled. "Then surely you must have the means to deal with these fugitives."

Ekalon stiffened, his unreadable expression never once wavering. "It doesn't work that way, Captain Da-gore."

What was it with these beings? They possessed powers beyond understanding, yet could not stop the fugitives? What stayed their hand? Certainly not the Oracle. He wanted the woman dead at all cost. A thought startled him. Was the Oracle as powerless to do the deed as were his emissaries? Did his only real power lie in bending men to do his biding? To do what he could not, or was forbidden to do? Now, that was a curious thought. "Where are the fugitives, Emissary Ekalon?"

"On the old road to Derbin-ee. The Oracle has amassed troops at Dragon Pass. He's ordered First Major Bair'tor to move his men eastward. You must stop them at Derbin-ee."

Da-gore nodded. The woman and her companions would be stopped. Afterward he would determine who was the real authority. He was a warrior, but he would not serve a puppet ruler.

Rhone found comfort in the darkness, away from the others. He was a man used to solitude, but there was more to it than that. There was something unsettling to his spirit about being around Mishah and her grandmother. He'd felt the same disturbance in the presence of the Mother as well.

He wandered down the dark forest road a short distance and found an old oak lying along the tangled floor, slowly decomposing. He sat upon the trunk and stared up at the stars through the gap in the forest roof left by the oak's demise. Was there really anything to the story Mishah had told? His inborn skepticism had developed a long, fracturing crack. He'd witnessed so much these last few days, things that did not make any sense in the world he thought he knew and understood. Beings that winked in and out like the opening and closing of a moonglass. An army seemingly always thwarted in its attempt to reach them. The Mother, a legend from childhood fables suddenly real. One man, one woman, and a whole world populated by their offspring.

He shook his head. There could be no denying any more that the woman existed. His own eyes had seen her. Were the Lee-landers correct after all? He became aware of a burning against his chest. It had been there for some time, he realized, but only now had it become uncomfortable—as it had when Mishah spoke of the lamb, and the sacrifice to save mankind. He took the twisted crystal pendant from around his neck and felt the warmth of it in his palm. Now in the darkness, he noticed a faint crimson pulse at its heart. Like the tall crystal in the Lodath's chamber, this too had beating life within it.

A shiver shook him. Why did he still carry it? Because the Lodath had promised him his freedom? Was that reason enough, now that he was away from Nod City? He clutched it and heaved back to throw it away.

At once the burning in his fist ceased and a warmth enveloped him. His head swam. A drunkenness filled his brain and shoved all concerns, all terror, every stress of the last days far into the background. Why should he be rid of it? Because it represented all that the Lee-landers opposed? What were these zealots to him anyway? He opened his hand. The pulsating was stronger. His breathing, which had quickened, now settled into an even, measured pace. He recalled when the Lodath had given the pendant to him. After a few moments of the crystal's heady effect, he had wanted to flee from it. Curiously, he didn't want to flee now. He relaxed deeper, the tension in his muscles melting. He wanted the sensation to last forever.

Release the crystal, Rhone.

Submerged beneath a wave of well-being, a niggling bubble began to rise to the top of his consciousness. What if he couldn't flee from it? He hardly cared ... yet something urged him to break the spell. Break it now, before it sinks its claws so deep you'll never wrest free of it.

Let it go.

The thought rising up through the euphoric miasma clouding his brain had a vaguely familiar sound to it.

Your soul is being contested for.

Rhone shook himself and opened his fist. The crystal's hypnotic pulse riveted his eye.

Resist the serpent and he will flee from you.

Resist. How could he? His fingers closed around it. He tried to put the pendant in his pocket, but something stayed his hand. He commanded his fingers to open, to no avail. The euphoria left him, replaced by a growing fear.

"I will not be controlled," he shouted aloud. His fingers sprang opened and the crystal fell from them, the thong catching on his thumb. Dangling there, the life seemed to ebb from it, then winked out. Rhone drew in a long, shaky breath. What had overcome him? *Resist.* The voice lingered like an echo in the back of his brain. But whose voice? It hadn't been his own. Sari'el! He remembered it now from the encounter on the road. He spun about. Nothing. No tall warrior, no wavering sheet of light, no rift in one world leading to another. His heart pounded his ribs and another long breath did little to settle it.

He looked at the pendant. It would be a simple matter to let go of it ... but ... he shoved it into his pocket.

❧

Mishah watched Rhone vanish into the darkness. What sort of man was he really? He seemed troubled. Had he felt her anger? Or had her story touched him in some way?

She winced at a sudden twinge and wrapped her arms around her large belly. She needed rest. Overexertion would do her no good. The pilgrimage was supposed to be an easy trip, first by boat, and then wagon. Not this rush, this flight from an enemy bent on her destruction. Her throat constricted. She shouldn't think about that. Her thoughts flashed on Lamech, imprisoned back in Nod City—she shouldn't think about that either. She stood. Amolikah's hand was there to help her.

"I'll prepare some food, dear. You need to keep your strength up."

"I'm going to build a fire." Kenock began gathering wood.

Bar'ack said, "Master Rhone wouldn't forbid it without good reason."

"I want a cup of tea, and I don't want it cold." Kenock looked at her. "What could it hurt, anyway, Mi?"

Cerah said, "I could use something warm to drink, too."

A warm cup of tea *would* help Kleg'l, and she could easily fall to such a temptation as well. Kenock glanced at Amolikah. When she didn't protest, he set about building the fire.

Mishah tried not to let her weariness show. "I'll just see how Kleg'l is." She went to where the good-man lay upon a blanket. "Asleep?" she asked softly.

"No, Mistress Mishah." He opened his eyes. "I'm feeling much better, really."

She frowned. "The Creator commanded us not to lie."

"But it's true."

"Un-huh. Let me be the judge of that."

"How can you judge how I feel?"

"My dear Kleg'l. All I need do is look into your face." She checked his bandage. The quintin powder had stopped the bleeding and the wound was reforming a scab across the stitches. "If you can take it easy, this might even heal."

"I must see to your safety, Mistress Mishah. I will take it easy afterward … when you can rest. You must think of yourself, and the child."

She ran a hand gently over his brow, feeling heat rising from it. "I am thinking of my child, Kleg'l. You have a fever. It's not high. It burns the poison from your wound."

She heard the crackle of the fire, smelled its smoke. Shadows played across the good-man's long face. After a while, Cerah and

Kenock came over. Kenock went to his haunches. "Lamech told both of us to see to Mi and Grandmother's safety. You're lying down on the job."

Kleg'l's wide mouth twitched into a grin.

Kenock gripped him by the arm. "Mi will take good care of you. She's the best."

Mishah groaned softly as she stood. Her baby was quiet within her. Asleep, no doubt, as they all should have been. She looked about for her healer's bag and spied it hanging from a low branch in the shadows just beyond the reach of firelight. She needed her moonglass to better examine the wound. Wincing at a sharp pain, she went to the case, removed the moonglass, and opened it. The light fell full upon the bearded face of a man standing not more than a span from her.

She gave a startled gasp. The man sprang from the shadows and grabbed her. Three other men burst from the shadows, wielding swords. One put a point to Amolikah's chest while a second man snagged Cerah as she dashed for their packs, near where Kleg'l lay. The third backed Bar'ack up against a tree. Kenock remained beside Kleg'l, stunned, watching the man who held Cerah and stood over Kleg'l.

Cerah struggled in his arms. He shoved her to the ground and held her there beneath the point of his sword.

Kenock crouched to spring. A warning look from one of the men held him back. Then the man barked a laugh. "What is this? Wayfarers alone in the Wilds?" A grin crawled across his face. Mishah squirmed. The arms of the man behind her tightened. She couldn't see his face, but the first frightful image of it was etched in her brain. She heard his breathing, felt the hot reek of it on her neck. He shoved her toward the others.

"Who are you?" Amolikah demanded.

"Moths drawn to your fire," the man over Cerah said.

Mishah pressed against the arms to no avail. Why hadn't they listened to Rhone?

"What is it you want?" Amolikah demanded.

Kleg'l tried to rise. The sword shifted and pushed him back down. In the darkness, all Mishah could tell was that two were bearded and two weren't. Their dress was that of Wildlanders, and their attitude that of men used to getting their way.

"For starters, you can hand over your pouches. Wayfarers don't travel without a handy supply of gold and silver glecks."

The man guarding Amolikah glared at Mishah. Something in his eyes turned her skin clammy.

As Bar'ack gaped at the steel against his chest, Kenock began to slowly back away from Kleg'l's side. What was he thinking? If he tried something now, he'd be dead in an instant. She had to do something. "Kleg'l, give him our pouch."

Kleg'l glanced at her, then at Amolikah. Amolikah nodded. Reluctantly, he reached inside his shirt.

"That's more like it." The man grabbed it from him and shoved it into a bag on his side. "Now the rest of it. I know there's more."

Amolikah said, "Kleg'l is our good-man. He carries the family pouch. You have all our money."

"Maybe I do, and maybe I don't. By your dress, I'd say you aren't peasant folk. What's in those packs?"

A panicked look pulled Cerah's face.

"Clothing and food is all," Mishah said. What would they do if they found the book? Destroy it? Cast it aside as of little worth? Master El-weel had warned them of highwaymen. Why hadn't they taken more care in setting up camp? If they'd only obeyed Rhone and hadn't built a fire, these four might have passed them by none the wiser.

The man guarding Amolikah stared at Mishah with glazed, unblinking eyes that reflected firelight in their large pupils. A low growl had begun to rumble in his throat. His sword now quivered in his grip. What was he thinking? Didn't anyone see? Mishah wormed in her captor's arms, but they only drew tighter about her.

Suddenly he turned on her. The man guarding Kleg'l glanced over. "Bel-oir? What is it?"

Bel-oir's lips shaped a snarl and saliva began drooling down his chin. Mishah's heart climbed into her throat.

"Bel-oir? What's wrong?" the man holding her demanded.

Without warning, Bel-oir lunged, his sword driving for her heart. Something moved off to the side of her. Steel clanged and Bel-oir's sword flipped from his fist. He wheeled as Rhone stepped from the shadows. A lion's growl roared from Bel-oir's throat and he attacked Rhone with the fierceness of a turnling, and the apparent strength of an ox.

Sidestepping Bel-oir's hunched shoulders, Rhone came around backhanded and drove the hilt of his sword into the wild man's skull, knocking Bel-oir unconscious.

Mishah was suddenly flung aside. Her captor lunged at Rhone. Rhone parried his thrust and stepped inside the man's outstretched arm. His blade found an unprotected chest and pushed clear through it. The brief clash had moved almost faster than Mishah could follow. He yanked free and the dead man toppled. The two remaining villains charged. Rhone leaped the fire, slashed down, and cut deep into the third man's neck. Without a break of motion, he ducked, spun back and drove through the fourth man.

Blood dripping from his sword, Rhone straightened. As he looked at the three bodies on the ground, Bel-oir charged out of the darkness, wielding the blade he'd lost. But it wasn't toward Rhone that his deadly rush was taking him, but straight for her.

Rhone heaved back and sent his sword whirling through the air. Once, twice, three times the heavy blade flipped. Mishah seemed to see it all in slow motion as the deranged man came for her. The

impact drove him back and impaled him to the ground. He con-
vulsed a moment, then his arms and legs slowly ceased their spasms
and the man went still.

※

With a roar of sheer fury and hatred, Pose wrenched himself
from the dead body and screamed skyward. In less than a day, he'd
found a tent to cover his nakedness, and had lost it. With anger and
self-pity mixing together, the spirit, undressed in its disembodiment,
burst through the dimension of man and flung himself at his master's
feet. "I am unclothed!"

"You have failed me again!" Lucifer's pearly glow suddenly
burned crimson. He strode around the groveling spirit, wisps of light
like flames leaping off of him.

"I tried, Master. I want only to do your will!" A dread thicker and
heavier than any he'd known filled him.

His master picked him up in one hand. Paroxysms of torment
surged through him. White hot heat followed by the deepest cold
galvanized him with raw pain. His agony exploded with a roar. "Send
me back, Master." Writhing in Lucifer's clutches, Pose pleaded,
"Send me back and I will not fail you."

"Back you will go! But no human for you this time. I will clothe
you in the body of my servant, Leviathan!" Lucifer reared back and
cast Pose down to the world of men, into the sea.

※

"I said no fire."

When no one made a reply, he scowled and dragged the bodies
out off sight.

Bar'ack jumped at the sounds of his returning footsteps. "I tried
to stop them, Master Rhone. They didn't listen to me."

Rhone put a purse in Kleg'l's hand. "I think this is yours."

"Thank you," the good-man said quietly.

Rhone glared at each of them. "Which way did they come from?" He'd been on his way back when he heard the trouble, but still too far to catch the direction they'd come from.

Mishah said, "They just appeared suddenly from the night."

"They saw the fire," Kenock said lamely. "That was my fault. I should have listened to you. If only I could have gotten my hands on a proj-lan—"

"You'd be dead now." Rhone turned toward the road and strode off.

"Where are you going?" Bar'ack called nervously.

He ignored him. His ears had detected another sound. He stepped out onto the road, a silvery-gray strip in the starlight, and started up it. What he'd heard had been horses. He found them about two hundred spans away, off the road beneath the dark trees, hitched to a wagon. As he suspected, men of a thieving nature usually had no trouble acquiring decent transportation. He stroked their muzzles. "Looks like you've changed owners."

When he rolled into camp, Kenock grabbed for a proj-lance. "Master Rhone, it's you," he said, relieved.

Rhone set the brake and hopped to the ground. "They left us transportation."

Cerah went to the horses, stroking their long manes. "These are fine-looking horses. I'm surprised men like that own such animals as these. We'll make Derbin-ee by nightfall tomorrow."

"Not nightfall. Morning. We're leaving now." He looked to Mishah. "You and your good-man will rest in the wagon bed."

Mistress Amolikah said, "In spite of our folly, the Creator has answered our needs again."

Kenock frowned. "He picks strange ways to answer them."

His grandmother shot him a glance.

Mishah peered in the direction Rhone had dragged the bodies as he helped her toward the wagon. "Those four won't bother you anymore."

"No. But who else might be prowling this road tonight?"

"Your fire may have attracted the giants. That's why we must leave now."

❦

Riding in the wagon, Mishah's pains lessened, yet she couldn't relax. Whenever she closed her eyes, there were giants. Then she'd awaken with a start and stare down the dark road and wonder if in the next moment they would appear behind them. Maybe the giants didn't know they escaped Chevel-ee. She couldn't count on that. If the Lodath pursued them so far from Nod City, what was he doing to Lamech, helpless in his prison? Mishah squeezed her eyes to stop the tears. She couldn't permit herself to dwell on the unknown. The Creator would protect him ... she hoped.

Finally she dozed, undisturbed by dreams of giants. When she awoke, dawn grayed the eastern sky. She checked Kleg'l's wound, satisfied by the color of the healing skin. He'd broken the fever and was resting comfortably.

Kenock walked with Cerah, talking, their shoulders nearly touching, occasionally permitting fingertips to brush. Bar'ack tried to join in, but this was clearly a case where three was one too many. Eventually he gave up and climbed into the wagon, huddled in a corner, and began snooping through baggage that had been left by the previous owners.

"Look." He held up a ring he'd discovered.

"Put it back," Amolikah said. "It doesn't belong to you."

He laughed. "The owners no longer need it."

Mishah cringed at his cool disregard for the four men killed. Maybe they deserved it, but human life was too precious to be treated so lightly.

With the coming of morning, the forest gave way to a patchwork of farms and the land dropped off a ridge and leveled toward the sea. The air held a curious, tangy smell, unfamiliar, yet somehow pleasant. Travelers they met along the way seemed friendly. Maybe because Derbin-ee was just ahead and villains didn't perpetrate their crimes so near to an outpost of civilization. But Mishah didn't believe that. Criminals plied their trade wherever they wanted to.

The sun stood midway to its zenith when the glinting, blue waters of the Border Sea came into sight. She had never seen anything so beautiful, like a million shards of splintered mirrors cast out across its surface. Derbin-ee, a tiny speck against the vast blue waters, was yet a good distance off. As they neared the village, a soft pink shimmer danced before her eyes. The buildings took on the shape of conch shells, their walls circular and adorned with bits of pink shell set in a bright white plaster. Every roof was an identical stepped cone of green clay tiles with a chimney vent at the very center. A low stone wall, with a gate and an arched entryway, encircled each palm-shaded home. Streets of crushed stone ran around the buildings in tight curves that perfectly matched the character of the village. Contrasting with the low architecture was a stone tower perched on a rock outcropping at the very edge of the water.

Mishah's eye latched onto the only straight feature in town. A ruler-straight street ran past the tower, down to the sea, and out onto a causeway of white stone that ran uninterrupted for maybe two hundred spans before curving back to shore to enclose a little harbor. A breach in the causeway, spanned by an arched bridge, opened onto the sea. Within the harbor lay maybe three fists of boats, motionless upon the perfectly still water.

A stench suddenly wrinkled her nose. Blocks of pressed seavine swarming with flies lay spread out in huge drying fields around the tower. She noted a scaffolding, and as she watched, a pallet of pressed seavine appeared as if from a mine shaft.

Folks on the streets stopped to look at them. Faces in open

windows stared. Perhaps visitors to Derbin-ee were a rare thing? This isolated village, far off any regular thoroughfares, lay in a land little traveled. Mishah knew such folks tended to be clannish ... like those of the Lee-lands of Morg'Seth, she thought ruefully. She tried not to let their suspicious looks bother her. But they did.

Rhone pulled to a stop in front of the town square, which, not surprisingly, was a circle—a large green orb of grass with four palm trees, a scattering of benches, and a white stone fountain. "These people don't like strangers."

"They're just clannish." She tried not to sound defensive. Did visitors to Morg'Seth have the same feeling?

Amolikah climbed down off the wagon. "We need to find some-place to eat. And a store." She sounded nervous. Had she sensed a new danger? "There." She pointed to a two-story building with a sign out front showing a bed and table.

They left the wagon at the town circle. The inn's surrounding wall of stone had an arched entryway formed of a bone from some huge creature. The decor inside was sparse; a few tables against the curving wall and a staircase up to the second floor. The door to a room beyond was closed. The floor was wood with no carpet to muffle the heavy thump of Rhone's boots.

"Anyone here?" he called.

The question went unanswered for a moment. Then at the sound of footsteps, they looked up. A woman came partway down the stair-case and peered at them. A suspicious scowl seemed to be something permanently etched into every face in Derbin-ee. "Looking for lodg-ing?" Her words were a monotone of suspicion.

Amolikah stepped forward. "Something to eat, and a place where we can buy more provisions."

The woman considered their number. "Take a table." She set a broom aside, descended the stairs, then stopped and looked at Mishah. "Are you all right?"

Her weariness must have been obvious. "We've traveled far."

The woman's stern face showed a glimmer of a smile. "My name is Deblia. It looks like you'll be a mother soon."

"I hope not too soon." She looked down at herself. "This traveling has not been easy on me, or the little one."

"A hearty meal will brighten your face." Deblia went through the back door.

Bar'ack fell into a chair. Kenock drew back one for Cerah, and another for Grandmother. Rhone took a chair against the wall facing the door and leaned his proj-lance near at hand. Mishah paced to the window, stared out, then went to the door.

"Come, sit." Kenock took her by the arm and guided her to a place between himself and Rhone.

"I see them coming in my dreams, Kenock."

Rhone said, "Now that we have transportation, we should keep ahead of them."

"The horses and wagon don't belong to us," Amolikah said. "Would you just take them?"

"Until they are claimed? Yes."

"No. We'll see about procuring other transportation. I will not show up at the Cradleland in a stolen wagon."

"How can it be stolen?" Bar'ack demanded. "The owners are dead."

Amolikah looked at him. "You don't really believe those men came upon such fine horses honestly?"

"Honestly or not. What does it matter?"

"It matters to me," Amolikah said.

"All right. Enough." Rhone leaned forward on his arm. "After we eat, I'll see about buying us another horse and cart."

That quieted them for a moment.

"You'll buy it?" Mishah asked, wondering why his eyes had caught her in just that way when he'd said it.

"Yes." He plopped the Mother's money pouch on the table and held her for a long moment in his view.

Mistress Deblia brought a steaming tureen of seavine stew, a pot of hot ferrisroot tea, and flagons of dark ale. The dinner was spicy and exotic, but it set well with Mishah. She ate faster than she normally did, keeping on eye always toward the window.

When they finished, Deblia told them where they might find a horse to buy or rent. Rhone paid her three shaved glecks before Kleg'l could get his pouch out.

"We are able to pay our own way," Mishah said.

He looked at the pouch the Mother had given him. "I had intended to return this to her on our way back. It seems now she has little use for glecks, shaved or otherwise."

Why was he doing this?

They started for the door when six men entered. They were armed with proj-lances, and like Mistress Deblia, weren't smiling.

Rhone placed himself before the woman.

A man wearing the gold shoulder braid of a chief gate warden said, "You the ones who came in that wagon out there?"

Rhone's back went rigid, his shoulders taut. Mishah breathed a sigh of relief when he conspicuously moved his hand away from the hilt of his sword and nodded. "We did."

"Put your weapons down and come with us."

28

The Tower Keep

The tower room was less intimidating than the dungeon beneath Government House in Nod City, but it was a prison cell none the less, and Mishah had seen more of such places in the last couple weeks than she ever thought she would.

"Not even a place to sit!" Bar'ack groused. He kicked at the dirty straw scattered about, put his back to the rough, stone wall and slid down to the floor. "How can they hold us like this without any proof?"

Complaining seemed to be his gift, and she'd about had her fill of Bar'ack. But he was just one of many irritations. The chief gate warden had taken everything they owned, including her healer's bag. How could she tend to Kleg'l without it? Fear shook her. She hugged herself to quell the shiver.

Rhone tried the ironwood bars but they were solid. A long locking bar, secured by a peg well out of reach, held the door.

She peered out at the vast sea far below. There were no bars on the window, but where could anyone go short of sprouting wings? From here, high up in the tower, she had a wide view of the sea and a narrow slice of the village below and to her left, its round buildings toylike from this elevation. Only they weren't toys, and she definitely was not having fun.

She clenched a fist, nails digging into her palm. How far behind were the giants? Somehow, they had to convince the chief gate warden of their innocence. And soon!

Kenock and Cerah came to the window. "I'll say it again, Mi. He picks strange ways to answers our prayers."

She glared at him, but bit her tongue. The Creator *would* take care of them! The baby squirmed within her and she folded her arms across her stomach. "His ways are not our ways, Kenock."

Kenock scowled, then shuffled away. Cerah looked back at her. "How are you feeling, Mishah?"

"The baby is impatient to be free of his prison." She winced. Why had she chosen *that* expression? Cerah encircled her shoulder and gave her a squeeze. Mishah turned back to the window. She heard Rhone walk up behind her. "How will this get straightened out?" she asked.

He came around her and put his hands on the rock sill, staring out to the sea. "I'll explain to the chief gate warden how we came by the wagon."

He made it sound so simple. She had her doubts. "He said the owner was murdered and the wagon stolen. How will you convince him we weren't the ones who did it?"

"If need be, I'll show him the bodies."

"Show him! And how long of a delay will that cause?"

"A few days." She heard in his voice that the delay was as unacceptable to him as it was to her.

"A few days and the giants might be at our doorstep."

"And they might not be."

She looked up into his face. The light slanting through the narrow window sculpted his strong features. How did they instill such sudden confidence? Somehow, they did. In spite of herself, she was drawn to him. Then a memory of Lamech filled her mind, and guilt took hold. She looked back out the window.

At mid-fourth quartering, the chief gate warden appeared on the landing and ordered the men's wrists shackled. Rhone tested the half-span of chain between his hands.

"Don't get no ideas," a guard warned.

Under a contingent of three armed men, they were escorted down two levels to a room and told to sit.

The women were not shackled. For Mistress Amolikah and Mishah, that was understandable, but Cerah was another matter. Rhone had watched her over the past few days. She possessed a warrior's spirit, even if she wasn't aware of it. Cerah would be a woman to reckon with if she or someone she cared about was in danger.

The chief gate warden, a man named Sentor, sat behind a table between two other officials. He introduced the one to his right as Witness Gar. Gar had a sullen face and strange, staring eyes. The other, Witness Fain'l appeared attentive and eager for the proceedings to begin as he propped his elbows upon the table, steepled his fingers at his chin. Sentor was a lean man with a high forehead, square jaw, and deep-set eyes so dark they might have been black. His skin had a dusky hue, his hands large and callused; the job of chief gate warden must have been a sideline. When not donning the official shoulder gold braid, Rhone suspected he wrestled a plow, or the rudder and oars of a seavine boat. He spoke in a slow, deep voice, working his thoughts completely through before uttering them.

Rhone's view returned to the man on Sentor's right. Something familiar about Gar's eyes ...

Sentor began without formality. "You say four men attacked you and your party, and that you killed them defending yourself." He addressed all of them, but it was to Rhone that his view went.

"That is what happened," Kleg'l said, looking uncomfortable on the hard, straight-back chair.

"All seven of you fended off these attackers?" Sentor asked.

"I did it."

His eyes widened with interest. "Alone, Master Rhone?"

Rhone nodded.

Sentor pursed his lips. "You're a Hodinite, aren't you?"

"I am."

"I've heard the stories of the fighting men from Atlan. They were without exception, large men and always well armed."

"It's a trait of my people."

"Did you know Master Gailen?" Sentor addressed the group.

Each shook his or her head.

Sentor indicated the table. A window in the curved wall dropped a shaft of light onto their belongings, including Rhone's sword and their proj-lances. Amongst their personal effects lay items that had been in the wagon when they acquired it. The stench of drying sea-vine from the window permeated the air.

"It was Master Gailen's wagon you were driving. Most of that belonged to him."

Bar'ack sprang to his feet. "We told you how we came into possession of it."

Sentor's finger shot toward him, sudden anger boiling in his voice. "You had Mistress Sofila's ring and broach in your pocket. Now sit back down."

Amolikah's scowling eyes bore into Bar'ack. He shrunk from her burning gaze.

Sentor paused, considering his words. "Master Gailen and his wife were well thought of by all of us. Their murder has kindled a fire in the hearts of the people of Derbin-ee. A fire that cries out for jus-tice."

"But … but I only found those things among the stuff in the wagon." Bar'ack's voice had suddenly gone weak.

"Master Bar'ack was wrong in taking them," Amolikah said, "but we had nothing to do with the death of those people."

"We punish thieves nearly as severely as murderers in Derbin-ee."

"The guilt is clear here," Gar said.

Sentor's view slid sideways. "Nothing is clear yet."

"I can take you to the bodies of the men who did the crime." As far as Rhone could see, that was going to be the only way to straighten this out.

"What will that prove? Nothing! You may have merely murdered innocent men along the road. You can claim anything."

Gar's eyes rounded, glinting bright green. "Death and destruction dog your footsteps."

What did that mean? How much did these people already know?

"What proof would you accept?" Mistress Amolikah asked.

"Is a man who is capable of thievery not capable of murder as well?" Sentor's view hitched briefly back to Bar'ack.

"I'm not a thief! You can't prove any of it."

Rhone put a hand to his arm. "Enough said, Bar'ack. My young friend is neither a thief nor a murderer. Taking the items was a poor decision. It is clear now the wagon had been stolen, but we did not steal it, nor did we harm those people."

"I might almost believe you, Master Rhone." Sentor folded his hands in front of him. "For the most part, Hodinites are honorable people, when they aren't causing treachery among themselves."

Rhone exhaled sharply, but held his tongue.

"I see I've touched upon a tender spot."

"The affairs of my people are not the issue here."

Sentor nodded. "Agreed. The issue is to determine your guilt or innocence." He paused and glanced at Cerah. "What holds your eye, Mistress? You've not taken it from that table since coming here."

"I had a book with me. It is very ... important. I don't see it there amongst the rest of our belongings."

Sentor's expression went flat. "I have the book and I have seen what it contains. How did you come by it?"

"It was given to me."

"Or stolen by you, or by him." He considered both her and Bar'ack. "Two thieves working together? If that book is what it appears to be, you have no right to possess it."

"She is not a thief!" Kenock said.

"Then perhaps you are?"

Mistress Amolikah rose and stepped forward. "It was given to her by the Mother. We were there to witness it."

Sentor leaned forward, his hands upon the table. "News travels fast, in spite of distances. Do you think we don't know what happened in Chevel-ee? Or Far Port?"

Witness Gar stood and crossed to the table. "The Mother was murdered, and the book stolen!" His eyes stood wide, his voice low, gravely. He lifted Rhone's sword from the table and turned the blade in the light from the window. "Even now, the soldiers of King Irad and the Lodath of the Oracle come." He pointed with the heavy blade. "They come for you."

Kenock said, "We've done nothing wrong."

"You were branded criminals in Nod City. You escaped and fled to Far Port where enemies of the king tried to protect you … and suffered the consequences for their rebellion." Gar started around behind them with Rhone's sword in his fist. "You next fled to Chevel-ee where you were welcomed. How did you repay their kindness? By stealing the book and murdering the beloved Mother."

"That's a lie!" Bar'ack cried.

Gar leveled the sword at Bar'ack. Rhone watched the eyes— those strange, piercing, overwide eyes. The eyes always gave a warning, but these were different somehow; as if they'd lost connection with the brain.

"Gar." Sentor stood. "Put down the sword."

Gar seemed caught in a war of wills, a battle he finally won—just barely. Lowering the point, he went on in the heavy, gravely voice, "Somehow you contrived an explosion that destroyed the evidence of your crime. The Lodath's Guard was too late to prevent it. You'd already made good your escape."

He circled behind them, his eyes fixed upon Mistress Mishah. "Then you came upon Master Gailen's farm, murdered him and his wife, stole their possessions and wagon. And now your flight brings you here. Finally, you've been stopped. Your treachery is at an end." Gar drew up behind Mishah, his hand trembling, the point of his sword rising slowly again.

The muscles across Rhone's back tensed. "How could you know all of this, Witness Gar?"

"How?" Gar hesitated. Rhone became aware of a low thrumming vibrating under the floor, as if heavy machinery turned far beneath his feet. "I received a message by bird."

"Show me the words that accuse us. If they are true, shouldn't we be permitted to read them?"

Sentor said, "Yes, Witness Gar. Neither have I read the messages you speak of. I want to see them."

"I haven't got them with me." The voice deepened with anger.

Witness Fain'l unsteepled his fingers. "Then go now and bring them to us."

A low growl snarled Gar's lips, his eyes suddenly narrowed and the sword drove for Mishah's spine. Rhone caught the blade in his chain and wrenched it aside. Sentor and Fain'l sprang to their feet. Gar let out a howl and yanked the sword free of the twisted links, striking toward Rhone.

Rhone ducked under the blade and drove his shoulder into Gar's chest. A pain like hitting a brick wall shot up his neck and down his arm. Gar's strength was far greater than his physique suggested. He threw Rhone back and swung the heavy sword as if it had no weight to it. Kenock dove for Gar's knees. Rhone dodged the whirling blade, catching it again in the length of chain between his wrists. He wrenched the chain tight and drove a foot into Gar's hand. Fingers sprang open and the sword came free.

Sentor and Fain'l closed in, hesitating, clearly caught in a dilemma. Gar barreled into Rhone like a rampaging bull, casting him back onto the table. His weight seemed tripled, his strength greater than any Makir who Rhone had fought. Even the warrior execution-ers in the Pit of Ramor had not shown this much might.

Sentor, Fain'l, and Kenock joined in the fray. Gar cast them off as if a garment. He grabbed Rhone's webbing knife from the table and went for Mishah again, who had backed against a wall with her grandmother and Bar'ack. Kleg'l shoved a chair in Gar's path. He stumbled and batted it aside. Sentor and Rhone each grabbed an arm. Gar flung Sentor off and turned the knife on Rhone. Rhone caught the wrist and held it with all his strength.

There was a movement, a swish of something moving through the air, and a hollow thump. Gar lurched and reeled headlong to the floor. Holding the proj-lance by the tube, Cerah hitched it back over her shoulder for a second swipe. But her aim had been perfect, her swing hard, and the blow delivered just right.

Gar was out cold.

Mishah sat upon the straw, her back against the stone of the wall, her cloak drawn up over her shoulders. Night was upon them, and she'd begun to chill. After what had happened, the bars of their cell were almost comforting. Did caged animals find safety behind their bars too? The smell of caked seavine wafting up from the drying yards below was as much a torment as her aching back and her skin that seemed at times to be ripping. But it was the sudden jolts of pain that had her worried. Just the same, there were others here not as well off as she.

Kleg'l reclined against the opposite wall across the small room, his head back and eyes closed, his lips giving a spasm every now and again. His bandaging needed to be changed, and he could use something to ease the pain, but without her healer's bag ... at times she wanted to scream. Frustration and fear warred within her. She was still shaking from what had happened at the hearing.

Bar'ack sat in deep shadows by himself. What was he doing here anyway? A fling with adventure? Right now he no more wanted to be here than she did. He'd cowered when Rhone needed him the most, and he now hung his head in shame. The adventure had turned sour, but there was no going home, not now, not anytime soon.

"You look pale, dear." Grandmother sat beside her and put an arm over her shoulder, drawing her near.

"I'm all right. I miss Lamech."

"Hearts once bound should never be separated." A note of sadness colored Amolikah's voice. She was thinking of Grandfather again, in the grave now more than twelve years.

Mishah said, "Do you believe what Witness Gar said? The soldiers are advancing on the village?"

She felt her grandmother quiver. "I don't know what I believe. I pray it is not so."

Rhone was examining the bars again, and the narrow passage beyond. His view lingered a long moment on the first few steps of a flight of stairs leading up and out of sight. What was he thinking? He crossed to the window and leaned out to examine something, reaching outside and feeling the stone wall.

Mishah ached all over. She straightened her spine and kneaded the palm of her hand into her back. "What do you think, Master Rhone?"

"I think I don't want to be here when they arrive." He cocked his head as if listening.

Kenock went to the window. "What happened to that man? His strength was … was unnatural."

Rhone shook his head. "I don't know. Much in this world is still a mystery." He looked out the window again. "The sea hides many mysteries, and dangers."

Kenock followed Rhone's eye. "It frightens me."

"As well it should. Few venture far out on the Border Sea. My people are great seafarers, but even the bravest of them holds a healthy caution when land drops below the horizon and nothing but timber and pitch separates him from creatures like Leviathan, the saw spine, or the gormerin—carrier fish. There are things in the sea that hate men. The sea spawned the first turnlings."

Rhone glanced at Kenock, his voice taking on the tone of remembering. "On moonless nights, seavine serpents rise up and slither into boats, devouring whole crews. We found a coastal barge once, adrift on the still sea, deserted except for one man who'd hidden in a savot barrel. His story turned brave men's blood to ice. No one goes to sea during the dark of the moon."

Cerah joined them. "You make it sound like the sea is filled with turnlings, Master Rhone. Not all of the Creator's creatures have turned. There is beauty in it, too."

"I didn't mean to paint it blacker than it is, Mistress Cerah. Who can deny the magnificence of prism coral, or a shoal of glimmer fish, like moonglass of every hue, gliding beneath the night waters." He looked at her. "I've yet to thank you for your help."

"You are welcome, Master Rhone." She took Kenock's arm. "The book. I must get it back." A fierce determination filled her face.

Kenock curled his hand around her hers. "We will."

Rhone fingered the junction between two blocks of stone.

"I need to stand." Mishah gave a soft grunt as she rose and went to the window. "The sea is dark. The moon nearly through its cycle." The stars were magnificent in the blackness.

"What do you see up there tonight?"

She looked at him. There was that curiosity again. Was it genuine? Or did he have something else on his mind? "What do *you* see, Master Rhone?"

"From here, I see Dagim."

"Yes. The fishes. Do you know what they speak of?"

"When the sun dwells in the fishes, harvest is over and we enter the time of the falling leaves."

"That's one interpretation. The fishes are a picture of an increase. They speak of a multitude of people, but exactly who those people will be has not been revealed to us. It is for another age." She wished she could explain it better, but the full meaning had been hidden from Lamech, and even from Enoch. "It's a true mystery, Master Rhone; one the Creator intends to reveal at a later time."

He studied her. "It's a picture thin on plot, isn't it?" He leaned out the window and looked downward where the waves gently lapped the stone cliff upon which the tower had its footing. "Are they all so ambiguous?"

"The twelve pictures weave together to make a complete story, Master Rhone. You cannot dissect one from the total and expect it to tell the whole story, any more than you could remove one chapter from a book and expect to get the full plot."

"No, I suppose not." He gripped the window's edge, leaned out, and stared up the outside wall toward the tower's top. Then he ran his hand along the stones as if feeling for something.

"Might I ask a question, Master Rhone?"

He drew back inside the dark chamber. "Ask what you like."

"What made you change your mind about the money? You said you intended to return it. Why?"

"Because it bothered you that I took it."

She scowled. Did he mock her now?

Amusement left his eyes, pale starlight revealing the determined set of his jaw. He gave her a thoughtful look, clearly struggling with what to say next.

"You told me of the sign of the lamb, remember."

"Yes. The Lamb, the Daughter of Splendor, and the sea monster."

He turned and stared a long moment at the dark sea. "You told me the name of the bright star in the monster's jaw, remember?"

"Mn'kir. It means bound. It speaks of a hook in the sea monster's jaw. The lamb's sacrifice will bind the serpent forever." Her words seemed to cause him pain.

"In Atlan we have a similar word with the same meaning. It is *Makir*."

"The Makir Warrior," she said, making the connection.

Rhone nodded. "You reminded me of the *Usito*, the Code of the Makir ... the oath I once swore to honor and defend. The Usito binds me now, even as it did in the past." His shadowed eyes fixed upon her. "The Mother was correct in all that she said about my grandfather, Hodin. He was a protector of the weak with a warrior's heart. Something happened many years ago, something he never spoke of, and the elders never mentioned, but it had changed him."

"Hodin's story is in the Book," Cerah said.

"Is it? I would like to read it someday."

"We must get the Book back, Master Rhone!"

Rhone continued. "When it was over, Hodin gathered his sons and his grandsons, those with a warrior's heart and his sense of honor. That was many years ago, long before I was born. He formed a society of protectors that became know as the Makir Warriors. Makir, from the word Mn'kir, Mistress Mishah. The same as the name of the star in the monster's jaw. And like him, they were bound. Bound to an oath. The Usito. One of the tenets of the Usito is that a Makir must never use his skills for pay."

Bar'ack had become suddenly interested in Rhone's explanation. "That's why you refused to watch those Makir Warriors' mock battle in Nod City."

"Yes, that, and because I knew those men, and they would have recognized me had they seen me. I did not wish to reveal that part of my life."

"Why did you leave it, Master Rhone?" Mishah saw it was difficult for him to speak of this time in his life, but the question had been on her mind since discovering his true nature back in the Mother's lodge.

"It was a family matter."

"Yes," she prodded when it appeared that was all he had to say.

He grimaced. "I was the Pyir, the chief among the Makir, and in line for the high seat on the Council of Ten—my father's seat. But my brother got a taste of power and craved more." He stopped again. It seemed painful to speak of it, but he had kept the story inside him so long, it came out anyway.

"My brother schemed against me with lies, and even murder. To clear my name, I was forced to leave. When I returned, my father was in prison, and my mother virtually a prisoner in her own home. I tried to bring Zorin to justice and free my father, but he had my father executed and I was taken prisoner and sentenced to the Pit of Ramor. Few have ever survived the Pit." He smiled briefly. "But then, no Makir had ever been condemned to it. According to Atlan law, he who survives the Pit must be spared. Zorin had to comply or face Council censure himself." He thought a long moment, then drew in a breath. "To protect my mother, I exiled myself."

His face went taut and his fist clenched.

"I would have returned anyway, to set the Council right and take my rightful place upon the high seat, but Zorin is ruthless, and our mother still lives."

Mishah said, "And so you've never returned?"

He shook his head.

"Pyir Rhone," Bar'ack said quietly as if trying the words out on his tongue.

"Do not call me that!" The sharp command of his voice startled Mishah. Bar'ack's head snapped up, his eyes wide with surprise, the look of embarrassment coming to his face.

"I am sorry, Master Rhone. I won't."

"So, you decided to help us because of the oath?"

"No. The oath compels us to help no one, Mistress Mishah. But once we have taken on a task, it compels us to see it through to the end."

She watched him from beneath raised eyebrows. "Then why have you chosen to take on this task?"

"In truth, I'm not sure. At first it was the money, but not any more. There is much going on here that is far from the normal experiences of mankind."

Amolikah crossed the dark cell and looked up into his shadowed face. "You are on the cusp of decision, Master Rhone. Mother Eve sensed it too—the Darkness struggles for your soul. Some decisions have eternal consequences."

❦

Rhone stared out the window across the dark sea. Somewhere beyond it lay the Cradleland. Once considered a mythical place, he wasn't so sure anymore. His thoughts were troubled. He remembered his first encounter with the Lee-landers on the Meeting Floor in Nod City; the voices in his head that weren't quite his own; the giants; and the being who called himself Sari'el. Then there had been the Mother. The earth had trembled and had swallowed up her enemies. What power did this Creator wield to control such forces? Was it the power of god-men as the Oracle claimed? Or something else … ?

Footsteps sounded on the stairs and a moment later Chief Gate Warden Sentor, carrying a lantern, appeared on the landing and studied them. "I wanted to apologize for what happened during the hearing."

"What *did* happen?" Amolikah asked.

Sentor shook his head. "Impossible to say. Gar has always been a quiet, thoughtful man. That's why he's a court witness. He's never had an outburst like that."

"Where is he now?" Rhone asked.

"At home, resting. Our healer has given him something to calm him and help him sleep. She's with him now. I will be questioning him once he is more himself."

"Our good-man needs a healer as well. Could I have my case back?" Mishah asked. "His bandage should be changed, and I want to give him something for the pain."

Sentor was plainly an honorable man who wanted to do right by his position. "I will permit it."

"And my book?" Cerah clutched the bars in desperate fists.

He shook his head. "That I'll hold onto for a while longer, until we know more."

"But I must have it back."

"In due time, Mistress. It is safely locked away."

Mishah wrapped her arms around her large stomach. "We don't have a lot of time."

The chief gate warden frowned. "If even part of what witness Gar said is true, this matter is beyond my jurisdiction. It is something the circuit warden will have to decide when he gets here."

"How long will that delay us?" Mishah tried not to let her fear show.

"A month, six weeks."

"We can't remain here that long!"

"Is there no other way?" Rhone asked.

Sentor looked at him. "No." He glanced back at Mishah. "I'll fetch your healer's bag."

When he'd left, Mishah slumped against the bars. "If those giants find us locked up in this tower, we're doomed. What will become of us? Of the prophecy? My child?"

Cerah said, "The Creator does not close one door without opening another."

And what door has he opened here? Rhone stared at the dark landing, his eye on those steps climbing upward.

"I want to believe it, Cerah, but I just don't see any—" Mishah stopped at the sound of Sentor's returning footsteps.

An armed guard accompanied him this time. He removed a peg and slid the locking bar from its catches, then held the proj-lance on them as Sentor opened the door and handed the case to Mishah.

"I've removed the knives from it. I trust you weren't planning any surgery on your good-man?"

"No surgery, but I will have to cut the bandages."

"I left the scissors."

"Thank you."

29

A Change of Plans

Rhone had watched the boats come in at the day's end, converging at a place below the cliff, out of sight from his vantage point. Some of the boats reappeared a little while later and rowed to the small harbor where men debarked, levered poles and packages upon their shoulders, and walked the causeway road into town. Stars appeared, and a waning sliver of moonlight rose above the water.

The industry appeared to be seavine harvesting. That explained the blocks of seavine drying along the cliffs. Somewhere below them, seavine was being stored and processed. He leaned out the window to study the dark water below the cliff.

Mishah, Cerah, Amolikah, Kenock, and Kleg'l had been debating who would arrive first, the circuit warden or the giants. In the end, they agreed the giants would be there first. Bar'ack remained apart from them, grasping the bars like a desperate animal.

The scraping of footsteps on the stairs brought instant silence to their discussion. A man paused on the landing and shone a lantern in on them. Bar'ack backed away, slumping against the wall. The man grunted and continued up the stairs. Rhone cocked his head to listen. Somewhere above them, metal hinges squeaked and a wooden door thumped. A while later, a beam of light stretched far across the dark water and the footsteps started down.

The man reappeared, held the lantern high and peered in on them again, then continued down.

Rhone stabbed a finger at the ceiling. "A navigation beacon. We're losing the moon. They're only lit during the dark of the month."

Mishah adjusted her cloak, drawing it together at her neck. "Master Rhone, you've said little about our situation. I was hoping you'd have—"

"An answer to the problem?"

She nodded. "Something like that."

"You're a Makir," Kenock said with a note of accusation in his voice. "You have training."

Rhone hitched his head toward the dark window. "No training I know of teaches a man to sprout wings like a bird."

Disappointment showed in all but Cerah's face. She went to the window and probed the same seam between the blocks he'd investigated earlier. "No bird, Master Rhone, but a squirrel perhaps?"

"Perhaps."

Now she smiled. They understood each other. He said, "We should get some rest."

Mistress Amolikah studied him.

Kleg'l said, "Rest? We haven't done anything all day to rest from."

The older woman glanced at Kleg'l. "Yes, we should rest." She looked back at Rhone with a question in her eyes, one she kept to herself.

❧

The first quartering folded into the second as the long night stretched out toward morning. Near mid-second quartering, Rhone stirred from his place and stood, quietly brushing the straw from his clothes. He leaned out the window. All was dark except for a lamp or two along the causeway, and the beam of light from the roof of the tower. He would have preferred it not to have been lit, but that couldn't be helped now. He felt the slim handholds between the stones. The tower had been skillfully made and the stones fitted tightly, but because it narrowed toward the top, each layer had been very slightly inset from the one below it.

In the night stillness, he heard the far-off rumble of heavy machinery, though he no longer felt the faint vibrations this high in the tower. Light flicked up the stairwell from the floor below, and muffled voices reached his ears. Since the lamplighter had left, no one had come up to check on them. "No time like the present," he mumbled softly to himself.

"What you're planning is dangerous." Mistress Amolikah's whispered quietly from the darkness. She rose and crossed to him.

Another shape moved too. Cerah came to him, her eyes wide and alert. She put her head out the window a moment. "The morning mist is rising. The stones will be slippery."

"What's going on?" Kenock mumbled sleepily, sitting up and scrubbing the sleep from his eyes.

Cerah went to him. "Speak softly. We're getting out of here"

Rhone removed his boots, sat on the sill, and swung one leg over, feeling for a toehold. The height was dizzying.

"Master Rhone." Cerah lifted the skirt of her jumper and drew a short dagger from a sheath on her left calf. "An extra claw for the squirrel."

A warrior's spirit, indeed! He hefted the blade. "Thanks." He eased his weight down onto the sharp rock, swung the other leg, and found a second toehold. He pressed his thick fingers into a narrow crack for a tenuous purchase on the steep wall. With toes clinging by a mere fold of skin, Rhone drew in a breath, cast his view upward to the glare of light above, and released the sill, groping for a slim gap.

The breeze off the sea was cold against his skin. Pushing, he rose half a span, reached, and found a new hold. He pushed again, fingers searching the stones, not finding enough purchase to support his weight. His grip broke, and he grappled for the sill and jolted to a stop. Cerah and Kenock grabbed onto his arm and held him until as he pull himself back through the window and dropped to the floor.

The fall had scraped his hands raw. "My fingers are too big and I'm too heavy." He muffled his anger, glaring at the blood on his hands. "This squirrel needs sharper claws."

Mistress Amolikah touched his arm. "There must be another way."

Cerah's mouth took a determined set. "I don't think so." She examined the gaps in the stones. "My fingers fit."

"It's too dangerous," Kenock whispered.

Bar'ack sat up, rubbing his eyes, looking around. "What are you three up to?"

"Keep your voice down," Rhone cautioned.

"Escaping," Cerah whispered, loosening her belt and pulling her jumper over her head. She shoved the dress into startled Kenock's hands. "What are you staring at?"

"You," he said, shocked.

Her shirt fell mid-thigh above a pair of green knit leggings. She tightened the belt about her waist. "Well, you can stop gawking. You didn't expect me to climb in that dress, did you?"

He shook his head, speechless.

She kicked off her shoes.

Rhone said, "Can you do this?"

"I can."

"And you can get yourself killed," Kenock croaked.

"I'll be all right, Kenock. What choice do we have?" She held out a hand.

Rhone placed the dagger in it. *A true warrior's spirit!*

Mishah stirred. Cerah lowered her voice further. "We do it tonight, or we face giants tomorrow. If we make good our escape, we'll be on our way to Dragon Pass by the time anyone knows we're gone."

Mistress Amolikah said, "And if you fall, you'll arrive at Adam's Bosom a day or two before we do."

Cerah made a wry face. "The decision really isn't all that difficult, put that way."

"I can't let you do this. It's a hundred spans to those rocks."

"Kenock, I must." She gave a quick smile. "I used to climb the walls of Chevel-ee when I was young."

"But those walls were only five spans high!"

"I'll be all right. I feel the Creator's strength." She turned to the window before he could argue further.

Rhone helped her onto the sill and held her until she'd gotten her grasp. "Don't look down."

"I never do." She drove the blade between two stones and started upward.

"She's going to be killed." Kenock wrung his hands.

Rhone leaned out the window, watching her creep slowly but surely up the side, the chink of steel striking stone coming at regular intervals. "If she does, it will be an honorable death." Moisture was thickening on the stone. Kenock began pacing. Rhone kept his eyes on the shadow against the wall. Suddenly the clink of steel stopped.

Kenock rushed to the window. "What happened?"

Rhone pushed his head back inside. "Some obstacle. She's searching. Keep your voice down. You'll make her nervous, and bring the guards up to investigate."

Cerah crept sideways a span and the strike of steal resumed. Kenock returned to his pacing. Rhone heard Mishah rise and come over. Mistress Amolikah whispered what was happening.

The sharp *snap* rang out in the still night and the blade clattered down the wall, past the window and past a window below them where a light shone. The dagger bounced away from the wall and made a soft, distant clink upon the rocky cliffs.

Kenock gasped.

"What was that?" Mishah whispered.

Rhone drew his head back inside. "She lost her knife."

"Creator, protect her." Kenock grasped his skull and collapsed against a wall.

When Rhone leaned back out the window, Cerah was no longer in sight. With sudden dread, he looked to the cliffs but the shadows were too deep to see details. Then the soft squeak of a hinge moaned from above. They rushed to the bars as her careful footsteps came down the stairs.

"Cerah!" Kenock shoved his arms through the bars and hugged her. Her face showed lingering terror, but she managed a smile in spite of it.

Rhone put a finger to his lips and pointed to the latch. She removed the pin and quietly pushed the beam through the catch. The door opened.

"Wait here." Silently, he descended to the next floor and peeked around the corner of a stone wall. Two men hunched over a dueling board, studying the gaming pieces arranged in battle formations— the lamplighter and other he didn't recognize. A proj-lance leaned against a wall and a sheathed sword hung from a hook. From a row of hooks hung the wrist shackles. A lantern on a shelf cast a pale light on their table, leaving the rest of the room in shadows. The lamplighter moved his black warrior.

"Ho, ho," the other man laughed. "That move will cost you a gate warden, Bilko."

Bilko rubbed his fingers. "Hummm. Didn't see that one."

Rhone crept quietly toward the sword.

The man removed Bilko's gate warden from the board and laughed again. Bilko studied the pieces and reached for a black priest. Rhone came silently up behind him and tipped over the priest with the point of his sword. They jumped.

"One word out of either of you," he whispered, "and you'll lose something more dear than a gate warden. Now, stand." They obeyed, eyes fixed upon the blade. Rhone inclined his head toward the stairs, gathering up wrist shackles as he went.

❦

The dark hallway was indented here and there with even darker alcoves, some empty, other containing bundles wrapped in tarps. The tower appeared deserted as they crept down the dark stairs. Mishah was still seeing the surprise on the guards' faces, shackled and gagged in the cell.

"If we're lucky we won't be missed until the third quartering," Rhone said.

"If so, luck won't have anything to do with it," Amolikah whispered. They came to the room where Bilko said they'd find their belongings. The packs and weapons were there, but not the Book. Cerah tossed aside sacks and rummaged through shelves. "It's not here! I can't leave without it."

Mishah cocked her head. "Do you hear that?"

Kenock whispered, "Machinery?"

Rhone nodded. "Somewhere beneath us." He started for the door, and looked back. "Mistress Cerah, you must come."

"I won't leave without the Mother's book!"

Kenock took her by the shoulders. She wrenched free of his grasp and glared at him. "She entrusted it to me! Don't you understand?"

"I understand, Cerah. But we can't stay."

"If I leave it, I've failed.

"If the giants kill you, you've failed too. And I won't leave without you, so we both fail."

She stood there, torn.

"We'll come back for it, Cerah. I promise."

She hugged him suddenly and nodded. Rhone took the lead again, down past the room where they'd met with the chief gate warden. Suddenly Cerah sprang to the closed door. It was unlocked and she dashed inside. Kenock threw a startled look at Mishah, and then dove after her. Misaha saw irritation in Rhone's scowl. "I'll get her," she said.

Inside the darkened room, Cerah was frantically searching for the Book.

"We can't delay," Kenock implored, but she wasn't listening.

"He said it was safely locked away," Cerah whispered, scanning the room. "There!" She rushed to a cabinet against the wall, but the door was locked. Kenock gave it a try. It didn't budge.

"It's no use, Cerah. We must go now!" he said.

"Not until I get the Mother's Book back," she said sharply.

Mishah heart pounded as she watched the door. "Kenock is right, Cerah. We can't delay any longer."

Rhone entered the room, saw Cerah struggling with the cabinet door, drew out his sword and thrust the blade in the crack by the lock. It sprang open.

Cerah gave a gasp. "Yes!" She grabbed up the heavy Book, clutching it to her chest.

"Move quickly," Rhone said. They flew down the stone stair to the next level. Mishah remembered this passage. It led to the tower door. They'd reached ground level. Rhone paused at the door and put an ear to it. He scowled suddenly, wheeled about, and hurried them into an alcove. The door opened and Chief Gate Warden Sentor entered with two other men.

"Something about this is very unnerving," Sentor was saying.

"You mean other than having King Irad's soldiers prowling our realm?" one of the men replied.

Sentor gave a short laugh. "Yes, other than this incursion into our territory." They paused before the alcove, their backs to it. Mishah stopped breathing. Rhone's arms crushed her and the others hard against the stone wall.

"What puzzles me," the third man said, "is why he has ordered his warders to Dragon Pass. According to the news I get, there are more than two hundred already in place. What is so important about Dragon Pass to warrant such numbers?"

Sentor grunted, a grave note entering his voice. "Some of what Witness Gar said just might be true."

"Is the healer still with him?"

"She left once he was asleep. She thinks he's much improved. Whatever got into him seems to have passed." Sentor laughed. "Let's hope it's not something in the water." They chuckled and resumed walking down the hall and up the stairs.

Rhone let go of a long breath and now led them back the way they'd just come. What was he thinking, following the chief gate warden? Mishah glanced at her grandmother and failed to catch the older woman's eye. Where Sentor had ascended the stairs, another flight continued downward into the tower's foundations. It was these Rhone turned down.

Hewn rock gave way to the rough cave walls, and the wooden stairs became natural stone. The sound of machinery grew louder as they went deeper; a rhythmic rumbling up through the soles of her shoes. Now she heard a new sound. Rushing water.

"Where are we going, Master Rhone?" Bar'ack asked.

Rhone paused where the narrow, moist walls pressed close. No light reached down this far, and only the dimmest hint of a torch flickered somewhere below. The breeze that funneled up from below carried the smell of the sea. Mishah hitched her cloak tighter. Rhone glanced to Cerah. "Is there another way through the mountains other than Dragon Pass?"

Mishah saw the shadowy movement of her head. "No. Dragon Pass is the only way, and through it we must go to circle the western edge of the Border Sea."

Rhone's voice remained low, thoughtful. "Somehow the Lodath knows our destination and has sent his warders to cut us off. If we attempt it, he'll have us in his grasp at Dragon Pass, or drive us into the sea."

"Either way, he wins," Amolikah said.

Kleg'l quietly said, "We cannot permit that."

"No," Kenock agreed.

"We won't." Rhone's determination sounded reassuring enough, but she wondered how could he protect them from so many. "Somehow the Lodath is able to track us," he went on.

Amolikah said. "He has the Oracle's ear, and the Oracle has his watchers everywhere." She paused. "We'll have to find another way around the sea."

Rhone nodded. "I have a feeling the 'other way around' lies at the bottom of this passage."

The chill drove deeper into Mishah. She couldn't stop shivering, even huddled in her cloak. Would Lamech have known a way out if he were here? She wanted to believe he would, yet how could he? He was a farmer. Rhone was a warrior. A Makir. If he didn't know, who would?

❦

The passage brightened, and suddenly they stepped out onto a flat, slick stone near an underground river. The crash of cascading water and the rumble of machinery shook the ground, filling the cavern with a teeth-jarring sound. Here and there, a lantern hung from iron stakes driven into solid rock. Rhone took one and held it aloft. Shadows shifted along the high, arching ceiling before the lantern's feeble light.

"What is that sound?" Mishah looked at the swift flow of water tumbling to the sea from the deeper recesses of the cave.

Indeed, what was it? A back door? "Let's see." Mist borne on a cold wind filled the air. Ahead, the tunnel took a sharp bend. They rounded it and came to a halt before a massive waterwheel turning beneath the gushing of an underground river. Huge wooden gears clacked, busily turning cams and levers, and two great grinding stones. Conveyor belts crisscrossed the mechanism, and racks of steel blades rose and fell, pounding timber blocks. At the far end, an elevator of buckets clattered upward into a shaft in the ceiling. Rhone recalled the workings on the surface, the mounds of drying seavine, chopped and pressed into blocks.

No back door. He frowned, aware of a burning against his chest, like a hot coal beneath his shirt.

Wheelbarrows filled with seavine lined the wall while two men lazily shoveled seavine from them onto one end of a conveyor.

Rhone motioned them back. The sea would be their only way out. As they turned, Witness Gar sprang from the shadows and pointed a proj-lance at Mishah.

Rhone grabbed Mishah aside the instant Gar fired. The proj screamed past his ear and burst into a ball of fire against the back of the cave. With a howl of rage, Gar charged them, whirling the proj-lance like a club.

Rhone swept up his proj-lance, slamming it against Gar's, and the two weapons skittered across the floor, into the rushing river. Rhone tackled the wild man at the knees, driving him to the floor. Gar somehow managed to cock his legs under Rhone and catapulted him across the cave.

Gaining his feet, Gar drove into Rhone with a power beyond

human. Rhone maneuvered Gar in a headlock, but he might as well have had a three-point in his arms. This strength wasn't human; it was like going hand-to-hand with one of the giants.

Gar lifted him overhead and slammed him into the wall. Rhone crumpled to the floor, his breath, pained gasps. The burning coal beneath his shirt seemed to have grown suddenly hotter.

Suddenly Gar turned toward Mishah. Kenock, yelling, plowed into him with windmilling fists. Gar batted him aside.

Rhone swayed to his feet.

Kleg'l reeled to the floor next, curling in pain and clutching his chest. Cerah leaped to Gar's back, but the wild man tore her off and cast her aside. Rhone grabbed an empty wheelbarrow and shattered it against Gar's back. He shrugged off the blow that would have stopped any normal man and went for Rhone's throat. The two locked, Rhone focusing every ounce of his strength on the fingers slowly squeezing the breath from him. His brain whirled and spots swam before his eyes, the burning against his chest now the glowing tip of iron worked in a forge.

Gar forced him toward the rumble of crashing blades and grinding wheels. Locked in this death grip, staring into eyes radiating a malevolent hatred, Rhone knew he was fighting something other-worldly, a battle no mere human could possibly hope to win. His strength began to fail, Gar's fingers an iron trap about his throat. Sari'el had said his soul was being contested for. Was that contest to end here and now? The thought terrified him.

He was vaguely aware that someone had attacked Gar from behind, but the effort seemed ineffective. The rumble of grinding stones was near his ears, their grittiness chafing his cheek. He felt himself slipping toward unconsciousness ...

In a flash of desperation, he let his feet go out from under him, too far gone to really feel hard stone pound his spine, or Gar's weight crash down on him. He got one foot on Gar's belly and with the last of his strength, levered him over his head. The deadly grip broke.

A cry shook the cavern, cut off by the crunch and grinding of flesh and bone. Someone was dragging him. Blood rushed back to his brain. Bar'ack and Kenock helped him to his feet, pain shooting up his spine and down through his hips. The world came back into focus. The mighty waterwheel still turned, the grinding stones unstoppable, but now they bore a long, bloody streak upon their surface, and Witness Gar was no more.

30

Daughter of Seth

Per fled the useless body that had once been Witness Gar, and in a moment of time, he stood before his master.

"I am naked again," he moaned, cowering before the burning glare in his master's eyes. Lucifer's anger drove out the light and filled the heavens with black, roiling clouds of smoke, tinged blood-red with his fury.

"You ruined the tent I'd given you!"

"Give me another," he pleaded, unable to look upon his master's furious rage. "Do not leave me like this, unclothed."

With footsteps of thunder, Lucifer paced his realm. The earth passed beneath his feet, infected with the blight, like mold spreading across a rotting peach. "The woman must be stopped." He drove his fists together with lightening exploding from them and lancing through the blackening smoke. "We cannot fail."

Lucifer grew in stature until his form overshadowed the miserable planet beneath him. He raised his fist to heaven and shook it at the throne room of the Tyrant of Old. "You will not win this! I am the god of this world. I wrenched it from your grasp, and I will not give it back!"

Per cringed as his master's rage crashed around him. Lucifer snatched him up and held him before his fiery glare, the hot breath of his hate more terrifying than the feared Lake of Fire, their final destination should they fail in this war. "Return to my realm. The people of the Tyrant will attempt a sea crossing. Should they succeed, you must stop them before they reach the Cradleland!"

Lucifer flung Per once again back to earth.

❧

Rhone hurried down the dark tunnel, stiff from the battle, but loosening up some now as he worked the kinks from his hips and back. The burning against his chest had lessened, but the pain of it was still there. He had one thing left to do, once he had himself and the others away from Derbin-ee.

Amolikah looked at him as they hurried toward the faint dawn showing in the mouth of the cave where it opened onto the Border Sea. "There is only one way left to us, Master Rhone. But the Mother warned us not to take it."

"Soon this whole area will be filled with seavine gathers, returning to work. Then this way will be lost as well. We have no choice." He appraised the boats docked up ahead, just inside the sea mouth.

"Do you know how to sail, Master Rhone?" Mishah sounded breathless. Kenock carried the heavy healer's bag, helping her along.

"I'm from the Island of Atlan; we are a seafaring people," he gave her a look that was the closest thing yet she'd seen to a grin, "among other things. Although I've not put my hands to oar or tiller since leaving my country, it's not something a man soon forgets."

Kleg'l staggering under renewed pain, managed to keep up, with Bar'ack lending a hand. Beyond the cave's mouth, gray water lapped the rocks. Five boats lay alongside a landing just inside the cave, three of them not much larger than skiffs. A fourth, a coastal barge with a large, flat deck, was still piled high with mounds of yesterday's seavine harvest. The fifth looked promising. As large as the barge, it had a sleek hull and six oars in the rowlocks. A mast with a sail furled against a spar reached nearly to the ceiling of the cave. It appeared unoccupied, and Rhone hustled them across the gangplank.

Somehow, Gar had known of their escape, and now the workers who'd fled at the beginning of the battle knew too. Surely they raised an alarm. There could be no pleading innocent this time. Fleeing Derbin-ee was their only hope ... was Mishah's only hope of reaching the Cradleland. His thoughts came to a sudden halt. When had he made the leap from mere curiosity to true concern?

"Everyone aboard!" Casting a glance back the way they had come, Rhone drew in the gangplank. "Bar'ack, throw off the aft line! Kenock, the bow hawser!" Released from its moorings, the boat lurched in the current and drifted with the flow of the underground river toward the arch of stone and the gray sea beyond.

All but Mishah and Kleg'l manned an oar. Rhone grabbed the tiller and took up a stout pole to fend them off the rocks.

The low door in the center deckhouse slammed open and a man rushed up the stairs, naked from the waist up, looking half asleep. "What in Dirgen's name are you doing on my boat?" He turned a surprised circle at seeing all of them there.

"We need it," Rhone said.

"You need it?" He snarled and spewed a stream of profanities that made even Rhone wince. "Off! All of you off my vessel!" He reached inside the hatch and drew out a proj-lance.

Rhone released the tiller and drove him into the cabin wall with the blunt end of the pole. "You can come with us and have it back once we reach our destination, or I'll toss you overboard now."

The boat bumped an underwater obstacle. Mishah grabbed the tiller. It heeled to port and corrected itself in midstream. They cleared the mouth of the cave, straightening out to sea as their clumsy rowing grew more synchronized.

"You'll end up behind bars for this."

"A minor concern now. What are you called by?"

"Ben'jor." His eyes narrowed. "You're on the run!"

"From charges more serious than commandeering a boat, Master Ben'jor."

"You're the ones being held in the Dirgen's Pillar." His eyes widened suddenly. "The ones what murdered Master Gailen, and got the king's Guards on your tail."

Rhone glanced toward the gray cliffs, the black maw of the cave shrinking. "The swim back is growing longer, Master Ben'jor. What will it be?"

Lips thinning, Ben'jor exhaled sharply out his nose and nodded. "I'll stay with my boat to see that nothing happens to her. But I don't see what good it will do you. Men can travel the coast road faster then we can row, or catch the breeze. They'll be waiting for you in Orin-ee when we get there, or Sarv-ee if you flee eastward. Flee as far as you can, the chief gate warden and the others will be always one step ahead."

"We won't be going west or east."

"Humph! There ain't no other—." His words came to an abrupt halt, his eyes narrowing to two dark slits. "Why ... why, you ain't taking my boat *across* the sea?"

Mishah said, "Eve's Weep, on the north coast."

Ben'jor's jaw dropped, his eyes all at once too large for his face. "Eve's Weep. Why in Dirgen's name go to a castoff place like that? Ain't nothing there but a few shacks and a rotting pier that ain't hardly safe to lay up to." He shook his head. "No, Mistress, nothing there worth risking our lives crossing this here jut of the sea for."

Her expression remained resolute.

Ben'jor's lip began to tremble. "I know of a hidden cove east of here. I can lay you safely ashore there. Can't hardly get to it off the coast road. The men after you won't even think to search for you there."

He shot a panicky look at the yellowish cliffs receding in the distance, catching the first golden rays of sunlight. His head swiveled around toward the horizon. "You don't want to take this boat out there. There's turnlings out there!" He shifted his near-frantic gaze from Mishah and Rhone. "Only the strongest boats ever venture out beyond the sight of land."

Rhone cast the pole aside and took the tiller from her. "Nevertheless, it's where we must go." He looked at Mishah. "Your Creator seems to have protected you this far. Would he do so only to let you perish at sea?"

She broke off the eye contact. "No, of course not." She took up her healer's bag and went to Kleg'l, leaning against the mast, folded slightly at the waist, a hand pressed to his chest.

※

The third quartering came and went with hardly a breath of a breeze moving upon the still waters. Hot, heavy air blurred the never-changing horizon. Kenock was not used to the heat of the sea. He glanced at his grandmother. Amolikah's strength had waned long ago; now she only went through the motions of rowing. Cerah had urged her to seek the shade of the deckhouse with Mishah and her good-man, but she'd refused to give up the oar.

He worried about her, and about his sister. Mishah's growing pains were not a good sign. She knew she must rest, yet wanted to be a part of the rowing. Rhone had forbidden it.

Cerah sleeved the sweat from her face, her clothes already drenched. Behind her, Ben'jor puffed and grunted with each measured stroke. Once convinced of the hopelessness of retrieving his boat from them, he'd taken the rowing bench across the deck from Rhone. He seemed particularly anxious to be across this narrow arm of the sea. His skill and power, coupled with Rhone's muscles, drove the slender bow through the still water at a good clip.

Mishah hauled a bucket of water from below and ladled out drinks for each of them.

"How are you feeling, Mi?" he asked her.

"I'm fine," she said brightly. But she wasn't. He could see that.

Later, she brought up food from Ben'jor's meager stores and passed it around. Moving alongside the cabin's low roof, she bumped a harpoon that clattered loudly to the deck.

Ben'jor's eyes shifted nervously. "Try not to make too much noise." He glanced across the still, flat water. "Dirgen prowl the sea for men foolish enough to stray into deep water."

Dirgen? Kenock glanced about the deck. Was this a new danger to prick them?

Cerah frowned. She must have noticed his worried look. "The sea holds many mysteries, and seafaring men are a superstitious lot, Kenock."

Amolikah reached for a cluster of withering grapes. "And filled with much nonsense," his grandmother added. "There is only one thing I fear upon the breathless face of the deep."

Cerah nodded as if she, too, understood the true danger here, but she chose to give encouragement instead. "Some of the Creator's cleverest and most beautiful handiwork is in the sea."

Ben'jor grumbled. "You'll change your mind in a splinter of time should we have the misfortune to meet with Dirgen's pet."

Was that a shudder his grandmother gave?

"Dirgen's pet?" Bar'ack grunted, pulling through another stroke. "What's that?"

Ben'jor's eyes rounded. "The Folded One. Leviathan."

"Leviathan?" Bar'ack swallowed hard.

Kenock wasn't surprised. It seemed that Rhone's apprentice had a streak of cowardliness through him.

"Leviathan, boy. Dirgen's fearful serpent." The seaman's view shifted around the rowers. "His scales are harder than any iron the

Tubal-Cain company forges, and they're doubled up too. A proj would ricochet off them, harmless as a stone from a sling. And they're locked together," he released his oar and twined his fingers, "tighter than this, they are." He looked at Rhone. "No Hodinite sword, not even one in the skilled hands of a Makir Warrior, can part them."

Even Ben'jor could not mistake Rhone's heritage.

The boat gave a gentle rock and Ben'jor went silent as they looked at each other. Cerah said, "Trying to frighten us will do you no good, Master Ben'jor."

"True, I am trying to frighten you, Mistress. To frighten and to drive some sense into all of you so that you'll turn this vessel right around and head back to the safety of shore. Leviathan is real, and I don't want to face him, not ever again." His eyes seemed to remember some terrible sight.

Kenock said, "How does one kill Leviathan?"

"You can't. That's what I'm trying to tell you. No one can! His scales are impenetrable. His mouth is larger than a dairy shed door, with rows of teeth longer than your arm and sharper than Master Rhone's sword. His back spines are a lumberer's saw. They'd gut this boat like it was paper and twine! You've never seen a monster like Leviathan. The eyes burn with the glare of the morning sun low on the sea, and from his mouth comes fire, like a burst beetle or pocket dragon, but a hundred times worse. The sea boils when it swims. And he leaves a wake a league long. He has the power of a regiment of men in his loins, and if you could—mind you I said *could*—set a hook in his jaw, no hawser made, whether woven of hempweed or spider silk, could hold the monster."

Ben'jor's cheeks trembled and there was a desperate pleading in his eyes. Cerah shook her head, disgusted. "See, you've only managed to frighten yourself."

Kenock decided not to mention that wasn't precisely true.

"Please, turn about and flee before Leviathan awakens!"

Rhone glanced at Mishah. She hadn't said a word, but it was clear the seaman's words had affected her. He stared at the misty distance. "How much farther is it?"

Ben'jor pulled himself together. "If we pick up a breeze, maybe two days. If not, our backs and shoulders will have us across this spit of sea in three, maybe four—that is, if Dirgen doesn't discover us first."

Amolikah's eyebrows pinched. "What about pursuit?"

He shook his head. "No one will come after you, not out here, they won't. No man's that foolhardy. There's a sea-crossing ship over at Wen's Slip, but it will take days to reach it, and then at least a week to bring it back, even with a full crew at the oars."

Mishah said, "Then it's only Leviathan we have to worry about."

His gave a short, uncertain laugh. "Leviathan's only the worst of it, Mistress. A hundred lesser things out here will kill you just as dead."

❦

Rhone split them into rowing crews so some could rest while they still maintained a slow progress. Kenock and Bar'ack remained at the oars as the others went into the cabin below deck. Ben'jor unfurled a chart and weighted it at the corners with plates and cups. He placed a magnetic pointer atop it, and began walking a pair of dividers across it. Rhone frowned out the window. Leviathan was known wherever seafaring men lived. What was the chance of it showing up here? Not much, yet …. He shrugged. Worrying wouldn't change anything. He grabbed at his chest, rubbing at a sore spot he hadn't noticed before.

Mistress Amolikah, Cerah, and Mishah sat by the good-man's cot—Kleg'l had taken a violent blow from Gar. The healer was explaining something to Cerah when he walked over.

"How are you, Kleg'l?"

"As well as can be expected. The wound didn't open, and for that I'm thankful."

"And so am I," Mishah said.

Cerah smiled, looking at Rhone as if seeing something the others had missed. "What weighs heavy on you, Master Rhone?" Her directness surprised him.

"Have you also the Mother's perception?"

"The Mother was very special. I am like everyone else, but it is plain you have a question."

"You are not like everyone else. And yes, I do have a question. Several."

"Perhaps you ought to pull up a chair," Amolikah suggested.

He did. "Tell me of the Book the Mother entrusted to you."

Cerah said, "The Book holds the true history of the world. The first part contains the words of the Creator, how he spoke our world into existence, how he formed the Mother and the Father from the dust of the earth. The second part is Father Adam's words, the story of his life in the Cradleland in the Before Time. The fellowship he had with the Creator, the Creator's messengers, and the animals."

Messengers. Would Sari'el have been one, he wondered? He grabbed at his shirt front, clutching the crystal in folds of material, feeling its heat grow in the palm of his hand.

"The third part speaks of the fall, and afterwards. It holds the history of his sons and daughters."

Here was the part he wanted to open up. "What of his children? Of Hodin? Can you tell me of him?"

"You don't know?"

"It was said Hodin guarded his past as a sten-gordon her nestlings. There was some trouble, but no one involved with it ever spoke of the matter."

"It was in there, all of it, but it's been a long since I've read it."

She paused, remembering. "Hodin was the fourteenth of seventeen sons. He had nineteen sisters. One died as a child, the others all had many children of their own. Like you, Master Rhone, he was a powerful man, with a kind heart, and Mother Eve loved him dearly."

"Does the Book tell why he fled to Atlan? There was trouble amongst his brothers, or so the story is told."

"I can't remember the details, but you are right." Cerah frowned. "Eve's children could not live near each other very long before trouble arose." Her mouth cocked to one side, her eyes narrowed in concentration. "What I do remember is that when Hodin came of age his eye fell upon a cousin named Atla. Atla was beautiful. Many wished to have her for a wife, including Gabli, son of Gert, son of Cain. When Atla married Hodin, Gabli gathered his brothers with the evil plan of murdering him. Though a mighty man and fierce warrior, Hodin did not wish to go to war. He and Atla moved to the land of Havilah, on the seacoast, to the village of his brother, Marin. Gabli found him there, and the two fought. Gabli died and was carried back to his father in the land of Nod.

"Gert and Cain raised an army from amongst their people and marched to avenge Gabli. Knowing Marin would be in danger if he remained, Hodin took his wife, a son, and twelve fighting men across the Border Sea to an uninhabited island to the east."

"Atlan," Rhone said.

"Yes. Atlan, though it wasn't called that back then. There Hodin made a stand and he routed his enemies. Afterward, he fortified the island, built a mighty city, and I suppose you know the rest."

"He trained his sons in the ways of war and bound them to the oath. No one has breached the shores of Atlan since." Rhone nodded, "The story is true to the character of the man history tells us Hodin was. That answers some questions, Mistress Cerah."

Mistress Amolikah's eyes took on a speculative look. "But were they the correct questions?"

"I don't understand."

"Was it only Hodin that sparked your curiosity, or something else?"

How could she know? The heat within his grasp grew. "You are perceptive, Mistress Amolikah. There was another question."

"I thought there might be."

He drew out the pendant and held it before them. "What is the true meaning of this? The Mother seemed to know." The crystal caught the sunlight, flashing colors around the cabin. "It burns to the touch. Sometimes I hardly notice it, and at other times it's quite painful."

Cerah caught a breath. "It's the pledge pendant of the Oracle. Some say it puts the wearer in touch with the Oracle. Some say he can control men by it. It holds evil. It attracts evil." She paused. "It burns, you say?"

"Touch it and tell me if it is not so?"

Cerah shook her head. "I will take your word for it, Master Rhone."

Kleg'l, his curiosity piqued, touched it, and said he felt nothing but cool crystal between his fingers. Ben'jor, overhearing, examined the pendant as well. Noting nothing out of the ordinary, he returned to his chart.

Mistress Amolikah extended a finger. Her hand recoiled as if struck by a serpent. "It's filled with evil."

Rhone frowned. "Curious. I feel it. You feel it. Kleg'l doesn't feel it." He looked at the man hunched over the chart. "Ben'jor doesn't feel it. Why do you suppose that is?"

Something like sudden understanding entered Cerah's eyes. Her view shifted to where his shirt now hid the pendant. "That pledge is the work of the Deceiver. Eve knew him, and she knew the feel of him close by. She perceived him when she spoke to you, Master Rhone.

"The Creator promised to send a Deliverer in the fullness of time; a man born of a woman to redeem mankind. Mother Eve didn't know the details of the prophecy, so when she birthed her first son, she thought him the Deliverer, but Cain wasn't. The prophecy was for a time still future. Yet, through one of her children he *would* come—but which? Even the Deceiver couldn't know that ... until now." She stared at Mishah, then back at him. "That line will become the target of the Deceiver's hatred. He will seek to destroy it. That line, it now appears, is Seth's." Her view shifted toward Amolikah. "That is why you felt the evil and Master Kleg'l did not. He is from Jalek."

"But it doesn't explain why I feel it," Rhone countered. "I'm from Hodin."

"Are you?" Her knowing look told him he'd missed something here. Something important.

And then he understood. "Atla."

She nodded. "A daughter of Seth."

31

Leviathan

Their boat crept across the flat gray water, north by west, the glaring sun burning down upon their weary shoulders. Mishah wanted to be of more help, but she could barely haul the water bucket up the stairs without her back screaming and her ribs aching at her spine. At times, she imagined her skin ripping open, and at other times it felt on fire. Her belly itched almost continually now.

Night brought a welcomed respite from the heat, but no rest from the oars. They worked in shifts. Ben'jor slept down in the cabin while Bar'ack, Kenock, Grandmother, and Cerah labored at the rowing benches. Two-sixths of a quartering, and they'd retire, leaving Rhone and Ben'jor to the task alone.

No moon brightened the sky, only the stars' brilliance speckled the blue-black dome of heaven. She hardly noticed, wearily making her rounds amongst the steady clack of the rowlocks and muffled, bone-tired grunts, offering water and slices of dried fruit from a basket over her arm. Their provisions were few, and she rationed them to last out four days, if need be. She hoped the crossing wouldn't take that long. Rhone stood alone at the bow, grasping a mast line, staring out at the blackness.

"You should be resting."

He looked at her. "I am."

More like watching out for danger. "A drink?"

He drank deeply from the ladle, then took the heavy bucket from her hand. The pendant hung outside his shirt now. Had it become too uncomfortable against his skin?

"Why don't you be rid of that thing? It's what you want to do."

He lifted the crystal by its thong and peered at the pale glow radiating from it. A faint, almost imperceptible red pulse from deep within it made her shiver. "Why do you keep it?"

"I tried to throw it overboard just a moment ago, but something stayed my hand."

She felt an eyebrow rise and forced it back down. She didn't want to appear skeptical. "You're a powerful man, Master Rhone. Is so simple a task beyond your abilities?"

"It has nothing to do with strength."

"Has it already taken such a hold of you?"

His view wavered, then broke contact with the crystal. "I felt its claws from the moment it was given to me."

"The time has come for your decision."

"I know." He made a wry smile. "Do your stars have a story of the Oracle's Mark, and how to be rid of it?"

She shook her head. "That's a story your own heart has to write, Master Rhone. I pray yours writes one with a good ending." She paused and narrowed her eyes past him toward something she couldn't quite make out.

He turned. "What is it?"

"Something on the water ahead."

He studied the black sea a moment. "It's only the floating tops of seavine. The sea must be shallow here."

"Are we nearing shore?"

He shook his head. "The sea floor rises and falls like the mountains and plains on land. It might be ten spans deep here, and a hundred spans deep a quarter league from here. It's of little concern, except that seavine will slow our progress."

Mishah laughed quietly, yet something troubled her. "Any slower and we'd be stopped."

They started for the stern, pausing amidships to check the compass binnacle in the light from a sliver of moonglass. He unlashed the rudder and held it slightly to one side to adjust their course, then secured it again.

Mishah scratched the side of her stomach, trying to be inconspicuous about it. A tiny foot or elbow poked her diaphragm. "Someone waking up?" she spoke lovingly to her extended belly.

Rhone smiled, and suddenly her heart ached. It ought to be Lamech's smile, not this tall warrior's—as helpful as Rhone had been. She'd gone almost the whole day without thinking of Lamech. Now his face swam into view. The weight of missing him settled like a stone in her heart. His baby would be born and grow to a tall lad before meeting his father. Stinging tears welled up. She was glad for the darkness so he wouldn't see.

The boat dipped gently to one side. Mishah put a hand against the cabin to steady herself. "I need to put these away." She lifted the basket. "We have to conserve what little we have. Master Ben'jor's pantry wasn't stocked to feed seven extra mouths."

Rhone peered suddenly out at the black sea and returned the water bucket to her in a mechanical fashion. "I'm sure our food supplies are in good hands," he said distractedly.

She started down the steps. The boat lurched hard, throwing her against the companionway wall. Bar'ack's voice shrilled in terror. She reversed her steps. Ben'jor was already plunging up the companionway, a harpoon in his hand. He rushed past her shouting, "Seavine serpents!"

She hurried after him. Something black and thick, like an immense worm, lay across the gunwale, one end of it still in the sea.

The worm moved, dark and glistening in the starlight. At the bow, a second cord of flesh crawled aboard, dipping it steeply toward the weedy water. A broad flat head reared. The rowers scrambled from their benches.

Ben'jor drew back and sent the harpoon into a gaping mouth. Rhone grabbed his sword from against the cabin wall and dove for the second serpent. A severed head thumped heavily to the deck and the writhing body slipped back into the sea.

"It's a swarm!" Ben'jor shouted. "We got to get out of these sea-vines!" A flash, an explosion, and a third seavine serpent collapsed to the deck. Mishah turned as Kenock reloaded the proj-lance, point it seaward, and fire again sending a spout of seawater raining bits of bloody flesh down on them.

Now seavine serpents began slithering aboard from every direction. Rhone leaped among the creatures, slashing coils thick around as a man, dodging striking fangs.

Ben'jor grabbed up an oar, and Cerah another. Kenock sent a proj hissing through the blackness. In the bright flash, the sea surface looked like boiling water. Bar'ack, momentarily frozen with fear, shook himself and went to help Cerah at the oars. Grandmother found a stout pole and backed against the mast, batting at a flat, broad head rising up above her. Its tongue licked out as its fangs unfolded like sleek, yellow daggers.

"Mistress Mishah, what's happening?" Kleg'l stood in the companionway behind her, holding one of the proj-lances. She grabbed it out of his hands and fired at the serpent attacking Amolikah. Its head thumped to the deck, striking blindly in the throes of dying.

Mishah looked back at Rhone. Coils of flesh had him about the waist, pulling him toward the edge of the boat. She broke open the breach and realized she hadn't another proj. "I need a weapon!"

Kleg'l clambered down the stairs and returned holding a harpoon. "This is all I could find, Mistr—"

She grabbed it and lifted it overhead. The barbed point sank through the tough muscle, burying itself in the deck beneath. The coils released Rhone and the serpent's head reared and whipped back and forth. Its red eyes locked on her with fangs unsheathing.

Rhone's sword shot around and drove up through the jaw, into the roof of the serpent's mouth, finding the small brain and cutting the signals to the body. The snake collapsed. He yanked it free, grabbed her hand, and swung her out of the way, wheeling the next instant, somehow knowing where his sword should strike next.

She staggered back into Kleg'l's arms. "That was a foolhardy thing to do, Mistress Mishah."

"Quickly! We must row! We have to get this boat out of these vines!" They scrambled over fallen serpents and mounted the rowing benches alongside Cerah and Ben'jor. Kenock fired his last proj and snatched up a harpoon. Rhone fought to the middle of the boat, his sword slashing with a wild precision, somehow managing to stay one jump ahead of the deadly fangs.

Slowly, they drew away from the swarm.

Exhaustion overtook Mishah as she pumped the oars. Rhone and Kenock repelled each renewed attack until finally the serpent swarm moved off in another direction.

Daylight found the boat free of the seavines and adrift. All aboard were exhausted beyond movement. Mishah slumped over her oar, hardly aware the night had passed. She lifted her head and brushed the tangle of hair from her eyes. A deep breath cut into her. She hugged her belly. *Please, not now, not here.* It was still too early—far too early.

She let the oar splash into the still water. The others abandoned their oars, staggering half dead to their feet. Rhone and Kenock had cleared the deck of dead serpents. Their clothes were splattered in red. She looked down at herself and made a face. She was too. Standing helped lessen the pain a little. A sharp stab buckled her.

Rhone caught her by the elbow. "You need to rest."

She nodded and squinted against the sun, low on the horizon. Not a seavine in sight … and no shore either. "You should, too."

"In due time."

She started to turn, then stopped, staring at the Oracle's pendant still about his neck.

He looked down at it.

"Have you decided?"

"I'd decided last night, but I remember becoming suddenly occupied."

She smiled, too weary to laugh. He gripped the pendant, then hesitated.

"It should be a small thing for a man who just fought a swarm of seavine serpents."

His lips thinned with determination. With a yank, he snapped the cord and stared at it. "It grows hot."

The pale glow reddened, the pulsing within growing stronger.

"Be rid of it now, Master Rhone. Quickly, before it can sink its claws deeper."

The line of determination turned grim, his hand shook, as if engaged in a physical battle. He curled his fingers, heaved back, and stopped again.

"You have the power within yourself to break its hold, Master Rhone." But would he? Could he?

"I will," he said softly. Setting his jaw determinedly, he flung the pendant far out to sea. It arched high and for a moment, seemed to hang in midair, then plunged soundlessly into the water.

She fixed upon the place where it had disappeared, and suddenly drew in a breath, as if it had been she who had flung the power of the Deceiver away. "There, it is done."

His view narrowed, then all at once went wide. She looked back. The sea where the pendant had disappeared had begun to churn.

The churning became a boiling, ripples radiating out, growing into waves, and waves into a roiling torrent.

"What?" she gasped. A head, half the size of their boat, reared up out the maelstrom, smoke billing from its nostrils, eyes like pools of molten gold glaring down on them. It rose from the sea on a thick body, dark green scales glinting in the morning sunlight, two rows of serrated plates, like the teeth of a saw, running down its spine, spilling water back to the sea.

"Leviathan!" Ben'jor wailed.

"Everyone below," Rhone ordered. The harpoons had been placed atop the low cabin roof. He grabbed up one in each hand. "Get proj-lances!" The monster rose until its foremost fins sliced above the water, each twelve spans or greater, dwarfing the boat.

"We have no more projectiles!" Bar'ack cried.

Mishah's hopes sank. Exhausted almost to the point of fainting as they all were, there could be only one end to this new menace. She squeezed her eyes shut and prayed. Someone grabbed her arm.

"Come, dear." Amolikah's urgent look belied her calm voice.

"I found one!" Kenock rushed up from the cabin, waving a proj. Amolikah tugged again. Mishah's feet refused to move. Rhone grabbed a proj-lance, slamming the proj into the chamber and aiming for the head. The fiery dart missed, exploding against an impenetrable scaly ridge above the eyes. The sea shook with Leviathan's roar. Golden eyes narrowed and it rushed the boat.

Rhone took up the harpoons and hurled one into the monster's chest, the heavy point merely glancing off the scaly armor.

"Mishah!" Amolikah tugged at her arm.

"No. If the boat should splinter, we'd be trapped down there." Her view fixed on Rhone as he readied the second harpoon. The wave ahead of the approaching beast drove into the side of the boat. They tumbled against the gunwale, grabbing at the railings to keep from being flung overboard.

"And if we stay, the creature will take us."

Mishah looked at Amolikah. "Would it be any different below? That monster will snap this boat like a bean pod." Just then Leviathan rammed the boat and Mishah's shoulders wrenched, but her grip held. She flung the seawater from her eyes. Rising coils and jagged fins lifted clear of the water. Slick, green scales glinted in the morning sunlight as the monster reared.

Rhone drew back for another throw, but it was a hopeless battle. No man could defeat such a creature! There was only one who could put a hook into Leviathan's jaw. Her view shot heavenward. *Creator, you've brought us this far. Surely you didn't do so only to have it end this way.*

The air shook as the creature hissed a stream of fire down onto the boat. Rhone seized that moment to send the harpoon sailing into the gaping mouth. Leviathan lurched backwards and its mouth snapped shut, teeth sheering the harpoon like a toothpick. It shook its head, then folded its coils one upon the other and sprang onto the boat, driving the stern under water. A wave hit Mishah like a fist, breaking her grip on the railing and lifting her off her feet. She gasped seawater into her mouth and nose as she plunged deeper and deeper. She hadn't time to take a proper breath. Her lungs burned, the burning becoming a raging fire inside her chest. She fought the urge to inhale, to fill her lungs with the warm water to quench the flames. Her downward descent slowed and instinctively she kicked and clawed toward the shimmering disk of light above her.

Her head broke the surface and she heaved in a breath and coughed up water. Seawater clouded her vision. She blinked desperately and didn't immediately see the boat, only the glaring golden orb of the sun low upon the water. Gasping for air, she looked around. There it was, tilted in the water, bobbing like a cork, smoking like a doused cook fire. Where was Leviathan? Her grandmother stood at the railing waving frantically. Bar'ack and

Ben'jor were there, holding tight and staring at her. But where was Leviathan?

She looked back. The glaring golden orb of the sun moved and a head the size of a small house lifted from the water's surface. It seemed to grin at her. Terror-stricken, she flailed toward the boat, but fear had seized her muscles. She wildly looked back at her companions, helpless upon the foundering boat.

Rhone leaped off the side and strove through the water with powerful strokes. The grin left Leviathan's maw. Had she imagined it? Swiftly, the monster lifted itself on green coils from the still sea, reared back and showed rows of sharpened teeth. She was too numbed to be terrified anymore. The mouth came rushing at her.

Rhone swept an arm around her, but it was too late …

Then something broke the surface, something orange and green, and immensely larger than Leviathan itself. This new sea monster leaped in front of Leviathan's deadly spikes. Its mouth, as large as Ben'jor's boat, closed over Mishah and Rhone, and all was suddenly darkness.

32

Gormerin

For an instant, Kenock's heart had stopped. His world had come crashing to an end and he stood as if dead himself, unable to move, unable to breath ... unable to even think! One moment Mishah was there, and the next she was gone.

Leviathan's roar brought reality back into sharp focus. Kenock lurched as the monster bellowed out across the water and began to rise on great coils, its molten eyes searching, then fixing upon him. Kenock's fists welded to the railing as the hellish creature moved through the water.

Leviathan's head suddenly snapped around. Its forward motion abruptly halted, it began thrashing like a fish on a hook, fighting some unseen line slowly but powerfully dragging it down into the deep. Leaping and churning waves that pummeled the foundering boat, its coils cleared the water then slapped the sea with a crack and disappeared beneath boiling water.

No one breathed as the final ripples of the battle leveled toward the horizon and the sea grew glass smooth.

"Great Dirgen!" Ben'jor whispered.

Kenock's grief rushed back. "She's gone." Tears choked the

words in his throat, filled his eyes, and streaked his cheeks. His breath came in raspy gasps.

Cerah hugged him, her tears wetting his cheek. "Taken from us now, but not forever."

He knew she meant to comfort him, but the words rang hollow after watching Mishah meet with such a horrible death. And Rhone! At least Rhone had tried to save her—Rhone had leaped to her rescue while he had stood helplessly by, too struck with shock and fear to lift a finger to help. A ragged breath shuddered though his body. Cerah took his hand. Her presence seemed distant and somehow detached from his world of anguish as he stared across the sea, calm now as if no tragedy had been played out upon its flat, gray stage.

"Kenock." Amolikah's voice yanked him from pain so fresh it still did not feel real. "We're taking on water. We need help down here."

He became aware of the sound of hammering from below. They were sinking, but somehow it didn't matter.

Cerah took him by the arm. "They need our help."

"What's the point?"

"Kenock! We cannot bring Mishah back. But we can save what's left of us." Her sternness surprised him.

Amolikah turned him by the shoulders. "We must get off this sea before that creature returns. And we can't do it without everyone's help."

"Off this sea? We're in shambles." He looked around the boat, at the charred stern section, at the mast lying along the deck. Splintered wood shot off at angles from the deck. "It's at least three days back. We'll never make it."

"It's only another day to Eve's Weep, and we *will* make it."

"Eve's Weep? We're still going forward? What's the point?"

Amolikah's green eyes narrowed. Where was the sadness? A grandmother's despair at watching her granddaughter perish? Her eyes held none of that. They showed anger, and unbending determination. "The Mother said we must reach the Cradleland. It is important to the Creator that we do so. To the Cradleland we will go."

"But Mishah's dead!" His eyes filled again.

Amolikah's mouth set a stern line. "But we aren't. We must continue."

He couldn't believe what he was hearing!

Her voice took on a gentler tone. "Kenock. I don't understand it anymore than you do. But we will continue to the Cradleland. Somehow, the answer lies there."

Two and a half days after leaving Chevel-ee, Da-gore arrived in Derbin-ee. First Major Bair'tor's troops from Dragon Pass were waiting. Bair'tor, an officer in King Irad's army, was a short, thickish man with a gray beard. Da-gore had met him a few times at official functions, but they'd never served together. The two officers held council outside the village where the smell of seavine was not so sharp, away from the hoards of flies swarming the drying blocks. The first major had brought Chief Gate Warden Sentor with him.

"Good to see you again, First Major Bair'tor." Da-gore guessed by the unsmiling face within the helmet that the fugitives had slipped past Bair'tor's troops.

"I heard what happened in Chevel-ee." Bair'tor glanced at the two giants, clearly impressed.

Da-gore frowned. "The fugitives have sympathizers, or some other power. How did they manage to get past this time?"

Bair'tor inclined his heat at the chief gate warden. "He'll tell you."

Sentor's stern mouth accentuated the squareness of his jaw. "They escaped this morning." He glanced at the tower looming above the sea cliffs. "Unfortunately, that's the only place in Derbin-ee to hold prisoners. It was never designed for the purpose. They killed a man and stole a boat. The owner of the boat is missing, presumed a hostage."

Bair'tor removed his helmet and wiped sweat from his forehead. "You've dealt with these people, Captain Da-gore. Tell me about them."

"They've shown an uncanny streak of luck, and I intend to break it." His eyes compressed slightly. "As far as the Lodath is concerned, we have a free hand in this matter."

Bair'tor nodded. "What makes these runaways so important?"

"I don't know. I only follow orders."

Bair'tor gave a thin smile. "Don't we all." He looked at Sentor. "They struck out to sea this morning? What lies on the distant shore?"

"A few small villages. Mostly Wild Lands. Once across the sea— if they make it that far—they could disappear into the Ruins of Eden without a trace. No one ever ventures there anymore, or travels much beyond the sea villages. To the east is the Land of Havilah; some big mining operations and a large shipping industry in Marin-ee, but Marin-ee is too far east."

"What's the nearest village they could reach?"

He thought a moment. "That would be Eve's Weep. An old stopping place for gold shipments from Havilah. Now that the ore is shipped on coastal barges from Marin-ee, Eve's Weep is mostly abandoned."

"Do you know of a place called the Cradleland?" Da-gore asked.

Sentor nodded. "I know the legends. Few if any know the way anymore. Even if it could be found, you can't enter it."

"Why is that?" Bair'tor settled his helmet back onto his head.

"It's guarded."

Da-gore narrowed his eyes. "By whom?"

"Not *whom*, by *what*, Captain Da-gore. Don't know what it's called, but the old stories say something more terrible than Leviathan. That's why no one ever goes there, why the location is lost, and the memory of it nearly faded."

Da-gore said, "We'll need boats to cross the sea."

Sentor's eyes widened. "You won't find anyone willing to cross it, Captain."

Bair'tor said, "Willing or not, we will take the boats we need."

"The sea is full of dangers. This being the dark of the moon, sea-vine serpents will be swarming."

Bair'tor said, "Ore barges cross from Marin-ee to Wen's Slip."

"They're big vessels and well armed. We have nothing like that here."

"Nevertheless," Da-gore said, "I'll want boats for my men."

By the day's end, they had requisitioned the two largest boats in the harbor, the others being too small to make the crossing. Only Da-gore and the giants and twenty of Bair'tor's men could be accommodated. The owners of the boats had refused at first, but quickly agreed at the point of a proj-lance. Supplies were taken aboard and the troops put to the oars, grumbling that they weren't seafarers.

It was dark when they finally struck out across the sea.

First Major Bair'tor and the rest of his troops, more than 180 men, had already started back to cross Dragon Pass and skirt the western edge of the Border Sea, then penetrate into the Ruins of Eden.

❦

Instinctively, Rhone clutched Mishah to himself as the giant fish leaped, snapped them up like flies on a millpond, and swallowed them down. Smoothly contracting muscles plunged them deep into the fish's gut. He held her tight. Death was easier when shared, and no doubt death awaited them as the muscles pushed toward the acid-filled bowels of this great fish. Where Leviathan had failed, this interloper had succeeded.

Although only an instant of time had passed, it seemed a lifetime. Images and regrets flashed across the canvas of his mind. He thought of his home, his mother, and all that remained unfinished in his life. Their passage slowed. In a moment, they'd feel the burning, and then it would be all over.

He hadn't heard even a whimper from Mishah. Had she fainted? Was she already dead? Suddenly the descent ended, the contracting passage opened up, and they tumbled into a faintly illuminated chamber. Mishah gasped. Like him, she'd been holding her breath.

"Master Rhone?" Her arms had locked like a vice around him.

As his eyes adjusted, he found her wide, confused gaze fixed upon him a nose-length away.

"We're not dead," she breathed.

"No." He felt the walls of the chamber. Only slightly moist. No digestion here. "At least not yet." The firm flesh, like a thick leather wineskin, undulated as if being worked against by the steady, rhythmic movement of muscles.

"I don't understand." A note of terror edged her words.

"I don't either. We're breathing, and that shouldn't be."

"Where is the light coming from?"

He untangled himself from her arms, but she remained tight against him as if the walls of the chamber were coated with deadly poison. They were inside a pouch large enough to comfortably hold the two of them.

"Is it coming from outside?" She looked around.

"No. We must be far under water."

"This is impossible." Terror was turning to wonderment.

"Impossible as it is, it's happening." His view of her was becoming clearer. The chamber was growing brighter. Lines of yellowish-green light had emerged from the darkness, running in bands along the chamber.

"It gives us light," she said. "It knows our needs and supplies it." Tentatively, she touched one of the lines. "Cold. Like the living fire of a lantern fly."

"*Gormerin!*"

She stared at him. "The carrier fish?"

"It can be no other." Rhone traced the lines of light with his finger. "They say carrier fish search the sea floor for those things man has lost and spit them up on the shore." The light now showed fine red and blue veins mottling the walls of the chamber.

Mishah put her nose near them and inhaled. She let her breath seep slowly out. "I think I understand." She looked at him. "Gormerin was prepared for us by the Creator." A look of peace filled her face and she closed her eyes, her lips moving silently.

The clear truth of that stunned him. The Creator had prepared this fish for *them*? "What power can do this thing?" He began to tremble. "How can nature be moved and controlled like a puppet, made to do one man's bidding?"

"The Creator is not a man, Master Rhone."

He pulled in a breath and willed himself calm. Could anyone be calm when faced with a power that went beyond understanding? "What sort of god can create a fish to sustain men?"

"What sort of God can create the Gormerin?" A small smile touched her lips. "The same God who spoke our world into existence, whose fingers made the stars and the heavens, whose hands fashioned you and me." She took his hand. "Do not fear, Master Rhone, for now I know my God is in control."

Her sudden tranquillity only sharpened the edges of his nerves.

She peered at the web of blood vessels just beneath the tough skin. "Lamech would be fascinated. He seeks out the wonders the

Creator has hidden in the world for man to find." Her finger traced a line of cold fire. "Lamech delights in discovery."

Rhone didn't understand, but he wasn't blind to truth when it confronted him. Too much had happened the last few weeks for him to deny a power was at work here. He had tried to ignore it at first, then to put it off when ignoring became impossible, but this—this was more than he could shrug off as mere curiosity or coincidence. By rights, he should be dead, yet he wasn't. He and Mishah had been saved in the belly of a great fish. The Oracle's giants had sacked Chevel-ee and the earth had opened up and swallowed them. Watchers from a dark realm moved unseen around him while the Creator's Messengers did battle to protect them. Cerah's messenger had guided her safely to them. And now this. The experience terrified him more than any he'd ever known, yet Mishah was suddenly at peace. What did she have that he didn't?

"Tell me of your God, of the Creator."

"There is so much, and I feel inadequate. If Lamech—"

"Lamech is not here. You are. I've heard you speak of these matters. You are capable in your own right."

She looked at him, the yellow-green glow highlighting her cheeks, the edge of her nose, the curve of her lips. Her shoulders took a determined set. "Very well. Foremost, the Creator is love. See how he has provided for us in our moment of need? We are safe from Leviathan, warm and dry far beneath the sea, breathing air taken from the water. I know not where we are being carried, but I know wherever it is, it will be exactly where the Creator wants me."

She'd said something that snagged his imagination. "… warm and dry beneath the sea, breathing air taken from the water." Could such a vessel be constructed to carry men? A boat that traveled under the water, not atop it? It was a fascinating idea, and he filed it away for future contemplation. That he was thinking of a future was a turn in the right direction.

"What of Grandmother and Kenock? And the others?"

"If your Creator can rescue us in such a manner, could he not do likewise for them?"

Her lips twitched. "See, your faith already grows."

"Where does the Creator get his power?"

"He has always had it. He has no beginning, and he has no end. He created man to be a companion to him, but Mother Eve and Father Adam severed the perfect relationship. Through their sin, death entered the world. This saddened the Creator, yet he knew beforehand, from the foundation of the world, what would happen, and had already formed a plan to redeem man from his fallen state."

"And when he does, we will live with him as he first intended?"

"Yes, and he will give us life such as he possesses. There will be no more death, no more tears or sorrow." She breathed deeply and looked away. "No more separation."

"Will everyone live undying?"

She shook her head. "No, only those who put their trust in the Redeemer to come."

"Who is the Redeemer to come?"

"The mystery is hidden from our eyes. We have no knowledge of it, except from the prophecy—" she jumped slightly, then smiled and patted her stomach, "—written in the stars."

"What of those who have already died?"

"If they have trusted in the Creator, the will be with him forever."

He still didn't understand all she was telling him, but he believed her. He thought of his mother, a captive in her own house. His father, betrayed and murdered by a son. He thought of his own exile from a people and land he loved. No separation? Life forever without tears? "Mistress Mishah," he indicated the chamber giving them warmth, light, and sustenance, "I cannot deny the power of your Creator. If he can prepare a fish to save us from Leviathan, and fashion worlds with but a spoken word, then I believe he can raise the dead and give them life as you claim." He didn't understand it, but he wanted to be part of it. "What must I do?"

Her expression widened. "Master Rhone, you've already done it. Believing is all that is required."

※

For the moment, at least, Mishah's discomfort had disappeared and she'd lost track of time—not that any sense of time could be had within the close walls of the carrier fish.

When the chamber began to compress around them, its walls moving rhythmically by the muscles within it, Rhone grabbed her arm. As the passage opened up, she gave a whoop of surprise, and the next moment her dress was heavy with seawater, dragging her down again. Rhone tugged her back to the surface, treading water for the both of them. The fish remained a moment, its upper half arching high above them, an eye staring hugely. The eye shut and opened as if winking, then with a swoosh, the giant fish turned back to sea. The wave of its sudden departure lifted them high and drove them into shallow water. Her feet found the sandy bottom, and as the wave rolled back, Rhone helped her ashore.

33

Eve's Weep

Kenock took a break from the bailing, leaving the damp belly of the boat and climbing up on deck. He stretched as he stood at the stern of the boat, his muscles stiff, his shoulders and back burning. They had only two oars left. Ben'jor and Bar'ack were working them. Kleg'l, weak as he was, managed the tiller.

The flood that had nearly sunk them had spoiled the food Mishah had so carefully rationed. His throat clenched. In spite of her own sufferings, she'd kept their needs ahead of her own.

"Thirsty?" Cerah asked. He thought she was still below helping Grandmother bail and hadn't heard her come up behind him. He quickly brushed at his eyes, took the ladle and drank deeply. "How is it down there?"

"We're keeping on top of it, barely," she said.

Did he even care? Tears grabbed at his eyes again. Cerah hugged him, offering no words, just her strength and love. He didn't want to burden her with his grief. She too was grieving, though she'd known Mi only a short time. In the days since their first meeting in Chevel-ee, he'd come to care deeply for Cerah, and she for him.

"I better see if anyone else needs a drink." She started to turn away, but something caught her eye.

"Kenock?"

"Yes?" He heard the dull monotone in his own voice. Nothing was important anymore. Eve's Weep? He couldn't understand his grand-mother's insistence on continuing on …

"What's that?" She pointed at a distant shimmer, snaking across the sea.

He shrugged. He didn't know and he didn't care.

"Master Ben'jor," Cerah called.

"Hum?" He glanced up from his rowing, opening his eyes as if he'd been roused from deep thought.

"Something is coming this way."

Ben'jor squinted out to sea. "Glimmer fish. And a fancy big shoal of 'em it looks like."

"Are they turnlings?" Bar'ack asked.

"Haven't turned far as I know." Ben'jor stood for a better view. "But they do seem to be heading right for us. Come full night, a shoal of glimmer fish meandering just under the surface like that will set the sea ablaze."

The school of fish came closer looking ever so much like a great swimming serpent; millions of them in a living band of cold phospho-rescence a hundred spans wide and at least two leagues long, perhaps more. As Kenock watched, the shoal came up behind them, parted, passed around the boat, and closed up ahead. With a lurch, their ves-sel began to move.

Amolikah pulled herself wearily up the stairs from below to see what had happened.

Bar'ack shipped his oar to join them at the stern rail.

"What in Dirgen's name!" Ben'jor grabbed for the railing. They had begun to pick up speed. "What have the gods in store for us next?"

"Dirgen doesn't have anything to do with this." Amolikah's face glowed from the phosphorescence off the surface of the sea.

Ben'jor's jaw fell. The boat was now keeping pace with the great shoal of fish. Kenock noted the wide eyes among all of them. Kleg'l released the tiller, which no longer steered the boat. The fish were now bearing them along. Ben'jor hurried to the binnacle and studied the compass. "North by west. They're taking us straight for Eve's Weep."

Amolikah bowed her head, her eyes closed, her face filled with peace.

❋

Mishah stepped into the forest that stood alongside the seacoast and stripped off her dress. She wrung it out and, in the fading daylight, examined the stains. Shiverthorn and hempweed made a practically indestructible material, and she certainly had put it to the test since leaving home. It had taken abuse and proved worthy, but even her plunges into the sea had not removed the smears of seavine serpents' blood from it. This single dress was all she had—and it was becoming too tight for her now. Everything else—her other dresses, her undegarments, her personal belongings—had been lost.

She pulled it on damp and reached for the buttons down her back. Where was Lamech when she needed him? No, she mustn't permit her thoughts to go there—not here, not now, at least.

Back on the shore, Rhone was peering toward the west. He pointed. "Lights. If I haven't misjudged your Creator—" he stopped himself—"*our* Creator, I'd say that's Eve's Weep. The fish dropped us off on its doorstep."

"The map is back with my case. How will we find the way?"

He tapped his head. "It's all up here now." They started up the beach.

The glow of the westering sun had left the sky by the time they reached the dark buildings, mostly abandoned and falling in to disrepair, separated by a weedy road. A scattered few showed lights behind curtained windows. A pier ran out into the sea, silhouetted against the dusky water. Even in the gloom, it was plain the rickety thing was in need of repair. She'd not want to walk out onto it in the dark where an unseen gap in the boards could drop her right back into the sea.

She peered at the dark windows, some lacking glass, some showing a sharp glint of starlight off a broken pane. The cool breeze, her damp dress, the strangeness of this place chilled her … her baby poked and prodded. She hadn't had a sharp twinge since the carrier fish had snatched them from the jaws of Leviathan. That at least was reassuring. She shivered and hugged her arms.

"You all right, Mistress Mishah?"

"Yes." Why did she whisper? Afraid of awakening the old bones of Eve's Weep? "There'll be no inn here, Master Rhone. Nothing."

"We shouldn't linger long. Pursuers cannot be far behind."

She was exhausted. Did he really plan to enter the Wild Lands tonight? To push into the Ruins of Eden without daylight to show the way?

"We'll try one of the houses. Perhaps we can find something to eat and a place to dry our clothes." Rhone took her arm and guided her through the dark toward the first squat structure showing a light. He knocked and they waited. A shadow moved past the lamp inside, then footsteps and the door opened a crack, a heavy chain keeping it from widening any further.

A man with a sea-weathered face peaked out. "Who are you?"

Mishah knew she must look like a piece of flotsam washed up on the shore; her soiled, soaked dress, her long hair undone in stringy tangled strands. The wet dress overemphasized her very pregnant condition.

"We were washed overboard," Rhone said. "We just came ashore now. We're hungry and wet and were hoping someone here would help us."

She'd held her breath. Wisely, Rhone did not mentioned

Leviathan, or the giants. They would have to tell him eventually. She didn't want to put this man and his family in danger.

"Humm. Took a dunk, did you. Humm." His eyes studied them with open suspicion. "Come ashore here at Eve's Weep, did you?"

"Down the beach a few hundred spans," Rhone pointed.

Mishah peered past the open gap. A woman stood inside, listening to this.

The man looked over his shoulder. Mishah couldn't tell for sure, but she thought the woman had nodded. He looked back. "Just you and the lady?"

"We're the only ones."

"What village you from? Don't recognize you from anyplace around these parts."

"I'm from Morg'Seth," Mishah said. "Master Rhone is from Nod City. He is escorting me."

"Morg'Seth? That's a long way off."

"Yes, and we're tired and hungry. Won't you please help us?"

The woman's face appeared beneath the man's. She looked at them then at her husband. "We can surely help these people, Willin."

The chain rattled and the door opened.

※

This was hardly something one easily got used to. Once night came, Kenock's amazement turned to wonderment. The glimmer fish luminesced in hues of green to yellow to orange, some showing a deeper red. All in all, this school that moved the boat along at a pace twice that of rowing was about the most beautiful thing he'd ever seen. It was nothing less than the hand of the Creator reaching down and helping them along. But when he'd mentioned that to Bar'ack, he'd only scoffed and said glimmer fish naturally swarmed foundering vessels. Ben'jor, however, seemed too stunned for Kenock to believe this was a natural occurrence.

His grandmother stood near the tiller, staring into the blackness. He went to her and hugged her shoulder. "What are you thinking?"

"What has the Creator planned for our lives, Kenock? He took Mishah, yet saved us, and now helps us like this. It was Mishah and her baby who should have been saved." She looked at him, her green eyes glistening. "His ways are too deep. How can mere man ever know his mind?" Tears choked her throat. Now it was coming out. For some, grief required a longer gestation.

"I don't understand any of it." His eyes began to fill too.

"All we can do is trust, Kenock. Trust in his goodness and his wisdom. His grace is sufficient."

He had heard those words from childhood, yet now they sounded empty and he found no comfort in them.

Ben'jor's boots gave a hollow thump upon the deck behind them. "At this pace we'll be on the other side come tomorrow evening, Mistress Amolikah." He scratched at his beard, and hesitated, unsure how to continue. "I've never been much good at honoring the sacrifices, and when the monthly time comes, it's always my wife dragging me to the altar to do as the Creator instructed our fathers. I know you Sethites cling to the traditions harder than most folks, and I used to consider that foolishness." He shook his head. "But I'll tell you this, Mistress Amolikah, after what I've seen today, after all that has happened, and now this shoal bearing us along like they be doing, well, I've had these old sea eyes opened up. Come next new moon sacrifice, I'm going to be there."

"We've all had our eyes opened," Amolikah said.

Had they? Kenock glanced at Bar'ack, standing alone at the bow of the boat, staring ahead where the stars came down to touch the sea. Bar'ack and Ben'jor had seen the same things, yet one had his eyes opened while the other seemed to find his hope in unbelief. And what did he himself believe?

Below deck, when not bailing the seawater that continued to leak through the hull, Cerah and Kleg'l attempted to get soggy firewood burning in the stove. A cup of hot tea would be a comfort. Kenock started down into the deck cabin to see if he could help when Ben'jor mumbled, "Now what queer thing is happening over there?" Ben'jor moved to the rail and peered into the night. "Never seen anything like that, though after today, nothing much will surprise me."

Kenock reversed his steps. "What is it?"

The boat owner pointed to the receding horizon. "There, where sky and water come together. Looks like a wind is whipping up the water something furious." He stared up at unobscured stars. "Yet here the air is still as dawn."

All Kenock could see of it was a distant blur against the horizon, obscuring the stars in that region of the sky. Not being a seafaring man, the phenomenon meant nothing to him. It wasn't enough to keep him from Cerah.

※

Captain Da-gore twisted a hand into lashing line to keep from being driven into the sea by the waves crashing over the sides. Turning the bow into the winds had not helped, for the wind kept shifting directions. The two boats were now separated and the other might already have foundered for all he knew.

"What is going on?" He shouted above the howl, his words driven off into the wind.

The boat captain's eyes stood wide, his lips tight and pale. "Never experienced anything like this," he shouted back, then lurched from the railing to the mast and grabbed hold of it to break his plunge. He drew himself near to Da-gore's ear. "It's Dirgen! He's conjured up this wind to sink us." The man glanced worriedly at the giants at the oars, rowing like machines, apparently unimpressed by the madness of the sea around them.

Could it be the feared sea god? Da-gore didn't know anymore.

Perhaps instead of superstition, the entity was real. Like the beings who'd sired the haflings at the rowlocks. Da-gore knew the men aboard feared the giants. Were even the gods rebelling against these monsters that the star-beings had procreated? One thing was certain. The Earth-Borns' muscles combined with the efforts of the other soldiers at the rowing benches were all that kept the boat moving ahead. Without them, they'd be tossed like a cork.

A wave rocked the boat onto its side. As it came back up, Da-gore swiped the seawater from his eyes. He was almost ready to believe anything. This storm, the waterspouts, the angry sea, none of it was natural. It had boiled suddenly to life half a quartering earlier with no forewarning, and showed no sign of ending.

"We must turn back," the boat captain implored.

"No. We go forward." Even if he didn't understand it, he was a soldier who followed orders. He'd already failed three times to get the fugitives. He wouldn't fail again.

❦

It was the fifth of the second quartering when she and Rhone made ready to leave. They'd spent most of the night with Willin and his wife, Sheble who, once they got over their natural suspicion of strangers, turned out to be amiable hosts, eager to hear all about their adventures. Willin had been keenly interested in the carrier fish and the attack of Leviathan.

Sheble filled a sack with dried fruit and nuts and a loaf of hard, black bread. She'd insisted on giving them a wedge of cheese, though it was plain her own scullery was anything but overflowing with food.

Mishah had slept part of the night and felt more rested than she had for days. Her dress was dry and her hair combed, braided, and bound with pins at the back of her head—a job that took almost two divisions of a quartering to accomplish. Sheble gave her clean undergarments left over from when she was having children of her own and a patched cloak to replace the one lost at sea. Willin had no weapons to give them except a rusted hatchet he never used anymore. The way Rhone hefted it, Mishah knew the short ax would be as deadly in his hands as the finest blade the Tubal-Cain company could forge.

"This here is the way into Old Eden." Willin pointed at a shadowed track splitting off the road through the village as they stood outside the little seaside cottage. "Bear in mind, it's not much of a road anymore. You'll find the forest has taken most of it back, and the mountains fight you at every turn. After the exile, man wasn't meant to go back. I seen that place you're going to from afar once when I was a boy, but my father dared not get close. The gate is guarded by cherubim; as unnatural a creature as those Earth-Born you spoke about."

Mishah wanted to linger a day or two in hopes Amolikah and Kenock would show up. She would not believe they had perished. But Rhone was determined to reach the Cradleland before their enemies could catch up with them.

Rhone cast toward the east where the sky had begun to gray. "How far is the Cradleland from here?"

"A strong man afoot might make it in two or three days. Being that Mistress Mishah is with child, you might figure on four. That is if the roads are still passable. I've not heard of anyone making the trip for years."

"Nearly dawn." Rhone grabbed up the sack of provisions and slung it over his shoulder. "Be aware of what I told you. You two are in danger for helping us. You and your whole village."

"You mean about the giants and King Irad's Guard?" Willin gave a short laugh and glanced toward the few buildings still in use. His voice took on a somber note. "We'll watch out for those giants, Master Rhone. It don't take much time to alert the handful of families that remain here, and even less for all of us to disappear into the forest a few days until the danger passes."

"Please watch for my family," Mishah said. Rhone and Willin exchanged glances, but she refused to accept that her family was lost at sea. Sheble said they would.

"We'll set them to the right road, if they show up." His face was still sober as if he'd begun to seriously think of leaving. "But considering all that has happened, they might have given you up for lost and turned back. I would have."

The same thought had occurred to her. "I pray not." Something inside said Grandmother wouldn't turn back, not now. "Thank you both for your hospitality." She looked at her tall companion. "Are we ready, Master Rhone?"

He patted the rusty hatchet in his belt. "I'll return it on our way back."

Willin merely nodded. Mishah suspected he didn't believe he'd ever be seeing it again.

⚜

The morning mist burned off beneath a hot sun, and by the first of the third quartering, a wet blanket of heat had settled over the land. A hazy blue sky showed in ragged patches through the treetops. Shade offered little relief from the heat. Although Rhone couldn't see the mountains through the forest, the ground was rising and the hint of a trail he'd been following was growing steeper. Early on, they'd passed through a flat plain of once-cultivated fields. Now only the low stone walls remained to mark where cultivated ground was once worked by men. The Ruins of Eden were just that ... ruins.

"This was where the first children of Adam and Eve settled," Mishah studied the tumbled walls along the track they were following. "The names of the villages are mostly forgotten, but the people were our forefathers. Seth settled here before moving farther south."

Seth was a name well known. His, and the names of all the first born, could be traced in their many alterations throughout the world. Up until now, however, Rhone had not given credence to the legends that each family tree went back to the original rootstock of Eden. Seth was now derided for his descendants' zeal and narrow-mindedness. It was a name Rhone would have never connected with his own blood-lines. Why had the secret been kept from him? The revelation that he was from the same line as the Lee-landers was still too fresh to be comfortable. But then, much of his thinking needed an adjustment since coming to trust in Mishah's God.

They stopped for a midday meal of bread and cheese. She was slowing down, and he could see her distress. "Are you all right, Mistress Mishah?"

"I haven't been right for days." She looked down at herself. "He's anxious to be born."

"Is it too early?"

A worried look shot across her face. "Yes. A few weeks more, at least."

She needed rest; impossible now with soldiers from the Lodath following, though he'd seen no sign of them. Yet, they couldn't be many days behind. "If he were to be born early?"

"Some born in their eighth month do well, others have difficulty breathing." She herself seemed to be having trouble breathing as she spoke.

"Could you not have postponed the visit? Isn't it usual to make the pilgrimage early on?"

"I was only into my sixth month when I left. A pilgrimage is not generally a burden, and boat travel is both rapid and comfortable. The trip from Far Port to Chevel-ee should have taken only two days by wagon. All together, I should have been home in three weeks. I had plenty of time. Who could have expected all that has happened?"

It was true. None of them could have foreseen how so simple a journey could have gone so badly awry.

"We'll travel easier now, as long as we can." He stared down the footpath they'd been following. It was impossible to spot danger in so thick a forest. The only thing that told him this had once been a broad road were the occasional stone ruins along it, no more than mounds of vines now, hardly recognizable at a casual glance.

He held her arm, helping her through the difficult parts. The odor of javian was strong here. This appeared to be still rich collecting grounds, and had it been a different time and under different circumstances, he'd be searching out the webs. Were the spiders of Eden as timid as the ones he'd encountered outside Far Port? He made a note to return on his next trip.

※

For a night and a day, wind and waves battered the boat. Then with the coming of night, the sea went suddenly still. One moment a tempest raged, and the next it all fell apart; not a breath of wind stirred the dead calm surface.

Captain Da-gore stood among seavine strewn across the deck, stunned at the abrupt change. His men at the rowlocks went still as stone, their oars frozen in position. In the sudden quiet, the creak of their tired vessel was like a low moan of relief.

Down below the clatter of buckets continued; a bucket brigade was all that had kept the hold from filling and sinking them. But at the abrupt hush, the boat's captain rushed up the steps and stared at the calm sea.

"Is this a common occurrence in these waters?" Da-gore asked.

"Not to my reckoning."

"I didn't think so." Again he was dealing with the unknown. He turned to the men at the oars. "We've lost a day's travel." They were exhausted and needed rest—even the giants who worked without a break—but Da-gore was not going to fail this time. "Put your backs to the oars, men. You'll have time to sleep once our mission is complete." He glanced at the boat's captain. "Get us back on course."

34

The Ruins of Eden

As they watched, the shimmering band of living light bearing them along suddenly exploded apart like a million fiery sparks. In an instant, the shoal of glimmer fish dispersed, their lights extinguishing into the depths of the sea. The boat came to a stop in the water.

Cerah squeezed Kenock's hand. "They've finished what the Creator has sent them to do."

He drew in a long breath. The beauty had been lost on him. He didn't want to hear platitudes. The only thing in the world he wanted to hear was Mishah's voice again. He should have thrown himself to Leviathan.

Ben'jor's footsteps scraped along the deck. "Finally left us, did they?"

Kenock nodded and peered at the stars where sky touched water.

"They brought us as far as they could, Master Ben'jor. If I haven't misjudged, those are men's lights." Cerah pointed.

"So they are. Eve's Weep straight ahead." He called down into the cabin, "Land in sight."

They had made it. It hardly seemed to matter.

❦

Mishah huddled in her borrowed cloak, trembling.

"Cold?"

She looked up. "I'm chilled."

"A fire wouldn't be wise, tonight."

"I know." How could she forget the incident on the Derbin-ee Road? "It's not a night chill." The temperature was still balmy from the heavy heat of day now past.

"Are you ill?"

She rubbed her arms. "I think it's exhaustion. If I had my case, I could take something for it."

He peeled a not-quite-ripe orfin and handed it to her. "You need to eat."

She nodded and took it from him. She did not look well. Was it physical? Emotional? Probably both. "Tonight we can sleep without fear." He turned his head and listened a moment. "The forest is settled. Take advantage of it. Tomorrow might be different."

"I'm worried about my grandmother ... and what Master Willin said."

It was clear to him that she still refused to give up hope, but now was not a time to feed other fears. "Do you believe she would turn back?"

She held him a moment in her wide gaze, then shook her head. "I don't know. Grandmother would press on if she thought the Creator still wanted it. But Kenock and the others might not."

"Your grandmother holds sway over your brother. If she insists, he will follow, and if he goes, Mistress Cerah will go too. And I can't imagine Kleg'l dissenting."

Her frown lifted at that. "Kleg'l, never. He's too loyal."

"That leaves only Bar'ack." He frowned. "Right now, I imagine Bar'ack is longing for the safety of his father's home in Nod City. Frobin entices young men with his tales of adventure, but never reveals what truly awaits in the Wild Lands. Bar'ack would turn back in a heartbeat, but he would never do so alone. So, it seems they have no choice but to press on."

"*If* Grandmother desires it." Her expression turned worried again. "If she believes us dead, what reason would she have?"

"Only that the Creator desires it." He sipped his water. "First, we'll reach the Cradleland and learn why you were told to go there. The Mother said you'd be safe. Afterward, we'll worry about Mistress Amolikah and the others."

A glint of humor brightened her eyes. "Just like that? We'll arrive in the Cradleland and all will be right?"

"You see a problem?"

"Only one, Master Rhone."

"That is?"

"Have you ever delivered a baby?"

He grimaced. "No, have you?"

"Many times, but always on the receiving end, never the other."

He cleared his throat and stared into his cup. "Well, that bridge must be crossed … eventually. Try to get some sleep."

"Will you keep watch all night?"

He nodded. "Even when I sleep, I keep watch."

She gave him a puzzled look. "May I ask you a question, Master Rhone?"

His guard went up. He forced himself to lower it. What could be so important now to keep from this woman who had become so close to him? "Yes."

"Back in the tower, you told us something of what happened to you in Atlan. You were a mighty warrior, from a powerful family, it seems. Yet, I sensed you were holding back."

"I told what was necessary." He hid a frown behind his cup.

"But not the true burden of your heart."

"Your perception is as keen as your surgical knife. It touches a wound that still festers."

"Your father's death by treachery?"

He nodded. "My father's fate, yes, and my mother, a prisoner in her own house. But more than that, there are my people."

"Your people?"

"Yes, my people. What I did not speak in the tower was that my father was not just an important ruler, but king of Atlan, and I … I was the heir apparent."

The sounds of prowling beasts and the occasional eyeshine of some timid but curious creature kept Rhone alert, but not worried. Was it this new faith of his—the faith of the Lee-landers—that brought ease to his mind? Or had he been lulled by it into a false sense of security? He lifted the hatchet and frowned. What he wouldn't give to have his sword back, or even a proj-lance.

Mishah had fallen into unsettled sleep, huddled inside her cloak. She was dreaming again, like the time at Mistress Leahia's boarding-house, mumbling something about a destruction and a flood. He considered waking her out of it, but she needed her rest. If exertion forced an early delivery, both she and the child would be in danger. Even if the delivery went without a problem, another life to protect against the Oracle's forces could make the difference between reaching the Cradleland or not. He lifted his eyes to a patch of sky through the treetops. Who was this Creator he'd decided was worthy to be followed? Mishah had said he was *the God who spoke our world into existence, whose fingers made the stars and the heavens, whose hands fashioned you and me.*

The stars are merely the work of his fingers while he himself required more effort; the work of his hands. There was something comforting in that thought. He closed his eyes and dozed, always just a twig-snap away from full consciousness.

❧

Ben'jor tossed a hawser out and lassoed a piling, which lurched dangerously at the sudden tug of the boat.

Kenock leaped to the wobbly structure, felt it sway beneath him, and began transferring their packs, swords, and proj-lances from the sinking boat. Cerah hopped up next, catching his outstretched hand. Bar'ack steadied Amolikah while gripping a piling, handing her off to Kenock who hauled her across to the pier. Kleg'l was next, and finally Bar'ack himself.

That left only Ben'jor standing on the listing deck, watching the sea slowly but certainly rising toward the gunwale. He shook his head and dashed down into the deck cabin, returning with two shiverthorn bags. He tossed them up to Kenock, and with a final look at his doomed boat, leaped across to the pier. "She was a fine vessel." He gave a heartfelt sigh and shook his head.

"She *was* a fine vessel, Master Ben'jor. She got us safely across the sea." Amolikah presented her money pouch to him. "It's all we have left."

He frowned and pushed it away. "You might need it to get back home."

"We took your boat. It's only right we pay for the damages."

"There was plainly a purpose in your taking it, and now a purpose for it to be beached here. Keep your money, Mistress Amolikah." He picked up his bags and started for land, the pier rocking beneath him with each step.

"We'd all better get off this thing before it dumps us into the sea." Kenock gathered their few belongings.

The morning mist was burning off fast, revealing the empty buildings of Eve's Weep. The place appeared abandoned. But then

Kenock spied a handful of people gathered around three carts, a fist of sheep, and three or four cows.

The townsfolk glared suspiciously at them as they stepped off the pier. Cerah took his arm. "Probably don't get many visitors."

"Looks like they're packing up to go somewhere," he said.

Ben'jor shook his head. "Peculiar." He was glancing at the abandoned buildings. "These people never go anywhere. If they did, they'd never come back to this dreary place."

One of the townsmen left the carts and approached. "What do you want here?"

Ben'jor pointed at his boat with only the upper curve of its gunwale and a corner of the cabin above water. "She ain't going to sail again. A little hospitality is all we ask."

The townsman's view shifted to the boat, then back to them. Something lit in his eyes. "Is one of you Mistress Amolikah?"

Kenock's attention riveted. How could he know that?

"I am Amolikah." The older woman pushed to the front. "How did you know?" Her voice held a guarded expectancy. Kenock felt Cerah's nails bite into his arm. His heart quickened, his breath catching in his throat. *Could it be?*

"Mistress Mishah asked me to keep an eye out for you all."

"Mishah!" he blurted. Mi was alive? The flower of hope burst open inside him. "Mishah! Where is she?"

Amolikah's eyes closed and her head turned skyward. She drew in a sudden breath. "I knew it."

"Where's my sister?" he demanded.

"She and Rhone left here yesterday morning."

"Master Rhone is alive, too?" Bar'ack's eyes bulged.

"They was both alive last me and my wife saw them. My name is Willin, and my wife, Sheble."

"Praise the Creator!" Kleg'l exclaimed.

Bar'ack stammered, "How is that possible?"

"They said it was a carrier fish."

"A gormerin! Of course!" Ben'jor declared.

"The hand of the Creator," Amolikah said.

Sheble gave a small smile. "That's what they said. We're all leaving for a few days to visit family in Havil. But we can give you some food for your journey. You all must be famished. Mistress Mishah said you were poorly stocked when you left—"

She was alive! Mi and Rhone alive! The rest of what Sheble said faded beneath the blur of Kenock's relief. At least Kleg'l and Cerah were paying attention.

Amolikah showed Willin the map. "Can you guide us?"

Willin shook his head. "Not me, not no one here. We don't go there no more. There're cherubim where you're heading."

"Cherubim?" Kleg'l asked.

"Fearsome creatures. No one goes there, and maybe you shouldn't be either."

Amolikah refolded the map. "We must."

"Then let wisdom be your guide, Mistress."

"He does." She glanced at Ben'jor. "We've put you in a dangerous way. You are not safe here, nor will you be where we are going."

"From all you've told me and all I've seen, truer words have not been spoken, Mistress Amolikah." He glanced at the edge of his boat rising above the water. "I guess I'll be making my way home on foot."

Kenock said, "You can't return by way of Dragon Pass. King Irad and the Lodath's Guards watch it."

"No way back over the sea from here," Willin said. "No boats this side of Marin-ee make the voyage."

Ben'jor bunched his lips and squinted at the rising sun, two hand-breadths above the sea. "Then it's east to Marin-ee. I can catch an ore barge across the Pillars of the Sun to Wen's Slip and from there make my way up the coast to Derbin-ee."

Amolikah took his hand. "Take care, Master Ben'jor. The Creator be with you."

"And with all of you, Mistress Amolikah."

❧

Long, greenish-yellow rows of thick, full leaves—tough, broad ovals smelling faintly of the vera-logia they held—seemed to stretch on forever. Mishah stood on the green knoll overlooking their fields, Lamech at her side, his hand softly encircling hers. Her hair hung loose about her shoulders, clean and fresh, like lilac and lemons. The child stirred within her and she placed a hand on her belly. "Soon your son will be born."

Lamech's hand squeezed hers. "He will be perfect in his generations."

She gave him a curious look. "He will be free of the sin that the Mother and Father imparted?"

"No man but the Redeemer to come will be born free of that sin, Mishah."

"Then what do you mean?"

"A blight enters the blood of mankind even now. The fallen messengers of the Deceiver have begun to mingle their seed with the seed of man. Indeed, if permitted to continue, there might not be a drop of human blood unpolluted by the tinkering of the Deceiver." He paused and looked at the vast farmland. The corners of his mouth dipped further. "The Creator cannot allow that to happen. The Redeemer must be born of a human woman pure in her generations. To stop this blight, the Creator will utterly destroy this world."

She shivered at the foreboding tone in his voice. "And what part will our son play?"

"Our son is destined to preserve humankind, and not only humankind but all with the breath of life in its nostrils."

"There is something terrible yet comforting in what you say."

"Comforting? Yes, there is comfort in it. And that is what we will call our son. His name shall be Noah."

"Noah. Comfort," she repeated.

A black cloud had begun to crawl up the horizon, beyond the peaks of the Hope Mountains that bordered their farm. It rolled across the sky drawing nearer and nearer. As she watched, the cloud took the form of a dragon. Smoke blacker than night billowed from its nostrils, and fire roared from its mouth. It swept toward them, moving faster, the wind suddenly chill, whipping her dress and tangling her hair.

She flung herself into Lamech's arms and buried her head against his chest as flames crackled in her ears. Something tried to wrench him from her arms. She held on with all her strength as claws sunk deep into Lamech and ripping him from her arms.

"No! Don't take him from me! Not again!"

She bolted up from the ground and heaved in a sharp breath.

"Mistress Mishah?" Rhone said, concerned.

She swallowed, looked around and began to breath again.

"Another dream?"

That was all it had been. A horrible dream—no, it wasn't horrible. She'd been with Lamech. That part had been wonderful. She squirmed, recalling seeing the claws sinking into Lamech's back. She reached around and plucked a sharp twig from her cloak, frowned, and tossed it away. "Yes."

"Like the others?"

This one had been different. This time she had not been alone. For a moment, she'd been in her lover's arms and the world had stood still. And the message about their son? It had been more real than any of the others. Even the horrible memory of the cloud transforming into a dragon couldn't spoil that part of it. "No. Not exactly."

"It's morning now." He smiled. "Put away the bad dreams. We are not far now from the Cradleland."

"Today?"

"Perhaps tomorrow if we move quickly."

Move quickly? That wasn't likely to happen. "I'll do my best." She winced at a sudden cramp. *Not yet, my little one.* The child was restless inside her. If it had been a dream, it had been real enough, right down to the squirming in her belly. *Perfect in his generations?* Of course it had been a dream—but so real.

All too soon, they were on the march again. She had trouble bearing her own weight early on. Rhone took her arm to help her along. Would he end up carrying her before the day was over? She wouldn't be surprised. She was waddling like a duck, her hips somehow oddly out of joint, or so they felt. The morning grew old and passed into the heat of the day. Rhone had begun to pause more and more to sniff the air and look around, his hand resting unconsciously upon the rusty short ax slipped under his belt.

What was he keeping to himself? She stopped herself from asking, not certain she wanted the answer. Late in the fourth quartering, she could not take another step. "I need to rest. It's so steep." Her hips ached, and the cramps were so severe she wondered if she wasn't beginning to have birthing pains. *Creator God, it's still too early.*

Rhone helped her to the ground. "Maybe we should eat."

"I'm not hungry."

"I am."

She should be, for the little she'd eaten and the distance she'd walked. He dipped up water from a stream and filled her cup. She forced down bread and cheese and rebelled at the sight of an orfin he'd peeled for her.

"We'll rest a while, but we need to keep moving. It's too early to stop for the night."

"Half a quartering?" She pleaded. She needed to be off her feet.

"No. We are being followed."

Her head snapped up. "How do you know?"

"I hear talk of it."

She looked around, then back at him. "Spiders?" She'd been aware of their distinctive scent for days.

He nodded. "They're all around us, but it is not us they fear."

"The giants?"

"I can only assume so. I've been trying to reach out to them. The fear I sensed in the Wild Lands east of Nod City and again above Far Port has not infected the spiders here in the Guarded Mountains. I sense many from the southlands have migrated into these mountains. They're wary of us, wondering why we are here. I've yet to touch the thoughts of—" He paused suddenly and cocked his head.

She stared past him and thrust out a finger. He turned, lifting his chin toward the treetops. A black orb streaked in scarlet lowered toward him on a fine silver thread spinning out from a posterior abdomen the size of a big melon. Rhone seemed not surprised.

The spider halted eye level with the webmaster, studying him with eight black eyes glinting as if from a thousand faceted planes. Its forelegs made slow, probing movements like a cat preparing to bed down. All eight legs were slender things, twice the length of its body, spread wide at first, but as Mishah watched, the hind pair began sawing together.

Without breaking eye contact, Rhone stooped to the ground and felt around until he'd found two sticks. Rubbing them together, he produced a sound similar to what the spider had just made.

A movement pulled her view upward. "Master Rhone!" Fists and fists of black spiders had begun to lower toward the ground. Wonderment seized her. Black orbs with stick legs dangled before her eyes; a curtain of black beads strung on the finest of threads, each probing, looking. Their cool, sharp claws gently touched her hair, her cheek, plucking at her cloak and dress. Hundreds more descended until the clearing showered them with black javian spiders.

It was a magical moment with sunlight glinting off a thousand silvery threads and shining as if through an ebony veil. She ran a finger along sleek, hard bodies.

They plucked at Rhone's vest and sleeves, examining the texture of his thick hair, loose about his shoulders. He tapped the sticks and moved slowly among them in a sort of ritual dance she didn't understand.

Finally he went still and dropped his hands to his side and let the sticks fall to the ground. One by one, the spiders ascended their single filament, drawing it up with them.

"You all right?"

"It was wonderful," she breathed, "but what was it about?"

"Curiosity." He grabbed up the pack and took her hand. "We have to move. Danger comes up behind us."

The peril of their situation came back to her. "I don't think I can. I might just stay right here and have this baby."

"What!"

She gave a short laugh. "I wondered what it took to get to you, Master Rhone. Giants and Leviathan apparently don't."

"No, but delivering that baby here and now does."

"That is out of my control." She stood with difficulty. "Yes, let's leave this place, and quickly." She looked at her stomach and patted it gently. "Ah, my little Comfort. If you grow up terrified by spiders, I'll know why."

Rhone hitched up an eyebrow. "Comfort? Is that what you call a baby?"

She smiled at him. "His name will be Noah."

"Isn't naming the father's role?"

"But he did. Last night in my dream. Only it wasn't a dream. It was more than that. Lamech said our son's name would bring comfort. His name will be Noah."

"Humm." His strong fingers wrapped about her arm, helping her along the trail.

With every step, with each passing league, the wilds grew more and more rugged and beautiful. The dense, green forest was broken here and there by waterfalls tumbling a thousand spans from forested cliffs high above. Flowers splashed colors throughout the greenery. The animals seemed less timid. Fortunately, no mansnatchers or sten-gordons. Dragonflies as large as children darted in the sunlight on lacy wings. Yellow-and-black butterflies larger than weaving looms yet delicate as the finest silk flitted silently overhead, their presence made known only by a golden shadow skimming along the trail.

With all the beauty, it was hard to keep the terror in mind. Yet she must not forget the giants. And what of her family? The not knowing was a bitter ache in her heart.

"What did the spiders tell you?" she asked suddenly.

He glanced at her. "Evil has entered the forest."

She stopped. "Already?"

"Yes." He got her moving again.

"They told you that?"

"Not in words. They are not reasoning creatures, but their fear was clear."

"Why did they come to you?"

He cast a sideways glance. "It seems my reputation has made it all the way to the Guarded Mountains. But they wanted to be sure I was who they thought I was. Somehow, I've changed." He frowned as if with a sudden thought, and went on without revealing what had just crossed his mind. "They had to touch me, to take in my scent, to know for sure."

And her, too? Their slender legs probing, examining—so that

was what they were doing. Suddenly, she cried out and buckled from the pain in her stomach.

"What?"

"Stop," she groaned

"You're not—"

The pain tore at her, then slowly subsided. "I don't know." She grimaced, concentrated on breathing, on willing the pain and contractions to cease. "Just give me a moment."

He nodded and turned to stare back the way they had come, his hand upon the rusty blade under his belt.

35

The Oracle's Forces

Ranged before Lucifer stood ten thousand of his warriors. Now, with a beauty that bordered on blinding, he rose from his throne. Ekalon's eyes latched onto the trailing violet and yellow streams of light as he strode across the blue vault of the heavens. Although his features were perfect to look upon, his heart was blacker than the Pit. Fury seethed just below that carefully controlled exterior. One might not notice the burning wrath by simply looking, but Ekalon had been with him since Leviathan had been subdued and chained to the bottom of the sea by Sari'el. The fugitives had escaped again. Pose had been driven from the beast and now wandered with the other spirits of the dead Earth-Born. Hatred boiled hot within his master.

"The time has come to rise again!" His voice thundered across the heavens, lightening flashing from his heel as he paced before his troops. "In the beginning I struggled for our freedom, winning it. The cost was heavy but the prize was this world, and I took it! Now the Tyrant of Old challenges my hand. He invades my world and throws up a hedge around these puny worshipers of his. He must be stopped!"

A roar erupted from ten thousand throats; as great a shout as was given when the cornerstones of the world had been fastened in place. Ekalon remembered that time, when they had all been shackled-ones.

Green merged with purple, becoming maroon, swirling around Lucifer, shooting down through the earth and upward, past the moon and stars. His anger was a crimson bolt piercing through all of creation.

"Even now, the Tyrant amasses his shackled-ones. The Lodath's troops are almost upon the fugitives, but the shackled-ones will try to protect them. The fugitives must not be allowed to enter the Cradleland. You must engage the shackled-ones, keep them from their task, and allow my servants time to reach the woman and kill her."

Again, a thousand times ten voices shook the heavens in support. Ekalon searched for satisfaction on his master's face. Instead he saw frustration. Hadn't power been given over to him with his victory in the Cradleland? Why did the Tyrant of Old challenge him now? Wasn't the time for begging at his throne past?

"You have your orders. You know the enemy. He gathers at the gate. Away now!"

Like missiles plunging to earth, Lucifer's warriors streaked for the gates of the Cradleland. He stalked back to his throne, maroon fading to violet, then to green.

Ekalon went to him. "What would you have me do, Master?"

"There is still one of them within my influence." Lucifer's fingers curled into a hard fist. "I have but to control him fully to crush the woman and her child." His eyes shifted, burning as if with yellow flames. "Collect the spirits from where they wander through the dry places. I yet have use of them."

"Yes, my lord."

Neither Kenock nor Cerah had any experience in the Wild Lands, but now that their fate had fallen upon his shoulders, he was glad she was at his side. Together they'd make it through ... somehow. Cerah was smart, pretty, and had nerves of dragon scales. He studied her determined face and the way her red hair caught the sunlight. He was in love and he wanted desperately to be alone with her, to talk freely of his feelings, for he was certain the attraction was mutual. Nevertheless, he was anxious to catch up with Mi and Rhone, to be rid of the burden of leadership, and once again under the protection of the Makir Warrior's sword that, ironically, he now carried. Once he dreamed of having authority. Funny, now that he had it, all he wanted to do was give it back. He glanced at the heavy weapon in his fist and marveled how anyone could lift it effortlessly, let alone wield it with such deadly precision as he'd seen Rhone do.

The land they traveled through gave the appearance of once having been tilled and productive. At a stone pile, the ruins of some ancient house or inn, his grandmother stopped him.

"Kleg'l is having difficulty, Kenock."

He hadn't noticed, and went back to help the good-man.

Amolikah prepared something from Mishah's healer's bag and made Kleg'l drink it down.

Kenock peered down the trail, expecting to see giants any moment. What would Rhone do?

"Why are we stopping?" Bar'ack's abrupt tone surprised him.

"Kleg'l needs a moment's rest," Amolikah said.

"We don't have time for that."

Cerah scowled at him. "A few moments won't matter now, Master Bar'ack. What would you have us do? Leave him behind?"

He seemed ready to say something, then turned away and stalked up the road carrying their two useless proj-lances over one shoulder, the second sword swinging lightly in his right hand.

"What's got him in such a mood?" Cerah asked.

"Nerves." Kenock lifted Rhone's sword and held it out one-handed a moment. Frowning, he let the point fall back to the weedy track. No doubt, this was a heavier sword than the one Bar'ack carried. He looked up to discover his grandmother's mouth pinched into a worried line, her green eyes narrowed up the road.

Amolikah looked away from Bar'ack. "Is that helping, Kleg'l?"

"I am fine, Mistress Amolikah."

"You're not. Your wound is bothering you, and you are exhausted as we all are." She dug through the sack of food the townspeople had given them and passed out dried fruit. "Master Bar'ack, come and eat."

He pretended not to hear her, and kept walking.

"What *has* gotten into him?" Kenock mumbled.

"Nerves," Cerah said, giving his earlier answer back to him.

He grinned at her.

His grandmother wasn't smiling.

※

Captain Da-gore gathered his men on the single street running through Eve's Weep and peered at the empty buildings, then turned for another look out to sea. The second boat had been lost in the storm. That left him with just his lieutenant, the two giants, and six of First Major Bair'tor's troops.

One of the soldiers came jogging back from the outskirts of the village where Da-gore had sent him. "The whole place is deserted. Not even a dog left behind, sir. They pulled out of here recently. By the tracks, no later than this morning. They left by way of the road to Havil. Shall I take some men and bring them back?"

"No." He didn't have time to waste running down and interrogating villagers. He knew where the fugitives were heading. He lifted his proj-lance and pointed with the barrel. "This is the way."

"Should we wait for First Major Bair'tor and the others to arrive?"

"Three woman and four men? Do you fear those numbers?" What sort of soldiers were these that First Major Bair'tor had put in his charge?

"No, sir," he answered quickly, then glanced about and lowered his voice. "One of them is a Makir, according to Chief Gate Warden Sentor."

Da-gore indicated the two giants standing a little way off, keeping apart from the humans. "And we have them."

"Yes, sir." But the uncertainty remained in the guard's eyes.

Only two of the fourth quartering, they could still make several leagues before dark if they didn't delay. Da-gore called his troops to marching order. They shouldered their weapons and supplies, and started on their way.

The ancient road, little used now, soon dwindled to a single track, sometimes disappearing altogether. But Da-gore had the fresh tracks to follow, and the giants, undependable as they were, like carefree adolescents out for some adventure, had keen eyes when things became hard to discern. Where the fugitives' tracks faded, it was generally Herc or Plut who found them again, keeping Da-gore's company on the correct course.

He pushed his men hard until the sun left the sky. When night finally overtook them, Da-gore made camp and set watchmen. By the signs, his quarry would not be far ahead. Tomorrow.

❧

Mishah gasped and pressed her palm hard against the side of her stomach. The sharp pain buckled her. Had it been a true contraction, or only another false start? As on the boat, exertion brought pain. She had to force herself to rest, to will her body to relax and wait. *Please, Creator, not yet. Not here.*

Rhone looked over from the brook where he cleaned fresh vegetables and roots he'd gathered before the darkness had swallowed up the forest. In the feeble starlight, a worried look narrowed his eyes. Perhaps he was thinking he would have to deliver this baby—and perhaps he would.

The pain eased. Mishah shifted her heavy body to a more comfortable position, half reclined on the ground with her back against the rough bark of a tree. "No, not yet," she said in answer to his unspoken question.

"What can I do?"

He'd asked that maybe ten times already. Unfortunately, there wasn't a thing he could do. If only she had her healer case with her, she could take something to stave off the contractions. "You can find harrow root and jins leaves, and boil them into tea." She had to smile at his blank look.

"Harrow doesn't grow anywhere but the southlands."

"I know." She struggled for breath with the baby pressing her diaphragm. "I was being facetious." But this was no time for humor. "Master Rhone." Her voice turned suddenly grave. "You may have to deliver this baby."

He gathered up the food. "Even if we make it to the Cradleland before you deliver, there is no one else to help you."

"Unless Grandmother comes."

He looked up. She could see he didn't expect the others. "We can't count on that happening."

She frowned. "Then perhaps I ought to tell you what to expect."

He put tin-sliced carrots into her hand. "This will make you feel better."

He didn't want to hear it. She sighed. *Well, he was going to.* "Once it starts there is no stopping it."

"The baby will come as all babies do, Mistress Mishah. I'm sure when it does, I'll figure out what to do."

It wasn't as if giving birth was a complicated matter. The Creator designed it to happen naturally, and it usually did without much fuss. She suppressed a nagging worry. If only she had Grandmother at her side! "When a baby threatens to come prematurely, I put the mother to bed and give her a tonic to stave off labor. I have no tonic here, Master Rhone, and I cannot afford the luxury of rest."

"Then the baby will be born."

"There is another problem."

His expression hardened. He didn't want to hear this either. "What?"

The concern had weighed on her spirit for days. She wanted it to remain unspoken, but he needed to know. "Sometimes when a baby is born prematurely, his lungs are not finished growing. He won't cry." Her lips trembled. She had to control herself. "He'll struggle to breathe, but can't. His skin will turn blue. He is suffocating."

Rhone stared at her. "What would I do?"

Tears stung the corners of her eyes. She didn't want to even consider this. "Here, in this place, with no help, with no medicines, all we could do is pray."

He flung his knife into the ground and stood. "Would the Creator permit it?"

"I don't know."

"What of the prophecy?"

"I don't know! I truly don't understand any of this!" Tears gushed in spite of her resolve not to cry. Rhone stood as if uncertain what to do, then knelt and took her into his arms and held her until the tears subsided. She needed a man's arms around her, to comfort her.

She wiped her eyes. He strode to the dark footpath, and stared into the night. "Will delivering your child in the Cradleland instead of here make a difference?"

"I can't see how." She sniffed, patting her eyes with a dirty sleeve.

"She said you'd be safe there."

Mishah looked around the dark forest and hugged herself. "Safe? The Cradleland has been abandoned over a thousand years. How could it be any different than right here after so much time? Surely the forest will have swallowed up whatever remained of the garden."

He stared at the dark treetops. When he looked back, she couldn't see his face, but a peculiar resolve had come to his voice. "The Creator kept you from the giants. He kept you from Leviathan. Would he abandon you now?"

So much faith in so little time. She marveled, drawing strength from it. He was right. She was trying to do this in her own power, but events had moved far beyond what she could control. "You are right, Master Rhone."

He came back and sat cross-legged in front of her. "Then we need to trust him."

"I may not be able to walk much farther, if these pains continue."

"I'll carry you."

"I will be a burden, even for your big arms."

"You've yet to be a burden that I cannot bear."

He was being kind, but she and her family had all been burdens, and he had not once protested. And she realized now she couldn't have made it this far without him. What would have become of them if Lamech hadn't been taken captive and they had not enlisted Rhone's help? Could Lamech have fought off the sea-vine serpents? Or Leviathan? And what of the giants? No. Only Rhone could have. Even in that, the Creator's hands were moving, though she hadn't seen it at the time. She had to believe he would continue to watch over her.

She shifted on the ground, searching for a comfortable position, and prayed for protection, not only for them and her son, but for her grandmother and the others, wherever they might be, and for Lamech, whatever he was doing.

❦

Amolikah cast an impatient glance to where Bar'ack sat before the fire, dragging another log into the flames. Kenock knew her worry, but what could he do? He'd warned Bar'ack once.

"How long are we going to put up with it?" She scowled. "A fire like this is a beacon to anyone looking for us."

He glanced at Cerah, beside him with her knees drawn up, arms wrapped about them. "Something's happened to him, Kenock. He frightens me."

So, this was the burden of leadership. "I suppose I need to mention it. *Again.*"

"Be careful." Cerah's view went to Bar'ack. "He's not himself."

Kenock grimaced and stood. How right she was. Rhone's timid apprentice had become a lion.

Bar'ack dropped a log into the flames and glared at Kenock as he came up, firelight dancing in his wide eyes. The crackling of unseasoned wood, filled with living sap, drove the night sounds into oblivion while the heat and smoke seemed to be trying to drive Kenock back to where the others waited. He hunkered down. "A fire this large is going to attract attention, Bar'ack."

"I like a big fire." The words rumbled up from deep inside his chest, the voice more powerful, more sure.

The sound sent a shiver through him. "Let it burn itself out. We shouldn't have a fire at all."

Bar'ack gave a low growl and reached for another piece of wood.

Kenock stood and put a foot atop the log.

Without warning, Bar'ack swung out, hitting him with the force of a mule. The blow drove him off his feet, and he curled into a ball as pain exploded through him.

"Bar'ack!" Cerah rushed to put herself between the two of them.

Bar'ack looked as if he were going to come at her, then walked into the shadows.

Cerah's eyes were wide with fear when she looked at him. "Are you all right?"

He gasped for a breath and nodded. "I think so." He sat up, wincing. "Bar'ack's stronger than he looks."

"I told you there was something wrong with him!"

Amolikah examined his ribs. "Nothing seems broken."

Cerah stared after Bar'ack. "We should get away from here."

He drew in another painful breath. Bar'ack was no longer the fainthearted man who had cowered in the fight under the tower at Derbin-ee, and again when the seavine serpents had swarmed aboard their boat.

"Cerah's right." Grandmother looked quickly about. "Let's distance ourselves from him and that fire. I'll not sleep all night with that man near us."

"The flames will certainly draw them to us," Kleg'l said worriedly.

Kenock nodded. "You're right. We must go. He can fend for himself for all I care."

A sharp crack, like a tree branch snapping, came from the forest. Then another. A moment later Bar'ack returned dragging two huge limbs behind him. He dropped them by the fire and began stripping limbs, feeding the roaring flames. He paused to look at them. "I like a big fire," he said, then went back to work.

Gathering up their things, they backed into the night. Bar'ack hardly noticed.

※

"Captain Da-gore."

Da-gore glanced up as the guard came into camp. "What is it?"

"One of the watchmen has spotted something. I think you should come and have a look."

He set his daybook and pen aside, closed the silver cap on his bottle of ink, and set the lapboard upon the ground. His men lounged on their waxed sleeping cloths; reading, writing, or just thinking. Three were occupied in a game of squares and hardly looked up as he left the camp. The giants, as usual, had billeted themselves apart from the humans. Herc had gathered a stack of poles and was hacking points onto them with his big knife. Plut sat with his great sword upon his knees, stroking a whetstone along the edge. They had only killing on their minds. *What an army I could have if only these giants could be brought under submission.* He sighed. *As though that would ever happen.*

He followed the guard away from the small fire, his eyes rapidly adjusting to the blackness. Insects chirped and buzzed while dark creatures on silent wings flitted across the night sky. The land rose to a cedar glade. The scented air cleared the smoke from his nostrils, and he inhaled deeply, relishing its freshness. His escort stopped, whistled, got a reply, and led him to a dark ledge where a guard waited. "There," the second man pointed.

A faint flicker of firelight showed among the trees, the distance impossible to judge; a league at the very least, maybe two. He let a smile move across his face. "So, they light a beacon for us."

"Do we move out tonight?" his escort asked.

Da-gore appreciated the enthusiasm, but he didn't intend to go tromping through Wild Lands at night, not knowing exactly where he was heading. "Get a bearing on their location." He glanced at the sky and judged the distant fire to be nearly due east of their location. "We'll move out at first light."

They were within his reach now. This time he would not fail.

36

Demons Within

The dream came back to haunt her; stones of fire whirling in their perpetual orbits, deep forests swallowing up the light and warmth, the darkness always somewhere close behind her, its black wings and clawed fingers stretching like long shadows over her. The Evil drew nearer each night, the dreams becoming more real and terrifying. She longed for Lamech at her side, but he never came. She was alone, so alone. Even the glorious being who, in the past, had accompanied her seemed to have abandoned her.

With the terror of the night still raw in her brain, Mishah awoke. The misty dawn had settled wetly upon her cloak. She turned sleepily and stared up into a wide gray nose and huge brown eyes peering down at her. Her startled cry instantly awakened Rhone, the hatchet leaping to his hand. She clawed herself away from beneath the face.

Rhone started for her, then stopped and looked around. Mishah put a tree to her back, her breathing coming in panicked gasps, her heart pounding her ribs.

The donkey lifted its long head and peered curiously at her.

Rhone gave a low laugh and strode about the campsite, peering behind trees and up and down the trail. Finding nothing, he slipped the rusty weapon under his belt and put out a hand. The donkey seemed unafraid.

Mishah began breathing again, her heart settling back, the rush of fear draining in small shudders from her body. Then, she laughed too. "What's he doing out here?" she stood, grabbing the tree for support.

Rhone ran a hand along the animal's back and looked the little animal over. The donkey seemed content to stand there, dipping its head to tug loose a tuft of grass. "Can't be from a farm. Must be wild."

"It doesn't act wild." She was embarrassed for her fright. But at the moment, coming directly from the dream … "I'm sorry I woke you."

He started collecting their things. "Just as well. We need to start right away." He tapped his head. "According to the map, we are near."

"Today?" Hope swelled within her.

"If we keep a steady pace."

She looked down at herself, large and awkward. For the moment, the pain was gone. The rest had helped. But as soon as she began exerting herself, she knew it would return. Even just standing there, her hips felt strange and weak. "I won't be able to hold a steady pace, Master Rhone." Did that mean another night in the forests? How much longer could she *will* this baby not to be born?

"Last night I said I'd carry you. Looks like the Creator has seen to even that detail." He scratched the donkey between the ears.

Her mouth fell open, momentarily stunned. It had to be so!

Rhone laughed. "Does he always answer your needs so promptly?"

"I've not noticed it so, but this trip has opened my eyes to so much. Lamech saw the Creator's hand in everything. I mostly doubted, putting it off to a vivid imagination and wishful thinking." She shook her head. "I won't be so quick to doubt ever again."

"When I first heard your husband speak out on the Meeting Floor, I thought he was a fool for taking such risks. Now I see that I was a fool for not believing in his Creator. Lamech is a wise man, Mistress Mishah."

She appreciated hearing that from him, but his words brought back the loneliness she'd been trying so hard to fight off. He must have seen it in her face.

"Once we've made it to the Cradleland, and your son is born and I've safely seen you home again with your family, I will return to Nod City and free Lamech."

Her heart leaped, hope filling the hole despair had dug. "Could you do such a thing? Alone?"

"I will, even if I have to raise an army."

She sat on the donkey sideways, her right hand propped against its rolling rump, the fingers of her left twisted into the short, coarse mane. The ride was surprisingly easy, the animal's gait gentle. Although it walked no faster than she could have, it was a steady pace, one that devoured leagues that would have defeated her. Yet all was not well. The pain had returned, and now, a cramping—somehow different from before. No matter how hard she willed herself to relax, no matter how many mental pictures she drew of her body stemming the onset of labor, the contractions had begun. She had to tell him.

Rhone seemed to be deep in concentration. The donkey followed him as a dog might its master, though no halter or lead rope connected them.

"What is it?" she asked. His silence had turned worrisome.

"They are all around us."

"They?" She looked side to side.

"The spiders."

She had smelled the strong javian odor.

"They are frightened."

"Of us?" She looked again, still seeing nothing.

"No. It's the same as when we came upon the spider on the road to Chevel-ee. I didn't understand it at the time."

"But you do now?"

"It must have been the Oracle's pledge crystal. Somehow, these spiders *are* sensitives. They felt the evil in it. That's why I couldn't get near that spider. It must be why they've begun to migrate away from Nod City. But here they have no fear of me."

"Yet there is fear, and you no longer have the crystal."

"No, *I* don't." He thought a moment. "But Bar'ack does."

The way he said it chilled her. "Then the others must be close behind us. Grandmother is coming!"

He stared at her. "More likely the giants. They must carry crystals as well."

He refused to let her hold onto hope, and she refused to let it go. "We need to hurry."

She felt a gush, and suddenly her dress was wet. *No, not yet, Creator!* "Master Rhone, it's started!"

�֍

Kleg'l sagged in Kenock's arms. Cerah rushed to his other side to support him. The good-man's skin had paled. He hung his head, breathing deeply, his facial muscles twitching with each painful gasp. Sweat beaded across his forehead and trickled over his gaunt cheeks.

Kenock lowered him to the ground at the side of the trail. "How can I help, Kleg'l?"

Kleg'l pressed a hand to the bandage on his chest, looked at his palm, and smiled weakly. "No blood. Mistress Mishah would be pleased." The exertion, the unceasing pace of keeping one step ahead of their pursuers, had taken a toll on his healing body.

"We can rest a while," Amolikah said.

"No. Mistress Mishah needs you."

Amolikah felt his forehead. "You've a fever, Kleg'l." Cerah opened the healer's bag for her.

He shook his head. "No more of your tonics, your stimulants, Mistress Amolikah. They keep me moving, but they're burning me up inside." To speak seemed an effort. His breath had gotten ragged at the edges, and Kenock thought for a moment he might topple. Kleg'l braced himself with a hand. "The time has come for you to go ahead and leave me."

Kenock recoiled at the notion. "No. We cannot do that."

"We won't leave you, Kleg'l." Amolikah removed a pouch from the bag.

"I won't take it."

Kenock stared, stunned. Kleg'l had never refused his mistress.

His words struck Amolikah, too. She returned the pouch and peered at him with widened eyes. "You know what it means if you stay." Not a question, but a statement.

Kleg'l nodded a solemn understanding. "I know I will only slow you down. You need to move swiftly. To keep up with *him*."

Kenock knew who *him* meant. Bar'ack had snapped. It must have been the stress of the trip. He had let it get to him and it had scrambled his brain! Kenock had awakened that morning to find Bar'ack staring at them. When he sat up, Bar'ack had fled. Now he was ahead, and the giants behind them. They could not afford to delay here.

"Surely Master Rhone will protect her." Kenock desperately needed to believe that.

Amolikah said, "I wonder." Her face paled. "His eyes ... that same vacant stare that had been in Gar's eyes. The same evil that had taken hold of Gar has touched Bar'ack."

"No!" Kenock grabbed up Rhone's heavy sword. If what had

possessed Gar had taken hold of Bar'ack, he had to go now. Rhone would need his help.

Amolikah's hand came down on his shoulder, fingers digging into the muscle. "Wait. You can't stop him. If he is possessed as Gar was, he has ten times your strength. He wanted to kill you last night. Now he will."

"Mishah and Master Rhone must be warned."

"Yes, they must." Amolikah turned to Kleg'l. "We are not far from the Cradleland. We will come back for you."

Kenock turned Kleg'l by the shoulders. "The Lodath's Guard can't be far behind us."

"Don't worry over me, Master Kenock. You must hurry."

Amolikah said, "First we must hide you."

"There is no time, Mistress."

She grabbed his hand. Cerah helped him to his feet. Off the road they found an overhanging ledge. Kenock slashed a willowbud apart and used the branches to disguise the opening. Then he took the good-man's hand and squeezed it in his. "I'll come back for you."

As unflappable as ever, Kleg'l merely smiled. He smiled! "Find Mistress Mishah. I hand over my half of Lamech's command, Master Kenock. You now have it all."

He had it all, but he didn't want it! It felt hollow. He would forsake the responsibility just to have Kleg'l well and his sister at his side. He stood, struggling to restrain the tears. His eyes stung, his voice cracked when he spoke. "Farewell, good-man."

Amolikah shoved a pouch into Kleg'l hand. "Take these. They'll help with the fever and the pain."

He put it into his pocket. "Hurry. Mistress Mishah needs you."

Kenock refused to look back. Kleg'l was going to be all right. Their good-man was going to be all right! He pounded that single thought into his head over and over, but his heart was telling him something else. And what of Mishah? He restrained himself from bursting into a jog. No doubt Cerah could keep pace with him stride for stride, but he wouldn't leave Grandmother behind. He'd already left one; he'd leave no more.

❀

He helped her off the donkey. Although great with child, she was still light in his arms as he set her feet on the ground. She took the sack with the extra clothes Mistress Sheble had given her and started for a large tree when all at once she bent and clutched herself. He started for her but she waved him back. He took the donkey up the trail a few paces to give her privacy. A short while later her voice summoned him back. A pile of what appeared to be undergarments lay off to one side. Her eyes showed desperation.

"Quickly. We must hurry. This baby is coming."

He helped her back onto the donkey. "How early will it be?"

"A month and a week."

From what little he knew of birthing a child, five weeks sounded dangerously young. But what difference could it make if the child was born here, or two leagues from here? With no medicines, with no skilled help, the infant faced the same perils. Rhone remembered that Mother Eve had called the Cradleland "the Sanctuary."

Might there be help there he did not know of?

He threw the packs over his shoulder and started up the trail, the donkey falling into step behind him. Mishah slumped forward on the animal's back and held on tight, now and again giving a muffled cry deep in her throat.

❀

Da-gore had broken camp well before daylight, and now, with the sun high in the sky and almost a quartering of marching behind them, he came upon the place the fugitives had spent the night. He held his hand near the pile of gray ashes, feeling the heat still in them while the giants prowled the spot, sniffing the air. Trampled vegetation leading away from the campsite told him his prey was not far ahead.

Herc lumbered over, shoved his sword into the earth and leaned forward on the hilt. "Pose was here."

"Pose?" Da-gore's eyebrows came together. Was this another of these Earth-Borns' juvenile games? "Pose is dead."

"The breath of him was here." The giant appeared serious.

The breath of him? Da-gore turned that over in his brain. "Speak plainly."

Herc's rumbling voice took on an impatient note. He rapped his chest. "In here. Breath. Essence ..." The giant's scowl darkened. "It wanders looking for a tent to dwell in, but wanders no more."

Breath ... essence ... ? "His spirit?"

Herc nodded.

"His spirit had found a tent—a body to dwell in?"

"One of the fugitives."

The notion that the spirit of one of these halflings might enter into a human body disgusted him. "Are you certain?"

"He was here. But he is here no more." Herc jutted his heavy jaw in the direction of the trail. "He is ahead, with the fugitives."

Da-gore didn't understand it. Much about this whole expedition had been a puzzle. And much had opened his eyes to things around him—unseen things—that he would never have believed a month earlier. "Does Pose know what to do?"

"He knows."

In that case, the woman might already be dead. *A body!* This time he would have her corpse to take back to the Oracle. No more mistakes, no more failures.

The freshness of the signs stirred his blood. Closing in on an enemy, even one as puny as these, had kindled a primal lust for battle within him; the very thing he'd missed all those years as the

Lodath's captain of the Guard. That there was a true warrior amongst these farmers only added savor to the anticipated clash.

※

Mishah cried out with a jolt and lost her balance. Rhone caught her as she fell off the donkey's back and laid her gently upon the ground.

"I can't go on." Her moan pulled at his heart.

"Is the baby—?"

"Soon," she gasped, panting as the contraction passed.

He was seeing the pattern develop, and had begun to count the time between each wave of pain. They were drawing closer together, each contraction seemingly more torturous than the last one.

She grabbed his arm, panic in her eyes. "I can no longer ride, Master Rhone! I need Grandmother!"

He'd have battled a dozen giants to give her Mistress Amolikah, but it was beyond his power. "The Mother said the baby had to be born in the Cradleland."

She gritted her teeth. "I can't control this."

The Cradleland had to be close. The map was clear in his mind, and if its distances were even close to accurate, they had to be very close. "I'll carry you."

"No." She was crying, her fingers clawing into his arm. He lifted her in spite of her protests. The donkey trotted along beside them. He moved more swiftly carrying her this way. He should have done so from the start. She was light in his arms; no heavier that the weights he'd trained with as a youth. His muscles responded now as if no time at all had passed, as if new life was being pumped into them. It was more than muscle. It was a mind-set the masters had taught him, and he had taught others.

Branches whipped past and vines clogged the ancient trail, but they did not slow Rhone much. The trail crested a hillock. He stopped. Ahead, it plunged down into a wide plain of scattered trees where beasts of the field grazed. He stopped, his breath caught away by what lay beyond the plain.

"Mistress Mishah, look."

She didn't speak, but he knew she saw. A wall of white stone, shimmering in the sunlight as if made of the purest white marble with bands of rubies and clear emeralds, rose in the distance maybe a league farther on. It stretched on and on until its ends disappeared in the gray mist of distance. The height soared skyward far above the low line of clinging vines, impossible to judge.

Mishah suddenly stiffened in his arms, her groan ripe with pain. It lasted longer this time. As it passed, leaving her breathless, a voice behind him growled his name.

Rhone wheeled at the sound. Bar'ack stood forty paces away, a drawn sword in his hand.

37

The Cradleland

What's that?" Amolikah stopped suddenly and pointed at a gangerberry shrub.

Kenock didn't see anything until she fell to her knees, reached under the bush, and dragged out what appeared to be gray undergarments and leggings. "Mishah's."

Amolikah felt the material then looked up with sudden urgency in her eyes. "She's gone into labor."

"Oh, no," Cerah breathed.

Their eyes told him this was bad. "Labor? How can she? It's not time."

Amolikah tossed the clothing aside. "It means the child will be born dangerously early. It means unless Master Rhone has had training as a healer, she is going to need me soon."

Cerah's eyes held the same frightened look. "I'm sure Master Rhone has no training in delivering babies."

"Then we must hurry!" All at once the forest went still. Kenock's head snapped up, a tingle shot up his spine. His view leaped back down the trail. What was it Rhone said? It was right there, but he couldn't pull it clearly into view. Then he remembered. *Birds will momentarily hush when disturbed.*

"The giants come!" He grabbed Amolikah's hand. Cerah flew past them as he and his grandmother hurried to keep up. Fear for Amolikah crushed down on him. His sister needed him, but so did his grandmother. How could a man choose?

❦

Bar'ack! He was alive! Rhone took a step toward him.

"Grandmother!" Mishah called, but no one else was there.

Rhone's momentary relief was suddenly tempered by a warning in his skull. Something was wrong. "Where are the others? Are they near?" What he really wanted to know was, were they still alive?

"Give me the woman and you may live."

Something *was* very wrong. That voice. Those eyes. This was not his friend's son. The body, perhaps, but the soul was different. He remembered where he'd seen those eyes before. "Gar!"

Bar'ack advanced. "I will have her."

Mishah's grip tightened. Rhone pried her fingers, placed her on her feet, and held her by the shoulders as she buckled to the ground. He placed himself before her. What damage had he done by agreeing to bring Bar'ack along? His heart ached for him, and for Ker'ack. But this was no longer Bar'ack. He couldn't permit himself to think of this as his friend's son. "I have fought you before, in the tower and the cave beneath it."

"You fought only one of us," the voice taunted. "We are many now." Bar'ack's sword swung back and forth in a light, fluid movement.

Many? Rhone slipped the hatchet from his belt. Fighting only one of them had almost ended in his death. Now there was more than one? He didn't understand. He inhaled the lush earthiness of the forest, the sharp tang of javian all around him. Putting it all out of mind, he centered his thoughts. This could not be a battle of strength. It would all pivot on skill. "I will not give Mistress Mishah to you."

Out the edge of his eyes, he watched her claw her way off to the side of the trail.

Bar'ack, or whatever it was that had possessed his young apprentice, raised his sword and gave a low growl. The blade whirred with a suddenness Rhone had not expected. He ducked as it passed a fraction of a span above him, and as he came up to intercept a second blow, Mishah cried, "Kenock! Kenock, help us!" But was he even near, or had Bar'ack murdered them all?

Steel rang against steel, the hatchet's blade spitting sparks. Seeing an opening, Rhone swept in low and quick. Bar'ack leaped back as the hatchet skimmed the material of his jerkin, and he struck back. Rhone caught his hand. Bar'ack flung him to the ground and slashed wildly, his blade chopping the turf as Rhone rolled to avoid each blow.

Rhone scrambled to his feet in time to deflect a powerful downward swipe. The blade bit deep into the hatchet's ironwood handle and drove it from his fist. Bar'ack swung again. Rhone threw himself aside. The blade caught him on the upper arm like a hot iron. A searing bolt shot into his shoulder and up his neck. He backpedaled, clutching the wound.

Bar'ack lunged for the kill. Rhone jerked sideways and grabbed the possessed man's sword hand. Bar'ack had the strength of a three-point. With a flick of his wrist he easily broke Rhone's grip, driving the hilt of the sword into his jaw and sprawling him to the ground.

Stunned, Rhone tensed for Bar'ack's killing blow.

Mishah screamed. As his eyes cleared, she was crawling in retreat, throwing stones harmlessly against Bar'ack's chest. He had stopped over her and was drawing the sword back double-handed.

Rhone shouted, "Bar'ack!"

Bar'ack ignored him.

The donkey dashed between them and gave a double hind-legged kick that hardly moved him. Bar'ack struck out at the beast, missing it. Rhone swayed to his feet. Bar'ack turned back to Mishah.

Somewhere deep in his subconscious, he sensed them there, but it wasn't until the black-and-red bodies plunged down on invisible strands of silk that he actually knew they were all around him.

Bar'ack raised his sword.

Mishah screamed and covered her head.

A filament of immensely strong web encircled Bar'ack's wrists. He spun around in surprise, searching for the source of this new intrusion. From above, javian spiders began spinning silvery threads, drawing his arms tight against his chest.

Bar'ack gave an unearthly cry of rage that rocked the forest. He dropped the sword and strained against the web, but the spiders had already thrown a score of loops about him. The web was stronger than he, and the more Bar'ack struggled the tighter the silk became.

Rhone swept up the dropped sword and rushed to Mishah. With wild panic, she fought him until she saw who it was, then flung her arms about his neck, sobbing uncontrollably.

A cocoon grew before Rhone's eyes and lifted into the treetops where the javians turned him round and round, encasing him as if he were a bead of puff-pollen.

"Master Rhone!" Cerah sprinted up the road and stopped, bending over to catch her breath. Her view went to the treetops. "Amazing," she panted. "Unbelievable."

The others?" Rhone asked.

"I need Grandmother!" Mishah blurted between sobs.

Cerah grasped Mishah's hand. "Behind me. They're behind me. And the giants," she got out between gasps. She looked at him. "You're hurt."

The wound was deep and bleeding freely.

Mishah yanked at the hem of her dress, tearing off a strip of cloth, and tying it above the wound to stem the flow.

"It can wait."

Kenock and Mistress Amolikah appeared, Kenock carrying Mishah's healer's bag and helping his grandmother.

"Mi!" He hugged his sister.

"Kleg'l?" Rhone asked, looking around.

"We had to leave him. He couldn't go on."

"Grandmother!"

Mistress Amolikah wrapped her arms around Mishah. "I'm here."

"It's started."

"I know."

Rhone glanced up at the cocoon of silk above them, Bar'ack struggling inside it, his cries of rage muffled. "We need to move now." He looked at the old woman. "Can you keep up?"

"You go ahead. I'll manage. It's more important Mishah makes it."

"Grandmother! I need you." Mishah's arms reached for her.

"I'll stay with Grandmother." Kenock glanced at the heavy sword in his hand. "Master Rhone, maybe we should trade."

It felt good to have his own sword back. "No one will stay behind." He swept Mistress Amolikah up, put her atop the donkey, and slapped its rump, then took up Mishah and set off at a jog for the gleaming wall rising in the far distance. An ornate portal pierced it, too far yet for him to make out except that it appeared to be braced by a pair of statues, glowing like molten bronze in the sharp, midday light.

They'd covered a quarter of the way to the wall when something made him look back.

The giants had arrived.

❦

Da-gore halted his men at the forest's edge as the people far down the road fled toward the walls. He had them now. Herc and Plut would run them down before they reached those distant palisades that, for the briefest of moments, had arrested his breath. What was it? An unknown city? A place where yet again, the fugitives would find refuge?

Herc's head came about and cocked to one side. "Pose?" The giant's nose twitched, sampling the air. At that same moment, Da-gore spied the bundle of shining silk swaying overhead.

Herc's dark eyes stretched. "Pose—! and Hepha?"

Da-gore shivered at a sudden chill. The giant was calling to beings Da-gore knew were dead.

Herc stretched his sword, severed the stands anchoring the bundle to the treetops, and caught it as it fell. To Da-gore's amazement, he proceeded to extricate the fugitive.

Plut drew the man from the bundle of silk. "Per!"

Da-gore motioned to his men. "Take him."

"No." Herc moved between them. "Our cousins dwell within this one."

Herc's statement stunned him. "Who dwells where?"

The fugitive cast off the remaining strands of silk and growled. "We three dwell in this tent." The voice had not emanated from human vocal chords. "I almost had the woman. Give me a weapon!"

Plut yanked a sword from one of Da-gore's startled guards and handed it to him. Herc hefted the bundles of spears he had made onto his shoulder.

The dead giants? Before Da-gore could continue his thoughts, Herc, Plut, and the fugitive, as if collectively hearing the voice of a different commander, started after the fleeing humans. He had no time to work out the paradoxes. He rallied his men and took up the pursuit.

❧

She'd never despised her body before, but just then Mishah would have given anything to be lithe and fleet-footed again … if only for the time it would take her to dash from here to the portal.

Although Rhone claimed her weight not a burden, his heavy breathing, his heart pounding as his strong arms held her against his chest, told her it was not the trivial thing he made it out to be. But she'd never make it on her own. Another cramp forced a moan from her throat. She must not have this baby here, in his arms! She had to hold off. But that was beyond sheer physical ability! The baby was coming, and there was nothing she could do now to dissuade him. As the contraction passed and she was able to breath again, she opened her eyes and cast past his shoulders. "They're gaining on us."

He nodded. His breath came in hot bursts. Sweat, heavy with the odor of his exertion, soaked his shirt and the shiverthorn jerkin.

The portal into the Cradleland, although still distant, had become clearer; jewel-encrusted ornamentation carved from the whitest of marble, sea-green chalcedony, and ebony onyx. But what had seized the breath in her lungs were the two statues bracing either side of the portal, fashioned as if from molten sunlight, as tall as the portal itself, each holding a golden sword crossed before the arching entry that had no gate. Curiously, what lay beyond was washed out in a glow of light, but not exactly light; a veil of sheer silk, perhaps.

The giants were closing. Her grandmother had moved ahead of them, leaning forward on the galloping donkey, her dress fluttering, her hair loose and scattered across her back. Kenock and Cerah kept pace as best they could. Kenock lagged, weighed down by a sword in one hand and her healer's bag over his left shoulder.

She squeezed her eyes as needles of pain racked her like a knife twisting in her gut. With a groan, her fingers dug into Rhone's flexing muscles. Tears moistened her cheeks and her teeth sawed into her lip until she was sure they drew blood.

The whistle of a proj screamed past and exploded into the ground alongside the road. She flinched. Flying dirt stung her face and arms. Rhone staggered, regained his footing, and plunged on with a renewed strength. The statues loomed nearer. The air seemed to vibrate all around her, the air wavering as if from bands of rising heat. The explosion must have stunned her.

The giants were almost upon them. Bar'ack too! Fear contorted all she saw, like her dreams. More men were behind the giants. A proj-lance flashed. She buried her face against Rhone's chest. The explosion and the cry of the donkey came as one. Mishah flung her head around. The animal had fallen forward onto its knees. Her grandmother was tumbling.

Cerah rushed to the older woman and helped her to her feet. Amolikah seemed stunned, but unharmed. Mishah looked back, fear squeezing the breath from in her chest. They weren't going to make it. Suddenly Rhone drew to a halt and set her down. Grandmother and Cerah grabbed her by each arm.

"Grandmother?"

Amolikah gathered her in a firm embrace "I'm all right." She and Cerah pulled her toward the golden statues towering before them. When did they get so close? Her brain whirled. A claw ripped her stomach muscles. Through a fog of tears Rhone turned to face the onrushing giants. Her brother seemed to hesitate. He leaped between her and the portal, now within striking distance. The lone warrior prepared to sacrifice his life to give life to her and her unborn son. Coming to a decision, Kenock rushed to Cerah, put the healer's bag into her hands and hugged her fiercely.

"I love you, Mi." He kissed her forehead and rushed back to Rhone's side.

It tore at her heart. Both men willing to die. How could she permit it? How could she stop it? *Oh, Creator, God. Why now when we are so close?*

One of the giants slipped a pointed shaft from a bundle on his shoulder and flung it—not at Rhone or her brother, but at her. Rhone's sword swept up and split the spear as it whirred past him, the pieces tumbling to the ground.

"We've got to move faster," her grandmother said. The air about her buzzed, the faint odor of brimstone, the remnant of that last exploding proj, no doubt, stung her nose. Her feet moved reluctantly forward as she craned her neck, her attention, fogged as it was, riveted on what was happening behind her. The giants fell upon her brother and Rhone. The clang of steel rang in the air—air that seemed suddenly to be boiling all around her. Not far behind the giants, men in green and purple rushed to join the fray.

It would be over in a moment. Her brother was no fighter, and a lone Makir Warrior could never hope to hold out against the giants, let alone the reinforcements not far behind them.

A shadow moved overhead. She was vaguely aware that they had passed under the statues' crossed swords. The portal was but a few steps now. Rhone's swift sword moved with a glare of reflected sunlight as the giants forced him back. Kenock was only just managing to avoid Bar'ack's crashing blows.

Farther back, the soldiers formed a line and shouldered projlances. Twin flashes burst almost simultaneously. Mishah gasped in a breath. The air around her vibrated with some unseen energy. In a movement too fast for the eye to follow, swords whirling like golden flames intercepted the projs, exploding them against a golden barrier.

Shock seized her. A contraction tore at her. The statues had stepped together in front of the portal. Suddenly Mishah understood. They hadn't been statues at all, but living creatures. Stunned by their sudden mobility, even the giants halted in their assault.

In the intervening heartbeat, Rhone grabbed Kenock and shoved him toward the portal. The giants shook off their astonishment. The one with the spears unleashed another at Mishah. Flaming swords shattered it as it lobbed in.

Cerah dropped Mishah's healer's bag, and running between the legs of the golden beings, rushed back out onto the road.

"Cerah!" What was she thinking? "Cerah!" Mishah called as her grandmother pulled her onward. A veil of light engulfed her, the humming that had been all around her suddenly faded to only a memory in her ears.

Past the golden beings' legs, Mishah watched Cerah catch Kenock in one arm and snatch his sword off the ground. Mishah's view went to the healer's bag now lying inside the portal. They would need her help. Cerah pulled Kenock, stumbling backward, and managed to get amongst the golden legs when one of the giants broke away from Rhone and rushed her.

A streak of sunlight shot from a golden sword and sliced the giant in half at the waist.

The remaining giant threw back his head and roared in rage. Rhone staggered, blood flowing from a fist of wounds, soaking his clothes, draining his seemingly inexhaustible strength.

As Kenock and Cerah rushed beneath the protective swords of the portal's guardians and collapsed, Rhone turned and made a dash for safety.

The giant launched a handful of spears. Rhone lurched, his arms flung wide. He staggered, three thick shafts of wood protruding from his back.

The golden beings closed behind him. He was through the portal. Cerah and Amolikah dashed to Rhone and caught him as he fell hard against the white marble portal, drawing a streak of red down the pure stone as he slumped to the ground. Grabbing at his back, he clutched a spear and drew it out.

"No, don't," Mishah cried, crawling toward him.

Amolikah and Cerah dragged him into the Cradleland. The

golden beings placed themselves side by side in front of the portal, their swords spinning golden flames to keep all else outside.

The contraction wrenched a scream from her throat. She ignored it and grappling her way toward him. "My bag," she ordered. "Bring my bag."

"It's too late," Amolikah said.

Rhone's eyes still moved, though strangely, as if searching an unknown territory. Cerah brought the bag to her as she reached the fallen warrior. The bleeding came fast. Organs had been burst by the spears. His breathing was ragged, growing shallower.

Another contraction paralyzed her. As it passed, she ripped open the case, fumbling for powders, tears blurring her vision as she worked.

Kenock staggered over, holding his arm, a gash in his head running blood into his eyes. Rhone grabbed Kenock's arm. "We inside?"

"We're safe. They can't get to us here."

Rhone's view shifted to her as she spilled powder into the wounds. He gave her a smile through his agony. "Don't. It's too late." His voice was but a breath. "I've done the Creator's will."

It couldn't be too late. It mustn't be too late! She gripped his hand, no strength remaining. "Don't give up."

His eyes shifted. "They're here. All around us."

Kenock went to his knee and turned Rhone's head toward him. "Who is here?"

"The warriors. Sari'el and the others. They are with us. They were with us all along." He coughed and his eyes fluttered.

Mishah bent over him, great sobs racking her body. It couldn't end like this. He had to live. "Awwah!" She arched and threw her head back. Amolikah was there helping her. Waves of pain washed over her. Instinctively, she squeezed his unresponsive hand with each contraction.

With a burst of intense pain and the shock of release, the child came into the world. Mishah fell back, trembling from emotion too powerful to contain, exhausted beyond exhaustion. What should have felt like joy was instead an overwhelming sadness.

Amolikah took Mishah's baby and cut the cord.

Mishah's tears flowed, the realization of Rhone's death a spike through her heart. Slowly, insidiously, another dread had begun to worm its way into her consciousness. She hadn't yet heard a cry from her baby.

"Grandmother!"

Amolikah wiped the baby's face in her dress and probed his mouth with a finger.

It's what she had feared. His lungs hadn't fully developed.

Her baby wasn't breathing!

38

The Gardener

Amolikah's face bore the look of panic held just barely under control. She grabbed the naked little body to her breast and patted the back, then put her mouth to his and blew gently to inflate the lungs, to stimulate breathing.

Through a haze of fear and exhaustion, Mishah's mind raced. What did she know of premature babies? She'd never delivered one; her only knowledge of the emergency is what Mistress Alveer had told her. Why couldn't she remember it now? Her brain blanked as she fumbled through her healer's bag. Nothing made sense.

Amolikah inflated his chest again. Not even a weak cry came from the not yet fully formed lungs.

"Give him to me." What could she do that her grandmother could not? She had to hold him. She had to try. She couldn't have him die in another woman's arms. *Lamech, I need you!*

Amolikah placed the still baby against her chest.

"Breathe, little one, breathe." Her hands encircled the tiny chest and she pressed lightly with her fingers and blew life into his mouth. Her training hadn't prepared her for this. It hadn't taught her how to separate herself from such paralyzing emotions. Her thoughts exploded in a hundred directions. Though her efforts were heroic, they were ineffective. The little lips were turning blue. The miniature hands and feet already an unnatural hue.

"Creator, help me! You said he was to be special! To bring comfort," she pleaded. Frantically she breathed life's breath into her child's lungs, feeling that life slipping away as she had Rhone's. And as with him, she was helpless to stop the spirit of death enveloping her son! Rhone dead. Kenock hurt and maybe dying. Her baby dying. None of it made sense!

Amolikah made a sudden, startled sound and her arm tightened around Mishah's shoulders.

In a fury of panic, Mishah looked up. They were not alone.

Cerah's eyes rounded and her mouth fell open. "The gardener?" she breathed, her words hushed with awe.

The man held a hoe and rested the blade on the ground, gripping the handle in both hands. "I've been expecting you."

"My baby!" Mishah cried.

The gardener's eyes turned to the little one.

"My baby is dying." Racking sobs choked her words.

The gardener set the hoe down and knelt. She thrust Noah into his hands. She didn't know what made her do it, just that here was her only hope.

He took the dying child into his rough hands and brought him to his chest. At once the infant gave a cry—a loud, healthy-lunged newborn cry. The blueness of his skin began to fade before her eyes.

Cerah's voice pitched even lower than before. "You are he. The Mother has told me."

The gardener held the baby at arm's length. "I rejoice at the birth of every child. Each one is precious to me." He smiled and placed her son back in her arms. "He's a healthy boy, Mishah."

Mishah clutched Noah and tears burst anew. They were crying together, and it was a wonderful sound. As her sobs diminished and her eyes cleared, she saw the gardener clearly for the first time. He was a tall, slender man, dressed in the common clothes of a farmer. But when he smiled, peace radiated from his eyes and reached out to her, as tangible as a hand touching her. She could tell he'd been kneeling, for his trousers wore dark ovals of rich black earth about the knees. His nails were caked with black dirt, as if he'd just come from working a row of orfins.

"He will grow to be a man after my own heart and will bring comfort to a weary people."

"Comfort." She hugged her baby as his cries ceased and he squirmed against her. "That's what Lamech said in a dream. He gave our son a name that meant comfort—Noah."

"Was it a dream, Mishah?"

His inflection gave her a start. She stared at him. "How could it not have been?" She held her son tight, his steady, strong breath a reassuring beat against her breasts. "It had to be. But it was so real. I miss him so."

The gardener smiled. "Then you will dream of him often, until you are together again."

He stood. "I have plans for this little one. Here in my garden he will be safe from the Evil. Here I will walk with him, and instruct him."

Kenock gave a low groan. Mishah had forgotten about him, and now she saw the flowing blood, his cheeks pale. His wounds were deep and needed immediate attention. The gardener put out a hand and stopped her as she reached for her healer's bag. He touched Kenock's forehead and the bleeding stopped. When he removed his hand, no scar remained where the skin had been laid open to the bone. The gash in his arm had been instantly healed also.

Kenock stood, his color back, not a trace of the wounds, nor any aftereffects. He stared at himself, at his arm, then at the gardener. With sudden understanding, he fell to his knees and buried his head in his hands, weeping. "Forgive me."

The gardener reached down and brought him to his feet. "Stand before me in righteousness, for your sins have been forgiven."

His sins had been forgiven? Who could forgive sins but ... Suddenly she understood! *The gardener was the Creator!*

She glanced through the portals, past the golden legs of the guardians. The enemy was still there, but unable to pass by the guardians—cherubim, Willin had called them. The soldiers had backed a respectable distance from the flaming swords, and stood helpless, speaking amongst themselves, every now and again pointing. The lone giant stalked before the towering beings, keeping well back from them. She saw them clearly, yet knew from the outside looking in, they could never perceive more than the shimmering veil. The beauty of the garden was forever hidden from their eyes.

And it was beautiful. The plantings blended in color and sound ... yes, sounds ... for she perceived that the plants were singing a soft melody; pleasant, yet not overwhelming. And she heard other voices as well. The voices of animals. Was this what men like Rhone heard when they spoke to the spiders, a lingering memory of a past glory? Her heart ached for him. She grasped his dead hand and pressed it to her heart. Fresh tears stung her eyes.

Gently she laid his hand across his still chest and looked up into the Gardener's face. "I thought all this was lost in the fall."

"I have tended my garden, keeping it as it was when my son and daughter were placed in it."

"Why?" What had emboldened her to ask that of the Gardener, the Creator?

"I have yet a use for it." His gentle view fell upon the baby against her chest.

"My son?"

"There is much I wish to teach him. Much he must know to fulfill his destiny."

She didn't understand it. Would Lamech have? Already a new

and deeper understanding had begun to fill her soul. She suddenly understood Lamech's fire, his passion. Here was the Creator, and he'd simply reached out a hand and healed not only her son, but her brother. He had a plan for her son. Surely he had a plan for her, and the others.

Her view fell upon Rhone, his dull, lifeless eyes staring into the clear blue sky. In spite of a strange, unexplainable joy, deep sadness filled her again. Had the Creator a plan for Rhone, too? Was death that plan? Had Rhone simply been a means for them to reach this place?

The Gardener seemed aware of her sudden heaviness. "What troubles you, Mishah?"

She drew in a long, trembling breath as tears welled up in her eyes, tracing warm streaks down her cheeks. "You were able to help us all—all but Master Rhone."

"Because of his faith, Rhone is free."

"Yes. Free. And by all that I believe, I know I will see him again, at the end of the ages, when all things are renewed." She gave another rattling breath. "But if you had only come sooner, he might have lived. You could have healed him as you did Noah and Kenock." She touched Rhone's cold hand, realizing how fleeting life really was.

"Mishah, weep not."

"I came to care for him deeply."

"Rhone is part of a greater plan."

She swallowed and put her sleeve to her nose. Blinking away her tears, she patted her eyes. "I know. Your ways are not our ways. Your thoughts are higher than ours." She withdrew her hand. "He has served your purpose, and now he rests with his fathers until the end times." She sniffed, feeling a heaviness at his death, yet joy at the baby squirming in her arms. It was all too much for her. It would take time, but somehow she knew she had the time. "I only wish Master Rhone had lived long enough to see the child he died protecting."

The Gardener smiled. "The warrior is not dead. He is merely asleep."

Asleep with the fathers. The sleep all life falls into eventually. She understood it, yet her heart still ached.

The Gardener turned his view to Rhone, and when he spoke, his voice held power—the power to form the universe, to shake it to its knees.

"Rhone, arise!"

Readers' Guide

*For Personal Reflection
or Group Discussion*

Flight to Eden
Readers' Guide

O ne thing is certain: we have been carefully programmed when it comes to the "truth" about mankind's beginnings. What comes to mind when you imagine what the first man must have been like? A stout, hunch-backed creature with a broad forehead and dazed expression? We've become convinced that our early ancestors could scarcely communicate, just barely survived with the most rudimentary of tools, and their single greatest achievement was learning to walk upright!

Who is right? Paleontologists' eyes may roll, but *Cro-Magnon Man, Illustrated* is not an accurate portrayal of man, created in God's image. Adam and Eve were made perfect in body and blameless in spirit. They talked and walked with their Creator and were clothed in his glory. If not for one significant mistake, they would still be alive today! But the more time that passes since the original sin, the greater the effect of the curse upon the earth. Much has changed since that beginning time, but some things have not—the serpent still "prowls around like a roaring lion looking for someone to devour" (1 Peter 5:8) and God, the Father and Creator of mankind, still contends for every soul.

Flight to Eden will challenge any preconceived notions about good and evil, the Creation and impending judgment, the consequences of the Fall and God's amazing plan of redemption through Jesus. We can sometimes forget that we are not the only "chosen" ones. Millions of people walked the earth before Christ came, yet they were not born to live without hope. Jesus died for all the saints that had gone before and all those yet to come. He paid the price for every man and woman who chose to love and worship the Creator—even Adam and Eve.

The details contained within this story are supported by Scripture, yet are rarely considered in the face of worldly "expert" opinions. Does something seem fantastically impossible? Search the Word of God and you may well find the answers to your doubts. It is our hope that the following questions will motivate you to dig deeper for truth and examine your own relationship with the Creator. Noah, Abraham, Isaac, and Jacob did not birth our spiritual heritage ... it began in the Garden.

Chapter 1

1. Rhone is a webmaster, skilled in his trade with acute instincts and tremendous strength. What is most surprising about his character and how is he different from the stereotypical "prehistoric cave-man"? In what ways is he far more "advanced" than a modern, twenty-first-century man?

2. Who gives Rhone direction and warns him of impending danger? Why is he not surprised to hear voices? Is it difficult to accept that God would be as actively involved in the lives of people before the time of Christ as he is today?

3. Lamech confronts the people of Nod on the floor of the Government House and delivers a damning prophecy. How do the people respond and what does this reveal about the spiritual condition of the time? What "swift and sure" end does Lamech foresee?

Chapter 2

4. This story takes place during a time when men coexist with dinosaurs and other "prehistoric" creatures, have built modern cities, and have many things that we associate with contemporary life: books, poetry, light, artistry, tools, and more. How does this contradict what evolutionists have taught? What evidence can be found in the Bible that would indicate this might be true? (Genesis 4:16-22)

5. Sol-Ra-Luce is a controlling, evil man. In what other ways does he personify the Serpent? What similarities exist between Sol-Ra-Luce and the Antichrist that the Bible prophesies will arise in the end times?

Chapter 3

6. Ker'ack is a successful businessman who pays homage to the Creator.

Does he really know the Creator, or has his faith become passive and stagnant? How, in such a relatively short amount of time, have the people managed to forget the Creator, some believing him to be only a myth? Others actually believe the Oracle to be the voice of the Creator. What does this reveal about the fallen nature of mankind, and how are we the same today?

7. Depravity has become commonplace in Nod City, as the Oracle has declared that "lifestyle differences" are to be honored. How is this similar to today's mainstream propaganda regarding "alternative lifestyles"?

Chapter 4

8. Rhone, Lamech, and Mishah come to realize that the condition of the world is changing. Things that were remarkable, gifts and abilities that mankind once possessed, and the old order of things are fading away. What is causing these changes? Is this merely the result of the curse—or something else?

9. Who are the "shackled-ones"? What irony can be found in the designation given by the Oracle's agents? Why do they know each other by name? Who is the "Elect One" that prevents Ekalon from marking Rhone?

Chapter 5

10. What message does Mishah receive in her dream? How does she come to realize evil is pursuing her unborn child? How is God warning her and preparing her for the days ahead? How can her son preserve mankind? Is it surprising that Mishah struggles with her faith?

Chapter 6

11. Lamech has a clearly defined sense of right and wrong. Why is he

unable to control his "outbursts" in public? Why does he speak so freely, even though he is aware of the hostility around him? Is he really being obedient to God, or is he acting foolishly? What consequences result from his choices?

12. King Irad is a ruthless tyrant—guilty of violence, treason, and murder. How have the sins of Cain "come home to roost"? Irad has joined forces with the Lodath to further his own agenda—but who is really in control? What is the inevitable end of such an alliance?

Chapter 7

13. Lamech is taken prisoner and sentenced to fifteen years of hard labor. How does he respond to the circumstances that he finds himself in? What reason might God have for allowing these events to take place?

Chapter 8

14. Shortly after Mishah and the others continue on their journey, Lamech is called before the Lodath. What natural evidence can be found of a battle waging in the spiritual realm? Why does Lamech feel an inexplicable desire to tell more than he should? Why must he be cautious—"wise as a serpent, gentle as a lamb"?

15. What role does Captain Da-gore play in the unfolding events? Despite faithfully serving the Lodath and having witnessed the Oracle's power firsthand, are there any seeds of doubt within him? What evidence suggests that there still remains the possibility of redemption in his life? What characteristics do Da-gore and Rhone have in common?

16. When the Oracle appears, he tells his own version of what happened in "the beginning." Is there any truth in what he says? What makes

the lies so appealing and believable? What "truths" does he proclaim that men still believe today? How do the deceptions of evolution, reincarnation, and mankind's inherent "glory" serve Lucifer's designs?

Chapter 9

17. Despite declaring that he does not wish to be pledged to the Oracle, Rhone accepts the crystalline pendant from the Lodath in order to be permitted to leave Nod City. What is familiar about Rhone's thought, "What harm could come from this?" When a decision to compromise is made passively or under duress, are the consequences any less severe?

18. Gleefully, the Lodath tells Kenock that he is different from Lamech, Mishah, Amolikah, and Kleg'l. Is he right? How does Kenock justify his choices? Is he a true believer? If so, why is he so affected by the Lodath's assessment?

Chapter 11

19. Rhone and Bar'ack both miraculously survive the wreckage of the sky-barge. Is it really a "quirk of fate" that Bar'ack lands in the only spot in the forest capable of breaking his fall? How does this "coincidence" affect Rhone?

20. Even though Rhone himself possesses special abilities, he still doubts the veracity of other, equally far-fetched "myths." Why is it easier for the world to believe that man is a cosmic accident of evolved algae, rather than made by a loving Creator? What commonly held beliefs are challenged by this story? (Genesis 1; Genesis 2:4-25)

Chapter 12

21. The Oracle claims that the shackled-ones were responsible for the destruction of the sky-barge. Is this truth or yet another lie? Why

would the Creator protect Rhone from the Oracle's agents, only to attempt to kill him? Why, if the Oracle intends to use Rhone for his own purposes against Mishah, would *he* attempt to have him killed? Who is really responsible for the attack?

22. Mishah struggles with discouragement and despair—wondering why they must suffer and wishing the Creator would simply leave them to their simple lives. What revelation does Amolikah share with her? What lesson can be learned about the purpose of suffering in the plan of God for our lives? (Psalm 30:5; 1 Corinthians 13:12)

Chapter 13

23. Kenock wonders how some men and women can be so certain of their beliefs that they never question them. Why does he wrestle so with truth? What evidence would satisfy his need for "proof" of the Creator's existence? What other men and women mentioned in the Bible have experienced similar struggles?

Chapter 15

24. When Kleg'l is attacked in the alley, Rhone is close at hand and intervenes. Is this just coincidence? Why is Rhone so involved in the lives of the Lee-landers? Is it possible for God to use someone who doesn't even believe in him?

Chapter 16

25. Mishah asks the Creator how this journey could be his will when so much evil has happened. What is the greater sign of God's hand at work: peace and tranquility, or tests and trials? When do we encounter more resistance—when we are accomplishing his will for our lives or when we are off course? Why would evil seek to hinder us in those moments? How should we respond when we come under attack? (Matthew 7:13-14; Ephesians 6:10-18; Philippians 3:12-14)

26. Bar'ack tells Rhone of the Oracle's plan to mingle human blood with the blood of "gods" in order to help mankind "ascend." What role do the Earth-Born play in fulfilling this goal? What is the true motive of the Oracle? How are Mishah and her unborn child a threat to the Oracle's designs? What biblical evidence supports this possibility? (Genesis 6:1-2)

Chapter 17

27. How does Lamech's absence from his family affect the course of events? How might circumstances be different if he were still traveling with them? Why is Rhone's journey intertwined with the Lee-landers? Is it possible Lamech's imprisonment was orchestrated by the Creator?

28. Why don't the Lee-landers eat meat? Was it part of God's plan for humans to eat animal flesh? Would this change in dietary practices explain the changes occurring in the animals—many of them becoming "turnlings"? (Genesis 1:29-30; Genesis 3:17-19)

29. Bar'ack now carries the Oracle's pendant, but what other signs indicate he has rejected his parents' faith? What has contributed to his deception? What does this reveal about the corrupting influence of the world?

Chapter 18

30. What prophecy has the Creator written in the heavens? Mishah claims that it is there for all to see, if they have "a willing eye and an ear to hear the truth." How has astrology contaminated the truth? What motive would Satan have for blinding the eyes of unbelievers? What else has the Enemy turned from its original purpose to serve evil?

Chapter 19

31. Da-gore is surprised to learn that the Oracle has some limitations. What is interesting about the Oracle's inability to "touch" the Lee-landers? Why is the Oracle so worried about a mere human child? How can his mere existence "endanger the Oracle's realm" if humans are really lesser beings? Who demonstrates the true characteristics of an all-powerful god—the Oracle or the Creator?

Chapter 20

32. Rhone possesses a unique ability to communicate with javian spiders. What is interesting about Mishah's statement, that "in the beginning-time, man and animals communicated freely. If it were not so, the Mother would not have been so easily deceived by the serpent." Is it realistic to assume that Eve would have been on guard if a formerly noncommunicative animal slithered up to her and suddenly began speaking? (Genesis 2:19-20; Genesis 3:1-5, 11)

Chapter 22

33. When Hepha is killed, Da-gore learns more pertinent information about the Earth-Born, and the consequences they suffer for serving the Oracle. As he considers the "unpleasant side of the Oracle's love," he begins to encounter truth. Why is he beginning to see the fallacies and question his allegiance, while others are still so completely blinded and deceived by the Oracle's lies? What divine purpose lies behind this subtle change? (Isaiah 42:5-7; Psalm 119:123-125; Romans 2:4)

Chapter 23

34. Having lived more than one thousand years, Mother Eve is still vibrant and extremely perceptive of spiritual things. She speaks of being ready to "go home and be with Adam. To walk with the Creator as we once did." Is this a surprising expectation, given her role in the

Fall? What is the significance of her still serving the Creator, living with hope rather than in abject shame?

35. The Mother tells Mishah that she must flee for the sake of her son, and cannot return to Morg'Seth. How are Mishah's circumstances similar to the plight of Mary and Joseph, following the birth of Jesus? What same destructive peril faces both families?

Chapter 24

36. What light does the Mother shed on the purpose and destiny of the Earth-Born? What warning does she give Mishah? What does she mean when she says that Rhone can be "perfect in his generation"? (Genesis 6:8–9)

Chapter 25

37. Cerah learns that her life's purpose is to protect the written Word of God. The Mother tells her that because this Word contains the truth of the creation, the deceiver wants to eradicate it from the world of men. God's Word has survived to this day, but by what other means has the Enemy sought to eliminate its influence? In what areas of our culture has he been successful? How effective have his efforts been to discredit the Word and those who believe it?

Chapter 26

38. Why do the giants resist Da-gore's instructions and leadership? Which army is singularly unified in purpose and focus—the Oracle's or the Creator's? How does this reflect on the nature of rebellion? What inevitable end is planned for the Enemy and his servants? (Mark 3:23-27; Revelation 11:15; Revelation 20:7-10)

Chapter 27

39. Rhone attempts to throw away the pendant, but is unable to resist its

power. Why is the pendant's pull so strong? How is Rhone's struggle similar to what many people experience today? What tools does the Enemy use to keep people in bondage? Does there come a point when these vices exact so much control that people can no longer break free on their own?

Chapter 28

40. Mishah grows increasingly frustrated as they are imprisoned in Derbin-ee. Once timid and terrified to be "sifted by the Creator," how has she changed? Was losing Lamech—whom Mishah considered her "strength"—a blessing in disguise? How have tests and trials strengthened her faith?

Chapter 29

41. Cerah is a righteous woman, dedicated to the Creator, yet has a "warrior spirit." Is this characteristic a gift from the Creator, or a result of the curse? What men and women of the Bible exhibited the same tendencies? Is there ever a time when natural warfare is justified—even necessary?

Chapter 30

42. What is Leviathan, called "Dirgen's pet"? Is it surprising that the Oracle would be able to possess a living creature—particularly a sea serpent? What Scriptures support the existence of such a monster? What more modern "myths" give heed to such a creature, and is it possible that something similar still exists today? (Job 41:1–34)

43. Rhone learns that he is a descendant of the line of Seth, like the Leelanders and Cerah. Why is this an illuminating discovery? What promise is Rhone a part of, the "first prophecy spoken by the Creator"? Why are the descendants of Seth marked for vengeance and destruction by the Enemy? (Genesis 3:15; Genesis 4:25-26)

Chapter 31

44. Following the attack of the seavine serpents, Rhone finally casts off the cursed pendant, but immediately Leviathan is upon them. Has this new evil been lurking beneath the surface in wait all along? What consequences stem from Rhone's earlier hesitation to break free from the Oracle's control?

Chapter 32

45. Philippians 2:12-13 says, "Continue to work out your salvation with fear and trembling, for it is God who works in you to will and to act according to his good purpose." How has the course of events—particularly the apparent deaths of Mishah and Rhone—changed Kenock? What "good purpose" might be behind his disillusionment with the world, himself, and his own abilities? What do we discover when we finally reach the end of ourselves?

46. Like Jonah, Rhone is given time for contemplation in the belly of a great fish. What causes him to finally acknowledge the power of the Creator? How does this same circumstance only serve to strengthen Mishah's confidence in the omnipotence of God?

Chapter 33

47. What is plainly evident about the town and people of Eve's Weep? Why do some still live in such a remote place of devastation and emptiness? How is this further evidence of the consequences of the Fall?

48. After coming to believe in the Creator, Rhone quickly comes to realize that his thinking needs some serious adjustment. Why do old mind-sets have such a stronghold upon man—often warring against the truth? The Bible tells us that if we are in Christ, we are a new creation (2 Corinthians 5:17). Why does this transformation not immediately change our thinking? Is it wise to rely on the mind—or

knowledge and intelligence—to determine truth? What does the Bible have to say about our thought life? (Romans 8:7; Mark 7:20-23; Philippians 4:7-9; Proverbs 23:7; Isaiah 26:3; Romans 7:21-25; Romans 12:2)

Chapter 35

49. Lucifer—the Oracle—rallies his troops for one final attack against Mishah and her unborn child. Is he truly ignorant of the inevitable outcome? Is he so skilled in deception that he has come to believe his own lies? Is Mishah right in believing that the Creator has brought them too far to abandon them now? Is the outcome secure, despite the danger and evil that pursues them?

Chapter 36

50. Exhausted and close to giving birth, Mishah awakens to find a tame donkey waiting nearby to carry her to the Cradleland. Is this a loving provision by the Creator? What prophetic significance can be found in this situation? (Zechariah 9:9; Matthew 21:1-5)

Chapter 37

51. Mishah and her companions take shelter just inside the Cradleland. Why do the cherubim who guard the gate permit them to pass? What was the main purpose behind Adam and Eve's banishment from the garden? (Genesis 3:22-24)

Chapter 38

52. Rhone, the mighty Makir Warrior, fights valiantly until the end and is successful in his mission to bring Mishah safely to the Cradleland. But after battling the giants and the troops of the Enemy, he is mortally wounded and dies. Is he correct in saying that he has "done the Creator's will"? If so, what motivates the Gardener to call him back to life?

The Word at Work Around the World

A vital part of Cook Communications Ministries is our international outreach, Cook Communications Ministries International (CCMI). Your purchase of this book, and of other books and Christian-growth products from Cook, enables CCMI to provide Bibles and Christian literature to people in more than 150 languages in 65 countries.

Cook Communications Ministries is a not-for-profit, self-supporting organization. Revenues from sales of our books, Bible curricula, and other church and home products not only fund our U.S. ministry, but also fund our CCMI ministry around the world. One hundred percent of donations to CCMI go to our international literature programs.

CCMI reaches out internationally in three ways:

- Our premier International Christian Publishing Institute (ICPI) trains leaders from nationally led publishing houses around the world.

- We provide literature for pastors, evangelists, and Christian workers in their national language.

- We reach people at risk—refugees, AIDS victims, street children, and famine victims—with God's Word.

Word Power, God's Power

Faith Kidz, RiverOak, Honor, Life Journey, Victor, NexGen — every time you purchase a book produced by Cook Communications Ministries, you not only meet a vital personal need in your life or in the life of someone you love, but you're also a part of ministering to José in Colombia, Humberto in Chile, Gousa in India, or Lidiane in Brazil. You help make it possible for a pastor in China, a child in Peru, or a mother in West Africa to enjoy a life-changing book. And because you helped, children and adults around the world are learning God's Word and walking in his ways.

Thank you for your partnership in helping to disciple the world. May God bless you with the power of his Word in your life.

For more information about our international ministries, visit www.ccmi.org.

Additional copies of *FLIGHT TO EDEN*
and other River Oak titles are available
from your local bookseller.

If you have enjoyed this book,
or if it has had an impact on your life,
we would like to hear from you.

❀ ❀ ❀

Please contact us at:

RIVER OAK BOOKS
Cook Communications Ministries, Dept. 201
4050 Lee Vance View
Colorado Springs, CO 80918
Or visit our Web site: www.cookministries.com

RIVEROAK®
Good News in Fiction